Compiler Design Using Java®

An Object-Oriented Approach

Fifth Edition

John I. Moore, Jr.
Professor Emeritus of Cyber and Computer Sciences
The Citadel, Charleston, SC

ISBN: 978-1-7341391-4-3

Table of Contents

Preface

Many compiler books have been published over the years, so why another one? Let me be perfectly clear. This book is designed primarily for use as a textbook in a one-semester course for undergraduate students and beginning graduate students. The only prerequisites for this book are familiarity with basic algorithms and data structures (lists, maps, recursion, etc.), a rudimentary knowledge of computer architecture and assembly language, and some experience with the Java programming language or a closely related language such as Kotlin, C#, or C++. Most undergraduate computer science majors will have covered these topics in their first two years of study. Graduate students who have never had a course in compilers will also find the book useful, especially if they undertake some of the more challenging project exercises described in Appendix B.

A complete study of compilers could easily fill several graduate-level courses, and therefore some simplifications and compromises are necessary for a one-semester course that is accessible to undergraduate students. Following are some of the decisions made in order to accommodate the goals of this book.

1. The book has a narrow focus as a project-oriented course on compilers. Compiler theory is kept to a minimum, but the project orientation retains the "fun" part of studying compilers.
2. The source language being compiled is relatively simple, but it is powerful enough to be interesting and challenging. It has scalar data types, strings, arrays, records (a.k.a., structs), control statements, procedures, functions, and parameters, but it relegates many other interesting language features to the project exercises. Most undergraduate students will find it challenging just to complete a compiler for the basic project language without any additional features. Graduate students will likely want to extend the basic project language with features outlined in the exercises and Appendix B.
3. The target language is assembly language for a virtual machine with a stack-based architecture, similar to but much simpler than the Java Virtual Machine (JVM). This approach greatly simplifies code generation. First, it eliminates the need to deal with general-purpose registers. And second, relative addresses for branch instructions are handled by the assembler, simplifying the amount of work that needs to be done by the compiler. Both an assembler and an emulator for the virtual machine are provided in the book's GitHub repository.
4. No special compiler-related tools are required or used within the book. Students require access only to a Java compiler and a text editor, but most students will want to use Java with an Integrated Development Environment (IDE) such as Eclipse, NetBeans, or IntelliJ IDEA. Compiler-related tools such as scanner generators or parser generators could simplify certain tasks involved in building a compiler, but I believe that the approach used in this book makes the structure of the compiler more transparent. Students who wish to use compiler-related tools are welcome to do so, but they will need to look elsewhere to learn how to use these tools. Examples of freely available compiler-related tools include ANTLR, Coco/R, Flex/Bison, Lex/Yacc, JavaCC, Truffle, and Eclipse Xtext. In addition, while the presentation of the book uses

Java, students are free to select an alternative implementation language. Languages that support recursion and object-oriented programming will work best with the approach used in this book. Examples include Kotlin, C#, C++, Python, Scala, and Swift.

5. One very important component of a compiler is the parser, which verifies that a source program conforms to the language syntax and produces an intermediate representation of the program that is suitable for additional analysis and code generation. There are several different approaches to parsing, but in keeping with the emphasis on a one-semester course, this book covers only one approach – recursive descent parsing with several lookahead tokens. A previous edition of this book used only one lookahead token, but changes to the source language motivated the need for additional lookahead tokens. Plus, it is instructive to learn how to implement a parser using multiple lookahead tokens, especially since multiple lookahead tokens can be implemented simply and efficiently.
6. Missing from the book are a lot of favorite compiler topics such as finite automata, bottom-up parsing, attribute grammars, heap management, register allocation, and data-flow analysis. What remains fits nicely into a one-semester, project-oriented course for undergraduate students and beginning graduate students.

Why Study Compilers?

Relatively few people write commercial compilers, but I believe that the study of compiler design is an important part of a computer science education since compilers and closely related language translators are the primary tools for software development. Having a fundamental knowledge of how compilers actually work can improve one's ability to write efficient programs. In addition, learning how to write a compiler gives experience on working with a moderately large program, and it makes an excellent case study for software engineering and good program design. And the techniques used in compiler design are useful for other purposes such as writing a test harness, a support tool for process control, or an interpreter for a small, special-purpose language. One of my former students applied compiler technology to a commercial tool for testing software.

The Course Project

This book discusses implementation of a compiler for a relatively small programming language named CPRL (for Compiler PRoject Language), which was designed for teaching the basics of compiler construction. The target language is assembly language for CVM (CPRL Virtual Machine), a simple stack-based virtual machine. Together we will build a compiler slowly, one step at a time, with lots of template Java code in the book and even more in the book's GitHub repository to guide you through the process. Students are expected to download and study the Java code from the book repository as part of their learning experience. The end result is likely the largest single program that most undergraduate students will encounter.

Appendix A describes the decomposition of the overall project of developing a CPRL compiler into 12 smaller subprojects (numbered 0-11). Students should complete the subprojects in the specified order since each one builds on the previous.

Also, we will build the parser in three separate subprojects, focusing initially on the syntax as defined by the context-free grammar, then adding error recovery, and finally constructing abstract syntax trees for subsequent phases of constraint analysis and initial code generation. In the real world we would likely combine all three steps into one, but the division into three separate subprojects has been shown to provide a better understanding of the concepts and overall process for students new to compiler design.

Appendix B describes several extensions or variations to the basic compiler project outlined in this book. Some are more challenging than others. Ambitious undergraduate students and most graduate students will want to attempt one or more of these exercises.

Changes in the Fifth Edition

The fifth edition retains the objectives, emphasis, and general structure of the first four editions, but there are several important changes in this edition as summarized below.

1. **CPRL Language Changes.**

    - The design and implementation of strings have been simplified, which eliminated the need for class `Padding` and provided an opportunity to add additional language features to CPRL without overly complicating the compiler project. In addition, the plus operator + can be used for string concatenation.

    - CPRL now supports conditional expressions using the ternary operator ?: as found in many C-based languages. So now we can write statements like the following.

      ```
      max := x > y ? x : y;
      ```

      An important language design issue is the precedence of this operator. In both C and Java, this operator has a very low precedence. For CPRL, rather than create a new precedence level, the conditional operator was assigned the lowest precedence that already existed in the language, the same precedence as the logical operators.

    - An additional numeric type was added. Type `Byte` is an unsigned numeric type that occupies exactly 8 bits. Many programming languages have an 8-bit numeric type, although some are signed; e.g., as in Java. `Byte` values are promoted to `Integer` when used in expressions.

    - The CPRL compiler now supports built-in subprograms, and three built-in functions were added to the compiler implementation.

    - And finally, CPRL now supports a simple form of enumerated types (enum types). An enumerated type is defined by listing the identifiers that are the actual values of the type. Each enumerated identifier defines a constant value that is scoped to the enum type. Here is an example.

      ```
      type Day = <Sun, Mon, Tue, Wed, Thu, Fri, Sat>;
      ```

A major language design decision is how the enum constants relate to integers. In some languages, they are simply integer constants. For CPRL the enum constants have some properties similar to integers, but enum types are considered to be distinct types. In particular, we can't assign enum variables or constants to integer variables, and integer variables or literals can't be assigned to variables declared as an enum type.

2. **CVM Changes.**

   - A heap pointer, `HP`, was added as an internal register. The heap pointer is used only when string values are read from standard input or when strings are concatenated. Memory management is essentially nonexistent. We use a simple bump allocator that allocates heap memory when needed, and heap memory is never reclaimed; i.e., it is never deallocated.
   - Five new opcodes/instructions were added to the CVM.
     1. `GETBYTE`: read a single binary byte from standard input
     2. `GETEOF`: used to detect end-of-file for standard input
     3. `CHAR2INT`: converts a character value to an integer
     4. `INT2CHAR`: converts an integer value to a character
     5. `STRCAT`: used for string concatenation

     Ideally these new instructions would be implemented using lower-level instructions, but doing so was not possible with the existing instruction set, and adding them as machine instructions kept things simple and easy to understand. Plus, with the addition of type `Byte` to CPRL, opcodes `BYTE2INT` and `INT2BYTE` are now used by the compiler. These opcodes were defined in the previous edition of the CVM, but they were not used by the compiler implementation.
   - Opcode `PUTBYTE` has been removed from the CVM. It printed was an integer-like value for the byte, and `PUTINT` works fine since byte values are promoted to `Integer` before they are printed.
   - Some of the instruction byte codes changed from earlier editions, so older source code based on earlier versions of the book might need to be recompiled and reassembled in order to work properly with the current version of CVM.

3. **Source Code Changes.**

   - Abstract syntax tree classes `SingleVarDecl` and `VariableExpr` have been removed, and all related functionality has been incorporated into classes `VarDecl` and `Variable`, respectively. The value added by the removed classes was minimal and did not fully justify their existence.

- The prefix "`edu.citadel`" was removed from all package names. For example, package `edu.citadel.assembler` is now simply package `assembler`, package `edu.citadel.common` is now package `common`, etc.
- The `main()` method for each major application of the compiler has been moved into a separate class. For example, the `main()` method for the compiler is now in class `Cprlc` (in package `cprlc`).

In addition, there are many new paragraphs, various rewordings to make the presentation easier to understand, and a few corrections. In developing this new edition, several other possible changes to CPRL were considered, implemented, and then rejected to keep the book at a reasonable length and level of complexity. Overall, I am extremely pleased with the resulting new edition of this book.

Structure of the Book

The book chapters are organized in a natural progression from general concepts to step-by-step details for implementing the compiler project. Each chapter builds on the previous chapters, and forward references have been kept to a minimum. A few sections can be omitted or postponed without loss of continuity, but in general, the book is designed to be studied from front to back.

The most difficult chapters are 3, 6, 8, and 13, so don't try to rush through those chapters. Not coincidentally, these are also the longest chapters. The good news is that the last four chapters covering arrays, enumerated types, strings, and records are relatively straightforward, assuming mastery of the preceding material. These last four chapters can be covered relatively quickly, and it is not uncommon for the strongest students to work ahead at this point and to finish related compiler subprojects early.

Chapter 1 introduces basic concepts and terminology in the study of compilers. Following the book by David A. Watt and Deryck F. Brown [Watt 2000], Chapter 1 uses tombstone diagrams as a visual aid to explain many of the concepts. Sections 1.2, 1.3, and 1.6 are required. The other sections can be omitted or postponed without impacting the material in subsequent chapters, but doing so is not recommended.

Chapter 2 presents an overview of the structure of a compiler. In a sense, it sets the context for the remaining chapters. It can be omitted or postponed, but I always spend one class period on this chapter.

Chapter 3 provides an overview of how programming languages are defined, with detailed coverage of context-free grammars. The complete context-free grammar for CPRL, the source language for the compiler project, is defined in Appendix D.

Chapter 4 gives a brief overview of CPRL. A more complete definition of CPRL is provided in Appendices C and D.

Chapter 5 presents the details of implementing a scanner for CPRL, including an overview of several related classes found in the book's GitHub repository.

Chapter 6 is the longest and one of the most complicated chapters in the book. It includes a discussion of grammar analysis to compute first sets and follow sets plus details on the implementation of a recursive descent parser for CPRL. As defined in the compiler project, the initial version of the parser concentrates primarily on verification that a source program conforms to the syntax defined by the context-free grammar for CPRL.

Chapter 7 extends the parser developed in Chapter 6 to perform error recovery so that multiple errors can be detected and reported by the compiler.

Chapter 8 contains a detailed discussion of abstract syntax trees. Abstract syntax trees provide an intermediate representation for source programs that can be used for additional analysis and code generation. In this chapter, the parsing methods are modified to construct an abstract syntax tree for the source program.

Chapter 9 uses the abstract syntax trees from Chapter 8 to perform constraint analysis, with emphasis on checking conformance to CPRL's type rules as defined for CPRL/0, a major subset of CPRL.

Chapter 10 gives a brief overview of the CVM, the virtual machine that serves as the target for CPRL programs. The CVM has a stack architecture that is similar to but much simpler than the Java Virtual Machine (JVM). Appendix E contains additional information about the CVM, including complete definitions for every CVM instruction.

Chapter 11 modifies the abstract syntax trees to generate assembly language for CPRL/0. The GitHub repository provides an assembler that can be used to generate the actual CVM machine code.

Chapter 12 presents an overview of code optimization. The assembler provided on the course web site implements several optimizations, but none of the compiler projects require mastery of the material from this chapter. Therefore, this chapter can be postponed if desired, but it should not be omitted.

Chapter 13 extends constraint analysis and code generation to handle subprograms. It includes additional coverage of scope and a detailed discussion of calling conventions and activation records. Similar to Chapter 6, this chapter is long and can be quite complicated for many undergraduate students. But mastery of this material is essential for a course on compilers, even if it means that less time is available for the last four chapters.

Chapters 14-17 extend constraint analysis and code generation for arrays, enumerated types, strings, and records, respectively. Projects corresponding to these chapters are somewhat simpler than most of the preceding projects and can be completed relatively quickly. Implementing records completes the compiler project, but students are always encouraged to attempt some of variations and extensions outlined in Appendix B.

Chapter Dependencies

As illustrated in the diagram on the next page, Chapters 2 and 12 can be covered any time after Chapter 1, and Chapters 14-17 can be covered any time after Chapter 13. Otherwise, most chapters should be covered in the order presented in the book. The recommended approach is to cover the chapters in order 1-17 using the appendices as supplementary material. Many of the exercises in the last four chapters assume that compiler subprojects for previous chapters have been implemented. For example, some exercises in Chapter 17 use concepts from Chapters 14-16.

Chapter Dependencies

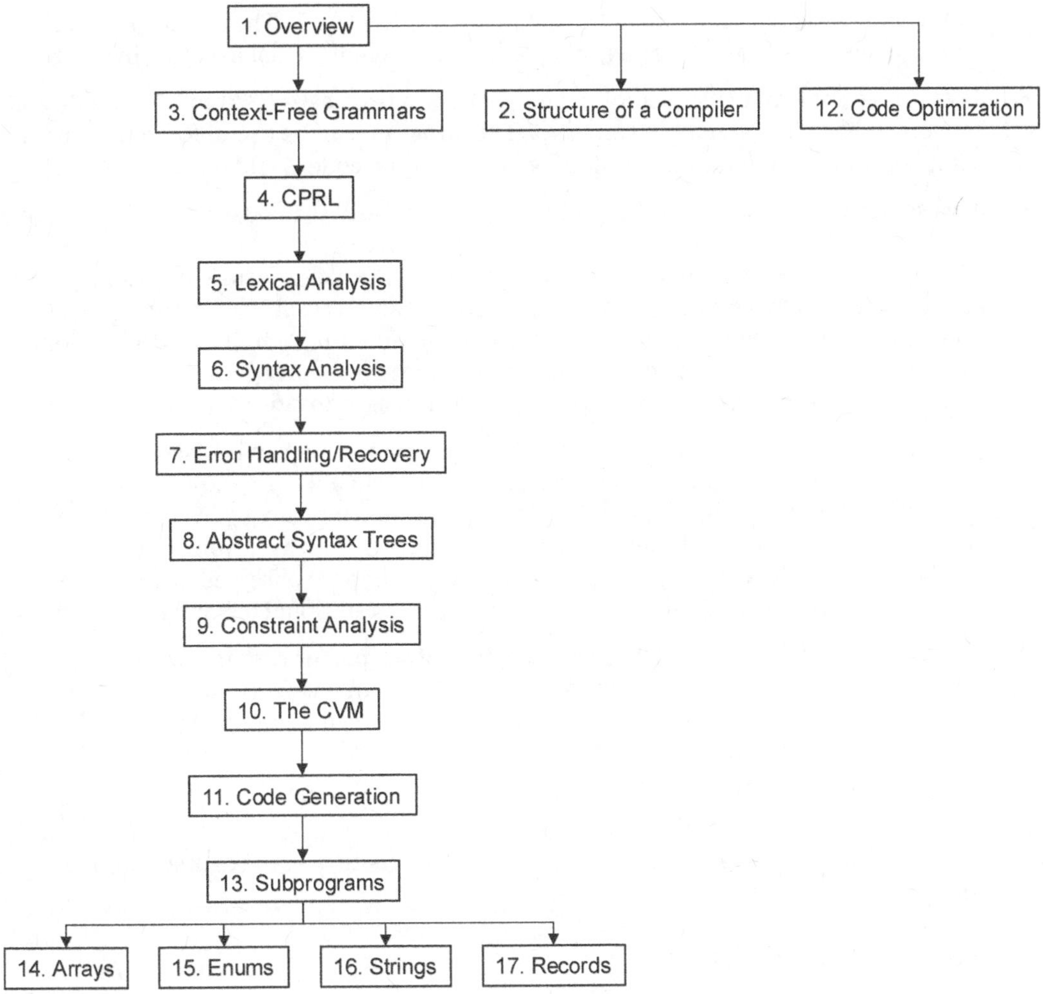

Book Resources

The repository for this book at https://github.com/SoftMoore/CPRL-Java-5th contains a number of related resources as follows.

- Java source code that implements the CVM, the target machine for the compiler project.
- Java source code that implements an assembler for the CVM. The compiler project targets assembly language for the CVM rather than actual virtual machine bytecode.
- Java source code for a disassembler; i.e., a program that takes CVM machine code and converts it back into assembly language. This program can be useful for debugging the compiler projects and for understanding how machine code is laid out in memory.
- Java source code or skeletal Java source code for many of the classes described in the book so that students don't need to start from scratch to create their compilers. Some of these classes suggest implementation ideas for other classes whose implementations are either not provided or are only partially provided. For example, source code for a procedure declaration might be relevant when implementing a function declaration. **Students should begin each phase of their compiler project by trying to understand the related Java source code that is provided.**
- Many examples of correct and incorrect CPRL programs that can be used to test a compiler. The final compiler should reject all incorrect CPRL programs with appropriate error messages, and it should generate semantically equivalent assembly language for all correct CPRL programs. Using the provided assembler and CVM emulator, all correct CPRL programs can be run to compare observed and expected results. Students are strongly encouraged to develop additional test programs.
- Sample Windows command scripts and Bash shell scripts for running and testing various stages of the compiler. For example, rather than trying to compile and test programs one at a time, there are command/shell scripts for running the compiler on all CPRL source files in the current working directory. These scripts are useful for testing the compiler against collections of correct and incorrect CPRL programs.

Appendix A provides additional details about the resources available on the book repository and how those resources fit into the overall structure of the course compiler project.

Java and Object-Orientation

As indicated in the book's title, the language used herein for implementing a compiler is Java, but other options are certainly possible. In fact, one of the project exercises listed in Appendix B is to write the compiler in a different language, and some of my former students have done this.

Since Java is an object-oriented language, every component of the compiler is structured in terms of classes and objects – the scanner is an object, the parser is an object, tokens are objects, etc. But the full power of "object-orientation" doesn't come into play until Chapter

8, where the details of abstract syntax trees are introduced. The approach used in this book for implementing abstract syntax trees fully exploits Java's object-oriented facilities for inheritance and polymorphism. As an example, consider that code generation for a list of statements looks like the following.

```
for (var stmt : statements)
    stmt.emit();
```

The list could include `if` statements, assignment statements, loop statements, etc., and therefore different statements generate code in different ways. But at the level of programming abstraction shown in this example, we only need to know that each statement has an `emit()` method that writes out the appropriate object code.

Similarly, the code to check constraints for a list of CPRL subprogram declarations looks like the following.

```
for (var decl : subprogDecls)
    decl.checkConstraints();
```

Note that the subprogram declarations in the list could be either procedure declarations or function declarations.

Which Version of Java?

The exposition in this book and the resources provided in the book's GitHub repository assume Java version 17 or later. In particular, interfaces `VariableDecl` and `Initializer` are declared to be sealed interfaces, and several classes make use of pattern matching for the `instanceof` operator.

The Java source code also makes use of the arrow syntax for switch statements and switch expressions, and Java source files frequently use local variable type inference with the keyword `var`, especially in conjunction with the `new` operator. Here is an example.

```
ArrayList<Statement> statements = new ArrayList<>(20);    // older style
var statements = new ArrayList<Statement>(20);            // using var
```

Formatting Source Code

Every programmer has his/her preferred way to format and indent source code. Should curly braces be aligned? Should code be indented 2, 3, or 4 spaces? What is the best way to format an `if` statement or a `while` loop? Sometimes arguments about how source code should be formatted seem to take on religious-like fervor. I avoid such arguments, for I have found the **one true way** that Java source code should be formatted. ☺ But if you are a nonbeliever, please feel free to reformat the Java source code according to your project standards or personal tastes. (FYI: The formatting style used in this book is loosely based on the GNU style, which is not very popular but which I have personally found to be the most readable. As the saying goes, "Beauty is in the eye of the beholder".)

Acknowledgements

When I was first learning about computers as a young man, I was in awe of compilers. That awe evolved into curiosity, which led to a lot of thought and study about how compilers are constructed, which led to a lot of contemplation about how best to teach an introductory course in compilers, which eventually led to my writing this book. Along the way I was guided and influenced by a number of teachers, colleagues, students, and books. I would like to acknowledge those who have been the most influential on my thinking.

I was first introduced to compilers many years ago when I "unofficially" audited a course on compiler design given by Richard LeBlanc at Georgia Institute of Technology (a.k.a. Georgia Tech). For reasons I no longer remember, I was unable to take the course for credit. But auditing it, especially under Richard LeBlanc, was enough to motivate me to learn more. I was fortunate enough to have Richard LeBlanc later on for another course on programming language design.

My next introduction to compilers came in a professional development course given by Frank DeRemer and Tom Pennello, with a guest lecture or two by Bill McKeeman. They will not remember me, but I am grateful to have learned more about compilers from teachers and researchers of their caliber.

I have also been inspired by several compiler books, especially two of them that took a pedagogical approach similar to this one. The first book is *Brinch Hansen on Pascal Compilers* by Per Brinch Hansen (Prentice Hall, 1985). That book is a little out of date now, but it had one of the most readable descriptions of compilers when it was first released. A second, more modern book is *Programming Language Processors in Java: Compilers and Interpreters* by David A. Watt and Deryck F. Brown (Prentice Hall, 2000). I follow their treatment of tombstone diagrams when explaining compilers and interpreters in Chapter 1. Many years ago I used the Brinch Hansen book as a textbook in my compiler courses, and I used the Watt-Brown book several times when it was first published.

It is important to acknowledge former students at Johns Hopkins University, the College of Charleston, and The Citadel, and to thank these institutions for allowing me to explore my ideas about writing compilers. I am particularly grateful to the following students who had the most influence on my thinking about how to teach compilers: Rob Ring, Scott Stanchfield, Logan Daigle, Zack Aardahl, Ben Hunter, Dalton Hazelwood, Gordon Finlay, Josh Terry, Davis Jeffords, Mike Dalpee, Matthew Blair, Mafer Contreras, Jared Johnson, Robert Roser, Shiloh Smiles, Noah Klepper, Robert Powell, Eddie Portelles, and Luke Tramontozzi. Some of the earlier students at Johns Hopkins suffered through my courses as I was trying to crystallize my approach to teaching compilers, and I am grateful for their feedback. They would barely recognize my course if they took it today.

In addition, I want to acknowledge Vince Sigillito, who served as Chair of the Computer Science program at the Johns Hopkins Part-Time Programs in Engineering and Applied Science, for first allowing me to teach a course on compilers many years ago. I remember telling Vince that I wanted to teach a course on compilers so that I could learn more about them. He had no objections and even indicated that he had done something similar in the past. Compiler Design has evolved into my favorite course.

I would also like to acknowledge the following individuals who provided invaluable advice and feedback on compilers in general and on the presentation and exposition in this book: Dr. Richard J. LeBlanc, Jr., Professor Emeritus, Georgia Institute of Technology and Professor Emeritus, Seattle University; Dr. Arthur B. (Art) Pyster, retired, former Professor of Systems Engineering, former Associate Dean for Research, George Mason University; Dr. Shankar M. Banik, Professor and Head, Department of Cyber and Computer Sciences, and Director of The Citadel DoD Cyber Institute, The Citadel; and Dr. George L. Rudolph, Professor and Chair, Department of Computer Science, Utah Valley University. I am most appreciative and humbled that they spent part of their valuable time assisting me with this effort.

A special acknowledgement goes to Dr. David Buzatto, Professor de Informática, Federal Institute of Education, Science and Technology of São Paulo, Brazil. Dr. Buzatto performed a thorough review of this edition of the book, uncovering many issues and providing numerous suggestions for improvement. I am ashamed to say that some of the issues he discovered have existed for several earlier editions. Thank you, Dr. Buzatto. I am eternally grateful for your assistance.

Finally, I would like to acknowledge Kayran Cox Moore, my wife of many years, for proofreading and providing invaluable feedback on several drafts of this book. She might not understand compilers or Java programming, but she has a deep understanding of English grammar and sentence structure, and she has no reservations about correcting my errors or improving my writing. Any grammatical errors remaining in this book are a result of my stubborn refusal to follow her advice, or, more likely, they were introduced after she proofread that part of the book. I also want to thank Kayran for being my anchor in life and the source for most of what is good about myself.

Chapter 1
Overview of Compilers and Language Translation

"... language is an instrument of human reason, and not merely a medium for the expression of thought ..." – George Boole

"There is a magical moment when a programmer presses the *run* button and the software begins to execute. Somehow a program written in a high-level language is running on a computer that is capable only of shuffling bits. Here we reveal the wizardry that makes that moment possible." – Jeremy Siek

1.1 The Role of Programming Languages

Mathematicians have long understood the importance of a good notation for communication and understanding, and the same can be said for programming languages. Programming languages serve as a means of communication among people as well as between people and machines, and they provide a framework for formulating the software solution to a problem. Moreover, programming languages can influence how we think about software design by making some program structures easier to describe than others. As an example, consider the fact that recursion was not available in early versions of Fortran, making it difficult for a programmer to "invent" a recursive solution to a problem even when such a solution might be the most natural.

In addition, programming languages provide a degree of machine independence and portability as they raise the level of abstraction used in problem solving. A good programming language lets us concentrate more on the problem being solved rather than on mundane implementation issues, thereby making us more productive.

> In the early days of object-oriented programming, I was often asked if one could "do" object-oriented programming in C. My response was that of course you could do it in C. You could even do it in assembly language. And if you were very, very patient, you could do it in 0's and 1's. The question is not *if* it can be done but how long it would take you to do it – how much support is provided by the programming language versus how much has to be implemented or simulated by the programmer.

1.2 Translators and Compilers

In the context of programming languages, a **translator** is a program that accepts as input text written in one language (called the source language) and converts it into a semantically equivalent representation in a second language (called the target or object language). If the source language is a high-level language and the target language is a low-level language, then the translator is called a **compiler**.

The figure below shows a simplified view of the compile/execute process as two separate steps. In reality, there can be other intermediate steps involved in creating an executable program. For example, many compilers do not actually create an executable program, but rather, a **linker** is used to combine several user-developed and system modules into an executable program. Compilers could be used to create the individual modules used by the linker. Additionally, another system utility called a **loader** would likely be used to copy the object program from disk into main memory.

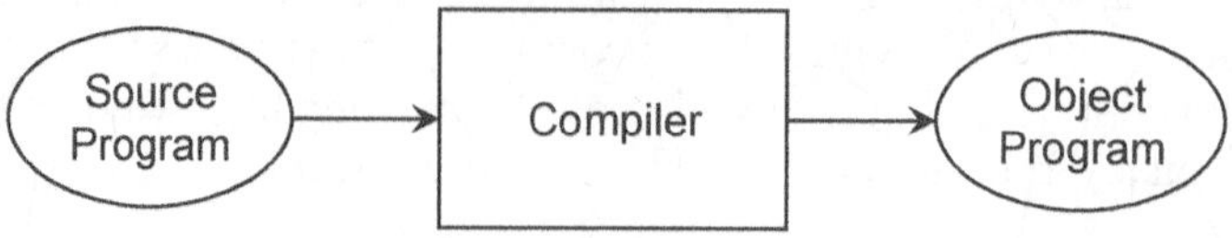

Compile

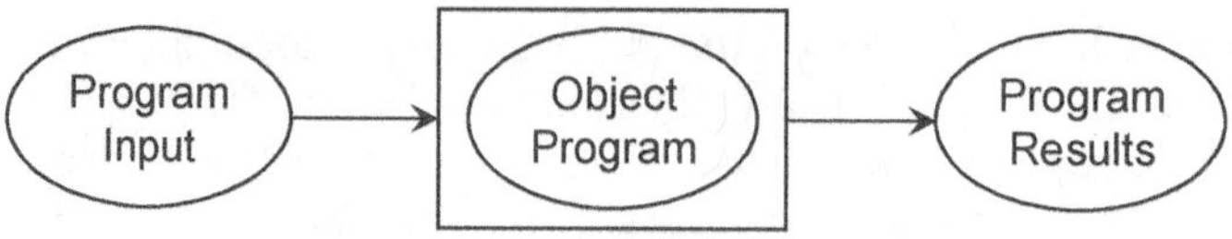

Execute

It is important to distinguish between the definition of a programming language and the implementation of that programming language in the form of a compiler. For example, some languages do not formally specify the sizes for basic integer and floating-point types. Instead, the compiler implementer is free to make these kinds of decisions, and implementation decisions are often driven by the compiler implementation approaches and the target hardware architecture; e.g., type `Integer` could be the "natural" size of integers for the target machine, which means that it could be 16 bits on one computer, 32 bits on another computer, and 64 bits on yet a third computer.

The Role of Compilers

A compiler must first verify that the source program is valid with respect to the source language definition. If the source program is valid, then the compiler must produce a **semantically equivalent and reasonably efficient** machine language program for the target computer. If the source program is not valid, the compiler must provide meaningful feedback to the programmer as to the nature and location of any errors. Feedback on possible multiple errors is usually desirable.

Other Language Processors

While the focus of this book is on compilers, it is important to recognize that there are a number of other language processors that perform similar functions. What follows is a brief discussion of some related language processors. Most are implemented using approaches similar to those of compilers.

An **assembler** is a translator that translates symbolic assembly language into binary machine code. Since assembly language is essentially a low-level representation of machine code, then the implementation of an assembler is usually much simpler than that of a compiler.

A **high-level language translator** (a.k.a. a **transpiler**) translates from one high-level language to another. For example, since C compilers were rather ubiquitous at the time, Bjarne Stroustrup originally implemented C++ as a translator to C. C++ programs were first translated to C, and then the C versions of the programs were compiled. Such an approach not only simplified the implementation of C++, but it made C++ immediately available on a lot of different computer systems. Due to the popularity of JavaScript for internet applications, today there are many languages that provide an option for JavaScript as a target language – examples include Dart, TypeScript, Kotlin, and Scala. In addition, there exist third-party translators to JavaScript from several other languages such as Ruby, Python, and Java.

A "pure" **interpreter** translates/executes source program instructions immediately. The interpreter does not analyze and translate the entire program before starting to run; rather, translation is performed one line or one instruction at a time as the program is being executed, and translation occurs every time the program is run. The source program is basically treated as another form of input data to the interpreter. Whereas compilation can be viewed as a two-step process (first compile, then execute), interpretation can be viewed essentially as a one-step process (execute), as illustrated below.

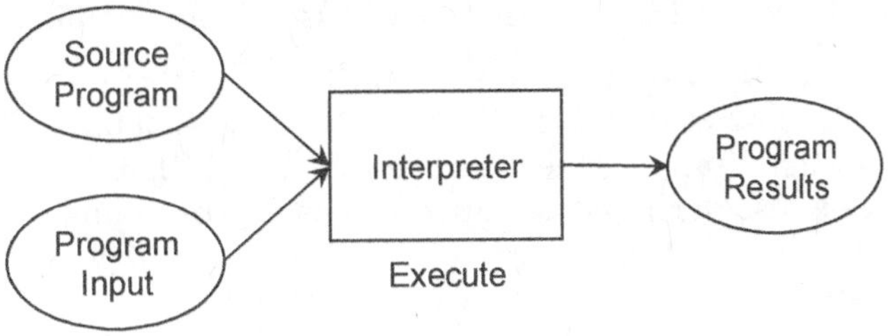

Examples of interpreters include most interactive command-line processors such as the bash shell (which can also run shell scripts), the Windows command-line interpreter (which can also run command files), and relational database interpreters for SQL. Early versions of LISP and BASIC were interpreted, and many language implementations come with a read-eval-print loop that is essentially an interpreter for language expressions.

In general, compilers provide earlier and better error detection, and the compiled programs generally run much faster, while interpreters can provide more rapid feedback to the user. Interpreters are sometimes preferred for prototyping and for highly interactive systems if the performance penalty can be tolerated.

An **emulator** or **virtual machine** is an interpreter for a machine instruction set. The machine being "emulated" may be real or hypothetical. The JVM is an example of an emulator for a hypothetical Java machine. Similar to real machines, emulators typically use an instruction pointer (program counter) and a fetch-decode-execute cycle. Running a program on an emulator is functionally equivalent to running the program directly on the machine, but the program will experience some performance degradation on the emulator. A real machine can be viewed as an interpreter implemented in hardware. Conversely, an emulator can be viewed as a machine implemented in software.

There are other variations on these themes. An **interpretive compiler** is a combination of a compiler and a low-level interpreter (emulator). The compiler translates programs to the instruction set interpreted by the emulator, and the emulator is used to run the compiled program. For example, Java is compiled to an intermediate, low-level form (Java bytecode) that gets interpreted by the JVM.

In addition, the JVM provides a **Just-In-Time (JIT)** compiler that translates Java bytecode into native machine code at runtime. The translation is performed for methods that are called frequently, and thereafter the JVM uses the compiled code directly instead of interpreting it. Use of the JIT compiler is optional, but it is enabled by default. Additionally, profiling is used to discover methods (hot spots) where additional optimization can be performed. Performance improvements can be significant for methods that are executed repeatedly. Note that Java's JIT compiler is part of the JVM, not the actual Java compiler that translates Java source files into bytecode.

Writing a Compiler

Writing a compiler involves three languages as follows.

1. The **source language**, which is the input into the compiler. Examples include C++, Java, or CPRL, the source language that we will use for our compiler project.
2. The **implementation language**, which is the language that the compiler is written in. This book uses Java as the implementation language, but other languages would have been just as appropriate. One interesting concept is that, for many compilers, the source language is also the implementation language. For example, a C++ compiler might be written in C++. Writing a compiler in the source language uses an approach known as bootstrapping, which will be explained later.
3. The **target language**, which is the output of the compiler. The target language for a compiler is usually assembly language or machine language, possibly for a virtual computer. The target language for the compiler project in this book is assembly language for CVM, a virtual machine designed to run CPRL programs.

1.3 Tombstone Diagrams

Tombstone diagrams provide a convenient notation to illustrate the three languages involved in writing a compiler.

This first diagram illustrates that program P is expressed in language L. L could be a high-level language, or, after compiling the program, L could be a machine language.

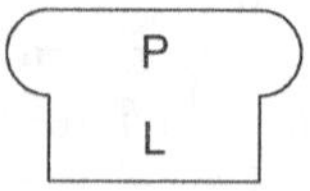

The second diagram illustrates that we have a machine (computer) M. Technically speaking, the concept of a machine involves several variants of an instruction set architecture and an operating system, but we will simplify everything and call this a machine.

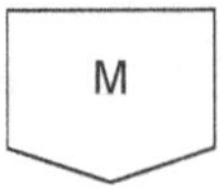

The third diagram illustrates an S-to-T translator expressed in language L. If L is a high-level language, then, after compilation, we would have a second version of this diagram, with L replaced by a machine language.

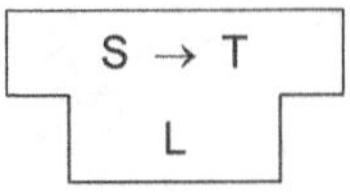

The figures below show several specific examples of these diagrams with actual program names, programming languages, and machines.

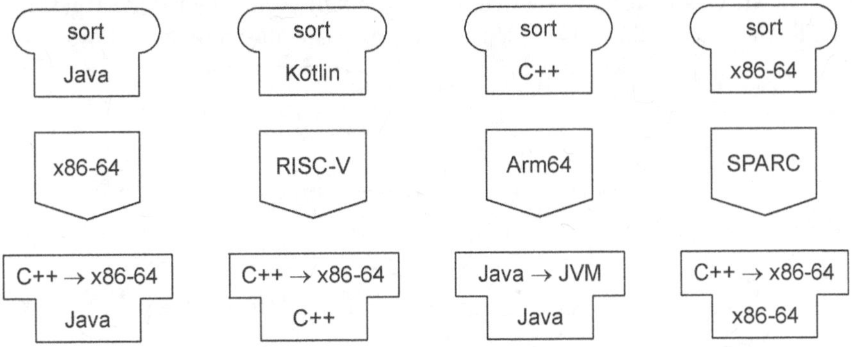

By themselves, these diagrams don't say a whole lot. The real power of these diagrams to illustrate concepts comes when we combine them. For example, suppose we have a program P that has been compiled to run on a particular machine M. We could illustrate the idea of a program running on a computer as follows.

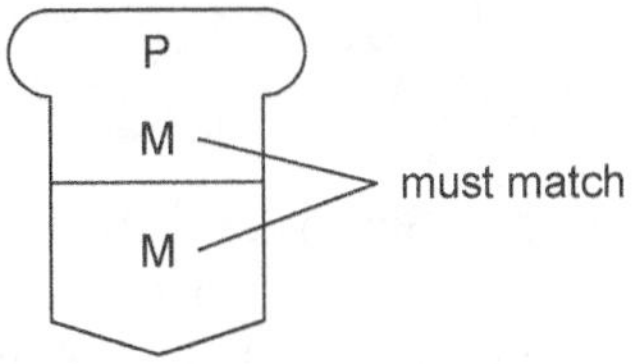

As indicated, the machine that the program has been compiled to run on must be the same as the machine actually running the program. So, for example, the combination below on the left is valid, but the combination on the right is not.

Now let's consider the idea of translating a program P, where the program is written in language S and the translator from language S to language T runs on machine M. The result of running the translator would be a semantically equivalent program in language T.

If S were a high-level language and T were a low-level language, then the translator would, in fact, be a compiler.

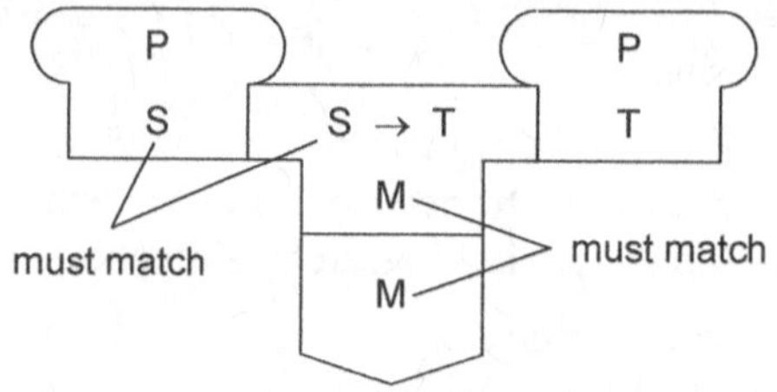

Let's illustrate with a sort program written in C++ using a compiler that targets an x86-64 computer. Then the two-step compile/execute process would look as follows.

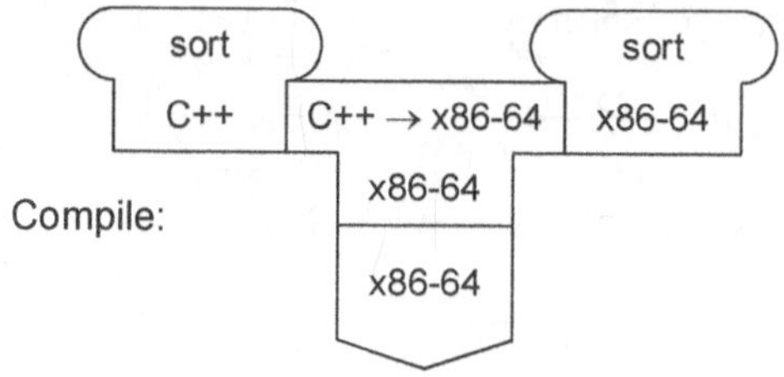

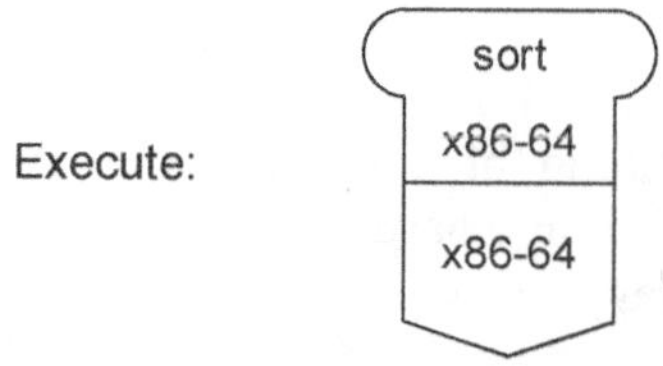

Two Versions of a Compiler

When we write a compiler in a high-level language, which is, by far, the most common approach, there are actually two versions of the compiler – the source code version written in the high-level language and the object code version obtained by compiling it. As an example, suppose that we have a Kotlin compiler written in C++ that targets an x86-64 machine. When we compile the Kotlin compiler, we then have one that runs on an x86-64 machine.

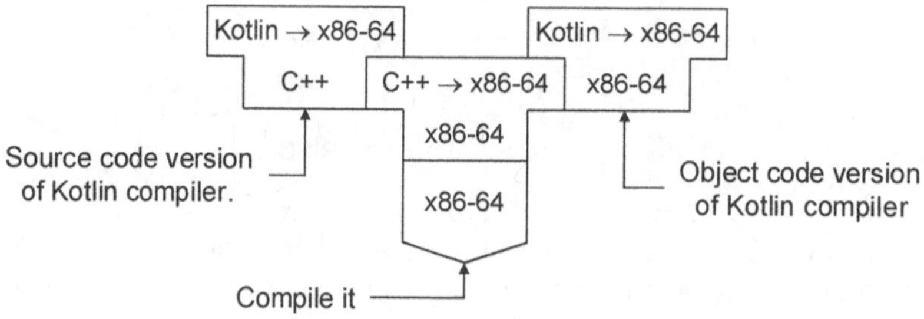

Cross-Compiler

A **cross-compiler** is a compiler that runs on one machine and produces target code for a different machine. The output of a cross-compiler must be downloaded to the target machine for execution. Cross-compilers are commonly used for embedded systems; for example, a small computer that might be embedded in a kitchen appliance or an automobile. Cross-compilers are also common for developing applications for mobile phones.

Using tombstone diagrams, we can illustrate the idea of a cross-compiler as follows.

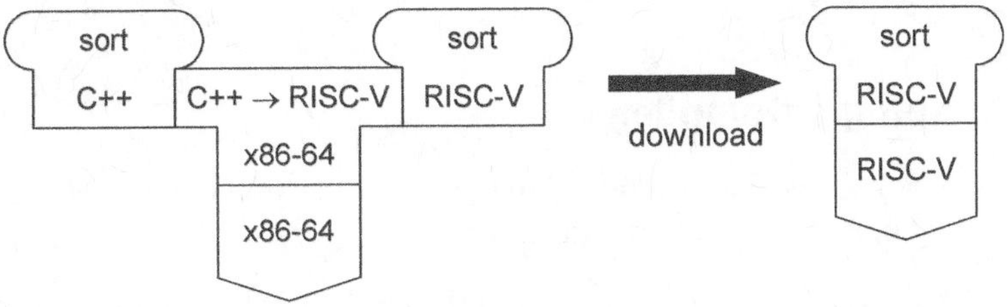

Two-Stage Compiler

We mentioned earlier that Bjarne Stroustrup originally implemented C++ as a high-level language translator (transpiler) to C. C++ programs were first translated to C, and then the C versions of the programs were compiled. As shown below, we can visualize this process using tombstone diagrams as a two-stage compiler. Note that the middle parts of the diagram could be viewed as being functionally equivalent to a C++-to-x86 compiler.

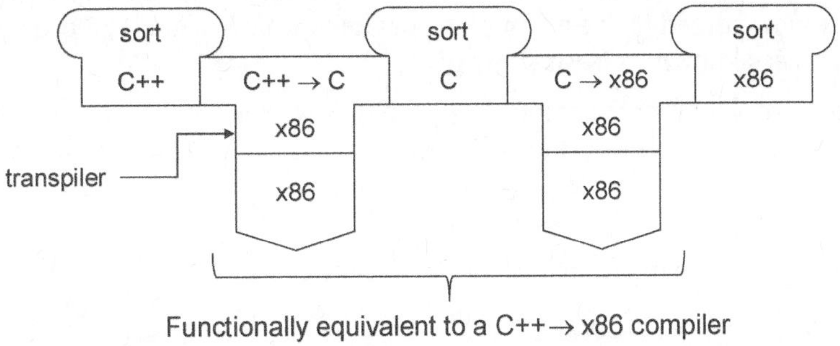

Similarly, as illustrated below, a compiler that targets assembly language is essentially a two-stage compiler, where the first stage translates from the source language to assembly language, and the second stage translates from assembly language to machine code.

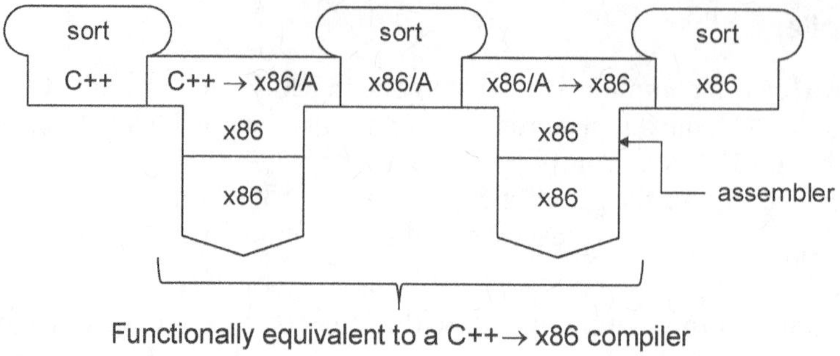

1.4 Bootstrapping a Compiler

It is common to write a compiler in the language being compiled; e.g., writing a C++ compiler in C++. Doing so has several advantages.

- The compiler itself provides a non-trivial test of the language being compiled.
- Only one language needs to be learned by compiler developers.
- Only one compiler needs to be maintained.
- If changes are made in the compiler to improve performance, then recompiling the compiler will improve compiler performance.

For a new programming language, how do we write a compiler in that language? This appears to be "a chicken and egg problem" in that we can't write a compiler for the new language unless we already have a compiler for the new language. The problem can be solved by a process known as **bootstrapping**.

Let's make the problem more specific. Suppose that we want to build a compiler for a programming language, say C#, that will run on machine M, and assume that we already have a compiler for a different language, say C, that runs on M. Furthermore, we desire ultimately that the source code for the C# compiler be C#.

The following tombstone diagrams illustrate this situation.

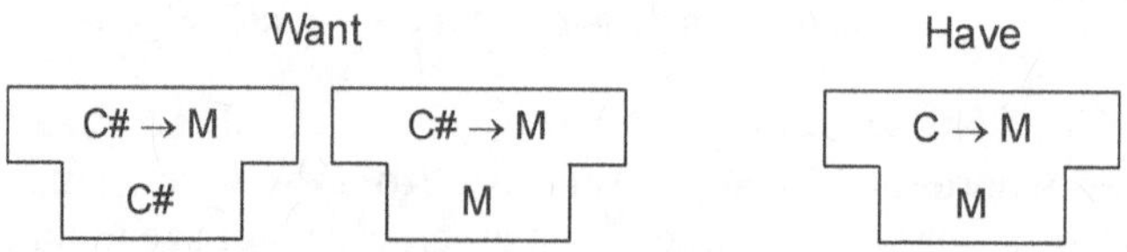

Bootstrapping a Compiler: Step 1

Start by writing a compiler for C# in C. At this point we don't necessarily need a compiler for the entire C# language, only for a subset of C# that is sufficiently complete for writing compilers. The result of implementing and compiling our C# compiler is illustrated as follows.

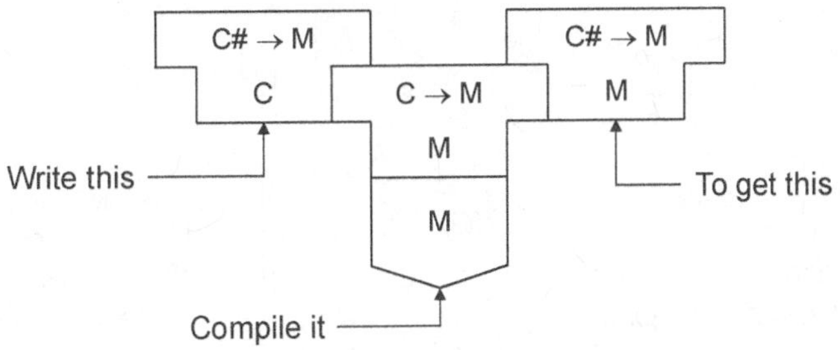

Bootstrapping a Compiler: Step 2

Now we write the full compiler for C# in C#, and then we compile it using the compiler obtained from step 1.

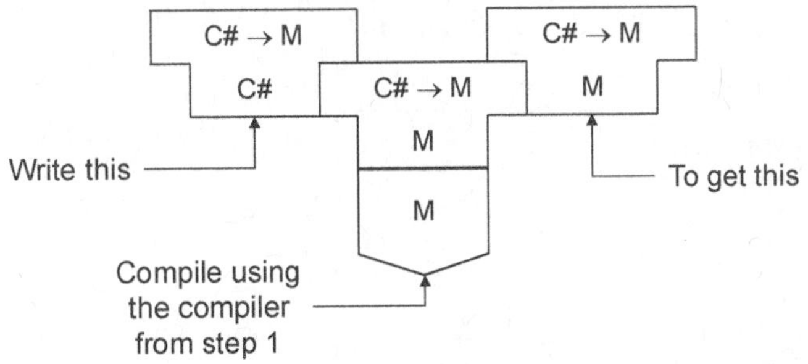

At this point we have exactly what we wanted – a C# compiler for machine M written in C#.

Efficiency of a Compiler

When we talk about the efficiency or performance of a program, we commonly refer to the speed at which it executes. The speed can be in absolute terms such as 12.31 seconds, or it can be in terms of asymptotic growth based on the size of the input. The latter is usually expressed using the big-Oh notation such as $O(n)$ or $O(n\ log\ n)$. Note that efficiency can also refer to the program's use of memory, and for application domains such as embedded systems, the efficient use of memory can be more important than the program's speed since it can affect product cost.

When we talk about the efficiency of a compiler, there are two aspects to consider: the efficiency of the compiler itself as a program and the efficiency of the object code generated by the compiler. For example, a compiler could run quickly but generate object code that is not very efficient.

Now suppose you have a compiler for a language (say C++) written in that language. If you modify the compiler to improve efficiency of the generated object code, then you can recompile the compiler to obtain a new compiler that generates more efficient code. This idea is illustrated in the following diagram.

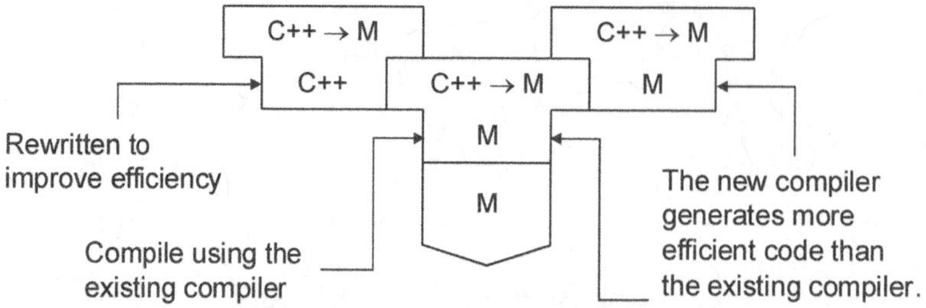

But at this point our new compiler (the compiled version) does not yet run with the efficiency improvements. If we want the compiler itself to be more efficient, we need to compile the C++ version one more time.

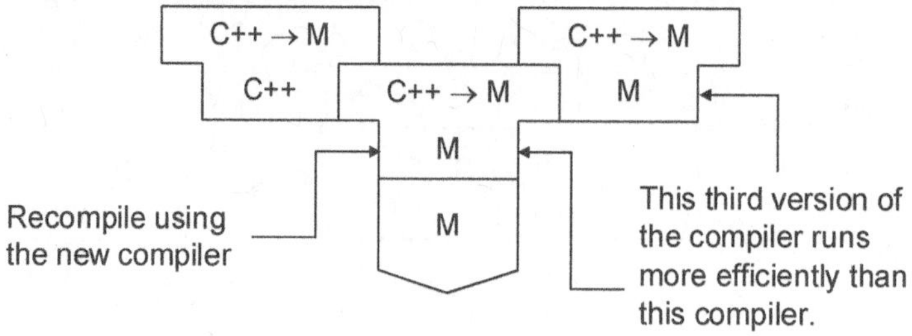

1.5 Interpreters

The tombstone diagram for an interpreter for language S expressed in language L is depicted as a simple rectangle. Note that L could be a high-level language or a machine language.

Here are three interpreter examples. The last two represent compiled versions that are ready to run on a specific machine.

The diagram on the right illustrates a BASIC interpreter running on an x86 machine.

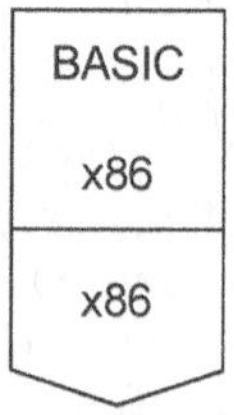

This is functionally equivalent to a "BASIC" machine; i.e., a machine that executes BASIC commands in hardware.

We can use the BASIC interpreter to run a sort program written in Basic.

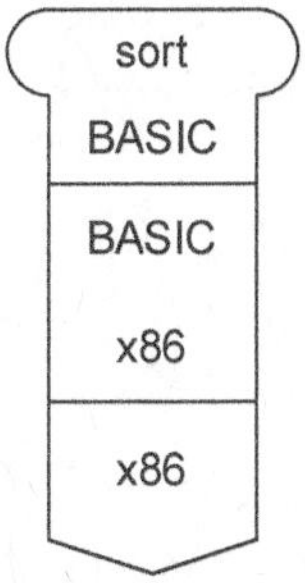

If we ignore Just-In-Time (JIT) compilation, we can think of Java programs as essentially being interpreted by the JVM. Thus, the compile/execute steps involved in using Java can be illustrated as follows.

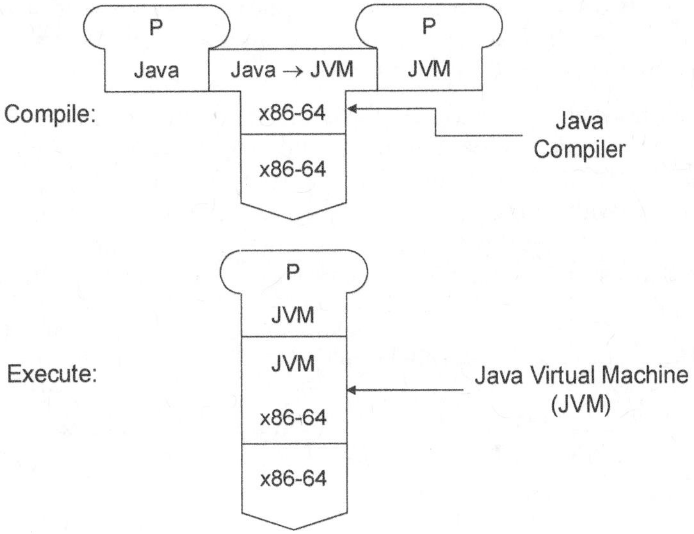

1.6 The Compiler Project

The compiler project outlined in this book uses a relatively small source language called CPRL (an acronym for Compiler PRoject Language), which was designed for teaching the basic concepts of compiler design. The target machine is a hypothetical machine called CVM (for CPRL Virtual Machine), but in order to simplify the process of writing a compiler, the target language for the compiler project is assembly language for CVM, not the actual machine language. It is easier to write a compiler for an assembly language than to write it for an actual machine, even a simple machine.

We denote the project's target language by CVM/A, where the "A" stands for assembly language. Thus, the project is to write a CPRL-to-CVM/A compiler in Java. When you compile your compiler, you will have a CPRL-to-CVM/A compiler that runs on a Java virtual machine. The process of writing and compiling a CPRL-to-CVM/A compiler is illustrated as follows.

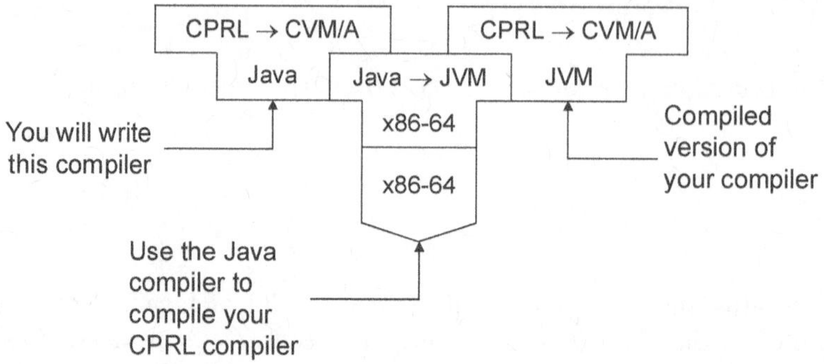

Note that there are two versions of your compiler, the source code version written in Java (shown on the left of the above diagram) and the compiled version that actually runs on the JVM (shown on the right of the above diagram).

Two important utilities are provided with the book resources, a CVM assembler and a CVM interpreter (emulator). Both of these utilities were written in Java and run on the Java virtual machine (JVM). Once your compiler is working, you can write test programs in CPRL, compile them with your compiler, and then assemble them with the CVM assembler. The diagram below illustrates the process of starting with a program written in CPRL and creating a compiled/assembled version of the program that will run on the CVM.

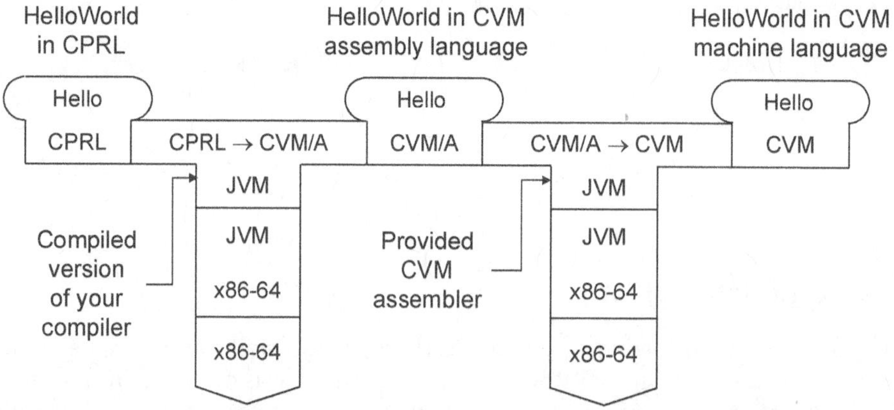

You can then execute your program using the CVM interpreter, as illustrated in the diagram below.

The program illustrated in these two diagrams is the typical first program in a new language that prints "Hello, world." to standard output. Using the naming conventions outlined in the course project, the actual file names for the three versions of the program would be `Hello.cprl` (for the CPRL version), `Hello.asm` (for the assembly language version), and `Hello.obj` (for the CVM version).

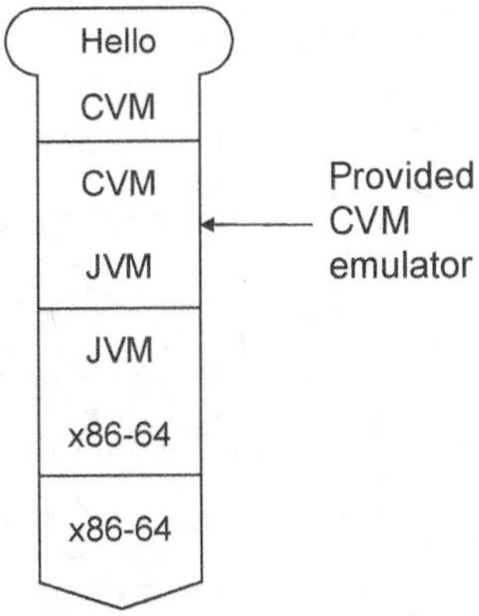

As outlined in Appendix A, source code for the CPRL compiler project is organized into four top-level packages, some of which have subpackages. Package `common` contains classes that are not directly tied to the CPRL programming language and therefore are useful on any compiler-related project. Package `cprlc` contains the classes that implement the actual CPRL compiler. We cover the classes in these two packages starting with Chapter 5.

Package `cvm` contains classes that implement the CPRL virtual machine (CVM) and a CVM disassembler, and a fourth package, `assembler`, contains classes that implement an assembler for CVM assembly language. We cover these two packages in more detail much later in the book starting with Chapter 10. Complete source code is provided for packages `common`, `cvm`, and `assembler`, but only portions of the source code are provided for the classes in package `cprlc`. Although students will need to refer occasionally to the other three packages in order to understand the roles their classes play in developing the CPRL compiler, all new development will take place only in package `cprlc`.

1.7 Essential Terms and Concepts

assembler	bootstrapping
compiler	compile/execute process
CPRL	CVM
cross-compiler	disassembler
efficiency of a compiler	emulator/virtual machine
high-level language translator	implementation language (for a compiler)
interpreter	interpretive compiler
Java bytecode	JIT
JVM	linker
source language (for a compiler)	target language (for a compiler)
tombstone diagrams	translator
transpiler	two-stage compiler

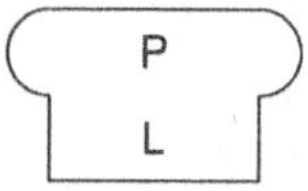

(program)

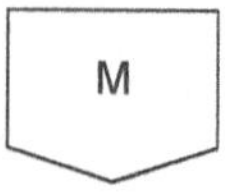

(machine)

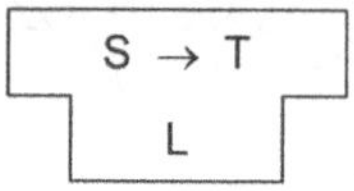

(translator)

(interpreter)

1.8 Exercises

1. Name and briefly describe the three languages involved in writing a compiler.
2. Describe several advantages of writing a compiler in the language being compiled (e.g., writing a C++ compiler in C++).
3. Explain the difference between a compiler and an interpreter. What are the relative advantages and disadvantages of each?
4. Draw a tombstone diagram representing a Fortran compiler for an x86-64 computer that is written in C++. Assuming that the C++ compiler runs on an x86-64 computer, draw a tombstone diagram for the "compiled" version of the Fortran compiler.
5. Describe the basic steps in bootstrapping a compiler. Assume that you have a C++ compiler for an x86-64 machine and that you want to write a Swift compiler for that machine. Use tombstone diagrams as part of your description.

6. A new computer called MACH-1 is being created, and you want to write a Kotlin compiler for the MACH-1. Assuming that you already have a C++ compiler for an x86-64 machine, explain how to use your existing C++ compiler to create a Kotlin compiler for a MACH-1 machine. Use appropriate tombstone diagrams as part of your explanation. Here are a couple to help you get started.

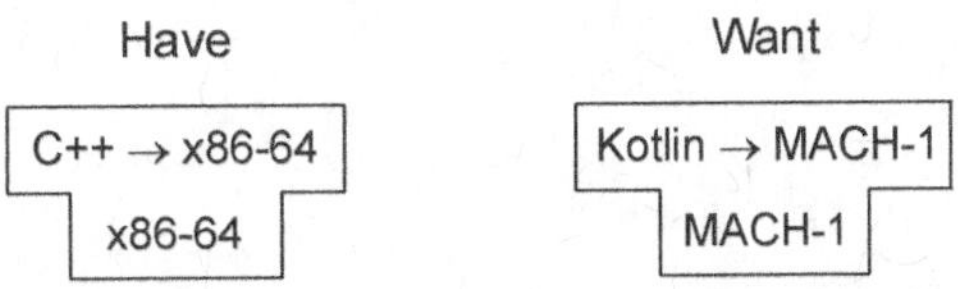

Hint: Review the concepts of cross-compiling and bootstrapping.

Chapter 2
Structure of a Compiler

The structure of a compiler generally has a form similar to the one illustrated in the diagram below. Details of the components or phases shown in this example will be covered in subsequent chapters, but here we present a general overview of this structure.

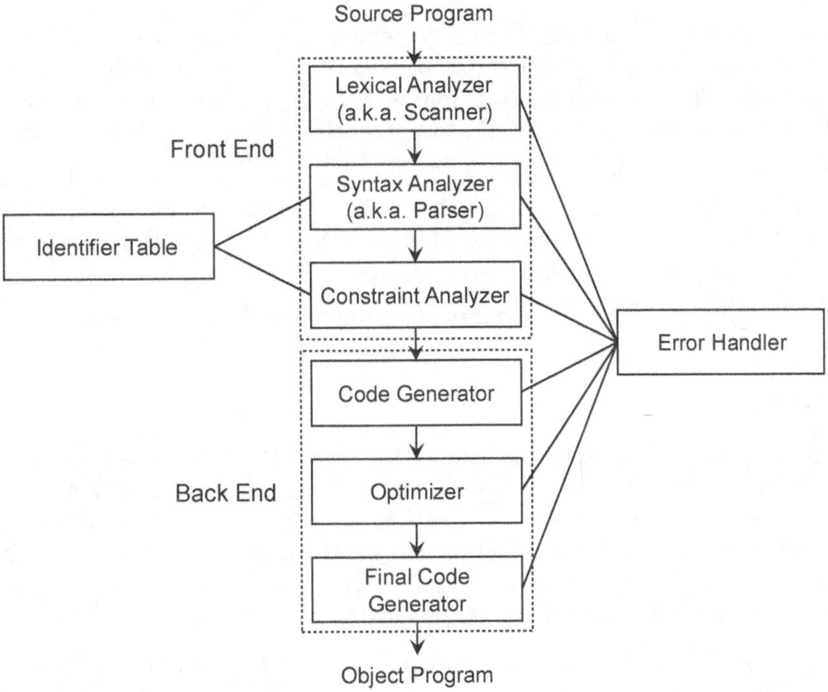

Think of the diagram as a general set of tasks that must be performed, and don't take the actual structure literally. Not every phase is required to be separated out as a distinct collection of code components in the compiler; e.g., parts of syntax analysis and constraint analysis might be intertwined, and similarly for optimization and final code generation. Also, optimization might actually be performed in several places within the compiler.

Not shown in the diagram above is the fact that most compilers use one or more intermediate representations during the compilation process. Common intermediate forms include abstract syntax trees, which provide a high-level intermediate representation of the basic structure of the program, and low-level intermediate code similar to machine code but often machine independent. Some compilers use both abstract syntax trees and low-level intermediate code. Note that some optimizations can be performed on the intermediate representations as well as on the final machine-dependent object code.

The lexical analyzer, syntax analyzer, and constraint analyzer – the first three components shown in the diagram – are collectively called the "front end" of the compiler. The front end performs analysis of the source code to determine whether or not it is valid according to the definition of the programming language being compiled. If the source code is valid, then the front end must determine its intended effect. The front end is heavily dependent on the source language but relatively independent of the target machine. The front end can include some high-level optimizations, but most optimizations are handled later in the compilation process.

The code generator, optimizer, and final code generator – the last three components shown in the diagram – are collectively called the "back end" of the compiler. The role of the back end is to generate efficient machine code that is semantically equivalent to the source code. The back end is heavily dependent on the target machine but relatively independent of the source language.

We sometimes summarize the roles of the front end and back end by saying that the primary focus of the front end is *analysis* of the source program, and the primary focus of the back end is *synthesis* of the object program.

Now let's examine each of the components of a compiler in a little more detail.

2.1 Scanner

The lexical analyzer is often called the lexer or the scanner. We will use the term scanner primarily in the remainder of this book. The scanner identifies the basic lexical units of the language, which are called the tokens or symbols of the language. These lexical units are often defined in terms of patterns called regular expressions. The scanner also usually removes extraneous whitespace and comments since they play no role in subsequent analysis or code generation, and it reports any errors encountered in the source code.

The diagram below illustrates the work of the scanner when it encounters a simple statement. Note that the scanner breaks the assignment statement into five lexical units and records the position (line number and column number) of each lexical unit.

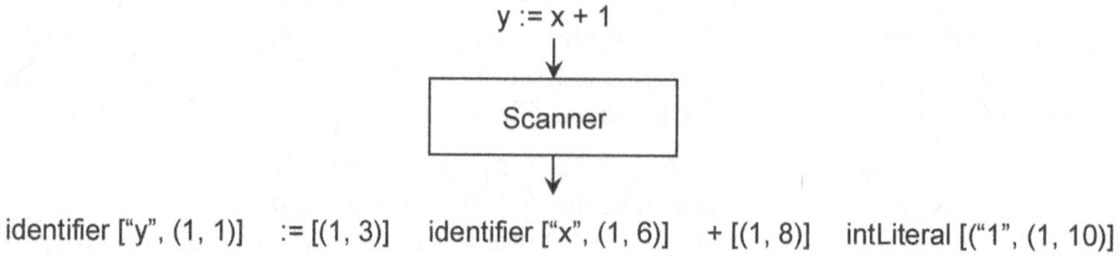

Chapter 5 provides a more complete explanation of the process of lexical analysis or scanning.

2.2 Parser

Using the lexical units produced by the scanner as input, the syntax analyzer or parser verifies that the grammatical rules of the language are satisfied. The grammar of a language is based on patterns called context-free grammars (a.k.a. BNF or Backus–Naur form). The parser also constructs an intermediate representation of the program that can be used for further analysis and code generation. The diagram below shows the parser constructing an abstract syntax tree (AST) for an assignment statement. The AST for an assignment statement consists of the left side, which in this case is an identifier, and the right side, which in this case is an adding expression.

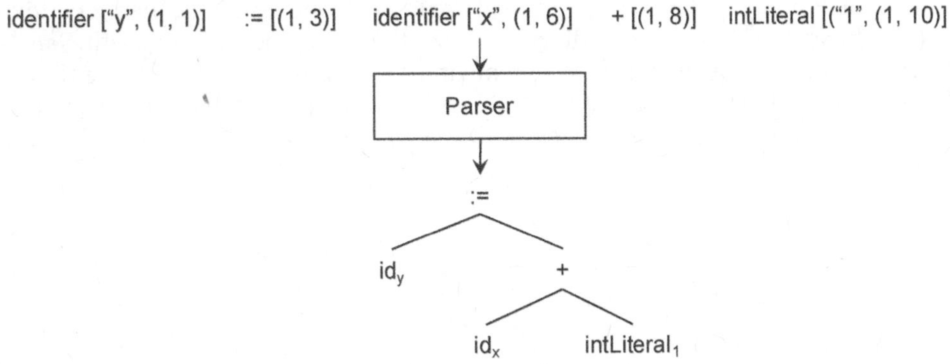

Chapter 6 provides a more complete explanation of the process of syntax analysis or parsing, while Chapter 8 provides a more complete explanation of abstract syntax trees.

2.3 Constraint Analyzer

The grammatical rules of a programming language are expressed in a notation called a context-free grammar, and the parser verifies that a program conforms to those rules. However, there are some language requirements that can't be expressed, or can't be expressed succinctly, in a context-free grammar. For example, we might have a rule that requires a `while` expression (as a prefix to a `loop` statement) to have type `Boolean`. Other rules might involve compatible types for an assignment statement. Type analysis is an essential part of constraint analysis. Usually the constraint analyzer just checks for validity, with little or no modification of the current representation.

Chapter 9 is devoted to the process of constraint analysis, with additional details in Chapters 13-17. Constraint analysis is sometimes referred to as analysis of static semantics, but constraint analysis seems to be a more appropriate term.

2.4 Code Generator

The role of the code generator is to create a low-level representation of the source program that is suitable for optimization and final code generation. The low-level representation can be based directly on the target machine, or it can be "machine-like" but somewhat independent of the actual target machine architecture. If the low-level representation is assembly language or if it is machine independent, then this component of the compiler is often referred to as an "intermediate" code generator.

The approach used in this book is to translate an abstract syntax tree into assembly language for the CVM, a stack-based virtual machine. Using this approach, our code generator encapsulates detailed knowledge of the target machine and is, therefore, highly machine dependent. The following diagram shows the code generator translating an abstract syntax tree for an assignment statement into assembly language for the CVM. Code generation is simplified since the CVM is somewhat simpler than a real machine, and it is further simplified by allowing generation of assembly language rather than actual machine code.

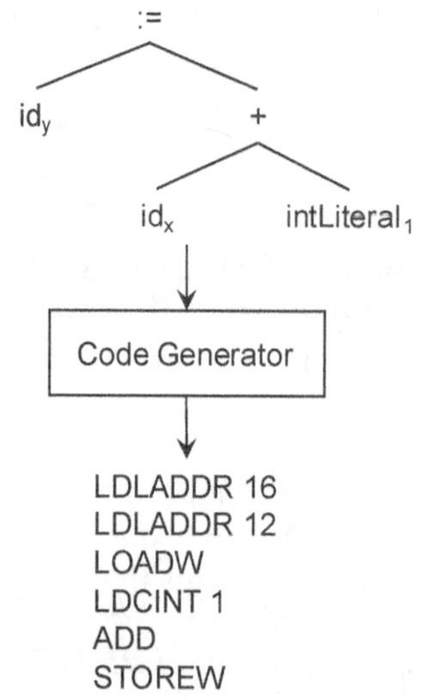

Chapters 11 and 13-17 cover code generation in more detail, with emphasis on generating code for the CVM. Some of the exercises in Appendix B discuss alternative targets such as the JVM or assembly language for the Intel x86-64 architecture.

2.5 Optimizer

The optimizer is concerned with improving the run-time performance of the object code. As discussed in the previous chapter, performance can involve both the speed at which the object code runs and/or the amount of memory used by the program. Some optimizations can improve both, but often there is a tradeoff between the two goals. Some compilers permit compiler directives or pragmas, where the programmer can provide guidance to the compiler as to how to resolve the tradeoffs.

The optimizer deals with issues such as allocation of machine registers, time/space performance of the code, moving invariant computations outside of a loop, and compile-time arithmetic. It is possible to perform optimization for different representations (e.g., intermediate versus object code optimizations) and at different levels (e.g., local versus global optimizations).

The diagram below shows the optimizer replacing instructions that "add 1" to an integer variable with an instruction to "increment" the variable. Most target architectures would support an increment instruction, and using such an instruction would result in minor improvements in both time and space performance of the object code.

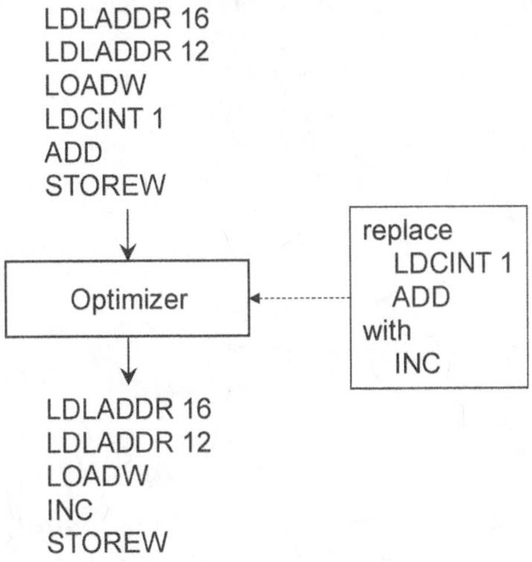

Chapter 12 provides additional details about code optimization.

2.6 Final Code Generator

The final code generator creates the object code file in a format that is ready to be loaded and executed on the target machine (or at least ready to be linked with other object code files). When the output of the compiler is assembly language, then the role of the final code generator can be performed by the assembler. The assembler provided in the course materials serves as the final code generator for the compiler project. It also performs a few minor optimizations such as the one illustrated in the previous section. The following diagram illustrates the role of the final code generator.

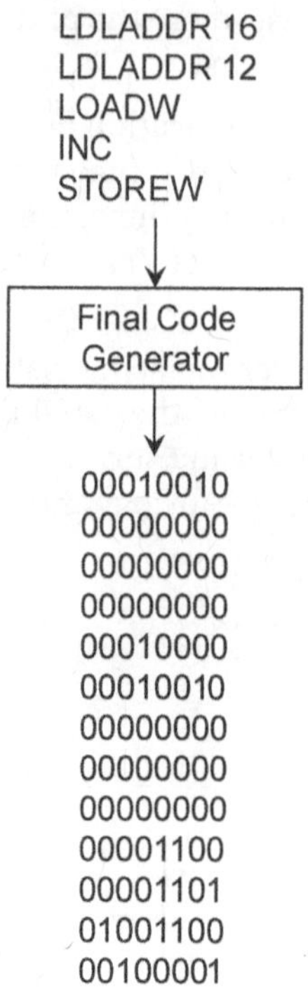

2.7 Tables and Maps

Tables and maps are used in various places by compilers. Some parsing techniques use table-driven scanners and parsers, where tables drive the compilation process. The basic idea for parsers is that a context-free grammar is used as input to a program that generates the tables, and then the tables are used as input to the parser.

The approach described in this book does not use a table-driven parser, but we will use maps (a.k.a. dictionaries or associative arrays) to record information about identifiers such as whether the identifier represents an integer variable, the name of an array type, or the name of a procedure. Most compilers will use something similar, which is often referred to as an identifier table or a symbol table.

2.8 Error Handler

The error handler reports the nature and location of errors. Error messages can provide important feedback to the programmer since, most of the time, a compiler is used to compile incorrect programs. The error handler usually tries to perform some type of error recovery so that multiple errors can be detected and reported. But, as we will learn in Chapter 7, error recovery can be difficult, and sometimes a compiler will produce a misleading error message. Most software developers learn quickly that all errors reported after the first error are suspect and should be approached with caution.

Here is an example of an error message generated by the project compiler when testing it against one of the incorrect CPRL programs.

```
*** Syntax error detected near line 7, character 4:
    Expecting ";" but found "else" instead.
```

Some compilers dispense with error recovery altogether, stopping with the first error. First released in 1983, Turbo Pascal was a blazingly fast compiler that used this approach, stopping at the first error encountered and bringing up an editor with the cursor positioned at the point of error. It was convenient and quick to fix the first error and then recompile. Today, many Integrated Development Environments (IDEs) and code editors have built-in compilers (or at least syntax checkers) that accomplish this in a more integrated fashion. IntelliJ IDEA, the Eclipse IDE, Apache NetBeans, Visual Studio, and VS Code are examples of IDEs/code editors that will flag programming errors and warnings while a program is being typed.

2.9 Passes

A **pass** is a complete traversal of the source program or an equivalent intermediate representation. A pass can involve disk I/O (i.e., reading and/or writing a file to disk), but the intermediate representation can be in memory. Some authors restrict the definition of compiler pass to a traversal that involves disk I/O, but we will use a more general definition. Using our definition, code that traverses the in-memory AST representation for a program will be considered a pass.

A single-pass compiler makes only one traversal of the source program, whereas a multi-pass compiler makes several traversals. A language must be carefully crafted in order to permit a single-pass compiler. For example, if an identifier can be used before it is formally defined, then it can be difficult to implement a single-pass compiler. The original definition of Pascal was designed for single-pass compilation, and some of the earlier Pascal compilers were implemented using a single pass. However, most modern languages are so complex as to preclude compilation using a single pass.

There are a number of advantages for using multiple passes in a compiler including increased modularity and improved ability to perform global analysis (optimization). Plus, multi-pass compilers often offer greater opportunity to exploit concurrency on multiprocessor architectures. And it is possible for a multi-pass compiler to use less memory at runtime if the passes are overlaid, but this advantage has less significance for most modern computers with large physical and virtual memories.

Disadvantages of multi-pass compilers can include slower compilation times, especially if extra disk I/O is involved, and they are usually larger (in terms of source lines of code) and more complex. In addition, a multi-pass compiler requires design of intermediate language(s)/representation(s).

The compiler project described in this book uses three passes.

- Pass 1 reads/analyzes source text and produces an intermediate representation (ASTs).
- Pass 2 performs constraint analysis on the intermediate representation.
- Pass 3 generates assembly language for the CVM.

Technically the assembler is not part of the compiler project since it is provided with the book resources, but the assembler also makes several passes, including some passes to perform optimizations.

2.10 Compiler Design Goals

As with any substantial software or engineering project, designing a compiler involves tradeoffs among potentially conflicting goals. However, there is one goal for a compiler that can't be compromised – the goal of reliability.

Compiler Design Goal #1: A compiler must be error free.

Since writing a compiler is a large, human effort, this goal might not be fully achieved, but it should always have the highest priority. Software developers must be able to trust that the compiler will produce semantically equivalent object code.

Other possible goals for a compiler include:

- Modularity/maintainability. The goal is that the compiler will support future changes. Examples include new features or enhancements to the source language or changes in the compiler operating environment such as a new release of an operating system.
- Portability. The goal is to design the compiler in such a way as to minimize the amount of work needed to port from one environment to a different environment. This goal is closely related to the one above. Portability is often achieved by using virtual machines such as the Java Virtual Machine (JVM) used by Java applications or the Common Language Runtime (CLR) used by Microsoft .NET applications.
- Fast object programs.
- Small object programs. This goal is especially important for embedded systems, where the size of the object code can affect the cost or usability of the product containing the software.
- Fast compilation times. This is often a requirement during prototyping or in the early stages of software development. It is also a useful goal for compilers used in academic environments, where students are learning how to program for the first time.
- Small compiler size.
- Good error diagnostics and error recovery capabilities.

- Minimize compiler development time, so that a working compiler is available as quickly as possible.

2.11 Essential Terms and Concepts

abstract syntax tree

back end (of a compiler)

code generator

constraint analyzer

error handler

final code generator

front end (of a compiler)

identifier (symbol) table

intermediate representation

optimizer

parser/syntax analyzer

pass (of a compiler)

scanner/lexical analyzer/lexer

2.12 Exercises

1. Name and describe the phases/components of a compiler.
2. What is the "front end" of a compiler? What is the "back end" of a compiler?
3. Discuss the relative advantages and disadvantages of a single-pass compiler versus a multi-pass compiler.
4. Which compiler goals from Section 2.10 might be more desirable for a compiler used in a teaching/learning environment such as academia? Which compiler goals might be more desirable in a production environment for commercial software? Which compiler goals might be more desirable in embedded system software?

Chapter 3
Context-Free Grammars

3.1 Specifying a Programming Language

The definition of a programming language must address the specification of three main properties of the language, which we will refer to as syntax, contextual constraints, and semantics (what actually happens at runtime). The specification of these properties can be formal, using a precise notation similar to mathematics, or informal, using descriptions in English or some other natural language. The tradeoff is that a formal notation, while precise, can require considerable effort to learn and fully understand the notation itself independent of the programming language being defined. On the other hand, while an English description might seem easier to understand, it can be difficult to make such a description sufficiently precise. The approach used in this book follows a common practice of using a formal notation to specify syntax and informal specifications for contextual constraints and semantics.

The syntax of a language is a definition of the basic language symbols (or tokens) and the allowed structure of symbols to form programs. For example, what is the structure of an `if` statement, a variable declaration, a function declaration, etc.? It is important for the syntax to be specified precisely, and for that purpose we will use a formal notation called a context-free grammar. Practically all programming language definitions use context-free grammars to define the language syntax, and while there are some alternatives for the details of the notation, it is usually relatively straightforward to switch from one notation to the other.

While context-free grammars are powerful, they are, well, "context free," and there are language requirements that either can't be expressed easily or can't be expressed at all in a context-free grammar. These language requirements essentially need some knowledge of the "context" in which they appear, and we call these requirements contextual constraints (a.k.a. static semantics). Contextual constraints consist primarily of type and scope rules, but they can include other miscellaneous rules that aren't directly related to types and scopes. An example of a contextual constraint would be that a loop's "`while`" expression must have type `Boolean`. Note that some languages allow numeric expressions in this context, for example, with zero corresponding to false and nonzero corresponding to true.

Finally, the semantics of a programming language address the meaning or behavior of programs when run on a real or virtual machine.

As illustrated in the diagram below, in general, each programming language is "approximated" by a context-free grammar. The outer cloud represents all possible programs that could be submitted to a compiler, including programs that are not valid according to the language definition. The outer circle inside the cloud represents all programs with valid syntax. As represented by the innermost circle, contextual constraints further restrict the approximating language to coincide with the desired language. It is possible for a program to be valid with respect to syntax but not with respect to contextual constraints. In terms of the diagram, programs having valid syntax but failing to satisfy contextual constraints fall in the region between the two circles.

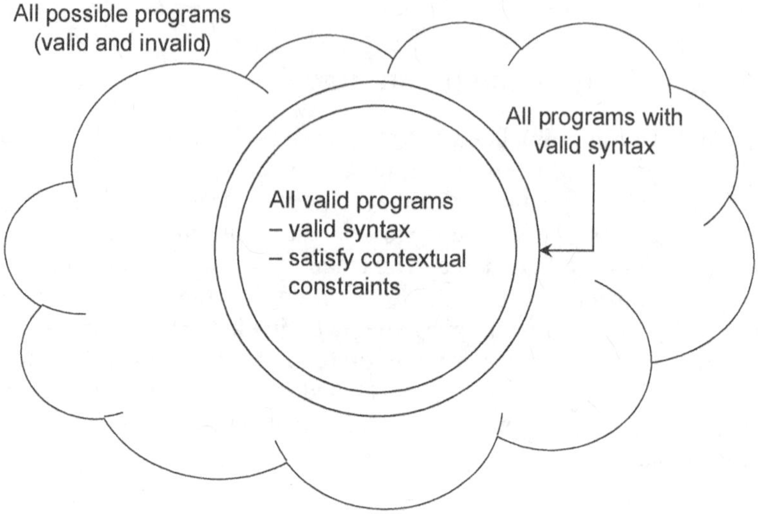

Here are two examples in CPRL that illustrate this point. Both examples are valid with respect to the context-free grammar that defines the CPRL syntax; but in the first example, the variable y has not been declared, which is required in CPRL.

```
var x : Integer;
proc main()
  {
    y := 5;
  }
```

In this next example, an attempt is made to assign an integer literal to a character variable, which is not permitted in CPRL (but is permitted in languages like C and C++).

```
var c : Char;
proc main()
  {
    c := 65;
  }
```

3.2 Context-Free Grammars

A context-free grammar, also known as a Backus-Naur Form (BNF) grammar or simply BNF, provides a formal notation for specifying the syntax of a programming language. A context-free grammar is sometimes called a syntactic metalanguage since it uses a finite notation to formally define the syntax for a programming language – it is essentially a language used to define programming languages. Context-free grammars show the structure of programs in the language, and they have been used extensively for almost every programming language since the definition of the programming language ALGOL 60.

They also drive scanner and parser development. For example, in our compiler project, most of the rules in the grammar are converted systematically into methods in the parser. Other approaches to parser development use compiler tools (so called "compiler compilers") that read the grammar as input and produce various parts of the scanner and parser, essentially automating much of the work outlined in Chapters 5 and 6.

There are many different (but similar) notations for defining context-free grammars. The notation that we use to define CPRL is a variation of a form called an *extended* context-free grammar or EBNF.

A **context-free grammar** (CFG) consists of four major components.

1. A finite set T of terminal symbols (a.k.a. the vocabulary) that represent the symbols appearing in the language. Examples include `2`, `a`, `i`, `<`, `=`, etc. These are the "atoms" of the language. Although these characters are not truly atomic since we can break them down into zeros and ones using a binary character code such as ASCII or Unicode, for the purposes of a context-free grammar we can consider them to be atomic. In addition, terminal symbols don't have to be single characters. For example, the keyword `while`, a variable named `average`, and the operator `<=` could be considered terminal symbols.
2. A finite set N of nonterminal symbols that represent the syntactic classes in the language. Examples include `declaration`, `expression`, `statement`, `loopStmt`, etc.
3. A start symbol (a.k.a. goal symbol), which is one of the nonterminal symbols, often something like `program` or `compilationUnit`.
4. A finite set of rules that define how syntax phrases are structured from terminal and nonterminal symbols. These rules are often called "syntax equations," "production rules," or simply "productions." They characterize possible substitutions for nonterminal symbols.

Format of Grammar Rules

Rules have the following form.

- An equals symbol "`=`" separates the left side of the rule from the right side.
- The left side of a rule is a single nonterminal symbol. Furthermore, we require that every nonterminal symbol appear on the left side of exactly one rule.
- The right side of a rule is a sequence of terminal symbols, nonterminal symbols, and other special symbols as defined below.
- A period "`.`" is used to terminate rules.

Here is an example of the rule for assignment statements in the context-free grammar for CPRL.

```
assignmentStmt = variable ":=" expression ";" .
```

ASCII, Unicode, and Character Encodings

The following is a very brief and overly simplistic discussion of character encodings.

There have been several standard character encodings in widespread use over the years. One of the earliest was the American Standard Code for Information Interchange or simply ASCII, which used seven bits to encode the English alphabet, digits, punctuation characters, and a number of control characters such as newline. Since most computer memories and external storage devices were organized around 8-bit bytes, ASCII was later extended by the ISO/IEC 8859 series of standards for 8-bit character encodings, the most popular of which was ISO/IEC 8859-1. The ISO/IEC 8859 series have now been largely replaced by Unicode, which originally used a maximum of 16 bits (two bytes) to encode characters but can now use up to 32-bits (four bytes). Unicode is capable of representing essentially all the characters used in different languages throughout the world as well as many historic scripts such as Egyptian hieroglyphs.

The current Unicode standard defines almost 300,000 code points (abstract characters) and several different ways to encode them. UTF-8 is a variable length encoding that uses a minimum of one byte to encode a character but can use up to four bytes for some characters. All characters in the ASCII subset are encoded in a single byte. UTF-8 is the most popular encoding, especially for transmission over the Internet.

UCS-2, an older two-byte encoding, was a popular encoding when Unicode was first developed, and the number of Unicode characters was small enough that they could all be encoded using only 16 bits. UCS-2 is still in use today, but it has essentially been superseded by UTF-16, which encodes each character using either two bytes or four bytes. Both UCS-2 and UTF-16 use the same encodings for characters that are encoded in only two bytes. While file systems can use different encodings, internally the Java virtual machine uses UTF-16 at runtime for characters and strings.

UTF-32 is a fixed length encoding that uses exactly 32 bits for each character. UTF-32 is not widely used since, on average, it requires significantly more space than other encodings.

All characters in the so-called Basic Multilingual Plane (BMP) of Unicode can be represented by 16 bits. For simplicity, CPRL, the source language defined in this book, restricts characters to this subset of Unicode. Each character in the Unicode BMP subset can be specified using four hexadecimal digits. The Unicode standard uses the notation `U+xxxx` to represent such a character, while Java, Kotlin, and many other programming languages use the notation `\uxxxx`. For example, English capital "A" is represented as `U+0041` or `\u0041`, and Greek capital sigma "Σ" is represented by `U+03A3` or `\u03A3`. Characters in the range `\u0000` to `\u007F` are the original ASCII characters.

In this rule, `assignmentStmt` is the single nonterminal symbol on the left side of the rule, and the right side of the rule contains nonterminal symbols `variable` and `expression` plus terminal symbols `:=` (assignment symbol) and `;` (semicolon).

Beyond terminal symbols and nonterminal symbols, the right side of a rule can make use of extra symbols to indicate notions of grouping, alternatives, repetition, and optional. It is the use of these additional symbols that makes the grammar *extended*. Our notation for context-free grammars adopts the following extra symbols from ISO/IEC 14977, an international standard for EBNF notation.

- A vertical bar "`|`" to separate alternatives. The vertical bar is read as "or".
- Parentheses "`(`" and "`)`" for grouping.
- Braces "`{`" and "`}`" to enclose a syntax expression that may be repeated zero or more times.
- Brackets "`[`" and "`]`" to enclose an optional syntax expression (i.e., one that may be repeated zero or one times).

The above rules do not use special symbols to indicate that a syntax expression should be repeated one or more times. Since "one or more" is equivalent to "one" followed by "zero or more", we can express "one or more" of syntax expression `E` as "`E { E }`". For the CPRL grammar, the requirement for "one or more" is used rarely. One such place is the lexical rule for `decimalLiteral`, which always includes at least one `digit`.

```
decimalLiteral = digit { digit } .
```

In addition to the above requirements, it is common to adopt certain conventions when writing grammar rules.

- Terminal symbols are (usually) quoted; i.e., we will use quotation marks to distinguish terminal symbols from nonterminal symbols.
- Set N consists of all nonterminal symbols appearing in the rules; i.e., any symbol that appears on the left side of a rule.
- Set T consists of all terminal symbols appearing in the rules; i.e., any symbol that does not appear on the left side of a rule. Most of these will be quoted.
- The start symbol is the left-hand side of the first rule.

Following these conventions, it is possible to specify a context-free grammar simply by specifying only the set of rules. We don't need to formally specify the set of terminal symbols, the set of nonterminal symbols, or the start symbols since that information can be derived by examining the set of rules.

> The CPRL grammar in Appendix D does not quite conform to these conventions since there are a few keywords that are reserved for possible use in the future. These keywords are essentially terminal symbols that do not appear in any rule.

Appendix D uses an extended grammar to specify the syntax for CPRL. Here are some of the rules listed in this appendix.

```
program = initialDecls subprogramDecls .
initialDecls = { initialDecl } .
initialDecl = constDecl | varDecl | typeDecl .
constDecl = "const" constId ":=" [ "-" ] literal ";" .

literal = intLiteral | charLiteral | stringLiteral | "true" | "false" .
varDecl = "var" identifiers ":" ( typeName | arrayTypeConstr )
          [ ":=" initializer ] ";" .
identifiers = identifier { "," identifier } .
... (See Appendix D)
```

The first rule says that a program consists of initial declarations (`initialDecls`) followed by subprogram declarations (`subprogramDecls`). The nonterminal symbol `program` is considered to be the start symbol since it appears on the left side of the first rule. Both `initialDecls` and `subprogramDecls` are nonterminal symbols and are further defined by other rules in the grammar.

The second rule says that the nonterminal symbol `initialDecls` (note the use of the plural form) is simply a list of zero or more `initialDecl` (note the singular form) symbols, where an initial declaration (`initialDecl`) is defined by the third rule as being either a constant declaration (`constDecl`), a variable declaration (`varDecl`), or a type declaration (`typeDecl`).

The last rule listed above defines the nonterminal `identifiers` as a list of `identifier` symbols, separated by commas. The list must include at least one identifier. Symbol `identifier` deserves additional explanation. As described shortly, we will actually create two grammars for CPRL, a lexical grammar and a structural grammar. Symbol `identifier` will be treated as a nonterminal symbol in the lexical grammar and a terminal symbol in the structural grammar. The rule that defines `identifier` is in the lexical grammar and is handled by the scanner, whereas rules in the structural grammar are handled by the parser.

If `N` is a nonterminal symbol and `E` is an arbitrary syntax expression, then a rule of the form

```
N = E .
```

means that the syntax expression `E` on the right side of the rule is an allowable substitution for the nonterminal `N` on the left side of the rule, regardless of the context in which `N` appears – hence the name *context-free*.

Lexical Versus Structural Grammars

It is common practice to separate the context-free grammar for a programming language into two parts, a lexical grammar that will be handled by the scanner and a structural grammar that will be handled by the parser. In effect, we will build two recognizers, a scanner that recognizes basic language symbols and a parser that recognizes the more complex language structure. Doing this allows us to reduce the complexity of the parser by moving some processing to the scanner. For a lexical grammar, we make the following restriction. It should be *possible* to define each nonterminal of the lexical grammar in a single rule using only terminal symbols and special symbols on the right side; i.e., no nonterminal symbols on the right side of the rule.

Consider the following excerpt from the specification of the Java programming language, where it discusses the separation of the grammar into two parts as described in this section.

2.2. The Lexical Grammar

A lexical grammar for the Java programming language is given in §3. This grammar has as its terminal symbols the characters of the Unicode character set. It defines a set of productions, starting from the goal symbol Input (§3.5), that describe how sequences of Unicode characters (§3.1) are translated into a sequence of input elements (§3.5).

These input elements, with whitespace (§3.6) and comments (§3.7) discarded, form the terminal symbols for the syntactic grammar for the Java programming language and are called tokens (§3.5). These tokens are the identifiers (§3.8), keywords (§3.9), literals (§3.10), separators (§3.11), and operators (§3.12) of the Java programming language.

2.3 The Syntactic Grammar

A syntactic grammar for the Java programming language is given in Chapters 4, 6-10, 14, and 15. This grammar has tokens defined by the lexical grammar as its terminal symbols. It defines a set of productions, starting from the goal symbol CompilationUnit (§7.3), that describe how sequences of tokens can form syntactically correct programs.

Chapter 18 also gives a syntactic grammar for the Java programming language, better suited to implementation than exposition. The same language is accepted by both syntactic grammars.

For the lexical grammar, we find it convenient to introduce the following additional notation to describe sets of characters.

- A single character will be enclosed in apostrophes (single quotes).
- Two periods (dots) will be used to indicate a range of characters.
- An unquoted plus symbol + will be used to indicate set union.
- An unquoted minus symbol - will be used to indicate set difference.

For example, suppose that we want a rule to describe the set of base 10 digits. Without additional character set notation, we could write this rule as

```
digit = "0" | "1" | "2" | "3" | "4" | "5" | "6" | "7" | "8" | "9" .
```

But with our new notation the rule can be shortened (without loss of understanding) to

```
digit = '0'..'9' .
```

The notation becomes even more useful for larger character sets. And while the notation of regular expression character classes could be used for this purpose, the notation chosen is sufficient for our needs and provides a somewhat more readable alternative, especially for complicated sets of characters. The CPRL grammar in Appendix D uses this notation for the lexical grammar, but it also provides the equivalent regular expression character classes in comments.

Here is an example of lexical rules using this notation.

```
identifier = letter { letter | digit } .
letter = 'A'..'Z' + 'a'..'z' .
digit = '0'..'9' .
```

Although we used three rules to define `identifier` above, we could substitute the definition of `letter` and `digit` into the right side of the rule for an identifier to create a single rule.

```
identifier = ('A'..'Z' + 'a'..'z') { ('A'..'Z' + 'a'..'z') | '0'..'9' } .
```

or equivalently

```
identifier = ('A'..'Z' + 'a'..'z') { 'A'..'Z' + 'a'..'z' + '0'..'9' } .
```

The definition using three rules is generally easier to understand, but the above illustrates the fact that it was *possible* to define `identifier` using only one rule after substitution.

Typically, the lexical grammar includes identifiers, reserved words, literals (e.g., integer literals, string literals, character literals, etc.), separators (e.g., parentheses, square brackets, commas, semicolons, etc.), and operators (e.g., +, -, <, <=, etc.). Note that the scanner will distinguish between a programmer-defined identifier (e.g., `average`) and a reserved word (e.g., `while`). The scanner will also recognize `<-` as a single symbol and not two separate single-character symbols. We will discuss these ideas in more detail in Chapter 5.

> Regular expressions describe concepts similar to those of context-free grammars, but they are more restrictive in that recursive rules are not allowed. Still, regular expressions are important enough that most modern programming languages and environments provide built-in support for regular expressions, usually as part of the standard library API. For example, Java support for regular expressions is provided by classes `Pattern`, `Matcher`, and `PatternSyntaxException` in package `java.util.regex`, and the standard C++ library provides support for regular expressions via the `<regex>` header. A common use of regular expressions is to define patterns that can be used in search or search/replace dialogs for applications such as text editors or text processing utilities. This book does not include a separate treatment of regular expressions, but several references and websites listed at the end of the book provide additional information.

The syntax or structural grammar rules handled by the parser are more complex rules that describe the structure of the language. These rules typically use recursive definitions. For example, the rule for a statement shows several alternatives, including a `loop` statement, as shown below.

```
statement = assignmentStmt | procCallStmt | compoundStmt | ifStmt
          | loopStmt       | forLoopStmt  | exitStmt     | readStmt
          | writeStmt      | writelnStmt  | returnStmt .
```

But in the body of a `loop` statement we can have another statement, which itself could be a `loop` statement or even an `if` statement that contains a `loop` statement.

```
loopStmt = [ "while" booleanExpr ] "loop" statement .
```

Hence we have used recursive definitions in the rules for statements. As we will see in Chapter 6, these recursive definitions give rise to recursive method calls in the parser.

Note that the parser treats the symbols returned by the scanner as terminal symbols. For example, consider the rule for a constant declaration.

```
constDecl = "const" constId ":=" [ "-" ] literal ";" .
```

In this rule, `constDecl` is a nonterminal symbol, the symbol `constId` is simply an identifier, and although it is not in quotes, the entire identifier is recognized and constructed by the scanner and is treated as a terminal symbol by the parser. The scanner handles all identifiers. The parser treats an identifier as if it were a terminal symbol in the part of the grammar that it handles.

As an analogy for the concepts of separating lexical and structural grammars, consider the progression that a child goes through in learning to read and write. The first step is to learn the alphabet, how the letters are put together to form words, and basic spelling. But the more complex part of learning to read and write is to master the structure of sentences in term of subjects and verbs, punctuation, and parts of speech (nouns, articles, adjective, adverbs, etc.). The lexical grammar, the part handled by the scanner, is analogous to the first step of learning the alphabet, forming words and spelling. The structural grammar, the part handled by the parser, is analogous to the more complex part of learning the structure of sentences, punctuation, and parts of speech. A similar analogy exists in mathematics, where the learning progression moves from numbers and counting to more complex mathematical expressions and formulas.

As specified in the rules for CPRL, a valid program ends with the last subprogram declaration. But what if a "candidate" program submitted to a compiler contains other characters or symbols after the last subprogram declaration? Grammar rules often use an **augmenting rule** to ensure that all input is matched; i.e., that there is nothing following a valid program other than an end of file. The following is an example of an augmenting rule.

```
system = program EOF .
```

In this rule, `system` is now the start symbol instead of `program`, and `EOF` represents "end of file". With an augmenting rule, there can be nothing meaningful in the file other than whitespace or comments after the last subprogram declaration. The augmenting rule may be explicitly listed as the first rule, or it may be simply "understood". We adopt the convention that an augmenting rule is "understood" and is not explicitly written as a rule in the grammar.

3.3 Alternate Rule Notations

There are a number of common variations or alternate notations for expressing rules. Here are some examples.

- Use "→", "::=", or simply ":" instead of "=" to separate left and right sides of rules.
- Use end of line (instead of period) to terminate rules. For this variation it is common to provide some way of expressing the fact that a long rule is continued to the next line.
- Use a postfix asterisk "*" to indicate a syntax expression that can be repeated 0 or more times. Similarly, use a postfix question mark "?" to indicate an optional syntax expression. These are the symbols used in regular expressions.
- Enclose nonterminal symbols in angle brackets "<" and ">" and omit quotes around terminal symbols.
- Use font highlights or changes such as bold instead of quotes to distinguish between terminal and nonterminal symbols.

Here are four examples of CPRL rules using an alternate notation.

```
<program> ::= <initialDecls> <subprogramDecls>
<initialDecls> ::= { <initialDecl> }
<initialDecl> ::= <constDecl> | <varDecl> | <typeDecl>
<constDecl> = const constId := [-] <literal> ;
```

These examples use `::=` to separate the left and right sides of the rule, they enclose nonterminal symbols in angle brackets, terminal symbols are not quoted, reserved words are shown in bold, and end of line is used to terminate rules.

Additionally, some non-extended (a.k.a. simple) grammar notations do not use the special symbols for "alternation," "zero or more," "optional," etc. A rule in an extended grammar that uses alternation is expressed as multiple rules. For example, this rule in our extended grammar notation for CPRL

```
initialDecl = constDecl | varDecl | typeDecl .
```

becomes three rules in a simple or non-extended grammar.

```
initialDecl = constDecl .
initialDecl = varDecl .
initialDecl = typeDecl .
```

Also, for simple (non-extended) grammars, the right side of a rule may be an empty string; e.g., "`N = λ`", where λ represents the empty string, and the concepts of "optional" or "zero or more" are expressed using recursion.

So, for example, this rule in our extended grammar notation for CPRL

```
identifiers = identifier { "," identifier } .
```

could be represented as three rules in a non-extended grammar notation.

```
identifiers = identifier identifiersTail .
identifiersTail = "," identifiers .
identifiersTail = λ .
```

The last three rules use recursion to specify that "`identifiers`" is a sequence of one or more identifier symbols, separated by commas.

While an extended grammar notation is usually more compact and easier to read for humans, some compiler tools require that the grammar be in this simple or non-extended format.

Syntax Diagrams

Syntax diagrams (a.k.a. railroad diagrams) provide a graphical alternative to textual representations for a grammar. Textual representations for a grammar are more easily processed by compiler tools, but syntax diagrams are more easily understood by humans.

The basic idea is to use a directed graph, where each diagram has an entry point and an end point. Terminal symbols are represented by rounded boxes, while nonterminal symbols are represented by square boxes. The syntax diagram describes possible paths between the entry and exit points by going through terminal and nonterminal symbols.

Below are two examples of syntax diagrams representing the CPRL rules for `loopStmt` and `initialDecls`.

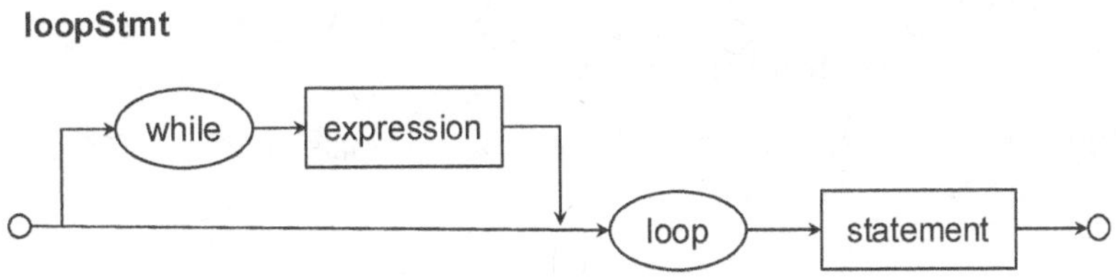

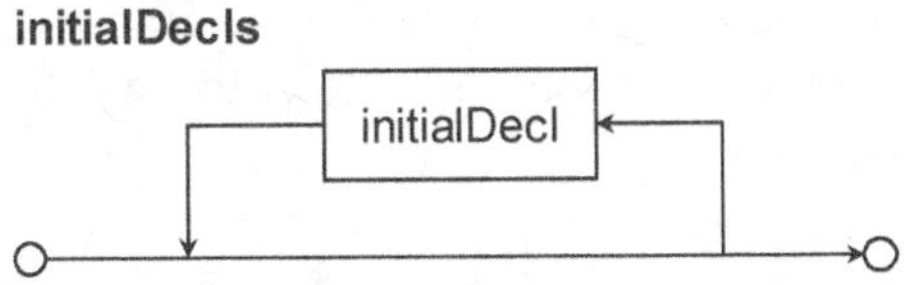

Use of Naming Conventions for Nonterminal Symbols

Language designers often use naming conventions for nonterminal symbols to convey contextual or semantic information in the grammar. This approach is illustrated by the following examples.

Example 1

```
functionCallExpr = funId "(" [ actualParams ] ")" .
funId = identifier .
actualParams = expressions .
```

Using substitution, these three rules are equivalent to the following single rule.

```
functionCallExpr = identifier "(" [ expressions ] )" .
```

From a language definition standpoint, there is no difference between the symbol `identifier` and the symbol `funId`. The use of `funId` is suggestive, but its use has no more effect on the language being defined than a comment has on source code. Similarly, there is no difference between `actualParams` and `expressions`.

Example 2

```
loopStmt = [ "while" booleanExpr ] "loop" statement .
booleanExpr = expression .
```

The name `booleanExpr` is chosen to indicate that the expression should have type `Boolean`, but as far as the grammar is concerned, there is no difference. With respect to the grammar, a `booleanExpr` is just an `expression`. Again, the use of `booleanExpr` can be interpreted as being roughly equivalent to a comment for the reader.

3.4 Grammar Transformations

There are some grammar transformations that do not affect the language being compiled. That is, although the grammar could look different, any program considered valid by the original grammar would be considered valid by the transformed grammar, and vice versa.

Substitution of Nonterminal Symbols

One such transformation is the substitution of nonterminal symbols. For example, suppose we have a rule of the form

```
N = X .
```

where the rule is nonrecursive and is the only rule for the nonterminal N. Then we can substitute `X` (the right side of the rule) for every occurrence of `N` in the grammar, thereby eliminating the nonterminal `N`. But the language designer may elect to leave the rule in the grammar. Here is an example used earlier.

```
booleanExpr = expression .
```

The symbol `expression` can be substituted for `booleanExpr` everywhere `booleanExpr` occurs in the grammar without affecting the language defined by the grammar. We don't really need `booleanExpr`. It is used simply to convey information that cannot be expressed formally in the context-free grammar.

Left Factorization

Another grammar transformation is left factorization. Suppose that the right side of a rule has alternatives of the form

```
X Y | X Z
```

We can replace these alternatives with the following equivalent expression.

```
X ( Y | Z )
```

Elimination of Left Recursion

Suppose that a rule has the form

```
N = X | N Y .
```

where X and Y are arbitrary expressions. A rule of this form is said to be left recursive since the nonterminal symbol on the left side of the rule is the first (left) symbol for one of the alternatives.

We can rewrite this rule to obtain an equivalent rule that is not left recursive.

```
N = X { Y } .
```

Example: Grammar Transformations

As a more concrete example, consider the following possible definition for `identifier`.

```
identifier = letter | identifier letter | identifier digit .
```

If we left factor the last two terms, we get

```
identifier = letter | identifier ( letter | digit ) .
```

Now we can eliminate left recursion to obtain the rule as it appears in the lexical grammar for CPRL.

```
identifier = letter { letter | digit } .
```

Grammars versus Languages

Understand the distinction between a language and a grammar. As illustrated above, different grammars can generate (define) the same language.

Two grammars are said to be **equivalent** if they generate the same language; that is, if every program that is syntactically valid according to one grammar is also syntactically valid according to the other grammar. Applying the grammar transformations discussed above will result in an equivalent grammar, but the general problem of determining whether or not two grammars are equivalent is known to be undecidable, meaning that there does not exist an algorithm that can examine two different grammars and always determine if they are equivalent.

3.5 Derivations and Parse Trees

Using the rules of a context-free grammar, we should be able to demonstrate that a sequence of symbols conforms to the grammar by systematically applying the rules one at a time, beginning with the start symbol. For example, consider the following simple grammar for expressions.

```
expr = expr op expr | id | intLit .
op = "+"   |   "*" .
```

Here we treat `id` (identifier) and `intLit` (integer literal) as terminal symbols for the purpose of this discussion, and we assume that they have the obvious meaning.

Using this simple grammar, we want to show that the string "`2 + 3 * x`" is valid with respect to the grammar. Beginning with the start symbol `expr`, we choose a valid replacement from the alternatives on the right side of the rule for `expr`, with the goal of eventually matching "`2 + 3 * x`". There are three alternatives on the right side of the rule for `expr`, but since neither of the last two can be expanded to match our desired target string, the only logical choice is the first alternative, "`expr op expr`". We write this as follows.

```
expr => expr op expr
```

The symbol `=>` means "derives." It shows that we have replaced `expr` by an alternative allowed in the context-free grammar.

Now we choose one of the nonterminals in the replacement sequence of symbols, say the first (left) appearance of `expr`. Then we choose the rule that has that nonterminal on the left side and replace the nonterminal with an allowed alternative on the right side of the rule. Replacing `expr` by `intLit` we now have the following.

```
expr => expr op expr
     => intLit op expr
```

Notice that we have underlined the nonterminal symbol that gets replaced in the next line.

Repeat this process until no nonterminal symbols remain. In order to show that "`2 + 3 * x`" is valid, we want to "derive" the sequence "`intLit + intLit * id`". For the steps below, we will always elect to replace the left-most nonterminal, and we will comment to show its replacement used in the next line.

```
expr => expr op expr                     // expr → intLit
     => intLit op expr                   // op   → "+"
     => intLit + expr                    // expr → expr op expr
     => intLit + expr op expr            // expr → intLit
     => intLit + intLit op expr          // op   → "*"
     => intLit + intLit * expr           // expr → id
     => intLit + intLit * id
```

The above series of replacements is called a **derivation**. At each step, the derivation simply replaced one nonterminal with one of its alternatives. Since we elected to always replace the left-most nonterminal symbol at each step of the above derivation, this is referred to as a **left-most derivation**. If we replaced the right-most nonterminal symbol at each step, we would have a **right-most derivation**.

We can view the derivation in a more graphical form using what is known as a parse tree. Instead of expanding the nonterminal using simply text, we put the replacement sequence of symbols below the nonterminal being replaced and draw a line from the nonterminal to each replacement symbol.

So, for example, instead of writing the first step as

```
expr => expr op expr
```

we draw the first level of the parse tree as follows.

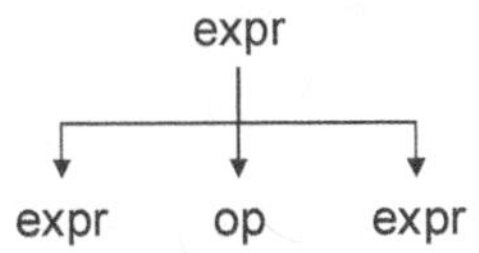

A **parse tree** (a.k.a. syntax tree) of a grammar G is a labeled tree with the following properties.

1. The leaves (terminal nodes) are labeled by terminal symbols.
2. The interior nodes (nonterminal nodes) are labeled by nonterminal symbols.
3. The children of an interior node N correspond in order to a rule for N.

Parse trees illustrate the rules used to recognize the input plus the terminal symbols. Below is the complete parse tree for the left-most derivation given above.

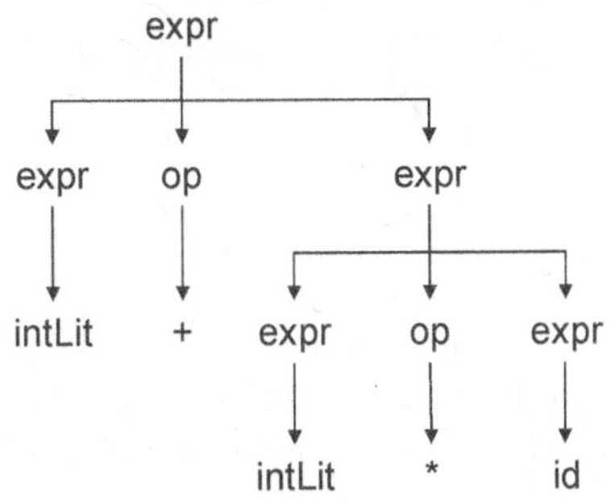

Note that the parse tree shows "`2 + 3 * x`" parsed with multiplication having a higher precedence than addition, which is what we want. But what if we were to choose a different alternative on the right side of a rule during the derivation? Would the corresponding parse tree always look the same? Let's see.

Using the same grammar, let's perform a different left-most derivation of "`2 + 3 * x`" by choosing a different alternative for `expr` in the beginning of the derivation process.

```
expr => expr op expr                        // expr → expr op expr
     => expr op expr op expr                // expr → intLit
     => intLit op expr op expr              // op   → "+"
     => intLit + expr op expr               // expr → intLit
     => intLit + intLit op expr             // op   → "*"
     => intLit + intLit * expr              // expr → id
     => intLit + intLit * id
```

Below we show the parse trees for these two derivations side by side.

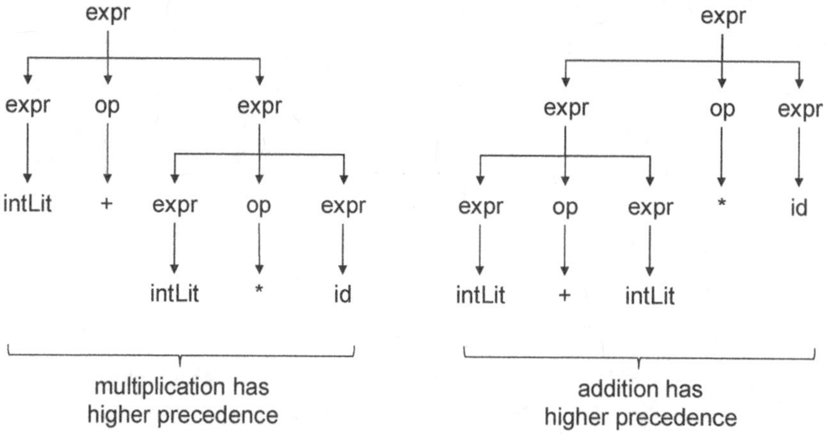

Clearly we have a problem. An **ambiguous grammar** is one for which some legal phrase has more than one parse tree. The simple expression grammar defined at the beginning of this section is ambiguous.

Specifying Operator Precedence

Operator precedence refers to the relative priority of operators in that it defines the order in which "adjacent" operators of different precedence levels are evaluated. For example, multiplication is generally given higher precedence than addition, so that "`2 + 3 * x`" is evaluated unambiguously as "`2 + (3 * x)`".

There are two general approaches to specifying operator precedence. We can define it within the grammar, or we can use an additional specification mechanism (e.g., a precedence table) separate from the grammar. In this book we will use the first approach in our definition for CPRL, but the second approach results in a simpler grammar and is supported by some compiler tools (e.g., yacc).

Consider the following grammar.

```
expr = term { "+" term } .
term = factor { "*" factor } .
factor = id | intLit .
```

The precedence of multiplication over addition is specified in the grammar itself. Below is a left derivation for "`2 + 3 * x`" using this grammar. Note that some of the steps in the derivation allow choices for repetition.

```
expr => term { "+" term }                      // replace term by factor
     => factor { "+" term }                    // replace factor by intLit
     => intLit { "+" term }                    // choose 1 repetition
     => intLit + term                          // replace term rule's right side
     => intLit + factor { "*" factor }         // choose 1 repetition
     => intLit + factor * factor               // replace factor by intLit
     => intLit + intLit * factor               // replace factor by id
     => intLit + intLit * id
```

We state without proof that, using the grammar above, the string "`2 + 3 * x`" can be parsed only one way. (Convince yourself that this statement is true by trying a different derivation, say a right-most derivation or one that is neither left-most nor right-most.) Below is the parse tree for "`2 + 3 * x`" using our non-ambiguous grammar.

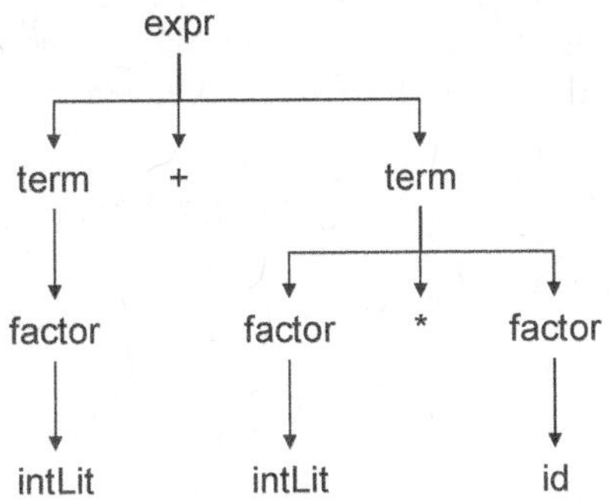

Note that "*" has higher precedence than "+" in this grammar.

Associativity

Closely related to the concept of operator precedence is that of associativity, which specifies the evaluation order of adjacent operators with the same precedence level when there are no parentheses. For example, in CPRL, the operators + and - are at the same precedence level and are *left associative*, meaning that `8 - 3 + 2` is evaluated as `(8 - 3) + 2`, which has the value `7`. If they had been *right associative*, then `8 - 3 + 2` would have been evaluated as `8 - (3 + 2)`, which has the value `3`. Since all operators in CPRL are left associative, we won't dwell on this topic except to point out a couple of examples of operators in other languages that are right associative.

Some languages support an exponentiation operator, and that operator is often defined as right associative. So for example, if the exponentiation operator is `^`, then `2^2^3` is evaluated as `2^(2^3)`, which is `2^8` or `256`, and not `(2^2)^3`, which is `4^3` or `64`.

As another example, the programming language C and some languages derived from C define assignment as an expression whose value is the value being assigned. The assignment operator `=` is defined to be right associative, so that `a = b = c` is evaluated as `a = (b = c)`.

Dangling `else`

Many languages, especially C-based languages, define an *if-statement* in a manner equivalent to the following.

```
ifStmt = "if" "(" expression ")" statement [ "else" statement ] .
```

Essentially this rule says that an *if-statement* can have an optional *else* clause. The problem with this rule as defined above is that it is ambiguous. (See exercise 12 at the end of this chapter.)

This ambiguity is known as the *dangling-else* problem. While it is possible to define the rules for an *if-statement* to avoid the ambiguity, doing so complicates the grammar. Language definitions that have a *dangling-else* problem usually just specify informally that, in the absence of braces, an *else* clause is associated with the nearest *if-statement* without an else clause. Most compiler tools will choose this option by default even if they complain about the ambiguity. Note that the grammar for an *if-statement* in CPRL exhibits the *dangling-else* problem.

```
ifStmt = "if" booleanExpr "then" statement [ "else" statement ] .
```

3.6 Abstract Syntax Trees

An abstract syntax tree is similar to a parse tree but without extraneous nonterminal and terminal symbols. An abstract syntax tree retains the "essence" of a language construct without the details of how it was parsed. Abstract syntax trees are covered in detail in Chapter 8. In this section we illustrate with a couple of examples.

Example 1. For binary expressions, we could omit all the additional nonterminal symbols introduced to define precedence – term, factor, etc. Once they have been parsed, all binary expressions would retain only the operator and the left and right operands. For the example used earlier, we show both the parse tree on the left and the (much simpler) abstract syntax tree on the right.

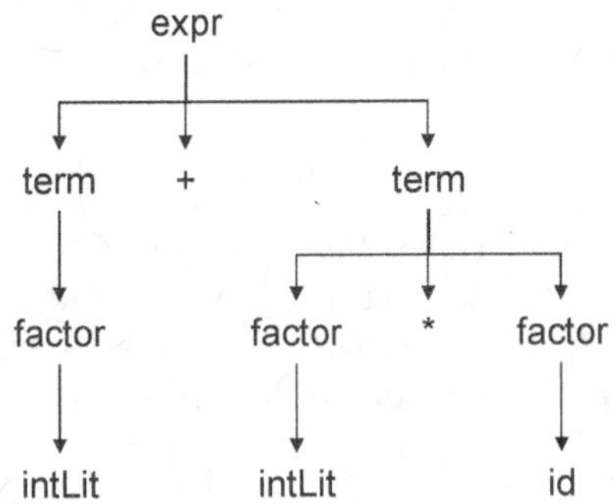

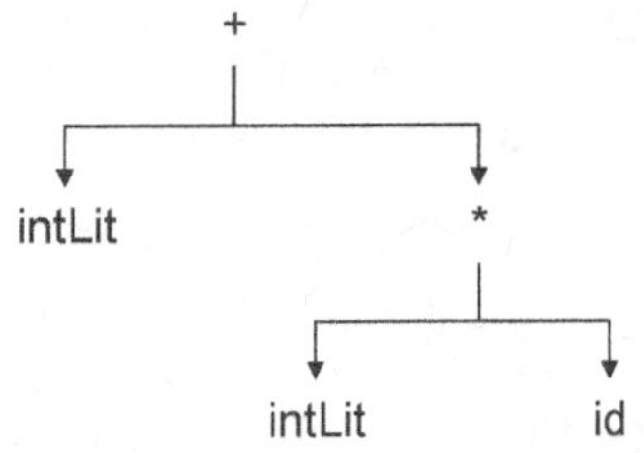

Example 2. Consider the following rule for a `while` statement.

```
whileStmt = "while" booleanExpr "loop" statement .
```

Once a `while` statement has been parsed, we don't need to retain the terminal symbols `"while"` and `"loop"`. The abstract syntax tree for a `while` statement would contain only `booleanExpr` and `statement`.

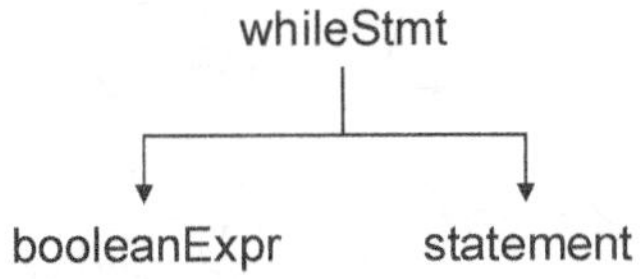

3.7 A Context-Free Grammar for Context-Free Grammars

We close this chapter by illustrating that the notation we use for defining a context-free grammar is powerful enough to specify its own syntax. Using our notation for character classes, here is one possible definition for the syntax of context-free grammars defined in itself.

```
grammar       = { rule } .
rule          = identifier "=" alternation "." .
alternation   = sequence { "|" sequence } .
sequence      = element  { element } .
element       = identifier | terminal | option | repetition | group .
option        = "[" alternation "]" .
repetition    = "{" alternation "}" .
group         = "(" alternation ")" .
identifier    = letter { letter } .
terminal      = "\"" { terminalChar | "\\" ( "\"" | "\\" ) } "\"" .
terminalChar = ' '..'~' - '\"' - '\\' .
letter        = 'A'..'Z' + 'a'..'z' .
```

In the above rules, `terminalChar` is defined to be any graphic ASCII character except double quote (") and backslash (\). An alternate definition of `terminalChar` using regular expression character classes would look as follows.

```
terminalChar = [ !#-\[\]-~] .
```

For simplicity, the grammar in the above example restricts the character set to the ASCII subset of Unicode, but that restriction could be relaxed. See, for example, the context-free grammar for CPRL as defined in Appendix D. CPRL essentially allows a string literal to contain any graphic Unicode character that can be represented in 16 bits.

3.8 Essential Terms and Concepts

abstract syntax tree (AST)	alternate rule notations
ambiguous grammar	ASCII/Unicode
associativity	augmenting rule
BNF/EBNF	CFG rules (productions)
context-free grammar (CFG)	contextual constraint
dangling else problem	derivation
elimination of left recursion	extended grammar
equivalent grammars	grammars versus languages
grammar transformations	left associative
left factorization	left recursion
left-most derivation	lexical grammar
nonterminal symbol	non-extended (simple) grammar
parse tree	precedence
right-most derivation	right associative
semantics	start (goal) symbol
structural (syntactic) grammar	substitution of nonterminal symbols
symbol	syntax
syntax diagram	`terminal symbol`
`E | F`	`{ E }`
`[ E ]`	`=>`

3.9 Exercises

1. Is it possible for a program to be valid with respect to syntax and still not be a valid program? Explain.
2. Is it possible for two different grammars to generate (define) the same language? Explain.
3. Rewrite the CPRL rule for an if statement (`ifStmt` – see Appendix D) using parentheses "`(`" and "`)`" plus postfix question mark "`?`" to enclose optional syntax expressions.
4. Fill in the blanks.
   a. When developing a compiler, we usually divide the grammar into two parts: a lexical grammar that is handled by the ______________________________, and a structural grammar handled by the ______________________________.
   b. With respect to context-free grammars, the left-hand side of a rule must be a single, ______________________________ symbol.
5. Consider the following simple (non-extended) grammar.

```
S = "0" S "1" .
S = λ .
```

   Describe in words the language (i.e., the allowable sequence of symbols) defined by this grammar.

6. Consider the following simple (non-extended) grammar.

```
S = "0" S "0" .
S = "1" S "1" .
S = λ .
```

   Describe in words the language (i.e., the allowable sequence of symbols) defined by this grammar. (Hint: What is a palindrome?)

7. Consider the following simple (non-extended) grammar.

```
S = A B .
A = "a" A1 .
A1 = "a" .
A1 = λ .
B = "b" B .
B = λ .
```

   a. Describe in words the language (i.e., the allowable sequence of symbols) defined by this grammar.
   b. Give an equivalent extended grammar definition.

8. Consider the following extended grammar.

```
S = { A } [ B ] .
A = "a" .
B = "b" .
```

Give an equivalent simple (non-extended) grammar definition.

9. Consider the following grammar for expressions.

```
expr = expr "+" term | term .
term = term "*" id | id .
id = "a" | "b" | "c" .
```

   a. Using this grammar, show a leftmost derivation for the following. `a + b * c`

   b. Draw a parse tree for the derivation obtained in part a.

10. In CPRL, the decimal representation for an integer literal is defined as a sequence of 1 or more digits.

```
decimalLiteral = digit { digit } .
digit = '0'.. '9' .
```

This definition allows a sequence of zeros at the beginning, as in `0000` and `0000095`. Rewrite the definition of an integer literal so that a sequence of zeros at the beginning is not allowed, but a single zero by itself should still be allowed.
Hint: Start by defining `nonZeroDigit` as follows.

```
nonZeroDigit = "1" .. "9" .
```

11. Look up the definition of the context-free grammar for a programming language that you are familiar with and compare its notation for rules to the notation used in this book.

12. *Dangling else.* CPRL defines an *if-statement* as follows.

```
ifStmt = "if" booleanExpr "then" statement [ "else" statement ] .
```

Essentially this rule says that an *if-statement* can have an optional *else* clause. Show that this rule is ambiguous by showing that a statement of the form

```
if (booleanExpr₁) then if (booleanExpr₂) then statement₁; else statement₂;
```

can be parsed in two different ways as shown below.

```
if booleanExpr₁ then
  {
    if (booleanExpr₂)
        statement₁;
    else
        statement₂;
  }
```

```
if booleanExpr₁ then
  {
    if (booleanExpr₂)
        statement₁;
  }
else
    statement₂;
```

Hint: For one derivation/parse tree, substitute an `ifStmt` without an `else` clause as the first statement in the above rule, and for a second derivation/parse tree, substitute an `ifStmt` without an `else` clause as the second statement in the above rule.

As discussed previously, this ambiguity is known as the *dangling-else* problem. While it is possible to define the rules for an *if-statement* to avoid the ambiguity, doing so complicates the grammar. Language definitions that have a *dangling-else* problem usually just specify that, in the absence of braces, an *else* clause is associated with the nearest *if-statement* without an else clause; that is, the first option (the option on the left) above is the one to be chosen.

Chapter 4
The Programming Language CPRL

This chapter provides an overview of CPRL, the source language for our compiler. Appendices C and D contain additional details of the language definition.

The name CPRL is an acronym for Compiler PRoject Language. Originally it was called simply CPL, but it turned out that a different programming language had been defined with that acronym in the early 1960's. Plus, Microsoft Windows used the extension "`.cpl`" for Control Panel files in the Windows system folder, so the name of the project language was changed to CPRL to avoid any confusion or conflicts.

CPRL is a small but complete programming language with statement-level constructs similar to those found in C-based languages such as Java, Kotlin, and C#. A few language constructs were patterned after similar features found in Ada. CPRL was designed to be suitable for use as a project language in an undergraduate or beginning graduate course on compiler design and construction. Its features illustrate many of the basic techniques and problems associated with language translation.

4.1 General Lexical Considerations

Identifiers in CPRL are case sensitive. Upper-case letters and lower-case letters are considered to be distinct in all tokens, including reserved words. Spaces may not appear in any token except character and string literals. In general, whitespace characters are used to separate tokens; otherwise, they are ignored. No token can extend past an end-of-line. Similar to most C-based languages, a comment begins with two forward slashes (//) and extends to the end of the line. Multiline comments are not available in CPRL, but it is not difficult to add them. In fact, that is one of the exercises described in Appendix B.

Identifiers

Identifiers start with a letter and can contain letters and digits.

```
identifier = letter { letter | digit } .
letter = 'A'..'Z' + 'a'..'z' .
digit  = '0'..'9' .
```

There are 37 predefined identifiers that serve as keywords in CPRL – examples include `array`, `const`, `if`, `else`, `loop`, and `while`. All keywords are reserved; i.e., a programmer is not permitted to use them as names for program entities such as variables, types, subprograms, etc. Some keywords such as `class` and `private` are not currently used in CPRL but are reserved for possible future use. Such keywords are essentially terminal symbols in the context-free grammar that do not appear in any rule.

Literals

Literal values for various types are described and illustrated as follows.

- Literal values for type `Integer` can be declared using decimal, hexadecimal, or binary notation. Examples include `100`, `0b1101`, and `0xFF`. Technically `-1` is not an integer literal but an expression – the unary negation symbol followed by the integer literal `1`. Integer literals can also be used with variables of type `Byte`, but their default type is `Integer`.
- Type `Boolean` has only two literal values, `true` and `false`.
- As with Java, Kotlin, and C#, a character literal is simply a single character enclosed by a pair of apostrophes (sometimes called single quotes). Note that a character literal is distinct from a string literal with length one. Examples of character literals include `'A'`, `'x'`, and `'$'`. The backslash character (`\`) denotes escape sequences within character and string literals; e.g., `\t` for the tab character, `\n` for a newline character, `\"` for a quote character within a string, and `\\` for the backslash itself.
- A string literal consists of zero or more printable characters enclosed by a pair of quotation marks (double quotes). Examples include `"Hello, world."`, `"Java"`, `"Kotlin"`, and `"Live long and prosper."`. As noted above, the string literal `"A"` is distinct from the character literal `'A'`; the two cannot be used interchangeably as permitted in some programming languages.

Other Symbols

The following symbols serve as delimiters, operators, and special symbols in CPRL.

```
// arithmetic, bitwise, and shift operators
+   -   *   /   |   ^   &   ~   <<   >>

// relational operators
=   !=   <   <=   >   >=

// assignment and punctuation symbols
:=   (   )   [   ]   {   }   ,   :   ;   .   ..

// special scanning symbols
EOF, unknown
```

4.2 Declarations, Statements, and Expressions

The three major syntactic categories in CPRL are declarations, statements, and expressions. Declarations introduce new names (programmer-defined identifiers) into the program. Examples include constant declarations, variable declarations, type declarations, and subprogram declarations.

Some languages distinguish between a declaration and a definition, but CPRL does not make such a distinction. In CPRL, there is no difference between a declaration and a definition. Also, in CPRL, initial declarations (declarations of constants, variables, and types) must take place before the name being introduced can be used, but this restriction does not apply to subprogram declarations. It is legal to make a call to a procedure or function before it has been declared.

Statements perform basic actions or control the flow of execution. Examples include assignment statements, loop statements, and if statements.

Expressions are syntactic entities that have values, and the values have types such as `Integer` or `Boolean`. Examples of expressions include literals such as `100` or `false`, variable expressions such as `i` or `max`, and compound expressions involving operators and operands such as `x + 7` or `i < 100`.

Unlike some programming languages, CPRL makes a strong distinction between expressions and statements. For example, in C, any expression followed by a semicolon is considered a statement. Thus, the following would be a valid statement in C but not in CPRL.

```
x >= 5;
```

Similarly, in most C-based languages including Java, Kotlin, and C++, we can call a function that returns a value without actually using the returned value. But in CPRL, all function calls return values, and all function calls are considered to be expressions. The value returned from a function call can't be ignored. On the other hand, a procedure in CPRL does not return a value (analogous to a `void` function in Java/C# or a `Unit` function in Kotlin) and a procedure call is considered to be a statement.

4.3 Types

Type Nomenclature

CPRL is a **statically-typed** language. This means that every variable, constant, or expression in the language belongs to exactly one type, and that type is a static property and can be determined by the compiler.

A **composite type** has individually-accessible components of other types. A common example of a composite type would be an array type. A **scalar type** does not have individual components (although technically we know that they are composed of bits and bytes). A common example of a scalar type would be type `Integer`.

The following diagram illustrates the type hierarchy of CPRL.

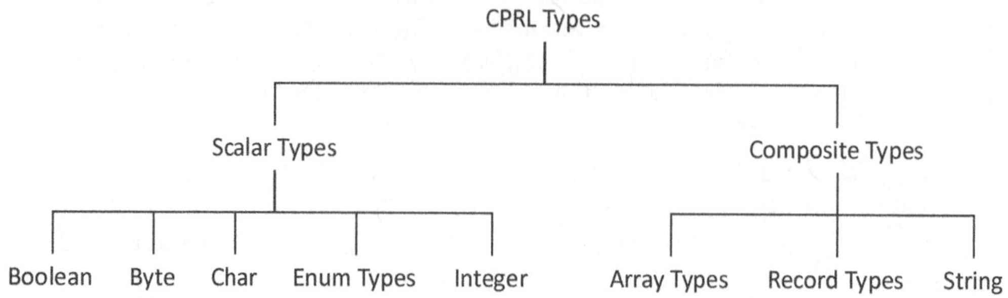

CPRL Types

As illustrated above, there are four predefined scalar types in CPRL – `Boolean`, `Byte`, `Integer`, and `Char`. Types `Boolean`, `Integer`, and `Char` are analogous to similar types found in most programming languages and have similar semantics. Type `Byte` is an **unsigned** 8-bit numeric type with values in the range `0..255`. Values of type `Byte` are promoted to type `Integer` when used as expressions.

An **enumerated type** is defined by listing the identifiers that are the actual values of the type enclosed in angle brackets. Each enumerated identifier defines a constant value that is scoped to the enum type.

Example

```
type Day = <Sun, Mon, Tue, Wed, Thu, Fri, Sat>;
```

A major language design decision is how the enum constants relate to integers. In some languages, they are simply integer constants. For CPRL the enum constants have some properties similar to integers, but enum types are considered to be distinct types. In particular, we can't assign enum variables or constants to integer variables, and integer variables or literals can't be assigned to variables having an enum type. Chapter 15 covers enumerated types in more detail.

In addition to scalar types, CPRL has three composite types – array types, record types, and `String`.

An **array type** is defined by the number of elements in the array and the component type. For an array variable `a` with `n` elements, the individual elements are accessed using the bracket notation, as in `a[i]`. Array indices range from `0` to `n-1`. Technically CPRL supports only one-dimensional arrays, but arrays of arrays can be declared.

Examples

```
type T1 = array[10] of Boolean;
type T2 = array[10] of Integer;
type T3 = array[10] of T2;
```

A **record type** is defined by specifying the fields in the record. Record types are similar to `structs` in C. Unlike arrays and strings, whose elements all have the same type, the fields of a record can have different types. Fields are accessed using the dot notation, as in `r.f`.

Examples

```
type Point = record
  {
    x : Integer;
    y : Integer;
  };

type Month = record
  {
    name    : String;
    maxDays : Integer;
  };
```

While it is possible to create multiple array and record types all having different names, there is only one string type named `String`, a predefined composite type similar to type `String` in Java and other programming languages. A string consists of a length followed by a sequence of characters. The string length is accessed using the dot notation, as in `s.length`, and individual characters in the string are accessed using the bracket notation, as in `s[i]`. Valid character indices range from `0` to `s.length-1`. The adding operator ("+") is used for string concatenation.

Constants and Variables

A constant is simply an identifier (name) associated with a literal value. As one would expect, the value for the constant cannot be changed at runtime. The type of the constant identifier is inferred to be the type of the literal.

For example,

```
const arraySize := 100;
```

declares an integer constant named `arraySize` initialized to `100`.

Variable declarations associate identifiers (names) with a type. The value of a variable is allowed to change as the program is running. A variable can be declared with an initial value. For scalar types, the initial value must be a constant; e.g., either a literal value or a previously declared constant. A `String` variable can be initialized with a string literal. Similar to many C-based languages, array and record variables can be initialized with composite constant values enclosed in braces "`{`" and "`}`". Nested composite literal values are used for nested composite types; e.g., an array of arrays or an array of records.

Also, for convenience, array variables can be declared without first having to create a new array type; e.g.

```
var a : array[10] of Integer;
```

In CPRL, constants, types, and variables must be declared before they can be referenced. Here are some examples illustrating constants and variables.

Example 1.

```
var x1, x2 : Integer;
var y : Integer := 13;

x1 := y + 1;
```

Example 2.

```
var found : Boolean := false;
```

Example 3.

```
const arraySize := 10;
type IntArray = array[arraySize] of Integer;
var table : IntArray := { 0, 1, 2, 3, 4, 5, 6, 7, 8, 9 };
table[0] := 999;
```

Example 4.

```
type Month = record
  {
    name    : String;
    maxDays : Integer;
  };
var month : Month := { "January", 31 };
```

String variables can be reassigned different values, but the length and sequence of characters of a string variable are immutable – they cannot be modified.

Example 5.

```
var name : String := "James";         // length = 5
writeln "first char = ", name[0];     // 'J'
writeln "length = ", name.length;     // 5
name := "John";                       // string variable reassigned
name.length := 3;                     // *** Illegal in CPRL ***
name[2] := 'a';                       // *** Illegal in CPRL ***
```

Operators and Expressions

CPRL has a fairly standard set of operators with common precedence. Here we point out a few differences between CPRL operators and those of other C-based languages such as Java, Kotlin, C#, and C++.

- The equality operator is `=`, not `==`. (Note that CPRL uses `:=` for assignment.)
- The boolean negation operator is the reserved word `not` instead of the exclamation point (`!`), but the relational operator for "not equal" is still `!=`.

- The modulo operator in CPRL is the reserved word `mod`, not the percent sign (`%`). Kotlin provides extension functions `rem` and `mod`, which yield different results when one of the operands is negative. Using `%` in Kotlin is equivalent to calling the extension function `rem`.
- The logical operators in CPRL are the reserved words `and` and `or` instead of the Java/Kotlin/C#/C++ operators `&&` and `||`.

For assignment and expressions with binary operators, both operands must have a numeric type or the same type. CPRL uses name type equivalence in that variables are considered to have the same type if and only if they are declared with the same type name or, for array types, they are declared using identical type constructors. Consider the following illustrative examples using arrays.

Example 1

```
var x : array[10] of Integer;
var y : array[10] of Integer;
```

In this example, `x` and `y` have the same type.

Example 2

```
type T1 = array[10] of Integer;
type T2 = array[10] of Integer;

var x : T1;
var y : T1;
var z : T2;
```

In this example, `x` and `y` have the same type, but `x` and `z` do not even though they have the same structure.

Expressions involving logical operators `and`/`or` use short-circuit evaluation.

Conditional Expression

Similar to Java, C#, and C++ (but unlike Kotlin and Python), CPRL has a ternary conditional operator "`?:`" that uses two symbols and three expressions as follows.

$$expr_1 \ ? \ expr_2 \ : \ expr_3$$

The first expression, $expr_1$, should have type `Boolean`, and the second and third expressions ($expr_2$ and $expr_3$) should have exactly the same type, not simply assignment-compatible types. If the first expression evaluates to true, then the value of the conditional expression is the second expression. Otherwise, the value of the conditional expression is the third expression.

As an example, to compute the maximum of two variables x and y, you can write

```
max := x > y ? x : y;
```

Both Kotlin and Python use a form of an *if-else* construct for this purpose. For example, in Kotlin (but using CPRL syntax), we would write something similar to the following.

```
max := if x > y then x else y;
```

4.4 Statements

Assignment Statement

The assignment symbol is "`:=`". An assignment statement has the following form:

```
variable := expression;
```

Example

```
i := 2*i + 5;
```

Compound Statement

A compound statement is a sequence of zero or more statements enclosed in braces "`{`" and "`}`". A compound statement can be used anywhere a single statement can be used. Compound statements are commonly used in conjunction with `if` statements and `loop` statements. For example, the body of a `loop` is exactly one statement, but it may be a compound statement.

Example

```
while i < length loop
  {
    writeln a[i];
    i := i + 1;
  }
```

compound statement

If Statement

An `if` statement in CPRL is similar to an `if` statement in C-based languages except that the boolean expression is followed by the keyword "`then`" and is not required to be enclosed in parentheses. An `if` statement can contain an optional `else` clause. Nested `if` statements can be used to implement a multiway branch.

Example 1

```
if x < y then
  {
    // swap x and y
    temp := x;
    x := y;
    y := temp;
  }
```

Example 2

```
if x >= y then
    max := x;
else
    max := y;
```

Example 3

```
if x < 0 then
    return -1;
else if x = 0 then
    return 0;
else
    return 1;
```

Loop and Exit Statements

A `loop` statement consists of the keyword "`loop`" followed by a statement, which is often a compound statement. A `loop` statement may be preceded by an optional "`while`" clause. An `exit` statement can be used to exit the innermost loop that contains it.

Example 1

```
while i < n loop
  {
    sum := sum + a[i];
    i := i + 1;
  }
```

Example 2

```
loop
  {
    read x;
    exit when x = SIGNAL;
    process(x);
  }
```

CPRL also permits an optional "`for`" prefix for a loop, which is especially convenient for looping over elements in an array.

Example

```
for i in 0..99 loop
    a[i] := a[i] + 1;
```

The `forLoop` variable, `i` in the above example, is implicitly declared as a variable having the same type as the range, usually type `Integer` but possibly an enumerated type. The loop variable is scoped to the loop; i.e., it is no longer accessible once the loop exits.

Input/Output Statements

CPRL defines only sequential text I/O for two basic character streams – standard input and standard output. The `write` and `writeln` statements can have multiple expressions separated by commas. Input is supported only for integers, characters, and strings.

Example

```
read x;    // assume that x was declared to have type Integer
writeln "The answer is ", 2*x + 1;
```

4.5 Programs

A program has an optional list of initial declarations (`const` declarations, `var` declarations, and `type` declarations) followed by one or more subprogram declarations. One of the subprograms must be a parameterless procedure named "`main()`", which serves as the starting point for program execution.

Example 1 (the smallest valid CPRL program)

```
proc main(){}
```

Example 2 (traditional "Hello, world." program)

```
proc main()
  {
    writeln "Hello, world.";
  }
```

4.6 Subprograms

CPRL provides two separate forms of subprograms – procedures and functions. A procedure (similar to a `void` function in C or C++) does not return a value; it is invoked through a procedure call statement. A function must return a value and is invoked as part of an expression. Keywords "`proc`" and "`fun`" are used to start the declarations of procedures and functions, respectively. Recursive invocations of subprograms are allowed. Subprograms are not required to be declared before they are called.

Procedures

Procedures are similar to void functions in C. Explicit `return` statements (which must **not** be followed by an expression) are allowed within a procedure body, but explicit returns from procedures are rare. Procedure calls are statements.

Example

```
proc writeBoolean(b : Boolean)
  {
    if b then
        write "true";
    else
        write "false";
  }
```

Assuming that `b` is the name of a `Boolean` variable, then the following statement would call this procedure and write out a textual representation for `b`; i.e., either `true` or `false`.

```
writeBoolean(b);
```

Functions

Functions are similar to procedures except that functions can (and must) return values. Function calls are expressions. A function returns a value by executing a `return` statement of the following form.

```
return <expression>;
```

Example

```
fun max(x : Integer, y : Integer) : Integer
  {
    if x >= y then
        return x;
    else
        return y;
  }
```

Assuming that we have two integer variables `a` and `b`, then the following would call this function and write out the returned value.

```
writeln max(a, b);
```

Parameters

There are two parameter modes in CPRL – value parameters and variable parameters. Value parameters are passed by value (a.k.a. copy-in) and are the default. Variable parameters are passed by reference and must be explicitly declared using the "`var`" keyword. Unlike other types, arrays are always passed by reference to subprograms regardless of whether or not they are declared as variable parameters.

Example

```
proc inc(var x : Integer)
  {
    x := x + 1;
  }
```

Functions cannot have variable parameters; only value parameters are permitted for functions (except that arrays are always passed by reference, regardless of how the parameter is declared).

> The terms *parameter* and *argument* can have different meanings in different programming languages, with *parameter* often used to refer to the variable defined in the subprogram declaration and *argument* used to refer to the value passed as part of the subprogram call. CPRL uses the term parameter generally for both meanings when the interpretation is clear from the context. When it is necessary to make a distinction, CPRL uses the phrases *formal parameter* (defined in the parameter declaration of the subprogram) and *actual parameter* (value passed as part of the subprogram call).

Return Statements

A return statement terminates execution of a subprogram and returns control back to the point where the subprogram was called.

A return statement within a function must be followed by an expression whose value is returned by the function. The type of the expression must equal the declared return type of the function.

A return statement within a procedure must not be followed by an expression – it simply returns control to the statement following the procedure call statement.

A procedure has an implied return statement as its last statement, and therefore most procedures will not have explicit return statements. A function requires one or more return statements to return the function value. There is no implicit return statement at the end of a function.

Type Compatibility

Variables and expressions in CPRL are considered to have the same type if and only if they have the same type name or they are declared using identical array type constructors. Thus, two types are considered different even though they may be structurally identical. This is referred to as "name equivalence" of types. We'll explore this concept in more detail in subsequent chapters when discussing user-defined types such as arrays and records.

Most of the time when we compare types, we want them to be equal. For example, when returning a value from a function, we want the value being returned to have the same type as the declared function return type. Similarly for passing parameters to a subprogram, we want the type of the actual parameter to be the same as the declared type of the formal parameter. For binary expressions, assignment statements, and variable initialization, CPRL weakens the requirement for "same type" slightly when it comes to numeric types `Integer` and `Byte`. Since `Byte` values are promoted to type `Integer` when used in expressions, we allow these two types to be mixed. For example, we can assign a variable of type `Byte` to a variable of type `Integer`.

Built-in Subprograms

Most real programming languages come with predefined standard libraries. Using the functionality in the standard library often requires that the program "import" or "include" the desired features, but some capabilities are usually available without any extra effort. For example, in Java, classes defined in package `java.lang` do not require an `import` statement. Similarly, Python has more than 70 officially documented built-in functions available in the global namespace that can be called without importing any modules.

CPRL currently has three built-in functions and one built-in procedure with the following signatures.

```
fun chr(n : Integer) : Char    // returns the character with the
                               // specified Unicode code point

fun eof() : Boolean            // returns true if standard input
                               // has reached the end of file

proc inc(var n : Integer)      // increments n

fun ord(c : Char) : Integer    // returns the ordinal value of a character
```

Functions `chr()` and `ord()` are patterned after built-in Python functions with the same name, and they provide the capability to convert between CPRL types `Char` and `Integer`. For example, `ord('A')` returns the value `65`, and `chr(0x20AC)` returns the Euro sign `'€'`. When calling `chr()`, there is no checking that the integer parameter is a valid Unicode code point, but if it is, the two functions are inverses of each other; i.e., if `c` has type `Char` and `n` has type `Integer` (and if `n` is a valid Unicode code point) then `chr(ord(c)) = c` and `ord(chr(n)) = n`.

Procedure `inc()` is patterned after a built-in procedure in Pascal-based languages, including Pascal, Ada, and Modula-2. It simply adds `1` to its variable parameter. It is essentially equivalent to writing `++n` as a single statement in C-based languages.

```
var n : Integer := 2;
...
inc(n);    // n now has the value 3
```

Function `eof()` is patterned after a built-in Pascal function with the same name. Normally in Pascal it would have a file parameter, but standard input is assumed if no file is specified. Since CPRL does not support files, the predefined function in CPRL has no parameter. To signal end-of-file from a keyboard, use the shortcut `Ctrl + D` on macOS/Linux or `Ctrl + Z` followed by `Enter` on Windows. Reading a file using the input redirection operator `<` works as expected, but the function does not detect end of file until a read is attempted. Following is an example function that reads and echoes the characters in a text file.

```
proc main()
  {
    var c : Char;
    loop
      {
        read c;
        exit when eof();

        // skip '\r' to make output consistent across Windows and Linux
        if c != '\r' then
            writeln c;
      }
  }
```

Assuming that the above program is in a CPRL source code file named `ReadChars.cprl`, you could run the following to echo the source code characters.

```
cprl ReadChars < ReadChars.cprl
```

A similar program could be used to echo the bytes in a binary file.

Code for the built-in CPRL functions is generated only if the functions are used in a program. Otherwise, no extra code is generated. Also, if a program defines a function with the same name, then the program-defined function is used, and code for the built-in function is not generated.

4.7 Essential Terms and Concepts

array	assignment statement
`Boolean`	built-in subprogram
`Byte`	`Char`
`composite type`	compound statement
constant	declaration
enumerated type	`exit` statement
expression	function
identifier	`if` statement
`Integer`	I/O in CPRL
literal (integer, boolean, character, string)	`loop` statement
operators (+, -, <=, etc.)	operator precedence
parameter (value versus variable)	pass by reference
pass by value	procedure
record	reserved word/keyword
`return` statement	scalar type
`String`	subprogram
variable	// (CPRL comment)

4.8 Exercises

1. **Project Assignment.** Implement **Project 0: Getting Started** as described in Appendix A. Read carefully the first few pages of Appendix A, where the organizational structure of the compiler into four top-level packages is described.
2. Explain what it means for a programming language to be statically typed.
3. Consider the following procedure.

```
proc inc(x : Integer)
  {
    x := x + 1;
  }
```

If `n` has the value `5`, then what value does `n` have after a call to the procedure of the form `inc(n)`? (Hint: How is the parameter passed for this procedure?)

4. Fill in the blanks.
   a. CPRL provides two separate forms of subprograms, ____________________ and ____________________.
   b. In CPRL, value parameters are passed by ____________________.
   c. In CPRL, variable parameters are passed by ____________________.
5. True or false.
   a. CPRL is case sensitive.
   b. CPRL defines certain reserved words that are not currently used within the language.
   c. CPRL is a statically-typed language.
   d. CPRL uses the operator "%" to denote the modulus operator; i.e., the remainder when one integer is divided by another.
   e. CPRL uses "=" as the assignment symbol.
6. Consider the following declarations.

```
type T1 = array[10] of Integer;
type T2 = array[10] of Integer;
var x : T1;
var y : T1;
var z : T2;
```

   True or false.
   a. In the above declarations, variables `x` and `y` are considered to have the same type.
   b. In the above declarations, variables `x` and `z` are considered to have the same type.
7. Write a CPRL function that uses integer arithmetic to compute the average of the first `n` integers in an array. Both the array and the value for `n` should be passed as parameters. The declarations for the array type and function should look something like the following.

```
type IntArray = array[100] of Integer;
...
fun average(a : IntArray, n : Integer) : Integer ...
```

   Note that the array is passed by reference even though the parameter is not declared as a `var` parameter. Discuss the performance implications of passing the array by value versus passing it by reference.

8. Write a CPRL function that implements integer exponentiation. The function should take two integer parameters and return the result of the first integer raised to the power of the second integer. The declaration for the function should look something like the following.

   ```
   fun pow(n : Integer, exp : Integer) : Integer ...
   ```

   Calling `pow(5, 3)` should return the value `125`.

9. Write a CPRL procedure that merges two sorted integer arrays. The two arrays and the number of items in each array should be passed as parameters, and the resulting merged array should be returned via a variable parameter. The declarations for the array type and procedure should look something like the following.

   ```
   type IntArray = array[100] of Integer;
   ...
   proc merge(a1 : IntArray, n1 : Integer,
              a2 : IntArray, n2 : Integer,
              var result : IntArray) ...
   ```

Chapter 5
Lexical Analysis (a.k.a. Scanning)

We are now at a place where we can (finally!) start to implement a compiler for CPRL. For most students, this is where the fun begins. We start with the scanner.

The role of lexical analysis or scanning is to identify the basic lexical units of the language, which are called the symbols or tokens of the language. The scanner also usually removes extraneous whitespace and comments since they play no role in subsequent analysis or code generation, and it reports any lexical errors encountered in the source code.

Our implementation of a scanner makes use of several helper classes including `Position`, `Source`, `Symbol`, `Token`, `BoundedBuffer`, `CharUtil`, and `ErrorHandler`, which are explained in this chapter. Classes `Position`, `Source`, `BoundedBuffer`, `CharUtil`, and ErrorHandler belong to package `common` since they are useful on any compiler-related project, not just the CPRL compiler. Classes `Symbol`, `Token`, and `Scanner` are specific to the CPRL compiler, and therefore these three classes belong to package `cprlc`.

5.1 Class `Position`

Class `Position` encapsulates the concept of a position in a source file, where a position is characterized by an ordered pair of integers representing the line number relative to the source file and the character number relative to that line. `Position` objects are used primarily for error reporting. Note that class `Position` is immutable; i.e., objects of class `Position` can't be modified after they have been created and initialized by a constructor.

The constructor and two key methods for class `Position` are as follows.

```
public Position(int lineNumber, int charNumber)

public int lineNumber()

public int charNumber()
```

5.2 Class `Source`

Class `Source` is essentially an iterator that steps through the characters in a source file one character at a time. At any point during the iteration you can examine the current character and its position within the source file before advancing to the next character. Class `Source` encapsulates a source file reader and maintains the position of each character in the source file. The input to class `Source` is a `Reader` (usually a `FileReader`), and the output is the sequence of individual characters and their positions within the file. Class `Source` implements Java's `Closeable` interface – the `close()` method of `Source` closes its `Reader`.

```
public final class Source implements Closeable
```

The constructor and key methods for class `Source` are as follows.

```
/**
 * Initialize Source with a Reader and advance to the first character.
 */
public Source(Reader sourceReader) throws IOException

/**
 * Returns an integer representing the current character in the source
 * file.  Returns EOF (-1) if the end of file has been reached.
 */
public int currentChar()

/**
 * Returns the position (line number, char number) of the
 * current character in the source file.
 */
public Position charPosition()

/**
 * Advance to the next character in the source file.
 */
public void advance() throws IOException
```

Class `TestSource` is used to test classes `Position` and `Source` before integrating them into the scanner. The main logic of `TestSource` is shown below.

```
var fileName = args[0];
var reader   = new FileReader(fileName, StandardCharsets.UTF_8);
var source   = new Source(reader);
var out      = new PrintStream(System.out, true, StandardCharsets.UTF_8);

try (source)
  {
    while (source.currentChar() != Source.EOF)
      {
        int c = source.currentChar();

        if (c == '\n')
            out.println("\\n\t" + source.charPosition());
        else if (c != '\r')
            out.println((char) c + "\t" + source.charPosition());

        source.advance();
      }
  }
```

We can test class `Source` by running the test program on its own source file `Source.java`. The results of testing class `Source` are as follows (read the first character vertically).

```
p       line 1, character 1
a       line 1, character 2
c       line 1, character 3
k       line 1, character 4
a       line 1, character 5
g       line 1, character 6
e       line 1, character 7
        line 1, character 8
c       line 1, character 9
o       line 1, character 10
m       line 1, character 11
m       line 1, character 12
o       line 1, character 13
n       line 1, character 14
;       line 1, character 15
\n      line 1, character 17
...
```

5.3 Class Symbol

The term **symbol** will be used to refer to a basic lexical unit returned by the scanner. Another common name for symbol is "token type". From the perspective of the parser, these are the terminal symbols.

Symbols include reserved words ("`while`", "`if`", "`proc`", ...), operators and punctuation ("`:=`", "`+`", "`;`", ...), identifiers, literals, and special scanning symbols `EOF` and `unknown`. To prevent name clashes with Java reserved words, class `Symbol` adopts the naming convention that all CPRL reserved words end with the "`RW`" suffix; e.g., `ifRW`, `whileRW`, etc. Symbols are defined using a Java `enum` class.

```
public enum Symbol
  {
    // reserved words
    BooleanRW("Boolean"),
    ByteRW("Byte"),
    CharRW("Char"),
    IntegerRW("Integer"),
    StringRW("String"),
    andRW("and"),
    arrayRW("array"),
    ...
    whenRW("when"),
    whileRW("while"),
    writeRW("write"),
    writelnRW("writeln"),
```

```
    // arithmetic operator symbols
    plus("+"),
    minus("-"),
    times("*"),
    divide("/"),
    ...

    // literal values and identifier symbols
    intLiteral("Integer Literal"),
    charLiteral("Char Literal"),
    stringLiteral("String Literal"),
    identifier("Identifier"),

    // special scanning symbols
    EOF("End-of-File"),
    unknown("Unknown");

    ...    // constructor and helper methods
}
```

In addition to the enum constants, class `Symbol` also contains several boolean-valued methods that will be useful later on for implementing the parser. Examples include `isStmtStarter()`, which returns true if the symbol can appear at the start of a CPRL statement, and `isRelationalOperator()`, which returns true if the symbol is one of the six relational operators such as `Symbol.equals` or `Symbol.lessThan`. The role of these methods will be discussed in more detail in the next chapter.

5.4 Class Token

The term **token** will be used to refer to a symbol together with additional information including the position (line number and character number) of the symbol in the source file and the text associated with the symbol. The additional information provided by a token is used for error reporting and code generation, but it is not used to determine if the program is syntactically correct.

Examples of the text associated with symbols are as follows.

- "`average`" for an identifier
- "`100`" for an integer literal
- "`"Hello, world."`" for a string literal
- "`while`" for the reserved word `while`
- "`<=`" for the operator "`<=`"

The text associated with a symbol is most meaningful for identifiers and literals (integer literals, character literals, and string literals) since, in all other cases, the text can be inferred directly from the symbol itself.

The constructor and three key methods of class Token are as follows.

```
public Token(Symbol symbol, Position position, String text)

/**
 * Returns the token's symbol.
 */
public Symbol symbol()

/**
 * Returns the token's position within the source file.
 */
public Position position()

/**
 * Returns the string representation for the token.
 */
public String text()
```

5.5 Class CharUtil

Class CharUtil provides several static methods used by the scanner for classifying characters. Most of the methods provide straightforward and efficient alternatives to regular expressions. Here are a couple of examples from this class.

```
public static boolean isLetter(char ch)
  {
    return (ch >= 'a' && ch <= 'z') || (ch >= 'A' && ch <= 'Z');
  }

public static boolean isDigit(char ch)
  {
    return ch >= '0' && ch <= '9';
  }
```

5.6 Class ErrorHandler

For consistency in error reporting, we use a class named ErrorHandler throughout all phases of the compiler. Here are two key methods in class ErrorHandler.

```
/**
 * Returns true if errors have been reported by the error handler.
 */
public boolean errorsExist()
```

```
/**
 * Reports the error.
 * @throws FatalException if the number of errors exceeds the maximum.
 */
public void reportError(CompilerException e)
```

As we will discuss in Chapter 6, version 1 of the parser does not implement error recovery. When an error is encountered, the parser will print an error message and then exit. Version 2 of the parser (Chapter 7) implements error recovery, whereby the parser will attempt to discover and report multiple errors within a single source program.

5.7 Class `BoundedBuffer`

Class `Scanner` creates the tokens for the parser, but occasionally the parser needs to see several tokens into the future. We accomplish this by storing the tokens in a bounded circular buffer. Our needs are simple and straightforward, and so we choose to implement the buffer directly as a generic class rather than reuse a more general version from a public source code library. Below is an outline of the class showing the constructor and the three methods.

```
public class BoundedBuffer<E>
  {
    ...

    public BoundedBuffer(int capacity) ...

    /**
     * Returns the capacity of this bounded buffer.
     */
    public int capacity()

    /**
     * Return the element at index i.  Does not remove the element.
     */
    public E get(int i) ...

    /**
     * Add an element to the buffer.  Overwrites if the buffer is full.
     */
    public void add(E e) ...
  }
```

While it is possible to include token buffering in the parser, we will include this capability within the scanner – the parser is already complicated enough. We declare the token buffer in class `Scanner` as follows.

```
// buffer to hold lookahead tokens
private BoundedBuffer<Token> tokenBuffer;
```

5.8 Class Scanner

Class `Scanner` is essentially a type of iterator that steps through the tokens in a source file one token at a time. At any point during the iteration, you can examine the current token and several tokens into the future before advancing to the next token.

Class `Scanner`

- Consumes individual characters from the source code file (via class `Source`) as it constructs the tokens.
- Removes extraneous whitespace and comments.
- Produces tokens (to be consumed by the parser) as output.
- Detects and reports lexical errors but doesn't throw exceptions back to the parser. Returns `Symbol.unknown` if a lexical error is encountered.

The following diagram illustrates the interaction between classes `Source` and `Scanner` to produce the tokens for a simple assignment statement. Note that the positions of the individual characters have been omitted from the diagram to save space, but they are shown as part of the output of the scanner.

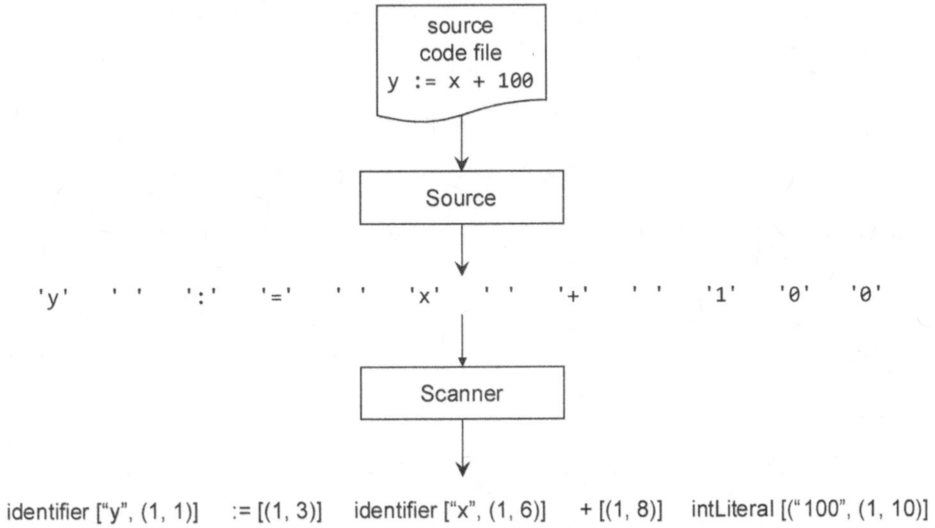

Similar to `Source`, class `Scanner` implements Java's `Closeable` interface.

```
public final class Scanner implements Closeable
```

The close() method of `Scanner` closes its `Source` object. Implementing `Closeable` allows us to use a try-with-resources statement to automatically close a scanner without having to explicitly close it in a `finally` block.

The constructor and key methods for class `Scanner` are as follows.

```
/**
 * Construct a scanner with its associated source file, number
 * of lookahead tokens, and error handler.
 */
public Scanner(File sourceFile, int k, ErrorHandler errorHandler)
    throws IOException

/**
 * The current token; equivalent to lookahead(1).
 */
public Token token()

/**
 * The current symbol; equivalent to lookahead(1).symbol().
 */
public Symbol symbol()

/**
 * The current text; equivalent to lookahead(1).text().
 */
public String text()

/**
 * The current position; equivalent to lookahead(1).position().
 */
public Position position()

/**
 * Returns the ith lookahead token.  Valid parameter values are in the
 * range 1..k; i.e., the first (current) lookahead token is lookahead(1).
 */
public Token lookahead(int i)

/**
 * Advance the scanner one token.
 */
public void advance() throws IOException

/**
 * Returns the next token in the source file.
 */
private Token nextToken() throws IOException
```

Internally the scanner uses a bounded buffer that can store up to `k` tokens, where the value of `k` is passed as a parameter to the constructor. For CPRL, `k` will have the value `4`, and so the CPRL parser can examine up to four tokens by calling scanner method lookahead() with parameter values in the range from `1` to `4`.

Methods `token()`, `symbol()`, `text()`, and `position()` are simply convenience methods since their values can be derived by calling method `lookahead(1)`; e.g., calling `symbol()` is equivalent to calling `lookahead(1).symbol()`. Most parsing decisions can be made by using the symbol returned from the scanner's `symbol()` method. Occasionally the parser will need to see additional lookahead tokens, and in those cases the parser will call the scanner's `lookahead()` method with a parameter value of 2 or more. Method `advance()` calls `nextToken()` and adds the returned token to the token buffer.

Method `nextToken()` is the longest and one of the more complicated methods in class `Scanner` since it is responsible for combining characters into tokens. Plus, it is also responsible for skipping extraneous whitespace and comments. Here is an outline of the logic for method `nextToken()`.

```
private Token nextToken() throws IOException
  {
    var symbol   = Symbol.unknown;
    var position = new Position();
    var text     = "";

    try
      {
        skipWhiteSpace();

        // currently at starting character of next token
        position = source.charPosition();

        if (source.currentChar() == Source.EOF)
          {
            // set symbol but don't advance source
            symbol = Symbol.EOF;
          }
        else if (CharUtil.isLetter((char) source.currentChar()))
          {
            var idString = scanIdentifier();
            symbol = getIdentifierSymbol(idString);

            if (symbol == Symbol.identifier)
                text = idString;
          }
```

```
        else if (CharUtil.isDigit((char) source.currentChar()))
          {
            symbol = Symbol.intLiteral;
            text   = scanIntLiteral();
          }
        else
          {
            switch((char) source.currentChar())
              {
                case '+' ->
                  {
                    symbol = Symbol.plus;
                    source.advance();
                  }
                case '-' ->
                  {
                    symbol = Symbol.minus;
                    source.advance();
                  }
                ...
                case '<' ->
                  {
                    source.advance();
                    if ((char) source.currentChar() == '=')
                      {
                        symbol = Symbol.lessOrEqual;
                        source.advance();
                      }
                    else if (source.currentChar() == '<')
                      {
                        symbol = Symbol.leftShift;
                        source.advance();
                      }
                    else
                        symbol = Symbol.lessThan;
                  }
                 ...
              }
          }
      }
    catch (ScannerException e)
      {
        ...
      }

    return new Token(symbol, position, text);
  }
```

Note that the one- and two-character symbols are handled by a large `switch` statement. If the scanner sees a "+" character as the next character in the input stream, it immediately recognizes a `plus` symbol. If the scanner sees a "<" character in the input stream, it needs to look at the next character in order to recognize the symbol. If the next character is "=", then the scanner recognizes a `lessOrEqual` symbol. If the next character is "<", then the scanner recognizes a `leftShift` symbol. If the next character is anything other than "=" or "<", then the scanner recognizes a `lessThan` symbol, and the character following the initial "<" is not consumed; i.e., it remains in the input stream.

In addition to one- and two-character symbols, the `switch` statement also recognizes a single quote (apostrophe) as the start of a character literal and a double quote as the start of a string literal. In both cases it calls helper methods as described below to complete the scanning of these two types of symbols.

> **Important observation:** The scanner always advances the `source` object whenever a symbol has been recognized, so that the `source` object remains one character ahead of the characters that have been consumed by the scanner.

There are four symbols that require special attention when scanning – identifiers, integer literals, string literals, and character literals. The bulk of the work in recognizing these four symbols is performed in separate methods, two of which are described below. Since the text for these four symbols needs to be retained as part of the token, and since the text can be several characters long, these methods use a `StringBuilder` object named `scanBuffer` to accumulate the token text. There is a simple helper method named `clearScanBuffer()` that reinitializes `scanBuffer`; i.e., makes it empty.

Additionally, there are several other helper methods in class `Scanner` such as `skipWhiteSpace()`, which skips over spaces, tabs, end-of-line characters, etc., and `skipComment()`, which skips over a comment.

Scanning an Integer Literal

Recall that integer literals can be expressed using decimal, hexadecimal, or binary notation. They are defined by the following lexical grammar rules.

```
intLiteral     = decimalLiteral | hexLiteral | binaryLiteral .
decimalLiteral = digit { digit } .
hexLiteral     = ( "0x" | "0X" ) hexDigit    { hexDigit } .
binaryLiteral  = ( "0b" | "0B" ) binaryDigit { binaryDigit } .
digit          = '0'..'9' .
binaryDigit    = '0'..'1' .
hexDigit       = digit | 'A'..'F' | 'a'..'f' .
```

When method `nextToken()` encounters a digit, it calls `scanIntLiteral()`, which examines the first couple of characters in the input stream to determine the format and then calls one of `scanDecimalLiteral()`, `scanBinaryLiteral()`, or `scanHexLiteral()` to complete the scanning process. For example, if the first character is the digit `0` and the second character is letter x or X, then scanIntLiteral() appends "0X" to scanBuffer and calls method scanHexLiteral().

The three methods scanDecimalLiteral(), scanBinaryLiteral(), and scanHexLiteral() implement scanning for integer literals expressed in decimal (base 10) format, binary (base 2) format, and hexadecimal (base 16) format, respectively. We illustrate with hexadecimal literals.

The lexical grammar rule for hexLiteral (shown above) requires one or more hexadecimal digits. This suggests that we scan a hexadecimal integer literal using a loop. The implementation is shown below. Note how the logic of the code parallels the grammar rule.

```
private void scanHexLiteral() throws ScannerException, IOException
  {
    // assumes that scanBuffer contains "0X"
    assert scanBuffer.charAt(0) == '0' && scanBuffer.charAt(1) == 'X';

    // check that the next character is a hex digit
    if (!CharUtil.isHexDigit((char) source.currentChar()))
        throw error("Improperly formed hexadecimal literal");
    do
      {
        scanBuffer.append((char) source.currentChar());
        source.advance();
      }
    while (CharUtil.isHexDigit((char) source.currentChar()));
  }
```

Although the lexical grammar rule for a hexadecimal literal allows a prefix of either "0x" (lowercase x) or "0X" (uppercase X), we only checked for the latter since the calling method, scanIntLiteral(), had already converted the prefix to use uppercase X.

Scanning an Identifier

Recall that an identifier is defined by the lexical grammar as a letter followed by zero or more letters or digits.

```
identifier = letter { letter | digit } .
```

The scanning of an identifier starts out simply enough. When method nextToken() encounters a letter, it calls method scanIdentifier() to complete the scanning process, similar to the way that scanIntLiteral() is called when nextToken() encounters a digit. The problem is that programmer-defined identifiers and reserved words "look" alike, and so after scanning an identifier, we still need to distinguish between CPRL reserved words and programmer-defined identifiers such as variable or procedure names. Here is one approach for making the distinction.

First, use a single method named `scanIdentifier()` to scan all identifiers, including reserved words. In other words, initially we don't make a distinction between programmer-defined identifiers and reserved words. This method returns a string.

```
/**
 * Scans characters in the source file for a valid identifier.
 */
private String scanIdentifier() throws IOException
```

Then, after calling `scanIdentifier()`, use an "efficient" search routine to determine if the string returned by `scanIdentifier()` is a programmer-defined identifier or a reserved word. The search will "look up" the string assembled by the above method to determine what type of symbol it is. If the string is "while," then the method will return `Symbol.whileRW` indicating the `while` reserved word. If the string is something like "average," then the method will return `Symbol.identifier` indicating a programmer-defined identifier, and the string "average" will be stored as the token's text.

```
/**
 * Returns the symbol associated with an identifier
 * (Symbol.arrayRW, Symbol.ifRW, Symbol.identifier, etc.)
 */
private Symbol getIdentifierSymbol(String idString)
```

One **very inefficient** way to implement `getIdentifierSymbol()` is to perform a sequential search (a.k.a. linear search) of all the reserved words, comparing the string parameter to see if there is a match. If so, you would return the appropriate reserved word symbol. If the entire list of reserved words is searched without a match, you would return `Symbol.identifier`. Here is one way to implement the logic for `getIdentifierSymbol()`. Its only advantage is that it is very easy to implement.

Create and initialize an array list of reserved word symbols.

```
private ArrayList<Symbol> reservedWords = new ArrayList<>(50);
...
for (var symbol : Symbol.values())
  {
    if (symbol.isReservedWord())
        reservedWords.add(symbol);
  }
```

We can visualize the contents of the array list as follows.

```
{
  BooleanRW,
  ByteRW,
  CharRW,
  IntegerRW,
  StringRW,
  andRW,
  arrayRW,
  ...
  whileRW,
  writeRW,
  writelnRW
}
```

Using this array list, the search method is implemented as shown below.

```
private Symbol getIdentifierSymbol(String idString)
  {
    for (var reservedWord : reservedWords)
      {
        if (idString.equals(reservedWord.toString()))
            return reservedWord;
      }

    return Symbol.identifier;
  }
```

We want method `getIdentifierSymbol()` to be as efficient as possible since it will be called many times, so the above implementation is too inefficient to be acceptable. One potential performance improvement is to use a binary search instead of a sequential search. Students are encouraged to explore other, possibly more efficient alternatives, and then to review the search algorithms discussed in Appendix F.

5.9 Handling Lexical Errors

There are several kinds of errors that can be detected by the scanner when processing a source file. Examples include failure to properly close a character or string literal (e.g., encountering an end-of-line before a closing quote), encountering a character that does not start a valid symbol (e.g., '#' or '@'), etc. As outlined in Chapters 6, 7, and 9, a lot of error handling is performed by the parser and within the abstract syntax tree classes, but the scanner needs to take action when encountering lexical errors.

In general, our compiler will use Java's exception handling mechanism to signal and report all errors. Lexical errors are encapsulated by class `ScannerException`, which is defined in package `common`. When any of the scanning methods detects an error, it calls a private method named `error()` with an appropriate error message. Method `error()` simply creates and returns a new `ScannerException` with that error message, and the exception is then thrown by the method that detected the lexical error. Method `error()` is overloaded; one version uses a specified position for reporting the error and the other version uses the current position in the source file.

```
private ScannerException error(String errorMsg)
  {
    return error(source.charPosition(), errorMsg);
  }

private ScannerException error(Position position, String errorMsg)
  {
    return new ScannerException(position, errorMsg);
  }
```

Most lexical errors are handled in the scanner method `nextToken()`, which, as shown earlier, has its processing logic enclosed in `try/catch` blocks. The `catch` block uses an instance of class `ErrorHandler` from package `common` to report the error, and then it sets the token's symbol to either `Symbol.EOF` (if end-of-file has been reached) or `Symbol.unknown`, so that the parser can handle it appropriately. The `catch` block at the end of method `nextToken()` is written as follows.

```
catch (ScannerException e)
  {
    errorHandler.reportError(e);
    // set symbol to either EOF or unknown
    symbol = source.currentChar() ==
                 Source.EOF ? Symbol.EOF : Symbol.unknown;
  }
```

Beyond the scanner exceptions handled in method `nextToken()`, both `scanCharLiteral()` and `scanStringLiteral()` contain special logic to handle an invalid escaped character. Recall that, like Java, certain characters can be escaped by prepending a backslash character ('\'). Escape sequences like '`\t`' and '`\n`' are valid, but not something like '`\x`'. Upon encountering an invalid escape sequence, these methods report the error and then attempt a weak form of error recovery so as to continue processing the string or character literal.

In addition to detecting and reporting errors in a CPRL source file, there are several checks for internal consistency throughout the compiler. Most internal checks within the compiler make use of Java's assert statement with a boolean expression and optionally a string. Assuming that assertions are enabled, if the boolean expression evaluates to true, then the statement takes no action. But if the boolean expression evaluates to false, then assert throws an `AssertionError` with the specified string used as an error message. `AssertionError` is an unchecked exception and therefore does not need to be handled or declared in a `throws` clause.

Assertions in Java

By default, Java assertions are disabled at runtime. They are enabled using a switch (either `-enableassertions` or `-ea`) to the java command, allowing the use of assertion checking during development and easy removal of assertion checking for production code or when efficiency concerns dominate. For example, the following command enables assertions checking for an application.

```
java -ea MyApplication
```

Note that source code does not need to be recompiled to enable or disable assertions on the JVM. Enabling or disabling assertions is a function of the class loader. Even when assertion checking is disabled, the assertions remain as useful comments in the code to document runtime assumptions.

For example, the scanner method `scanIdentifier()` assumes that `source.currentChar()` is the first letter of the identifier to be scanned, and so a check is performed to ensure that the character is, in fact, a letter. This is illustrated in the following excerpt from method `scanIdentifier()` in class `Scanner`.

```
// assumes that source.currentChar() is first letter of the identifier
assert CharUtil.isLetter((char) source.currentChar());
```

The above code simply checks that this condition is satisfied and that the compiler has not made an erroneous call to `scanIdentifier()`. Internal compiler assertions represent problems with the implementation of the compiler and should never occur if the compiler is implemented correctly. By default, Java assertions are disabled at runtime, but they can be enabled using a command-line switch. A normal scenario is to enable assertion checking when developing a compiler and to turn it off when the compiler goes into production. Even when they aren't enabled, assertions serve to document assumptions and inner workings of your compiler.

Most IDEs have a way to enable or disable Java assertions. For example, Eclipse creates a "run configuration" when you run a Java program, and you can enable assertions for a specific run configuration as follows.

- From the menu select **Run** and then **Run Configurations...**
- Select the run configuration for the application you want to edit, and then click on the **Arguments** tab. In the text area for **VM Arguments**, simply type `-ea` or `-enableassertions`.

A similar approach is used to enable assertions using IntelliJ IDEA.

5.10 Testing Class Scanner

It is important that we fully test the scanner before trying to integrate it with the parser. The book repository includes a test program `TestScanner.java` that can be used for this purpose. Omitting error handling, the basic logic of class `TestScanner` is as follows.

```
var fileName     = args[0];
var sourceFile   = new File(fileName);
var errorHandler = new ErrorHandler();
var scanner      = new Scanner(sourceFile, 4, errorHandler);
Token token;

try (scanner)
  {
    do
      {
        token = scanner.token();
        printToken(token);
        scanner.advance();
      }
    while (token.symbol() != Symbol.EOF);
  }
```

As shown below, method `printToken()` is used to print out the text associated with each token, using special logic to print the text for identifiers and literals.

```
private static void printToken(Token token)
  {
    out.printf("line: %2d   char: %2d   token: ",
        token.position().lineNumber(),
        token.position().charNumber());

    var symbol = token.symbol();

    if (symbol.isReservedWord())
        out.print("Reserved Word -> ");
    else if ( symbol == Symbol.identifier
           || symbol == Symbol.intLiteral
           || symbol == Symbol.stringLiteral
           || symbol == Symbol.charLiteral)
        out.print(token.symbol().toString() + " -> ");

    out.println(token.text());
  }
```

The book repository contains a directory named `ScannerTests` with subdirectories `Correct` and `Incorrect` containing several CPRL scanner test examples (not necessarily complete CPRL programs). In addition, there are a Windows command script and a Bash shell script that can be used to invoke `TestScanner` from the command line. Below are the results of testing the scanner with file `Correct_01.cprl` as input.

```
line:  2   char:  1   token: Reserved Word -> Boolean
line:  2   char: 11   token: Reserved Word -> Byte
line:  2   char: 21   token: Reserved Word -> Char
line:  2   char: 31   token: Reserved Word -> Integer
line:  2   char: 41   token: Reserved Word -> String
line:  2   char: 51   token: Reserved Word -> and
...
line:  8   char:  1   token: Reserved Word -> write
line:  8   char: 11   token: Reserved Word -> writeln
line: 11   char:  1   token: +
line: 11   char:  5   token: -
line: 11   char:  9   token: *
line: 11   char: 13   token: /
...
line: 20   char:  1   token: :=
line: 20   char:  6   token: (
line: 20   char: 10   token: )
line: 23   char:  1   token: Identifier -> x
line: 23   char:  5   token: Identifier -> y
line: 23   char:  9   token: Identifier -> x1
line: 23   char: 14   token: Identifier -> i
...
line: 32   char:  1   token: Integer Literal -> 1
...
line: 37   char:  1   token: Char Literal -> 'a'
...
line: 38   char:  1   token: String Literal -> "a"
...
line: 41   char:  1   token: End-of-File
```

5.11 Essential Terms and Concepts

`BoundedBuffer` (class)

`ErrorHandler` (class)

integer literal

`lookahead()` (method)

`Scanner` (class)

string literal

symbol

token

character literal

immutable class

keyword/reserved word

`Position` (class)

`Source` (class)

`Symbol` (enum class)

`Token` (class)

5.12 Exercises

1. **Project Assignment.** Implement **Project 1: Scanner** as described in Appendix A.
2. Explain the difference between the terms "symbol" and "token" as used in this book.
3. True or false: The scanner typically removes extraneous whitespace and comments from the source file.
4. As described in Section 5.1, a class is said to be **immutable** if instances (objects) of that class can't be modified after they have been created and initialized by a constructor. Class `Position` is immutable. Name several classes defined in Java that are immutable. (Hint: You can find several in package `java.lang`.)
5. Consider the **first three lines** of the following CPRL source code.

   ```
   while x1 <= 2*y loop
     {
       writeln "less than";
       ...
     }
   ```

   List the symbols that will be identified by the scanner. (Omit the ellipsis "..." and the closing brace.) Just list the text part of the symbols. (Hint: In the first three lines there are 11 symbols, and the first symbol is `while`.)
6. Many programming languages allow the use of an underscore character (_) as part of an identifier. Rewrite the definition of an identifier to allow underscores after the first initial letter (i.e., the first character must still be a letter). Rewrite the scanner method `scanIdentifier()` to accommodate this change.

7. Most C-like languages use two forward slashes (`//`) to start a comment and then ignore anything from that point until the end of the line. But Java has an added requirement for the compiler to process Unicode escape characters before any other lexical translation, even within comments. To see the implications of this, consider the following Java program that prints "Hello, world.".

```
public class TestComments
  {
    public static void main(String[] args)
      {
        System.out.print("Hello");
        // Comment?  \u000A System.out.println(", world.");
      }
  }
```

   a. Pick another programming language and test whether or not the analogous program will print "Hello, world." or simply "Hello".

   b. It is possible to write an entire Java program using only Unicode escape characters. Write a complete "Hello, world." program using only Unicode escape characters.

Chapter 6
Syntax Analysis (a.k.a. Parsing)

> This is one of the longest and arguably one of the most challenging chapters in the book. Students should read every word, parse every sentence, and try to fully understand each paragraph, example, section, etc., before continuing. (Note how I managed to sneak the word "parse" into the previous sentence. ☺)

First and foremost, the role of a parser is to verify that the grammatical rules defined by the context-free grammar are satisfied. Additionally, a parser should implement some form of error handling and recovery, and it should create an intermediate representation of the source code suitable for additional analysis and code generation.

The overall structure of the parser is based on the context-free grammar for the language. Using the approach outlined in this book, most rules in the grammar translate directly into methods in class `Parser`. Input to the parser is the stream of tokens from the scanner. From the perspective of the parser, each token is treated as a terminal symbol. Output from the parser is an intermediate representation of the source code. For our project we will create abstract syntax trees. We can visualize the work of the parser as follows.

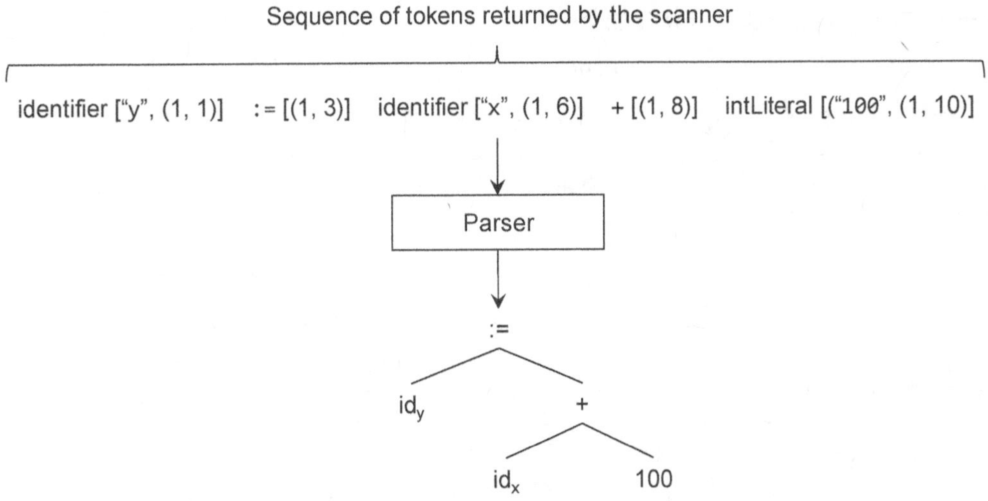

As outlined in Appendix A, we will build a parser in three separate projects. Version 1 of the parser will only check for valid syntax. If a program is not syntactically valid, then version 1 of the parser will print an error message and exit, stopping at the first error it encounters. Version 2 of the parser will add error recovery so that multiple errors can be detected and reported. Version 3 of the parser will generate abstract syntax trees, which will be used as the basis for additional analysis and code generation. The separation of parser construction into three separate projects is for educational purposes. Once you have learned how to write a parser you can combine all three versions into one project.

The primary focus of this chapter is language recognition; i.e., verification that the program submitted to the compiler conforms to the context-free grammar. The next two chapters will address error recovery and generation of abstract syntax trees.

6.1 Example: Implementing Method `parseLoopStmt()`

The parsing technique used in this course is called recursive descent with k lookahead tokens. We will use k=4 for CPRL, but the ideas presented work well for smaller or larger values of k. Most rules in the grammar will be implemented directly as methods in the parser. When implementing a method for a rule, if the right side of a rule references another nonterminal symbol, we simply call the parsing method corresponding to its rule. Since the rules contain recursive references to nonterminal symbols, the parser methods contain recursive calls to other parser methods. Most decisions made by the parser about what to do next are based on looking at only the next symbol in the input stream, but we will need to look several symbols ahead (using scanner method `lookahead()`) in a couple of places.

While there are a lot of details to be covered, a brief example should illustrate recursive descent parsing and provide an overview of where we are headed in this chapter. Don't worry if you don't initially understand every detail of this section. Just try to focus on the big picture. We will cover the details later in this chapter.

Consider the grammar rule for `loopStmt`.

```
loopStmt = [ "while" booleanExpr ] "loop" statement .
```

We will continue to refer back to this rule as we implement its corresponding parse method named `parseLoopStmt()`.

```
private void parseLoopStmt() throws IOException
  {
    ...
  }
```

The right side of the rule starts with an optional syntax expression that begins with the reserved word `while`. Since this part of the rule is optional, that suggests that we use an `if` statement. But what should we use for the condition? This is where we look ahead at the next symbol in the input stream. If the next symbol is `while`, we know that we want to parse the optional part. So now we have the following.

```
private void parseLoopStmt() throws IOException
  {
    if (scanner.symbol() == Symbol.whileRW)
      {
        ...    // parse optional while clause
      }
    ...        // parse rest of the rule
  }
```

At this point we need to stop and explain two "helper" parsing methods named `match()` and `matchCurrentSymbol()` that we will use to recognize terminal symbols. Implementations for these methods are shown in the next section.

Method `match()` has a single parameter of type `Symbol`. It simply verifies that the next symbol in the input stream has the same value as its parameter, and if so, it advances the scanner. If the next symbol in the input stream does not match the parameter, it signals an error by throwing an exception, an instance of `ParserException`.

Method `matchCurrentSymbol()` is used when we already know that the next symbol in the input stream is the one we want. This method takes no parameters and doesn't throw an exception. It simply advances the scanner. We could use `match()` for this purpose, but `matchCurrentSymbol()` is slightly more efficient.

For version 1 of the parser, methods `match()` and `matchCurrentSymbol()` are the only two parser methods that advance the scanner to the next token. All other parser methods use these two methods when recognizing terminal symbols. An additional method in parser versions 2 and 3 advances the scanner as part of a special case for error recovery.

Now back to the implementation of parsing method `parseLoopStmt()`. Since the `if` condition at the beginning of the method has already checked that the next symbol in the input stream is the reserved word `while`, we can use the more efficient `matchCurrentSymbol()` to handle this symbol. Method `parseLoopStmt()` now becomes the following.

```
private void parseLoopStmt() throws IOException
  {
    if (scanner.symbol() == Symbol.whileRW)
      {
        matchCurrentSymbol();
        ...
      }
    ...
  }
```

Looking back at the grammar rule for `loopStmt`, we see that the reserved word `while` must be followed by `booleanExpr`; i.e., a boolean expression, which is simply an expression based on the rule

```
booleanExpr = expression .
```

Since expression is a nonterminal symbol, parsing the boolean expression is handled by calling another parsing method `parseExpression()`. So now we have the following.

```
private void parseLoopStmt() throws IOException
  {
    if (scanner.symbol() == Symbol.whileRW)
      {
        matchCurrentSymbol();
        parseExpression();
      }
    ...
  }
```

We will have to wait until a later chapter to see how to check that the expression does, in fact, have type `Boolean`. For now, the best we can do is to call `parseExpression()`.

Continuing with our implementation of method `parseLoopStmt()`, let's return to the grammar rule. Note that the two symbols after the boolean expression are the terminal symbol `loop` and the nonterminal symbol `statement`. We can call method `match()` to handle the terminal symbol, and we will call another parsing method, `parseStatement()`, to parse the nonterminal symbol `statement`.

Ignoring exceptions that correspond to invalid syntax for the CPRL program being parsed, the basic flow of our method for parsing loop statements now becomes the following.

```
private void parseLoopStmt() throws IOException
  {
    if (scanner.symbol() == Symbol.whileRW)
      {
        matchCurrentSymbol();
        parseExpression();
      }

    match(Symbol.loopRW);
    parseStatement();
  }
```

Let's stop for a minute and summarize how the structure of the parsing method is derived directly from the grammar rule.

```
loopStmt = [ "while" booleanExpr ] "loop" statement .
```

- The nonterminal on the left side of the rule, `loopStmt`, gives rise to the name of the parsing method, `parseLoopStmt()`.
- On the right side of the rule, the optional part, `[ "while" booleanExpr ]`, is converted to an `if` statement. Within the body of this `if` statement,
  - reserved word `while` is handled by calling helper method `matchCurrentSymbol()`.
  - nonterminal `booleanExpr` is handled by calling parsing method `parseExpression()`.

- Reserved word `loop` is handled by calling helper method `match()`.
- Nonterminal `statement` is handled by calling parsing method `parseStatement()`.

Of course, we don't really want to ignore syntax errors, so we enclose our parsing logic in a `try` block whose corresponding `catch` block reports the error and then calls helper method `recover()`. In the next chapter we will learn how to use method `recover()` for error recovery by passing in a parameter that is a set of symbols. For now we pass an empty set. For this version of the parser, method `recover()` will ignore its parameter, print an error message, and exit the program. As stated in Section 5.6, error reporting will be handled by an instance of class `ErrorHandler`.

Our final version of `parseLoopStmt()` is shown below.

```
private void parseLoopStmt() throws IOException
  {
    try
      {
        if (scanner.symbol() == Symbol.whileRW)
          {
            matchCurrentSymbol();
            parseExpression();                          parsing
          }                                             logic

        match(Symbol.loopRW);
        parseStatement();
      }
    catch (ParserException e)
      {
        errorHandler.reportError(e);                    error
        recover(emptySet);                              handling
      }
  }
```

Note how the basic parsing logic inside the `try` block corresponds directly to the terminal and nonterminal symbols of the rule in the context-free grammar. Terminal symbols are handled by calling either `match()` or `matchCurrentSymbol()`, while nonterminal symbols are handled by calling a corresponding `parseN()` method. Also note that method `parseLoopStmt()` needed to look ahead at only one symbol in order to decide whether or not to handle the optional `while` clause. While one symbol will often suffice, occasionally we will want to look ahead at more than one symbol.

This approach is easy to comprehend, and it is easy to implement if the context-free grammar meets certain criteria. The grammar for CPRL as defined in Appendix D meets all of the criteria needed for recursive descent parsing with four lookahead tokens. But it is technically possible to refactor the grammar and use fewer lookahead tokens. (See Exercise 9 at the end of this chapter.)

6.2 Recursive Descent Parsing

Recursive descent parsing uses recursive methods to "descend" through the parse tree (top-down parsing) as it parses a program. The parser is constructed systematically from the context-free grammar using a set of programming guidelines. In addition, we want to use lookahead symbols to help us make *correct* parsing decisions with respect to syntax expressions of the form `[ E ]` (optional), `{ E }` (zero or more), or `E | F` (alternatives). We want to avoid **backtracking**, whereby an "educated" guess is made with respect to parsing alternatives, and then parsing restarts with a different alternative if the previous choice fails.

In general, a grammar needs to have certain "nice" properties if it is to be used for recursive descent parsing. Not all grammars are suitable for this purpose, but sometimes we can perform certain grammar transformations to make the grammar more suitable without changing the language being defined. That is, as discussed in Chapter 3, even though the two grammars appear to be different, any program considered syntactically valid by the first grammar will also be considered syntactically valid by the second grammar, and vice-versa.

Starting with a context-free grammar, the first step is to separate lexical grammar rules from structural rules. We will let the scanner handle simple rules such as reserved words, operators, identifiers, integer literals, etc. Symbols composed by the scanner are treated as terminal symbols in the grammar for the parser.

Additionally, we would want to simplify the grammar by substituting nonterminals where appropriate. So, for example, since syntactically a `booleanExpr` is simply an `expression` and a `varId` is simply an `identifier`, we could substitute `expression` for `booleanExpr` and `identifier` for `varId` within the rules, thereby eliminating nonterminals `booleanExpr` and `varId`. The CPRL grammar defined in Appendix D does not make the substitutions, but we will mentally make them as we implement our parser.

There are several properties that we want our grammar to have if we are going to use it to implement a recursive descent parser, and we express these properties in the form of grammar restrictions. Here are the first two.

Grammar Restriction 1: Each nonterminal appears on the left side of exactly one rule.

Grammar Restriction 2: Left recursion has been eliminated. (See Section 3.4.) Some approaches to parsing can handle rules with left recursion, but left recursion is problematic for recursive descent parsers since it leads to infinite recursion within the method calls. Additional grammar restrictions will be discussed in more detail later in this chapter.

We will learn how to build a recursive descent parser systematically by providing a set of programming guidelines based on the rules in the context-free grammar. These guidelines were followed for the example in Section 6.1.

Parsing Guideline 1

For (almost) every rule in the grammar

```
N = ...
```

we define a parsing method with the name

```
parseN()
```

As examples, for the rules

```
program = ...
initialDecl = ...
functionDecl = ...
assignmentStmt = ...
```

we define parsing methods

```
parseProgram() ...
parseInitialDecl() ...
parseFunctionDecl() ...
parseAssignmentStmt() ...
```

The caveat "almost" for Guideline 1 refers to the fact that some very simple rules in the grammar are not implemented as parsing methods. As previously discussed, the rules

```
booleanExpr = expression .
```

and

```
constId = identifier .
```

have no corresponding parsing methods. We simply make a mental substitution for these symbols as we write the parsing methods.

In other words, we parse the rule

```
constDecl = "const" constId ":=" [ "-" ] literal ";" .
```

as though it had been written originally as

```
constDecl = "const" identifier ":=" [ "-" ] literal ";" .
```

Similarly, the rules

```
addingOp   = "+" | "-" | "|" | "^" .
```

and

```
multiplyingOp = "*" | "/" | "mod" | "&" | "<<" | ">>" .
```

have no corresponding parsing methods, but there are helper methods in class `Symbol` that check whether or not a symbol has one of these properties; e.g., methods `isAddingOperator()` and `isMultiplyingOperator()`.

In general, the `parseN()` methods of the parser function as follows.

- Scanner method `symbol()` provides one lookahead symbol for the parsing methods. Additional lookahead symbols can be examined by using the `symbol()` method of tokens obtained from scanner method `lookahead()`; e.g., `lookahead(2).symbol()`.
- On entry into the method `parseN()`, the symbol returned from the scanner should be a symbol that could start on the right side of the rule `N = ...`
- On exit from the method `parseN()`, the symbol returned from the scanner should be a symbol that could follow `N`. (We will use this idea to implement error recovery in the next chapter.)
- If the production rules contain recursive references, the parsing methods will also contain recursive calls.

Parsing the "Right" Side of a Rule

We now turn our attention to guidelines for the systematic implementation of the `parseN()` methods by examining the right side of the associated rules. As an example, we will illustrate how to implement method `parseAssignmentStmt()` by examining the rule

```
assignmentStmt = variable ":=" expression ";" .
```

Parsing Guideline 2

A sequence of syntax factors $F_1\ F_2\ F_3\ \ldots$ is recognized by parsing the individual factors one at a time in order. In other words, the algorithm for parsing $F_1\ F_2\ F_3\ \ldots$ is simply

- the algorithm for parsing F_1 followed by
- the algorithm for parsing F_2 followed by
- the algorithm for parsing F_3 followed by
- ...

For example, the algorithm used to parse the right side of the rule for `assignmentStmt`

```
variable ":=" expression ";"
```

is simply

- the algorithm used to parse `variable` followed by
- the algorithm used to parse `":="` followed by
- the algorithm used to parse `expression` followed by
- the algorithm used to parse `";"`.

Parsing Guideline 3

A single terminal symbol `t` on the right side of a rule is recognized by calling the "helper" parsing method `match(t)`, where method `match()` is defined as follows.

```
private void match(Symbol expectedSymbol)
    throws IOException, ParserException
  {
    if (scanner.symbol() == expectedSymbol)
        scanner.advance();
    else
      {
        var errorMsg = "Expecting \"" + expectedSymbol
                + "\" but found \"" + scanner.token() + "\" instead.";
        throw error(errorMsg);
      }
  }
```

As an example, the algorithm for recognizing the assignment symbol ":=" is simply a call to this method with `Symbol.assign` as a parameter.

```
match(Symbol.assign);
```

Note that `match()` calls a method named `error()` to create the exception. Actually there are two overloaded methods named `error()`. One takes a single string parameter for the error message and returns a `ParserException` using the current scanner position. The second version takes two parameters, both an error message and an explicit position to be used in creating the `ParserException`. The latter version is useful for reporting the position of an error associated with a previously recognized token. There is a third similar method named `internalError()` that can be used to create an `InternalCompilerException`. Similar to the use of assertions, internal compiler exceptions are used to represent problems detected within the implementation of the compiler and should never occur if the compiler is implemented correctly. In other words, they represent logic errors within the compiler implementation and not errors in the program being compiled.

As mentioned in the previous section, in addition to `match()` there is a similar helper method named `matchCurrentSymbol()` that can used when we already know that the next symbol in the input stream is the one we are expecting. Method `matchCurrentSymbol()` is slightly more efficient in that it takes no parameters and doesn't throw an exception. It simply advances the scanner. Method `matchCurrentSymbol()` is implemented as follows.

```
private void matchCurrentSymbol() throws IOException
  {
    scanner.advance();
  }
```

In order to simplify explanation of the parsing methods, we will temporarily ignore exceptions thrown by the helper parsing method `match()`. Just assume that, instead of throwing an exception, the helper method simply prints an error message and then exits. We will return to the handling of exceptions near the end of this chapter.

Parsing Guideline 4

A nonterminal symbol `N` on the right side of a rule is recognized by calling the method corresponding to the rule for `N`; i.e., the algorithm for recognizing nonterminal `N` is simply a call to the method `parseN()`.

For example, the algorithm for recognizing the nonterminal symbol `variable` on the right side of the rule for `assignmentStmt` is simply a call to the method `parseVariable()`. Similarly, the algorithm for recognizing the nonterminal symbol `expression` on the right side of the rule for `assignmentStmt` is simply a call to the method `parseExpression()`.

Let's consider applying all of these parsing guidelines for the rule

```
assignmentStmt = variable ":=" expression ";" .
```

Using our initial approach to error handling, the basic parsing method for recognizing an assignment statement can be implemented as follows.

```
private void parseAssignmentStmt() throws IOException
  {
    try
      {
        parseVariable();
        match(Symbol.assign);
        parseExpression();
        match(Symbol.semicolon);
      }
    catch (ParserException e)
      {
        errorHandler.reportError(e);
        recover(emptySet);
      }
  }
```

Using only the guidelines already discussed, you should be able to write the basic parsing method for any rule where the right side is simply a sequence of terminal and nonterminal symbols. We illustrate with one more simple example. From the rule

```
compoundStmt = "{" statements "}" .
```

we derive the following parsing method.

```
private void parseCompoundStmt() throws IOException
  {
    try
      {
        match(Symbol.leftBrace);
        parseStatements();
        match(Symbol.rightBrace);
      }
    catch (ParserException e)
      {
        errorHandler.reportError(e);
        recover(emptySet);
      }
  }
```

6.3 First and Follow Sets

Before we can provide additional parsing guidelines, we need to perform additional analysis of the context-free grammar. Let's begin by discussing first and follow sets.

First Sets

The set of all terminal symbols that can appear at the start of a syntax expression `E` is called the first set of `E` and is denoted `First(E)`. We are especially interested in first sets for nonterminal symbols since they provide valuable information that can be used to guide decisions during parser development.

> Caution: In the remainder of this chapter, we will use braces "{" and "}" both to denote "zero or more" within a rule of a context-free grammar and to enclose elements of a set, as is common in mathematics. The interpretation of braces should be clear from the context where they appear.

Let's consider some relatively straightforward examples from CPRL.

constDecl:

```
    constDecl = "const" constId ":=" [ "-" ] literal ";" .
    First(constDecl) = { "const" }
```

varDecl:

```
    varDecl = "var" identifiers ":" ( typeName | arrayTypeConstr )
              [ ":=" constValue] ";" .
    First(varDecl) = { "var" }
```

```
arrayTypeDecl:
    arrayTypeDecl = "type" typeId "=" "array" "[" intConstValue "]" "of"
                    typeName ";" .
    First(arrayTypeDecl) = { "type" }   // similarly for records and strings
typeDecl:
    typeDecl = arrayTypeDecl | recordTypeDecl | enumTypeDecl .
    First(typeDecl) = { "type" }

initialDecl:
    initialDecl = constDecl | varDecl | typeDecl .
    First(initialDecl) = { "const", "var", "type" }
procedureDecl:
    procedureDecl = "proc" procId "(" [parameterDecls ] ")"
                    "{" initialDecls statements "}" .
    First(procedureDecl) = { "proc" }

functionDecl:
    functionDecl = "fun" funId "(" [parameterDecls ] ")" ":" typeName
                   "{" initialDecls statements "}" .
    First(functionDecl) = { "fun" }

subprogramDecl:
    subprogramDecl = procedureDecl | functionDecl .
    First(subprogramDecl) = { "proc", "fun" }

compoundStmt:
    compoundStmt = "{" statements "}" .
    First(compoundStmt) = { "{" }

loopStmt:
    loopStmt = [ "while" booleanExpr ] "loop" statement .
    First(loopStmt) = { "while", "loop" }
```

This last example requires a little more explanation. A loop statement can begin with the terminal symbol "`while`", but since the `while` part is optional, a loop statement can also begin with the terminal symbol "`loop`". Therefore, `First(loopStmt)` = { "`while`", "`loop`" }.

At this point we give a slightly more formal presentation of the rules used to compute first sets. While the presentation might seem a little daunting at first, the actual application of these ideas is usually more straightforward, as evidenced by the examples above. Using the set notation of mathematics ($\cup$ for union, $\subseteq$ for subset, etc.), and assuming that `E` and `F` are arbitrary syntax expressions, following are some basic rules for computing first sets.

- If `t` is a terminal symbol, `First(t)` = { `t` }.
- `First(E|F)` = `First(E)` ∪ `First(F)`.
- `First({E})` includes all terminal symbols in `First(E)`; mathematically we write `First(E)` ⊆ `First({E})`. As an example from CPRL, `First({initialDecl})` includes `First(initialDecl)`, which is the set { `"const", "var", "type"` }.
- `First([E])` includes all terminal symbols in `First(E)`; equivalently, `First(E)` ⊆ `First([E])`.
- Since `{E}` can occur zero times, `First({E} F)` includes all terminal symbols in `First(E)` and all terminal symbols in `First(F)`; equivalently `First(E)` ∪ `First(F)` ⊆ `First({E} F)`.
- Similarly, since `[E]` can occur zero times, `First([E] F)` includes all terminal symbols in `First(E)` and all terminal symbols in `First(F)`; equivalently `First(E)` ∪ `First(F)` ⊆ `First([E] F)`.

As a general strategy for computing first sets, we recommend using a bottom-up approach; i.e., start with the simplest rules and work toward more complicated (composite) rules.

Follow Sets

The set of all terminal symbols that can follow immediately after a syntax expression `E` is called the follow set of `E` and is denoted `Follow(E)`. Understanding follow sets is important not only for parser development but also for error recovery. If `N` is a nonterminal, we will use `Follow(N)` during error recovery when trying to parse `N`. To compute `Follow(N)` for a nonterminal `N`, you must analyze all rules that reference `N`. Computation of follow sets can be a bit more involved than computation of first sets.

Let's start with a relatively simple example from CPRL. What can follow a subprogram declaration? Consider the following rules.

```
subprogramDecls = { subprogramDecl } .
subprogramDecl  = procedureDecl | functionDecl .
procedureDecl   = "proc" procId ...
functionDecl    = "fun" funId ...
```

The first rule tells us that a `subprogramDecl` can be followed by another `subprogramDecl`, and from the next three rules we know that `subprogramDecl` can start with "`proc`" or "`fun`". Therefore the follow set for `subprogramDecl` must contain both "`proc`" and "`fun`".

Now consider the rule for `program`.

```
program = initialDecls subprogramDecls .
```

From this rule we know that anything that can follow `program` can also follow a subprogram declaration. But what can follow `program`? Recalling the augmenting rule we know that the only thing that can follow a program is `EOF` (end of file). Putting everything together we conclude

```
Follow(subprogramDecl) = { "proc", "fun", EOF }
```

Using a similar analysis, we can determine that both `procedureDecl` and `functionDecl` have the same follow set; i.e., `{ "proc", "fun", EOF }`.

As a second example, let's consider the follow set for `loopStmt`. ... (This one is left as an exercise, but here are a couple of hints. First, any statement can follow a loop statement, and therefore `Follow(loopStmt)` can include any terminal symbol that can start another statement. Second, a loop statement could appear as the last statement at the end of a procedure. Here is the answer. See if you can analyze the grammar to get this result.)

Conclusion:

```
Follow(loopStmt) = { identifier, "if", "else", "while", "loop", "for",
                     "read", "write", "writeln", "exit", "{", "}", "return" }
```

Again, using a similar analysis, we can conclude that the follow set for any statement is the same as the follow set for a loop statement. Therefore

```
Follow(statement) = { identifier, "if", "else", "while", "loop", "for",
                      "read", "write", "writeln", "exit", "{", "}", "return" }
```

Additional details and examples of follow sets are presented in the next chapter where we discuss the topic of error recovery.

Assuming that `N` is a nonterminal and `S`, `T`, and `U` are arbitrary syntax expressions, here are some basic rules for computing follow sets for `T`.

- Consider all rules similar to the following, where `T` is followed by `U` in a rule.

  ```
  N = S T U .      N = S {T} U .      N = S [T] U .
  ```

  In all of these cases, `Follow(T)` includes all terminal symbols in `First(U)`; equivalently,

  `First(U)` ⊆ `Follow(T)`. Additionally, if `U` can be empty, then `Follow(T)` also includes `Follow(N)`; equivalently, `Follow(N)` ⊆ `Follow(T)`.

- Now consider all rules similar to the following, where `T` is at the end of a rule.

  ```
  N = S T .      N = S {T} .      N = S [T] .
  ```

  In all these cases, `Follow(T)` includes all terminal symbols in `Follow(N)`; equivalently `Follow(N)` ⊆ `Follow(T)`.

- If `T` occurs in the form `{T}`, then `Follow(T)` includes all terminal symbols in `First(T)`; equivalently, `First(T)` ⊆ `Follow(T)`.

As a general strategy for computing follow sets, we recommend using a top-down approach; i.e., start with first rule (the one containing the start symbol), then the rules containing nonterminals in the first rule, and so on.

Parsing Guideline 5

This guideline handles the case where a syntax expression is enclosed in braces "{" and "}"; i.e., where syntax expression can be repeated zero or more times. Repetition zero or more times suggests that we need a loop. Therefore, a syntax expression of the form `{E}` is recognized by the following algorithm.

```
while <condition involving lookahead symbols for E> loop
   apply the algorithm for recognizing E
```

Most of the time, the condition can be formulated using only the first lookahead symbol. But what if a terminal symbol in `First(E)` could also follow `{E}`? In that case we would not know whether to continue looping or to exit the loop and parse the input following `{E}`.

Grammar Restriction 3: The condition involving lookahead symbols for `E` must be false for syntax expressions that follow `{E}`. For the case involving only one lookahead symbol, this means that `First(E)` and `Follow({E})` must be disjoint; in mathematical terms,

```
First(E) ∩ Follow({E}) = ∅.
```

Example: Parsing Guideline 5

Consider the rule for `initialDecls`.

```
initialDecls = { initialDecl } .
```

The first set for `initialDecl` is the set of three reserved words `constRW`, `varRW`, and `typeRW`. Therefore, the CPRL method for parsing `initialDecls` can be implemented as follows.

```
private void parseInitialDecls()
  {
    while (scanner.symbol() == Symbol.constRW ||
           scanner.symbol() == Symbol.varRW   ||
           scanner.symbol() == Symbol.typeRW)
      {
        parseInitialDecl();
      }
  }
```

In CPRL, the symbols `constRW`, `varRW`, and `typeRW` cannot follow `initialDecls` (plural form), and therefore the loop will exit appropriately whenever all initial declarations have been parsed. (Exercise: Which symbols can follow `initialDecls`? We'll cover this in the next chapter but try it on your own now.)

Class `Symbol` provides several boolean-valued helper methods for testing properties of symbols. Examples include the following.

```
public boolean isReservedWord()
public boolean isInitialDeclStarter()
public boolean isSubprogramDeclStarter()
public boolean isStmtStarter()
public boolean isRelationalOperator()
public boolean isLiteral()
```

For example, method `isInitialDeclStarter()` is implemented as follows.

```
/**
 * Returns true if this symbol can start an initial declaration.
 */
public boolean isInitialDeclStarter()
  {
    return this == constRW || this == varRW || this == typeRW;
  }
```

Using the helper methods in class `Symbol`, we can rewrite the method for `parseInitialDecls()` as follows.

```
private void parseInitialDecls()
  {
    while (scanner.symbol().isInitialDeclStarter())
        parseInitialDecl();
  }
```

For the CPRL grammar in Appendix D, all syntax expressions of the form `{E}` can be parsed using only one lookahead symbol.

Parsing Guideline 6

This guideline handles the case where a syntax expression is repeated one or more times. Since "one or more" is simply "one followed by zero or more", this guideline is for syntax expressions of the form `E{E}`. A syntax expression that can be repeated one or more times is recognized by the following algorithm.

```
apply the algorithm for recognizing E
while <condition involving lookahead symbols for E> loop
    apply the algorithm for recognizing E
```

Equivalently, the algorithm for recognizing `E{E}` can be written using a loop that tests at the bottom. In Java, the loop structure that tests at the bottom is called a `do-while` loop, so the algorithm implemented in Java would more closely resemble the following.

```
do
    apply the algorithm for recognizing E
while <condition involving lookahead symbols for E>
```

As an aside, note that the *structural* grammar for CPRL does not use "one or more" in any rules, and the *lexical* grammar for CPRL uses "one or more" in only three rules

```
decimalLiteral = digit { digit } .
   // one or more digits
hexLiteral = ( "0x" | "0X" ) hexDigit { hexDigit } .
   // one or more hexDigits
binaryLiteral = ( "0b" | "0B" ) binaryDigit { binaryDigit } .
   // one or more binary digits
```

Parsing Guideline 7

This guideline handles the case for an optional syntax expression enclosed in brackets "`[`" and "`]`". Optional suggests that we need an if statement, so a syntax factor of the form `[E]` is recognized by the following algorithm.

```
if <condition involving lookahead symbols for E> then
    apply the algorithm for recognizing E
```

As before this leads to another grammar restriction.

Grammar Restriction 4: The condition involving lookahead symbols for `E` must be false for syntax expressions that follow `[E]`. For the case involving only one lookahead symbol, this means that `First(E)` and `Follow([E])` must be disjoint; in mathematical terms,

```
First(E) ∩ Follow([E]) = ∅
```

Example: Parsing Guideline 7

Consider the rule for an `exit` statement.

```
exitStmt = "exit" [ "when" booleanExpr ] ";" .
```

We parse the "`when`" clause of an `exit` statement as follows.

```
match(exitRW);
if (scanner.symbol() == Symbol.whenRW)
  {
    matchCurrentSymbol();
    parseExpression();
  }
```

first check for optional when clause (→ `if (scanner.symbol() == Symbol.whenRW)`)

slightly more efficient than `match(Symbol.whenRW)` (→ `matchCurrentSymbol();`)

Note that the first set for the optional when clause is simply { "`when`" }, so we use the reserved word `when` to tell us whether or not to parse a when clause.

Questions: What is the follow set for the optional `when` clause? What problem would we have if it contained the reserved word "`when`"?

For the CPRL grammar in Appendix D, all syntax expressions of the form `[E]` can be parsed using only one lookahead symbol.

Parsing Guideline 8

This guideline applies when we have alternatives and need to decide which alternative to choose for parsing. A syntax factor of the form `E|F` is recognized by the following algorithm.

```
if <condition involving lookahead symbols for E> then
    apply the algorithm for recognizing E
else if <condition involving lookahead symbols for F> then
    apply the algorithm for recognizing F
else
    parsing error
```

Grammar Restriction 5: The condition involving lookahead symbols for `E` must be false for F, and vice versa. For the case involving only one lookahead symbol, this means that `First(E)` and `First(F)` must be disjoint; i.e., `First(E)` ∩ `First(F)` = Ø. (Why?)

Example: Parsing Guideline 8

Consider the rule in CPRL for `initialDecl`.

```
initialDecl = constDecl | varDecl | typeDecl .
```

We parse the alternatives on the right side of `initialDecl` as follows.

```
if (scanner.symbol() == Symbol.constRW)
    parseConstDecl();
else if (scanner.symbol() == Symbol.varRW)
    parseVarDecl();
else if (scanner.symbol() == Symbol.typeRW)
    parseTypeDecl();
else
    throw internalError("Invalid initial declaration.");
```

Alternatively, we could use a "`switch`" statement in Java instead of nested "`if/else if`" statements.

6.4 LL(k) Grammars and Recursive Descent Parsing

If a context-free grammar satisfies all grammar restrictions outlined above, and if all parsing decisions involve at most k lookahead symbols, then the grammar is called an **LL(k)** grammar. Thus, an LL(1) grammar is one for which all parsing decisions can be made by considering only one lookahead symbol. Note that LL(k) is a property of the grammar, not the language. As we will explain later, the grammar for CPRL is LL(4), but using left factoring it is possible to write an equivalent grammar for CPRL that is LL(1).

Recursive descent parsing using k lookahead symbols can be used only if the grammar is LL(k). The interpretation of the characters in LL(k) is as follows.

- First 'L': left-to-right parse (read the source file from left to right)
- Second 'L': leftmost derivation (descend into the parse tree from left to right)
- Number 'k': number of lookahead symbols

Not all grammars are LL(k); e.g., any grammar that has left recursion is not LL(k). In practice, the syntax of most programming languages can be defined, or at least closely approximated, by an LL(k) grammar; e.g., by using grammar transformations such as eliminating left recursion and left factoring.

> In his book *Language Implementation Patterns* [Parr 2010], Terence Parr had this to say about using additional lookahead symbols. "Having more lookahead is like being able to look farther down multiple paths emanating from a fork in a maze. The farther we can see ahead, the easier it is to decide which path to take. More powerful parsing decisions make it easier to build more powerful parsers. We don't have to contort our parsers (or grammars) as much to suit a weak underlying parsing strategy".

The phrase "recursive descent" refers to the fact that we descend (top-down) the parse tree using recursive method/function calls. The "recursive" part of the phrase "recursive descent" is easy to understand. For example, suppose we have nested loop statements.

```
loop
  {
    loop
      {
        ...
      }
    ...
  }
```

To parse the outer loop we call method `parseLoopStmt()`. But this method will call `parseStatement()`, which will call `parseCompoundStmt()`, which will (eventually) call `parseLoopStmt()` again – recursively.

To understand the "descent" part of the phrase "recursive descent," consider the following simple program.

```
var x : Integer;

proc main()
  {
    ...
  }
```

A portion of the parse tree for this program can be visualized as follows.

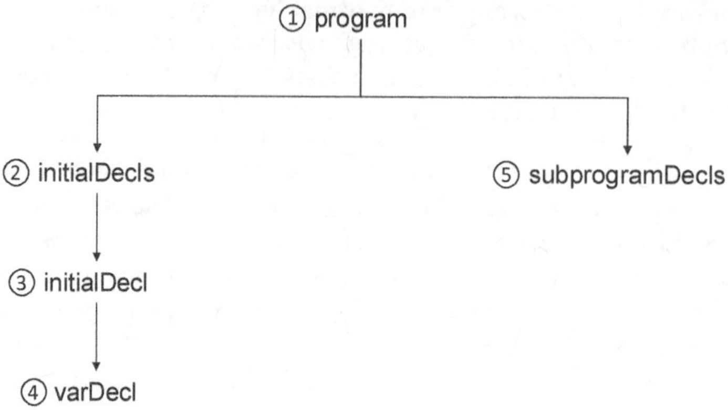

The numbers on the nodes of the parse tree correspond to the order of calls to parsing methods; i.e., these are the first five parsing methods called when parsing the program.

```
parseProgram()
parseInitialDecls()
parseInitialDecl()
parseVarDecl()
parseSubprogramDecls()
```

Note how these method calls "descend" the parse tree in a preorder traversal.

Developing a Parser

As outlined in Appendix A, we divide the parser implementation into three major projects.

1. Parser version 1 (Project 2 in Appendix A): Language recognition based on a context-free grammar, with minor checking of language constraints.
2. Parser version 2 (Project 3 in Appendix A): Add error-recovery.
3. Parser version 3 (Project 4 in Appendix A): Add generation of abstract syntax trees.

Based on this chapter, version 1 of the parser focuses primarily on language recognition. Using the parsing guidelines discussed earlier, we need to verify that the grammar restrictions are satisfied by the grammar for CPRL. This means that we will need to analyze the grammar to compute first and follow sets.

6.5 Variables versus Variable Expressions

Consider the two grammar rules below.

```
variable = ( varId | paramId ) { indexExpr | fieldExpr } .
variableExpr = variable .
```

From the perspective of the grammar, there is no real distinction between a variable and a variable expression.

The syntax expression `( varId | paramId )` is there to remind us that the identifier can be declared as a variable or as a parameter, but both `varId` and `paramId` are simply identifiers as far as the grammar is concerned. Therefore, using substitution, we could rewrite the first rule as

```
variable = identifier { indexExpr | fieldExpr } .
```

Nonterminals `variable` and `variableExpr` are parsed exactly the same way, but we make a distinction based on the context. For example, consider the assignment statement below.

```
x := y;
```

The identifier "`x`" represents a variable, and the identifier "`y`" represents a variable expression. Loosely speaking, `x` is a variable because it appears on the left side of an assignment statement, and `y` is a variable expression because it is used as an expression.

When a variable is used on the left side of an assignment statement, we need to know the **address** of the variable. But when a variable is used on the right side of an assignment statement, we need to know the **value** of the variable. Some programming languages use the terms **l-value** and **r-value** to describe this difference, where these terms are derived from the idea of left and right side of an assignment statement. As we will discuss in Chapter 13, similar concepts apply when a variable is passed by value or by reference to a subprogram.

The distinction between a variable and a variable expression will become important later when we consider the topics of error recovery and code generation. The error recovery and code generation are different for a variable than for a variable expression.

6.6 Handling Grammar Limitations

As specified in Appendix D, the grammar for CPRL is almost LL(1), but not quite. For example, consider the rule for a statement.

```
statement = assignmentStmt | procedureCallStmt | compoundStmt | ifStmt
          | loopStmt       | forLoopStmt       | exitStmt     | readStmt
          | writeStmt      | writelnStmt       | returnStmt .
```

The body of method `parseStatement()` will need a multiway branch to select the alternative parsing method to call; e.g., `parseCompoundStmt()`, `parseAssignmentStmt()`, `parseIfStmt()`, etc. Can we decide which of these parsing methods to call using only one lookahead symbol?

- If the lookahead symbol is "`if`", we know that we want to call `parseIfStmt()`.
- If the lookahead symbol is "`while`" or "`loop`", we know that we want to call `parseLoopStmt()`.
- If the lookahead symbol is "`return`", we know that we want to call `parseReturnStmt()`.

- If the lookahead symbol is "`identifier`", we know that we want to call either `parseAssignmentStmt()` or `parseProcedureCallStmt()`, but which one? Symbol `identifier` is in the first set of both an assignment statement and a procedure call statement.

A similar problem exists when parsing a factor.

```
factor = ("not" | "~") factor | literal | constId | variableExpr
       | enumConstValue | functionCallExpr | "(" expression ")" .
```

Symbol `identifier` is in the first set of `constId`, `variableExpr`, `enumConstValue`, and `functionCallExpr`.

Yet another similar problem exists when parsing a type declaration.

```
typeDecl = arrayTypeDecl | recordTypeDecl | enumTypeDecl .
```

Each alternative on the right side of the rule starts with the same terminal symbol "`type`". In fact, each alternative starts with the same three symbols.

```
"type" typeId "=" ...
```

In each of these three cases – `statement`, `factor`, and `typeDecl` – we can't simply use one lookahead symbol to determine which alternative to choose.

There are several possible approaches to solving these kinds of dilemmas. Below we describe four such approaches.

Approach 1: Use Additional Lookahead Symbols

In `parseStatement()`, when trying to decide whether to call `parseAssignmentStmt()` or `parseProcedureCallStmt()`, suppose that we could look two symbols ahead; i.e., that we could look at the symbol following the identifier.

- If the symbol following the identifier were "`[`", "`.`", or "`:=`", we would know to call `parseAssignmentStmt()`. (Symbol "`[`" could follow an array variable, and symbol "`.`" could follow a record variable.)
- If the symbol following the identifier were "`(`" , we would know to call `parseProcedureCallStmt()`.
- If the symbol following the identifier were anything else, we would know that the program is not valid according to the rules of the context-free grammar.

If a grammar meets all of our restrictions for parsing except that it requires 2 symbols of lookahead, then the grammar is said to be LL(2).

Similarly, in method `parseTypeDecl()`, the three alternatives differ in the fourth symbol.

- If the fourth symbol is the reserved word `array`, we would know to call `parseArrayTypeDecl()`.
- If the fourth symbol is the reserved word `record`, we would know to call `parseRecordTypeDecl()`.

- If the fourth symbol is the less-than symbol <, we would know to call `parseEnumTypeDecl()`.
- If the fourth symbol is anything else, then the program is not valid with respect to the rules of the context-free grammar.

So we will need to look 4 symbols ahead in order to make the parsing decision in the body of `parseTypeDecl()`. (See, also, Exercise 9 at the end of this chapter.)

Approach 2: Rewrite/Factor the Grammar

A second possible solution to our problem is to use factoring to rewrite the grammar. For example, since both an assignment statement and a procedure call statement start with an identifier, let's factor out the identifier part and create a different kind of statement called `idStmt` that encompasses both, so that the rule for `statement` becomes the following.

```
statement = idStmt       | compoundStmt | ifStmt    | loopStmt
          | forLoopStmt  | exitStmt     | readStmt  | writeStmt
          | writelnStmt  | returnStmt .
```

Now when parsing a statement, if the lookahead symbol is an identifier, we would know to call `parseIdStmt()`.

We *could* define `idStmt` as

```
idStmt = identifier ( assignCompletion | procCallCompletion ) .
```

where `assignCompletion` and `procCallCompletion` are defined as follows.

```
assignCompletion = { ( "[" expression "]" ) | ( "." fieldId ) }
                   ":=" expression ";" .
procCallCompletion = "(" [ actualParams ] ")" ";" .
```

Approach 3: Use an Identifier Table

A third possible approach to solving our parsing problem is to use an identifier table to store information about how the identifier was declared; e.g., if the identifier was declared as a constant, a variable, a procedure name, etc. Using this approach, when trying to decide whether to call `parseAssignmentStmt()` or `parseProcedureCallStmt()`, we could extract the text for the identifier, look up the text in the identifier table, and then use information about how it was declared to determine which parsing method to call. This approach is especially useful if all identifiers are required to be declared before they are used. In CPRL, initial declarations (declarations of constants, variables, and types) must take place before the name being introduced can be used, but this restriction does not apply to subprogram declarations. A call to a procedure or function can appear before the procedure or function has been declared.

Approach 4: Make Two Passes Over the Source Code

A fourth approach is to use an identifier table in conjunction with two passes over the source code. During the first pass, we can process all subprogram declarations, so that the identifier table would contain the names of all subprograms. During a second pass we could parse the complete program using the identifier table as described in approach 3 above.

Although approach 1 (use additional lookahead symbols) is sufficient for our purposes, we will use a combination of approaches 1 and 3 in this book; i.e., we will use both an identifier table and multiple lookahead symbols to make parsing decisions. The identifier table will be needed for purposes other than parsing, so we might as well introduce it when we first construct the parser. However, since the CPRL grammar is "almost" LL(1), most parsing decisions can be made directly without using the identifier table or the extra lookahead symbols. With respect to approach 2, too much refactoring not only makes the grammar less transparent, but it can also complicate construction of the parser. Plus, it should be noted that refactoring was used several times during creation of the CPRL grammar. Approach 4 was not chosen since we don't need it for CPRL and it tends to be less efficient.

6.7 Scope and Visibility

The term "scope" has been used several times without explanation under the assumption that developers reading this book are somewhat familiar with the term, but this section provides a more detailed explanation.

Identifiers provide names for entities in a program – constants, types, variables, subprograms, parameters, fields, and enumerated constants. It is possible for an identifier to have a predefined meaning in a programming language, but names created by the programmer are introduced via declarations. The basic idea of scope is the region of a program where a user-defined identifier can be used. More precisely, a declaration binds an identifier with an entity such as a variable, type, or function; and scope is the part of a program where this binding is valid.

An **applied occurrence** of an identifier is a reference to the identifier in a context other than its declaration; e.g., in a statement or as part of a different declaration. So scope addresses the notion of where an applied occurrence is permitted by the programming language. Closely related to the concept of scope is that of visibility. An identifier is generally visible within its scope, but with nested scopes it is possible for one identifier to "hide" or "shadow" another one with the same name.

One important scope-related issue is whether or not the declaration for an identifier must physically appear in the file prior to any applied occurrence. For example, in CPRL, initial declarations must appear before any applied occurrence. Contrast this with programming languages that support classes, where the declaration for a field or property of a class can appear anywhere in the class, and the name can be referenced anywhere within the class, including before its declaration. Note that applied occurrences for subprograms in CPRL (i.e., calls to subprograms) can appear before the subprogram has been declared.

When we encounter an applied occurrence of an identifier in a program, what entity does the identifier represent; or equivalently, exactly which declaration introduced the identifier? Scope and visibility rules allow the compiler to determine which declaration corresponds to an applied occurrence of an identifier. One way to avoid issues of scope is to require all identifiers in a program to be unique and to require that all identifiers be declared before they can be used, but these requirements would be too restrictive for all but the simplest of programming languages.

More generally, a declaration introduces an identifier (name) into a scope, and from the perspective of the compiler writer, a scope can be implemented as a map from identifiers to their declarations, with each scope having its own map. There are two fundamental rules for scopes.

1. Every identifier must belong to a scope.
2. The same identifier can't be declared twice in the same scope. (But the same identifier can be declared in different, possibly nested scopes.)

CPRL requires three scopes.

- **Global scope**. An identifier has global scope if it is not declared within a subprogram, as a field in a record, or as one of the enumerated constants in an enum type declaration.
- **Local scope.** An identifier has local scope if it is declared within a subprogram but not as a field in a record or as one of the enumerated constants in an enum type declaration. Parameter names are also considered to have local scope. Each subprogram declaration introduces a different scope.
- **Record scope.** An identifier has record scope if it is declared as a field name within a record type declaration. Each record type declaration introduces a different scope.

In the next few chapters, we will concentrate primarily on global and local scopes. Record scopes will be covered more thoroughly in Chapter 17. There is essentially a different type of scope for enumerated constants, but we don't need to declare it as such since it is checked entirely within the parser.

Let's consider a couple of CPRL examples illustrating the concepts of scope and visibility.

Example 1.

```
var x : Integer;
var y : Integer;

proc main()
  {
    p();        // which p?
    x := 8;     // which x?
  }

proc p()
  {
    var x : Integer;
    var n : Integer;

    x := 5;     // which x?
    n := y;     // which y?
  }
```

In this example, the identifiers `x` and `y` declared at the beginning of the program have global scope, as do identifiers `main` and `p` (the procedure name). Identifiers `x` and `n` declared inside procedure `p()` have local scope.

In the assignment statement

```
x := 5;
```

in procedure `p()`, the name `x` refers to the integer variable with local scope declared in procedure `p`.

In the assignment statement

```
n := y;
```

in procedure `p()`, the name `n` refers to the integer variable with local scope declared in procedure `p`, but the name `y` refers to the integer variable declared at global scope.

For the assignment statement

```
x := 8;
```

in procedure `main()`, the name `x` refers to the integer variable with global scope declared at the start of the program, not the one declared in procedure `p`. Note that an identifier declared at local scope can "hide" the same identifier declared at global scope, as illustrated in example 1 above, where identifier `x` declared in procedure `p()` hides identifier `x` declared at global scope. Some programming languages have a scope operator, e.g., `::`, that can be used to access a variable in an enclosing scope. So, for example, in procedure `p()`, the identifier `x` (unmodified) would refer to the variable with local scope, but `::x` would refer to the variable declared at global scope. CPRL does not have a scope operator.

Note that each subprogram, record declaration, or enum type declaration introduces a different local scope – the same identifier can appear in different scopes without conflict.

Example 2.

```
type Point = record
  {
    x : Integer;
    y : Integer;
  };

proc main()
  {
    var x, y  : Point;

    x.x := 5;
    x.y := 2;
    writeln "Point(", x.x, ", ", x.y, ")";

    y := x;
    writeln "Point(", y.x, ", ", y.y, ")";
  }
```

In this example, identifiers `Point` and `main` have global scope, while identifiers `x` and `y` declared in procedure `main()` have local scope. Field identifiers `x` and `y` have record scope.

Within procedure `main()`, the identifiers `x` and `y` can represent variables of type `Point` or fields in type `Point`. The meaning should be clear from the context, but the fact that the same identifier can refer to two different things in the program means that the same identifier belongs to two different scopes.

6.8 Class `IdTable`

For version 1 of the parser, we will create a preliminary version of an identifier table – class `IdTable` – to help track the kinds of identifiers that have been declared. This class will be augmented in subsequent chapters to contain more information, and the changes will allow us to perform a more complete analysis of CPRL type rules; but for now we will keep things as simple as possible.

We start by defining a simple Java enum class to represent the identifier type.

```
enum IdType
  {
    constantId,   variableId, arrayTypeId, enumTypeId, enumConstId,
    recordTypeId, fieldId,    procedureId, functionId
  }
```

For our current purposes, we don't need to distinguish between subprogram parameters and variables; all will be assigned an `IdType` value of `variableId`.

Handling Scopes within Class `IdTable`

A declaration introduces an identifier (name) into a scope, and it is possible to have different entities with the same name in different scopes, as illustrated in the previous section. The implementation of class `IdTable` needs to track which identifiers belong to different scopes, so we introduce another enum class to represent the three scope levels in CPRL.

```
public enum ScopeLevel
  {
    GLOBAL("global"),
    LOCAL("local"),
    RECORD("record");

    private String text;
    ...
  }
```

Since our compiler will need to search for names within a scope, we create a scope class that maps from the text of an identifier to its `IdType`.

```
public class Scope extends HashMap<String, IdType>
  {
    private ScopeLevel scopeLevel;

    public Scope(ScopeLevel scopeLevel)
      { ... }

    public ScopeLevel scopeLevel()
      { ... }
  }
```

We implement class `IdTable` as a stack of scopes (i.e., a stack of maps). "Opening" a scope creates a new scope object that is pushed onto the stack. Searching for an entity involves searching within the current scope (logically the top scope in the stack) and then, if necessary, within enclosing scopes (scopes logically under the top).

Key methods in class `IdTable` are as follows.

```
/**
 * Opens a new scope for identifiers.
 */
public void openScope(ScopeLevel scopeLevel)

/**
 * Closes the outermost scope.
 */
public void closeScope()
```

```
/**
 * Add an identifier and its type to the current scope.
 *
 * @throws ParserException if the identifier already exists
 *                         in the current scope.
 */
public void add(Token idToken, IdType idType) throws ParserException

/**
 * Returns the identifier type associated with the identifier name
 * (type String).  Returns null if the identifier is not found.
 * Searches enclosing scopes if necessary.
 */
public IdType get(String idStr)
```

Adding Declarations to `IdTable`

During parsing, when an identifier is declared, the parser will attempt to add its token and `IdType` to the table's current scope. If an identifier with the same name (same token text) has been previously declared in the current scope, then an exception will be thrown indicating that the program being compiled has an error since all entities declared in the same scope must have unique names.

Important: Add entries to the identifier table only when parsing declarations.

As an example, consider the following excerpt from method `parseConstDecl()`.

```
var constId = scanner.token();
match(Symbol.identifier);
...
idTable.add(constId, IdType.constantId);
```

Calling `idTable.add(constId, IdType.constantId)` will throw a `ParserException` if an identifier with the same text as `constId` is already defined in the current scope.

Using `IdTable` to Check Applied Occurrences of Identifiers

For an applied occurrence, the parser can check to see if the identifier has been declared, and if it has, then the parser can use the information about how the identifier was declared to facilitate correct parsing.

Consider the rule for factor, a type of expression.

```
factor = ("not" | "~") factor | literal | constId | variableExpr
       | enumConstValue | functionCallExpr | "(" expression ")" .
```

When implementing method `parseFactor()`, there are several cases to consider. For example, if the next symbol is the reserved word `not`, then the parser simply "matches" `not` and makes a recursive call to `parseFactor()`. Similarly, if the next symbol is "`(`", then we match "`(`", call `parseExpression()`, and match "`)`". And if the next symbol is a literal, we know to call `parseConstValue()`. But what if the next symbol is an identifier? An identifier could correspond to a constant value (a name declared as a constant), a variable expression (a variable used as an expression), an enum constant value, or a function call.

CPRL requires that identifiers introduced in initial declarations be declared before being used, so we can use the identifier table to decide whether to parse a constant value, a variable expression, or an enum constant value. But CPRL does not require that subprograms be declared prior to being called, so if the identifier is the name of a function, then it might or might not already be in the identifier table. If the function has been declared, then we can use the identifier table. If not, then we can use a lookahead symbol to decide if we have encountered a function call or if we have an error.

Below is an excerpt from method `parseFactor()` illustrating how we use the identifier table and the lookahead symbol in parsing.

```
if (symbol == Symbol.notRW || symbol == Symbol.bitwiseNot)
  {
    matchCurrentSymbol();
    parseFactor();
  }
else if (scanner.symbol().isLiteral())
  {
    // Handle constant literals separately from constant identifiers.
    parseConstValue();
  }
else if (scanner.symbol() == Symbol.identifier)
  {
    // Four possible cases: a declared constant, a variable
    // expression, a function call expression, or an enum
    // constant value.  Use lookahead tokens and declarations
    // to determine correct parsing action.
    var idStr  = scanner.text();
    var idType = idTable.get(idStr);

    if (scanner.lookahead(2).symbol() == Symbol.leftParen)
        parseFunctionCallExpr();
    else if (idType != null)
      {
        if (idType == IdType.constantId)
            parseConstValue();
        else if (idType == IdType.variableId)
            parseVariableExpr();
        else if (idType == IdType.enumTypeId)
            parseEnumConstValue();
        else
            throw error("Identifier \"" + idStr
                      + "\" is not valid as an expression.");
      }
```

```
      else
          throw error("Identifier \"" + idStr
                    + "\" has not been declared.");
    }
  else if (scanner.symbol() == Symbol.leftParen)
    {
      matchCurrentSymbol();
      parseExpression();
      match(Symbol.rightParen);
    }
  else
      throw error("Invalid expression.");
```

Alternatively, we could have used Java "`switch`" statements instead of nested "`if/else if`" statements to implement multiway branching in the code above.

Additional Examples Using `IdTable`

The rule for a procedure declaration is as follows.

```
procedureDecl = "proc" procId "(" [parameterDecls ] ")"
                "{" initialDecls statements "}" .
```

The following is an excerpt from method `parseProcedureDecl()`.

```
match(Symbol.procRW);
var procId = scanner.token();
match(Symbol.identifier);
idTable.add(procId, IdType.procedureId);
match(Symbol.leftParen);

try
  {
    idTable.openScope(ScopeLevel.LOCAL);

    if (scanner.symbol().isParameterDeclStarter())
        parseParameterDecls();

    match(Symbol.rightParen);
    match(Symbol.leftBrace);
    parseInitialDecls();
    parseStatements();
  }
finally
  {
    idTable.closeScope();
  }

match(Symbol.rightBrace);
```

Procedure name is defined at current (global) scope, but its parameters and initial declarations are defined at the local scope of the procedure.

Note that the procedure name is added to the identifier table at the current (global) scope, but parameters and initial declarations are defined within the local scope of the procedure. Also note the use of `try` and `finally` blocks to ensure that an open scope is always closed even when an exception is thrown by interim statements. A similar approach should be used when parsing function declarations, and a similar but slightly simpler approach will be used when parsing record type declarations and enum type declarations. They all require opening scopes, adding identifiers to the new scope, and closing scopes.

Similar to the excerpt above from `parseFactor()`, the following excerpt from method `parseStatement()` shows the use of the identifier table and lookahead symbols when deciding whether to parse an assignment statement or a procedure call statement based on the type of an identifier. Recall that variables must be declared prior to use in an assignment statement, but CPRL does not require that procedures be declared prior to being called. With respect to the lookahead symbol, observe that the identifier in a procedure call statement must be followed by a left parenthesis, but the variable identifier for an assignment statement can be followed only by a left bracket, a period (dot), or the assignment symbol.

```
if (scanner.symbol() == Symbol.identifier)
  {
    // Two possible cases: an assignment statement or a
    // function call.  Use lookahead tokens and declarations
    // to determine correct parsing action.
    var idStr = scanner.text();
    var idType = idTable.get(idStr);

    if (scanner.lookahead(2).symbol() == Symbol.leftParen)
        parseProcedureCallStmt();
    else if (idType != null)
      {
        if (idType == IdType.variableId)
            parseAssignmentStmt();
        else
            throw error("Identifier \"" + idStr
                      + "\" cannot start a statement.");
      }
    else
        throw error("Identifier \"" + idStr
                  + "\" has not been declared.");
  }
else
  {
    switch (scanner.symbol())
      {
        case Symbol.leftBrace -> parseCompoundStmt();
        ...
  }
```

You will also need to use additional lookahead symbols to implement method `parseTypeDecl()`, but that code is left for you to do. (Hint: You will need to look more than 2 symbols ahead in order to implement `parseTypeDecl()`, but if you have been reading this chapter carefully you should already know how far ahead to look.)

6.9 Parsing Variables and Variable Expressions

Recall the grammar rules for `variable` and `variableExpr`.

```
variable = ( varId | paramId ) { indexExpr | fieldExpr } .
variableExpr = variable .
indexExpr = "[" expression "]" .
fieldExpr = "." fieldId .
```

The first two rules tell us that variables and variable expressions are equivalent with respect to the context-free grammar, but we make a distinction since error recovery and code generation are different for a variable than for a variable expression. However, with respect to language recognition, the basic logic for parsing a variable is identical to the logic for parsing a variable expression.

To implement methods `parseVariable()` and `parseVariableExpr()` we use a helper method named `parseVariableCommon()` to provide the common logic. The helper method does not handle any parser exceptions but instead throws them back to the calling method where they can be handled appropriately. Both `parseVariable()` and `parseVariableExpr()` call the helper method to parse the grammar rule for variable. An outline of this helper method is shown below. Note the use of `Symbol` method `isSelectorStarter()`, which returns true whenever the symbol is left bracket or period (a.k.a., dot). A left bracket or period would denote an array index or a field reference, respectively.

```
private void parseVariableCommon() throws IOException, ParserException
  {
    var idToken = scanner.token();
    match(Symbol.identifier);
    var idType = idTable.get(idToken.text());

    if (idType == null)
      {
        var errorMsg = "Identifier \"" + idToken
                     + "\" has not been declared.";
        throw error(idToken.position(), errorMsg);
      }
    else if (idType != IdType.variableId)
      {
        var errorMsg = "Identifier \"" + idToken
                     + "\" is not a variable.";
        throw error(idToken.position(), errorMsg);
      }
```

```
    while (scanner.symbol().isSelectorStarter())
      {
        if (scanner.symbol() == Symbol.leftBracket)
          {
            // parse index expression
            match(Symbol.leftBracket);
            parseExpression();
            match(Symbol.rightBracket);
          }
        else if (scanner.symbol() == Symbol.dot)
          {
            // parse field expression
            match(Symbol.dot);
            match(Symbol.identifier);
          }
      }
  }
```

As shown below, method `parseVariable()` simply calls this helper method to parse its grammar rule.

```
private void parseVariable() throws IOException
  {
    try
      {
        parseVariableCommon();
      }
    catch (ParserException e)
      {
        errorHandler.reportError(e);
        recover(emptySet);
      }
  }
```

Method `parseVariableExpr()` is implemented similarly.

We are now ready to implement version 1 of the parser, as described in Project 2 of Appendix A. Start with the skeletal code provided in the book's GitHub repository and fill in the missing parts to implement the parser.

6.10 Class Parser

We will augment class `Parser` in the next two chapters, but for now it consists primarily of the following members.

- Parsing methods such as `parseProgram()`, `parseVarDecl()`, `parseProcedureDecl()`, `parseExpression()`, and `parseLoopStmt()`.
- Helper methods such as `match()`, `matchCurrentSymbol()`, `recover()`, and `error()`.

- Properties `scanner`, `idTable`, and `errorHandler`. There is also a temporary property named `emptySet`, which is needed for version 1 of the parser but will be removed in the next chapter.

Other than the constructor and method `parseProgram()`, all members of class `Parser` are private.

The constructor for class Parser is defined as follows.

```
public Parser(Scanner scanner, IdTable idTable,
              ErrorHandler errorHandler)
  {
    this.scanner = scanner;
    this.idTable = idTable;
    this.errorHandler = errorHandler;
  }
```

Class `TestParser` will be used to test the three versions of the parsers as created in this chapter and the next two chapters. Starting in Chapter 9, class `Cprlc` will be used to create and test the full compiler, including the `Parser`. In both `TestParser` and `Cprlc`, creation of a parser is performed similar to the following steps (some details omitted).

```
var errorHandler = new ErrorHandler();
var sourceFile = new File(fileName);
var scanner = new Scanner(sourceFile, 4, errorHandler);
var idTable = new IdTable();
var parser  = new Parser(scanner, idTable, errorHandler);
```

Once a parser has been created, calling `parser.parseProgram()` will parse the program contained in the source file.

6.11 Essential Terms and Concepts

applied occurrence (of an identifier)	`ErrorHandler` (class)
first set	follow set
global scope	`IdTable` (class)
LL(1), LL(k)	LL(k) grammar restrictions
local scope	`lookahead()` (method)
`match(Symbol expectedSymbol)` (method)	`matchCurrentSymbol()` (method)
`parseN()` (where `N` is a nonterminal)	`Parser` (class)
record scope	recursive descent parser
scope	variable
variable expression	visibility

6.12 Exercises

1. **Project Assignment.** Implement **Project 2: Language Recognition** as described in Appendix A.
2. True or false.
   a. All context-free grammars are LL(1).
   b. The context-free grammar for CPRL is LL(1).
3. What is the primary programming language construct used to parse a syntax expression of the form
   a. `{ E }`
   b. `E { E }`
   c. `[ E ]`
   d. `E | F | G`

   > Hint: Your answers should be something like "while loop," "do-while loop," "if statement without an else part," etc.

4. What is the primary role of a parser that is addressed in this chapter?
5. Describe the alternative approaches outlined in Section 6.6 for handling the issue where both nonterminals `assignmentStmt` and `procedureCallStmt` start with an identifier, and therefore the grammar for CPRL is not LL(1).
6. Explain the difference between the terms "variable" and "variable expression" as used in this book.
7. Explain the role of methods `openScope()` and `closeScope()` in class `IdTable`.
8. For this exercise, treat symbols recognized by the scanner as terminal symbols with respect to the parser. For example, in addition to operators and reserved words quoted in the CPRL grammar, the following are all terminal symbols with respect to the parser: `identifier`, `intLiteral`, `charLiteral`, `stringLiteral`, and `EOF`.

   Using the grammar for CPRL, compute the following first and follow sets.
   a. `First(program)`
   b. `First(initialDecl)`
   c. `First(loopStmt)`
   d. `First(simpleExpr)` (Hint: There are 11 terminal symbols in the answer.)
   e. `First(statement)` (Hint: There are 11 terminal symbols in the answer.)
   f. `Follow(statement)` (Hint: There are 13 terminal symbols in the answer.)
   g. `Follow(parameterDecls)`
   h. `Follow(constDecl)`
   i. `Follow(factor)` (Hard! Hint: There are 25 terminal symbols in the answer.)

9. Consider the following grammar rules in CPRL.

```
typeDecl = arrayTypeDecl | recordTypeDecl | enumTypeDecl .
arrayTypeDecl  = "type" typeId "=" "array"  "[" intConstValue "]"
                           "of" typeName ";" .
recordTypeDecl = "type" typeId "=" "record" "{" fieldDecls "}" .
enumTypeDecl   = "type" typeId "=" "<" identifiers ">" ";".
```

A grammar containing these four rules would not be LL(1) since the first set for each of `arrayTypeDecl`, `recordTypeDecl`, and `enumTypeDecl` is { "type" }, so there is no way to choose among the three alternatives for `typeDecl` using only one lookahead token. (Convince yourself of this by trying to implement method `parseTypeDecl()`.)

a. How many lookahead symbols are needed to parse a grammar that contains these four rules?

b. Refactor this grammar so that it is LL(1). (Hint: Review "Approach 2" in Section 6.6.)

Chapter 7
Error Handling/Recovery

Using the concepts explained in the previous chapter, we were able to build version 1 of the parser. The primary purpose of version 1 is to check that a CPRL program is valid according to the rules expressed in the context-free grammar. In addition, using class `IdTable`, version 1 of the parser can also detect certain scope errors. For example, it detects an attempt to declare the same identifier name twice within the same scope.

If a program fails to satisfy the CPRL rules checked by version 1 of the parser, the parser stops at the first error and prints an error message. In this chapter we implement version 2 of class `Parser` by adding error recovery to version 1, so that multiple syntax errors can be detected and reported during compilation. When a compiler is integrated with an editor or as part of an integrated development environment (IDE), it might be acceptable to stop compilation after detecting the first error and pass control to the editor. But in general, even if integrated with an editor, a compiler should try to detect and report as many errors as possible.

7.1 Types of Compilation Errors

When defining the CPRL language, we can categorize compilation errors into four general groups.

- Lexical/Syntax errors – violation of the language syntax as defined by a context-free grammar; e.g., invalid or missing tokens such as a missing semicolon, a string literal missing a closing quote, or using "`=`" instead of "`:=`" for assignment.
- Scope errors – violation of language scope rules; e.g., declaring two identifiers with the same name within the same scope.
- Type errors – violation of language type rules; e.g., the expression following "`if`" does not have type `Boolean`.
- Miscellaneous errors – other errors not categorized above; e.g., declaring a parameter as `var` in a function.

Version 1 of our parser was able to detect syntax errors and scope errors. While version 1 could reject many invalid CPRL programs, it did not check for all possible errors. Detection of most type errors and miscellaneous errors will wait until Chapter 9 where we cover constraint analysis.

As an alternative to categorizing errors based on the general type of error as described above, we can also categorize errors based on when and where they are detected during the compilation process. So, for example, lexical errors are detected by the scanner and syntax errors are detected by the parser. As outlined in Chapters 5 and 6, we will use exception classes to assist with error handling. Following is a diagram of the inheritance hierarchy for the exceptions used by the CPRL compiler.

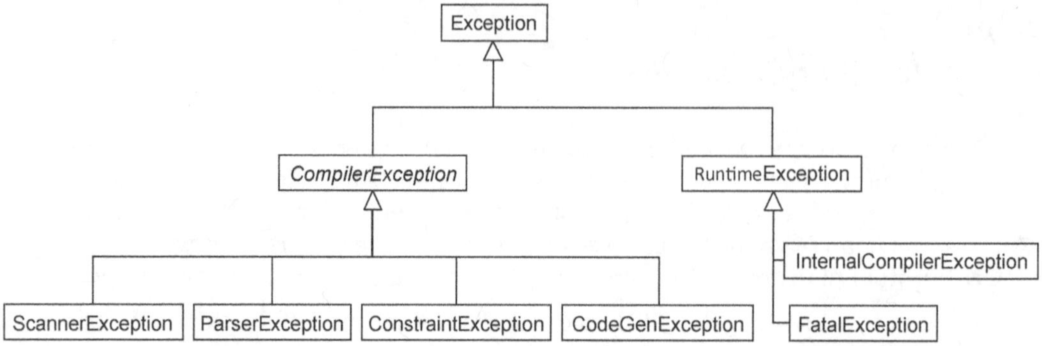

Class `CompilerException` is an abstract class whose functionality is inherited by four classes – `ScannerException`, `ParserException`, `ConstraintException`, and `CodeGenException`. All four subclasses of `CompilerException` are checked exceptions in Java.

As indicated by their names, `ScannerException` is used to encapsulate errors detected by the scanner, `ParserException` is used to encapsulate errors detected by the parser, `ConstraintException` is used to encapsulate errors detected during constraint analysis, and `CodeGenException` is used to encapsulate errors detected during code generation. Instances of `CodeGenException` should be rare compared to the other three types of exceptions.

Checked versus Unchecked Exceptions

Java makes a distinction between checked and unchecked exceptions. Any exception that derives from class `Error` or class `RuntimeException` is called an *unchecked* exception. All other exceptions are called *checked* exceptions. In the above diagram, `InternalCompilerException` and `FatalException` are unchecked exceptions.

There are two special situations involving checked exceptions. If a call is made to a method that throws a checked exception, or if a checked exception is explicitly thrown, then an enclosing block must either handle the exception locally or else the enclosing method must declare the exception as part of its exception specification list. Unchecked exceptions may be declared in the exception specification list or handled, but doing so is not required.

Class `FatalException` is used to signal errors for which compilation should be abandoned; e.g., too many errors in a single source file.

Instances of `InternalCompilerException` represent problems with the implementation of the compiler and should never get thrown if the compiler is implemented correctly. As outlined in Section 5.9, we will continue to use Java's `assert` statement to signal most of the internal errors within the compiler.

7.2 Handling Errors

The phrase **error handling** means finding errors and reporting them to the user. The phrase **error recovery** means that the compiler attempts to resynchronize its state and possibly the state of the input token stream so that compilation can continue normally. The purpose of error recovery is to find as many errors as possible in a single compilation, with the goal of reporting every error exactly one time.

Effective error recovery is extremely difficult. Any attempt to resynchronize the state of the compiler and/or the input token stream means that we are trying to make an educated guess as to what the programmer was trying to do at the point where the error was detected. Therefore, programmers learn early in their careers that any error reported by a compiler after the first error should be considered suspect. Correcting the first reported error could reveal new errors that were not detected before, or it could eliminate "false" errors reported previously by the compiler.

Recall that version 1 of the parser used an instance of class `ErrorHandler` to report errors. When an error was detected, we threw an exception, reported the error in a `catch` block, and then exited the program. For version 1 of the parser our `catch` blocks looked like the following.

```
catch (ParserException e)
  {
    errorHandler.reportError(e);
    recover(emptySet);
  }
```

Note that `errorHandler` is an instance of class `ErrorHandler`.

With error recovery we don't want to exit after encountering an error. Instead, we try to *recover* in order to detect/report additional errors. But what if we encounter many compilation errors? We don't want to overwhelm the programmer with an excessive number of error messages. Therefore, class `ErrorHandler` keeps track of the number of errors reported, and it exits compilation after a fixed number of errors have been reported.

Here are two key methods in class `ErrorHandler`.

```
/**
 * Returns true if errors have been reported by the error handler.
 */
public boolean errorsExist()

/**
 * Reports the error.
 * @throws FatalException if the number of errors exceeds the maximum.
 */
public void reportError(CompilerException e)
```

7.3 Error Recovery

Here is our general approach to error handling and recovery. As with version 1 of the parser, we will enclose the parsing code for each rule with a `try` block, and when errors are detected, we will throw an exception so that control transfers to the corresponding `catch` block. The `catch` block will report the error by calling appropriate methods in class `ErrorHandler`. But here is the main change for error recovery. Instead of exiting the program after reporting an error, the `catch` block will skip tokens until it finds one whose symbol is in the follow set of the nonterminal of the rule being parsed. The catch block will then return from the parsing method for that rule, so that the next token in the input stream will be valid as if no errors had been detected.

For example, consider the nonterminal symbol `procedureDecl`. The corresponding parser method is `parseProcedureDecl()`. In Section 6.3 we found that `procedureDecl` could be followed by `functionDecl`, another `procedureDecl`, or end-of-file (`EOF`); i.e.,

```
Follow(procedureDecl) = { "proc", "fun", EOF }
```

If there are no compilation errors in the program being compiled, then when `parseProcedureDecl()` returns, the next symbol in the input stream **should** be one of those symbols. If there are compilation errors, then we skip over all tokens until we encounter one of those symbols. So when `parseProcedureDecl()` returns, the next token in the input stream is valid just as though `parseProcedureDecl()` had not detected any errors.

More generally, when we return from method `parseN()`, we want the next token in the input stream to have a symbol in `Follow(N)`.

Method recover()

Method `recover()` implements error recovery by skipping tokens until it finds one in the follow set of the nonterminal defined by the rule. The follow set is implemented by a set of symbols, which is passed as a parameter to method `recover()`. Here is the complete implementation for method `recover()`.

```
/**
 * Advance the scanner until the current symbol is one of the
 * symbols in the specified set of followers.
 */
private void recover(Set<Symbol> followers) throws IOException
  {
    scanner.advanceTo(followers);
  }
```

Using these ideas, a possible implementation of `parseProcedureDecl()` **with error recovery** would look like the following.

```
// procedureDecl = "proc" ... "}" .
// Follow(procedureDecl) = { "proc", "fun", EOF }
private void parseProcedureDecl() throws IOException
  {
    try
      {
        match(Symbol.procRW);
        ...
        match(Symbol.rightBrace);
      }
    catch (ParserException e)
      {
        errorHandler.reportError(e);
        recover(EnumSet.of(Symbol.procRW, Symbol.funRW, Symbol.EOF));
      }
  }
```

Shared Follow Sets

When several nonterminal symbols have the same follow set, it is convenient to declare the set of "followers" once as a property within the parser and then reference it as needed, rather than repeat the construction of the set of followers in all catch blocks. For example, a function declaration has the same follow set as a procedure declaration. Rather than repeat construction of the set of follower symbols in methods `parseProcedureDecl()` and `parseFunctionDecl()`, we declare it once in the parser.

```
/** Symbols that can follow a subprogram declaration. */
private final Set<Symbol> subprogDeclFollowers = EnumSet.of(
    Symbol.procRW, Symbol.funRW, Symbol.EOF);
```

The set `subprogDeclFollowers` can be used for error recovery in both parsing methods; i.e., in `parseProcedureDecl()` and `parseFunctionDecl()`.

Using the idea of shared follow sets, the implementation for `parseProcedureDecl()` now becomes the following.

```
private void parseProcedureDecl() throws IOException
  {
    try
      {
        ...
      }
    catch (ParserException e)
      {
        errorHandler.reportError(e);
        recover(subprogDeclFollowers);
      }
  }
```

Note use of shared follow set.

Error Recovery for `parseStatement()`

Method `parseStatement()` handles the following rule.

```
statement = assignmentStmt | procedureCallStmt | compoundStmt | ifStmt
          | loopStmt       | forLoopStmt       | exitStmt     | readStmt
          | writeStmt      | writelnStmt       | returnStmt .
```

Error recovery for `parseStatement()` requires special care when the symbol is an identifier since an identifier can not only start a statement but can also appear elsewhere in the statement such as in an expression. Consider, for example, an assignment statement. If, during error recovery, we advance to an identifier, we could be in the middle of a statement rather than at the start of the next statement.

Since the most common identifier-related error is to declare or reference an identifier incorrectly, we will assume that this is the case and advance to the end of the current statement before implementing error recovery. The end of the current statement will be either a semicolon or (for a compound statement) a right brace.

Assuming that `stmtFollowers` is the name of the shared follow set for statements, we implement error recovery in `parseStatement()` as follows.

```
try
  {
    ...
  }
catch (ParserException e)
  {
    errorHandler.reportError(e);
    scanner.advanceTo(EnumSet.of(Symbol.semicolon, Symbol.rightBrace));
    recover(stmtFollowers);
  }
```

Note use of shared follow set.

Error Recovery for Initial Declarations

Finally, for a more complicated example, let's consider what can follow an initial declaration. From the rule

```
initialDecls = { initialDecl } .
```

we know that another `initialDecl` can follow `initialDecl`, so the follow set for `initialDecl` includes the first set of `initialDecl`; i.e., "`const`", "`var`", and "`type`".

Now consider two cases – the case where `initialDecl` appears as a global declaration and the case where `initialDecl` appears locally within a subprogram. For the first case the relevant rules are as follows.

```
program = initialDecls subprogramDecls .
subprogramDecls = { subprogramDecl } .
subprogramDecl  = procedureDecl | functionDecl .
```

From these rules we know that `procedureDecl` or `functionDecl` can follow an `initialDecl`, and therefore the follow set for `initialDecl` also includes "`proc`" and "`fun`". So for the first case we know that `Follow(initialDecl)` contains "`const`", "`var`", "`type`", "`proc`", and "`fun`".

For the second case where `initialDecl` appears within a subprogram, the rules for both `procedureDecl` and `functionDecl` contain the following phrase at the end.

```
... "{" initialDecls statements "}" .
```

Therefore, for this case, an `initialDecl` can be followed by a statement, and so the follow set for `initialDecl` contains the first set of `statement`. And since `statements` can technically be empty (it's **zero** or more `statement`), the follow set for `initialDecl` can also include `"}"`. Observe that `First(statement) + "}" = Follow(statement) - "else"`. We will use this identity when computing the follow set for `initialDecl`.

We could combine both cases to get a single follow set for `initialDecl`, but based on how we use follow sets in the parser, we will compute the follow set for `initialDecl` dynamically based on the two separate cases, as determined by the scope level. Here is how the shared follow set for `initialDecl` is implemented as a method in the parser.

```
private Set<Symbol> initialDeclFollowers()
  {
    // An initial declaration can always be followed by another
    // initial declaration, regardless of the scope level.
    var followers = EnumSet.of(
                        Symbol.constRW, Symbol.varRW, Symbol.typeRW);

    if (idTable.scopeLevel() == ScopeLevel.GLOBAL)
        followers.addAll(EnumSet.of(Symbol.procRW, Symbol.funRW));
    else
      {
        followers.addAll(stmtFollowers);
        followers.remove(Symbol.elseRW);
      }

    return followers;
  }
```

Error recovery for an initial declaration will look like the following, but the actual set of followers will be different depending on whether the initial declaration appears as a global declaration or whether it appears locally within a subprogram.

```
try
  {
    ...
  }
catch (ParserException e)
  {
    errorHandler.reportError(e);
    recover(initialDeclFollowers());
  }
```

Implementing Error Recovery

Not all parsing methods will need a `try/catch` block for error recovery. For example, method `parseInitialDecls()` does not need a `try/catch` block.

```
private void parseInitialDecls() throws IOException
  {
    while (scanner.symbol().isInitialDeclStarter())
        parseInitialDecl();
  }
```

Similarly, method `parseStatements()` will not need a `try/catch` block, and neither will method `parseExpression()`. But which parsing methods need a `try/catch` block for error recovery?

Only three methods throw a `ParserException` back to the caller.

```
match()
parseVariableCommon()    // called only by parseVariable()
                         //     and parseVariableExpr()
add()                    // in class IdTable
```

Any parsing method that calls one of these three methods will need a `try/catch` block for error recovery.

Duplicated Error Messages and Undeclared Identifiers

Consider the following incorrect CPRL program.

```
const i := 2;
var x : Integer;

proc main()
  {
    x := i;
  {    // wrong brace symbol
```

In this example, the programmer accidentally typed a left brace instead of a right brace to end the program. But when the parser sees the left brace, it calls `parseCompoundStmt()`, statement, resulting in two identical error messages.

```
*** Syntax error detected near line 8, character 1:
    Expecting "}" but found "End-of-File" instead.
*** Syntax error detected near line 8, character 1:
    Expecting "}" but found "End-of-File" instead.
```

The first error message is generated as the parser tries to match the closing right brace at the end of `parseCompoundStmt()`, and the second identical error message is generated as the parser tries to match the closing right brace at the end of `parseProcedureDecl()`. We can eliminate duplicated error messages by checking for them in the error handler.

Now consider another incorrect CPRL program.

```
var x = Integer;    // uses '=' instead of ':'

proc main()
  {
    read x;
    x := x + 1;
    write x;
  }
```

The variable declaration in the first line of the program is syntactically incorrect since it has an equals symbol instead of a colon. Using the parsing approach outlined in the previous chapter, version 1 of the parser will correctly report this error and then exit. However, since the error occurs within the variable declaration, identifier `x` is never added to the identifier table. When we implement error recovery, every applied occurrence of `x` will generate an error message stating that `x` has not been declared; that is, version 2 and all subsequent versions of the parser will report that `x` has not been declared four different times as shown below.

```
*** Syntax error detected near line 1, character 7:
    Expecting ":" but found "=" instead.
*** Syntax error detected near line 5, character 10:
    Identifier "x" has not been declared.
*** Syntax error detected near line 6, character 5:
    Identifier "x" has not been declared.
*** Syntax error detected near line 6, character 10:
    Identifier "x" has not been declared.
*** Syntax error detected near line 7, character 11:
    Identifier "x" has not been declared.
```

Similar to the way we handled repeated error messages, we let the error handler save the names of all identifiers with "`has not been declared`" error messages, and then we suppress any future error messages of this nature for the saved variable name.

We implement a private method within class `ErrorHandler` that checks for both repeated error messages and undeclared identifiers.

```
/*
 * Checks for repeated error messages and messages of
 * the form "Identifier \"x\" has not been declared.".
 * Returns true if this error message should be printed.
 */
private boolean shouldPrint(String message)
```

The error handler calls this method before printing an error message to determine if it should be printed.

7.4 Additional Error Recovery Strategies

Here we briefly describe a couple of additional possible error recovery strategies.

One common strategy is to first report the error and then replace the token that caused the error with one that might be allowed at that point in the parsing process. Here are two examples.

- Replace "`=`" by "`:=`" when parsing an assignment statement in a CPRL compiler. The assumption here is that the programmer might have experience with other languages that use "`=`" as the assignment symbol.
- Replace "`=`" by "`==`" when expecting a relational operator in a C++ or Java compiler. Every programmer who first learns a C-like language misuses "`=`" to mean equality at some point, and therefore this error recovery strategy would be appropriate most of the time.

The following code shows how to replace "`=`" by "`:=`" in method `parseAssignmentStmt()` for CPRL by enclosing the call to `match(Symbol.assign)` in its own `try/catch` block.

```
// replace match(Symbol.assign) by the following try/catch block
try
  {
    match(Symbol.assign);
  }
catch (ParserException e)
  {
    if (scanner.symbol() == Symbol.equals)
      {
        errorHandler.reportError(e);
        matchCurrentSymbol();   // treat "=" as ":=" in this context
      }
    else
        throw e;
  }
...   // continue parsing
```

Instead of simply calling `match(Symbol.assign)`, we use a nested `try/catch` block that treats "`=`" as "`:=`".

Another common strategy is to first report the error and then insert a new token in front of the one that generated the error. Specific examples include the following.

- When parsing an `exit` statement, after matching "`exit`", if a symbol encountered is in the first set of an expression, then report the error, insert "`when`", and continue parsing. The assumption here is that the programmer forgot the "`when`".
- When parsing an expression, if a right parenthesis "`)`" is expected but a semicolon "`;`" is encountered as the next symbol, report the error and then insert a right parenthesis with the expectation that the semicolon will likely terminate a statement. The assumption here is that the programmer forgot the closing parenthesis.

Of the four specific examples described above, the only one actually implemented in the compiler project is the replacement of "`=`" by "`:=`" in method `parseAssignmentStmt()`.

7.5 Essential Terms and Concepts

checked exception	`CodeGenException` (class)
`CompilerException` (class)	`ConstraintException` (class)
`ErrorHandler` (class)	error handling
error recovery	miscellaneous errors
`ParserException` (class)	`recover()` (method)
`ScannerException` (class)	scope errors
syntax errors	type errors
unchecked exception	

7.6 Exercises

1. **Project Assignment.** Implement **Project 3: Error Recovery** as described in Appendix A.
2. Fill in the blank.
   Given a grammar rule for a nonterminal `N`, our general approach to error handling involves enclosing the basic parsing code of `parseN()` in a `try/catch` block. When errors are detected, control transfers to the `catch` block, which will report the error and then skip tokens in the input stream until it finds a token in the
   ______________________________ of `N`.

3. True or false.
   a. All parsing methods should have a `try/catch` block for error recovery.
   b. All parsing methods that call `match()` should have a `try/catch` block for error recovery.
   c. All parsing methods that call the `add()` method of `IdTable` will need to have a `try/catch` block.
4. Name, describe, and give examples for the four general types of compilation errors as discussed in this chapter.
5. Explain the concept of shared follow sets and their roles in error recovery.
6. Explain why we decided to take a slightly different approach to error recovery for the method `parseStatement()`. (Why didn't the general approach used in other parsing methods work very well in this case?)
7. Explain why we decided to take a slightly different approach to error recovery when parsing initial declarations. (Why didn't the general approach used in other parsing methods work very well for initial declarations?)
8. Describe the *special* error recovery strategy used when trying to match the assignment symbol (`:=`) as part of parsing an assignment statement in CPRL.

Chapter 8
Abstract Syntax Trees

In this chapter we will describe the final modification to class `Parser` so that, as it parses the source code, it will also generate an intermediate representation of the program known as abstract syntax trees (ASTs). Once the parser is successfully generating abstract syntax trees, work on the parser will be complete. All remaining work for the compiler will take place in the AST classes, which provide the framework for performing constraint analysis and code generation.

8.1 Overview of Abstract Syntax Trees

An abstract syntax tree is similar to a parse tree but without extraneous nonterminal and terminal symbols. Abstract syntax trees provide an explicit representation of the structure of the source code that can be used for additional constraint analysis (e.g., for analysis of type constraints) and code generation. We will use different classes to represent different node types in our abstract syntax trees. Most AST classes correspond to a rule in the grammar, and the name of the class is often the name of the nonterminal symbol for the rule. Examples of AST classes that we will develop include `AssignmentStmt`, `LoopStmt`, `Variable`, and `Expression`. Each AST class has named instance variables (a.k.a., fields or properties) to reference its children. These instance variables provide the "tree" structure. Occasionally we also include additional properties to support error handling and code generation.

> In his book *Language Implementation Patterns* [Parr 2010], Terence Parr refers to this type of AST structure as an irregular (named child fields) heterogeneous (different node types) AST.

Abstract Syntax Trees: Example 1

Consider the grammar for an assignment statement.

```
assignmentStmt = variable ":=" expression ";" .
```

The important parts of an assignment statement are the variable (the left side of the assignment) and the expression (the right side of the assignment). We create an AST node for an assignment statement with the following structure.

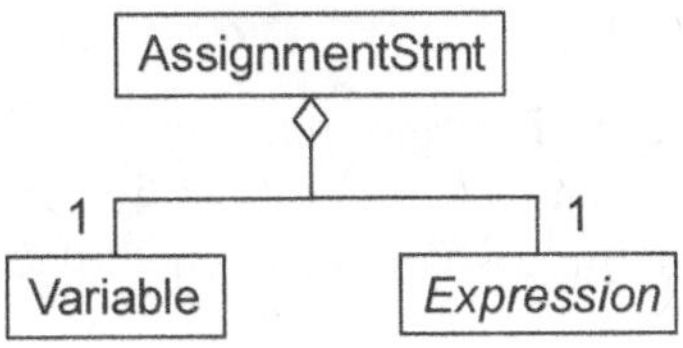

Here is an outline for the implementation of class `AssignmentStmt`.

```
public class AssignmentStmt extends Statement
  {
    private Variable   variable;
    private Expression expr;
    private Position   assignPosition;   // for error reporting

    public AssignmentStmt(Variable variable, Expression expr,
                          Position assignPosition)
    ...
  }
```

Note that parameter `assignPosition` in the above constructor is the position of the assignment symbol (`:=`), which is not actually part of the "tree" structure but is used in error reporting.

Abstract Syntax Trees: Example 2

Consider the rule for a loop statement.

```
loopStmt = [ "while" booleanExpr ] "loop" statement .
```

Once a loop statement has been parsed, we don't need to retain the terminal symbols. The AST for a loop statement would contain only the statement in the body of the loop and the optional boolean expression. We can visualize the AST for a loop statement as follows.

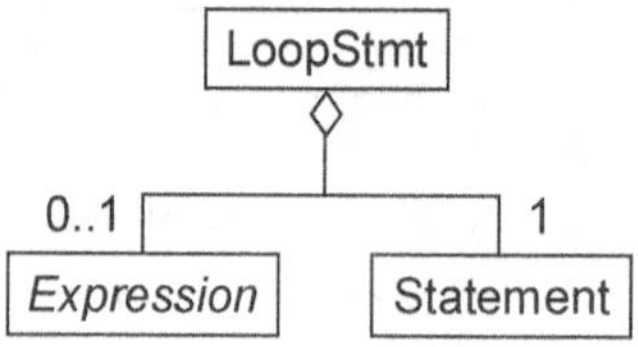

The notation 0..1 in the above diagram is UML notation for optional (`0` or `1`).

Here is an outline for the implementation of class `LoopStmt`.

```
public class LoopStmt extends Statement
  {
    private Expression whileExpr;
    private Statement  statement = EmptyStatement.instance();
    ...
  }
```

Note that `whileExpr` can be `null` to indicate that the optional boolean expression is not present. Also, property `statement` is initialized to an instance of `EmptyStatement`, which is a subclass of `Statement` that passes all constraint checks and generates no code.

Abstract Syntax Trees: Example 3

Consider the grammar for a `forLoop` statement.

```
forLoopStmt = "for" varId "in" expr ".." expr "loop" statement .
```

While it is possible to fold the syntax of a `forLoop` statement into the rule of the more general `loop` statement, we have separated the two since doing so simplifies parsing, constraint analysis, and code generation. However, AST class `ForLoopStmt` is implemented as a subclass of `LoopStmt`, thereby allowing us to inherit part of the implementation of `LoopStmt` and to treat both types of loop statements uniformly when working with loop contexts. (More on this later.) Beyond the statement in the body of the loop, which is inherited from `LoopStmt`, the important parts of a `forLoop` statement are the loop variable and the two integer expressions defining the starting and ending values of the `forLoop`. We can visualize the AST of a `forLoop` statement as follows.

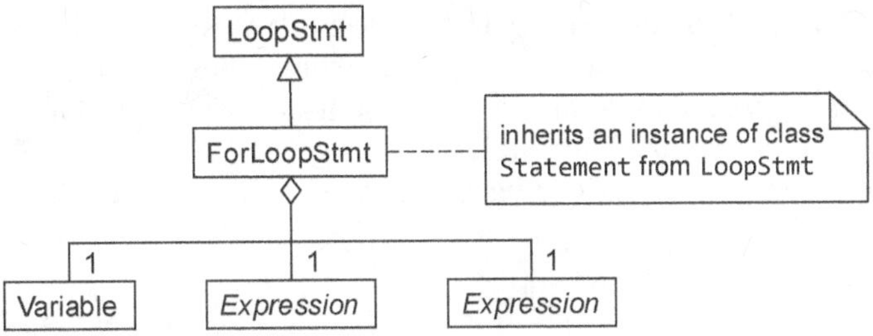

Here is an outline for the implementation of class `ForLoopStmt`.

```
public class ForLoopStmt extends LoopStmt
  {
    private Variable   loopVar;
    private Expression rangeStart;
    private Expression rangeEnd;
    ...
  }
```

The `forLoop`

```
for i in expr1..expr2
    statement;
```

is essentially equivalent to the following pseudocode.

```
open a new local scope
var i : Integer;    // variable i is implicitly declared
i := expr1;
while i <= expr2 loop
  {
    statement;
    i := i + 1;
  }
close scope
```

When parsing a `forLoop` statement, the parser will

- open a new local scope at the start of the parsing method's `try` block.
- create an implicit variable declaration of for the loop variable and add it to both the new scope and the identifier table.
- create a loop variable (an applied occurrence) to be used in the construction of a `ForLoopStmt`.
- close the scope in a `finally` block.

Details are provided in the project repository.

Abstract Syntax Trees: Example 4

For binary expressions, part of the grammar exists simply to define operator precedence. Once an expression has been parsed, we do not need to preserve additional information about nonterminal symbols that were introduced solely to define precedence (`relation`, `simpleExpr`, `term`, `factor`, etc.). A binary expression AST would contain only the operator and the left and right operands. The parsing methods would build the AST so as to preserve operator precedence. We can visualize the AST for a binary expression as follows.

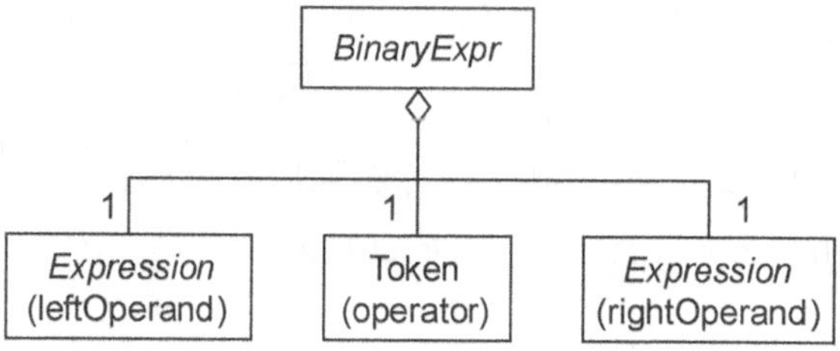

Here is an outline for the implementation of class `BinaryExpr`.

```
public abstract class BinaryExpr extends Expression
  {
    private Expression leftOperand;
    private Token      operator;
    private Expression rightOperand;
    ...
  }
```

Note that `BinaryExpr` is an abstract class. Concrete subclasses include `AddingExpr`, `LogicalExpr`, `MultiplyingExpr`, and `RelationalExpr`.

> Caution: The word "abstract" is used in two different ways in this chapter. It is used as part of the name for the intermediate representation known as abstract syntax trees, but it is also used in the object-oriented sense of an abstract class; i.e., a class for which instances cannot be created. The meaning should be clear from the context of the term.

8.2 Structure of Abstract Syntax Trees

There is an abstract class `AST` that serves as the superclass for all other abstract syntax tree classes. Class `AST` contains implementations of methods common to all subclasses plus declarations of abstract methods required by all concrete subclasses. All AST classes for the compiler will be defined in package `cprlc.ast`.

> Note the use of `AST` (in monospaced font) for the specific class and AST (in normal font) as an abbreviation for "abstract syntax tree".

Here is an outline of class `AST` showing two of its most important methods.

```
public abstract class AST
  {
    ...

    /**
     * Check semantic/contextual constraints.
     */
    public abstract void checkConstraints() ...

    /**
     * Emit object code.
     */
    public abstract void emit() throws CodeGenException ...
    ...
  }
```

Implementations of abstract methods `checkConstraints()` and `emit()` "walk" the tree structure using recursive calls to subordinate tree nodes. These methods are used in constraint analysis and code generation, respectively, and will be covered in more detail in subsequent chapters.

We will create an inheritance hierarchy of classes, some of which are abstract. All classes in the hierarchy are direct or indirect subclasses of `AST`. Each node in the abstract syntax tree constructed by the parser will be an object of a class in the AST hierarchy. Most classes in the hierarchy will correspond to and have names similar to the nonterminal symbols in the grammar, but not all AST classes have this property. See, for example, the earlier discussion about binary expressions. We do not need abstract syntax tree classes corresponding to nonterminal symbols `simpleExpr`, `term`, `factor`, etc.

In addition, some parsing methods simply return lists of AST objects.

```
private List<InitialDecl>    parseInitialDecls()    throws IOException
private List<SubprogramDecl> parseSubprogramDecls() throws IOException
private List<Token>          parseIdentifiers()     throws IOException
private List<Statement>      parseStatements()      throws IOException
private List<Expression>     parseExpressions()     throws IOException
```

Our AST classes adopt the following naming conventions.

- Most AST classes have names similar to nonterminal symbols in the grammar.
- The parsing method for that nonterminal will create the corresponding AST object.
  - `parseProgram()` returns a `Program` object
  - `parseVarDecl()` returns a `VarDecl` object
  - `parseLoopStmt()` returns a `LoopStmt` object
  - etc.
- Parsing methods with plural names will return lists of AST objects. (Note that we wrote the grammar so that related nonterminal symbols have this property.)

As examples, we will create classes `Statement` and `LoopStmt`.

```
public abstract class Statement extends AST ...
public class LoopStmt extends Statement ...
```

The parsing method `parseLoopStmt()` would be responsible for creating the AST node for `LoopStmt`. Instead of returning `void` as we did in the previous chapters, method `parseLoopStmt()` will return an object of class `LoopStmt`.

Similarly, the parsing method `parseStatements()` will return a list of `Statement` objects, where each `Statement` object is either an `AssignmentStmt`, a `LoopStmt`, an `IfStmt`, etc.

Methods `parseWriteStmt()` and `parseWritelnStmt()` are special cases in that both parsing methods return an instance of AST class `OutputStmt`. Otherwise, we would have to create two separate but nearly identical AST classes `WriteStmt` and `WritelnStmt`. Similarly, methods `parseVariable()` and `parseVariableExpr()` both return an instance of AST class `Variable`. We don't create a separate but nearly identical class named `VariableExpr`.

Method `parseLiteral()` is another special case. The grammar rules define `literal` to be one of the following: `intLiteral`, `charLiteral`, `stringLiteral`, `"true"`, or `"false"`. Since all of these literals are tokens returned from the scanner, method `parseLiteral()` simply returns a `Token`. There is no AST class named `Literal`.

```
private Token parseLiteral() throws IOException
  {
    ...    // returns a default (empty) token if parsing fails
  }
```

A <u>partial</u> inheritance diagram for the AST hierarchy is shown below. Names for abstract classes are shown in italics. Note the AST classes `Declaration`, `Statement`, and `Expression` representing the three major syntactic categories in CPRL programs as discussed in Section 4.2.

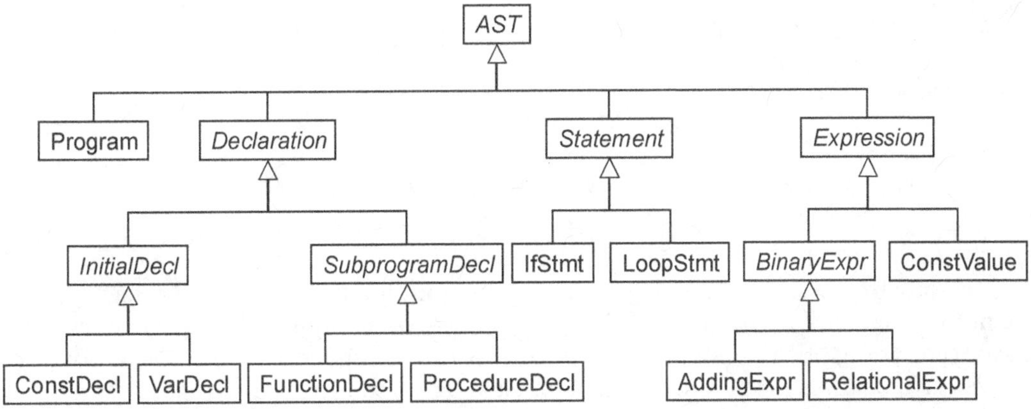

8.3 Extending Scopes with References to Declarations

There are a number of language constraints associated with identifiers that are not expressed in the context-free grammar for CPRL, and a parser built using only the set of grammar-related parsing rules will not reject programs that violate these language constraints. Examples of such constraints include rules such as the following.

- A variable must be declared before it is used.
- For an assignment statement, the variable on the left side of the assignment symbol and the expression on the right side must have assignment-compatible types.
- For an if statement, the expression following keyword `if` must have type `Boolean`.

So, for example, the following programs would be valid with respect to syntax but not valid with respect to contextual constraints.

Example 1

```
var x : Integer;
proc main()
  {
    y := 5;   // y has not been declared
  }
```

Example 2

```
var c : Char;
proc main()
  {
    c := -3;   // can't assign an integer value to a character
  }
```

Example 3

```
var x : Integer;
proc main()
  {
    x := 5;
    if x then      // expression must have type Boolean
        writeln "true";
  }
```

We will modify classes `Scope` and `IdTable` to help track not just the general category of identifiers that have been declared but their complete declarations. Scopes will now map Java type `String` (identifier name) to type `Declaration`, not `String` to `IdType` as done previously. Below is the new declaration for class `Scope` showing the change.

```
public class Scope extends HashMap<String, Declaration>
  {
    ... // same as before
  }
```

We no longer need class `IdType`; it was simply a bridge to simplify the implementation of earlier versions of the parser. While the original version of `Scope` allowed us to catch the error in Example 1 above, the new version will put us in a position to catch type errors as shown in Examples 2 and 3. Details of the approach to catching type errors will be covered in the next chapter, where we discuss constraint analysis in more detail.

We modify class `IdTable` to handle `Declaration` instead of `IdType`. Class `Declaration` is part of the AST hierarchy. A declaration object contains a reference to the identifier token (the name of the entity being introduced by the declaration) and information about its type. We will use different subclasses of `Declaration` for different kinds of declarations; e.g., `ConstDecl`, `TypeDecl`, `ProcedureDecl`, etc. For the new version of class `IdTable`, methods `scopeLevel()`, `openScope()`, and `closeScope()` are unchanged. Here are declarations for the two modified methods.

```
/**
 * Add an identifier token and its declaration to the current scope.
 *
 * @throws ParserException if the identifier already exists
 *         in the current scope.
 */
public void add(Token idToken, Declaration decl) throws ParserException

/**
 * Returns the declaration associated with the identifier name
 * (type String).  Returns null if the identifier is not found.
 * Searches enclosing scopes if necessary.
 */
public Declaration get(String idStr)
```

As previously discussed, `ScopeLevel` is defined in Java as an enum class with three constants, `GLOBAL`, `LOCAL`, and `RECORD`. Additional details of the scope level of a declaration are discussed in the next section and in subsequent chapters on code generation for variables. As illustrated later in Chapter 13, within a subprogram, different code is generated for variables declared at `GLOBAL` scope than for variables declared at `LOCAL` scope.

Parsing Variable Declarations

Declarations for constants, types, procedures, and functions all contain a single identifier as the name of the entity being declared. For example, in method `parseArrayTypeDecl()`, we get the type identifier, create an instance of `ArrayTypeDecl`, and add the identifier token and the type declaration to the identifier table.

```
var typeId = scanner.token();
...
var typeDecl = new ArrayTypeDecl(typeId, elemType, numElements);
idTable.add(typeId, typeDecl);
```

But variable declarations can declare several identifiers, all with the same type.

```
var x, y, z : Integer;
```

When parsing a variable declaration, method `parseVarDecl()` will need to add **all** identifiers in the declaration to the identifier table.

```
var identifiers = parseIdentifiers();
var varDecl = new VarDecl(identifiers, varType, ...);

for (var identifier : identifiers)
    idTable.add(identifier, varDecl);
```

Initializers

Recall that variables can be initialized at the point where they are declared. For scalar types, initializers are simply constant values, but for composite types, things get more complicated, especially when working with nested composite types. Review examples of variable declarations with initializers in Chapter 4 and Appendix C.

Since composite types can be nested (e.g., an array of records), initializers for composite types can also be nested. Therefore, initializers are implemented using a variant of the **Composite Pattern**. Here are brief descriptions of the AST classes involved in initialization. Additional details are provided in subsequent chapters.

1. Interface `Initializer` allows us to treat different forms of initializers uniformly. It is a sealed interface implemented only by classes `ConstValue`, `CompositeInitializer`, and `EmptyInitializer` described below.
2. Class `ConstValue` is used to initialize scalar types. A constant value is either a named constant, a literal, or possibly a minus sign followed by an integer literal.

3. Class `CompositeInitializer` is used for initializing composite types. Composite initializers are enclosed in braces, which can be nested for initialization of nested composite types.
4. Class `EmptyInitializer` is used when there is no initializer for a variable or as a return value when an error occurs in parsing an initializer.

The following diagram shows the relationships between these classes.

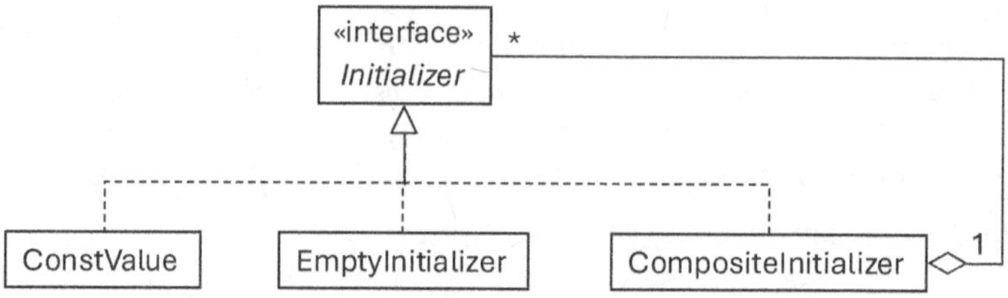

The three grammar rules pertaining to initializers and their corresponding parsing methods are outlined below. Implementations of the first and third of these three methods are provided in the book's GitHub repository.

```
// initializer = constValue | compositeInitializer .
private Initializer parseInitializer() throws IOException

// compositeInitializer = "{" initializer { "," initializer } "}" .
private Initializer parseCompositeInitializer() throws ...

// constValue = ( [ "-" ] literal ) | constId .
private Expression parseConstValue() throws IOException
```

Interface `VariableDecl`

Recall the grammar rule for `variable`.

```
variable = ( varId | paramId ) { indexExpr | fieldExpr } .
```

Since `varId` and `paramId` are just identifiers, we could have written the rule more simply as follows.

```
variable = identifier { indexExpr | fieldExpr } .
```

The reason for writing the rule using different identifier names was to *suggest* that the variable could have been declared using a `VarDecl` or a `ParameterDecl`.

As an example, consider the following assignment statement.

```
x := y;
```

The variable `x` could have been declared in a **variable declaration** or a parameter declaration, and similarly for the variable expression `y` on the right side of the assignment symbol.

Even though variables could have been declared using variable declarations or parameter declarations, there is a need to treat both types of declarations uniformly at several points during parsing. We achieve this uniformity by creating a sealed interface `VariableDecl` and specifying that AST classes `VarDecl` and `ParameterDecl` implement this interface. Interface `VariableDecl` contains five methods common to both `VarDecl` and `ParameterDecl`.

```
public Type type();
public int size();
public ScopeLevel scopeLevel();
public void setRelAddr(String idStr, int relAddr);
public int relAddr(String idStr);
```

The size of a `VariableDecl` is just the size associated with its type except for a variable parameter, whose size is always the size of a memory address (4 bytes in the CVM).

Relationships between interface `VariableDecl` and classes `VarDecl` and `ParameterDecl` are shown in the following UML diagram.

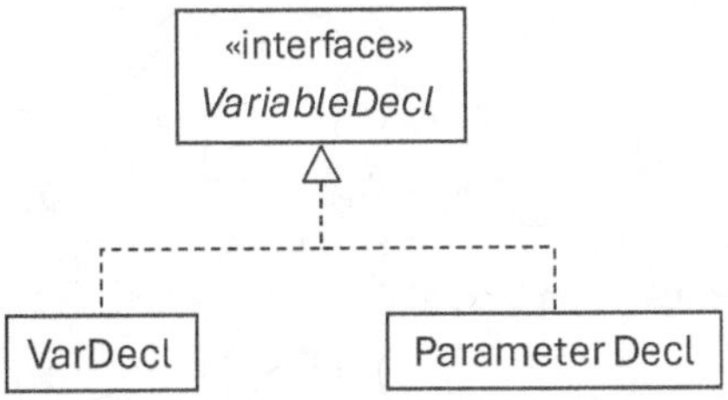

As an example of where `VariableDecl` is used during parsing, consider the following excerpt from `parseStatement()`, where we have encountered an identifier and are trying to decide whether to parse an assignment statement or a procedure call statement.

```
if (scanner.symbol() == Symbol.identifier)
  {
    var idStr = scanner.text();
    var decl  = idTable.get(idStr);

    if (decl != null)
      {
        if (decl instanceof VariableDecl)
            return parseAssignmentStmt();
    ...
```

Using `IdTable` to Check Applied Occurrences of Identifiers

When an identifier is encountered in a context other than its declaration (e.g., as part of an expression or subprogram call), the parser will check to see if the identifier has been declared. If it has, the parser will then use the information about how the identifier was declared to facilitate correct parsing (e.g., you can't assign a value to an identifier that was declared as a constant).

As an example, consider the following excerpt from method `parseVariableCommon()`.

```
var idToken = scanner.token();
match(Symbol.identifier);
var decl = idTable.get(idToken.text());
if (decl == null)
  {
    var errorMsg = "Identifier \"" + idToken.text()
                 + "\" has not been declared.";
    throw error(idToken.position(), errorMsg);
  }
else if (!(decl instanceof VariableDecl))
  {
    var errorMsg = "Identifier \"" + idToken.text()
                 + "\" is not a variable.";
    throw error(idToken.position(), errorMsg);
  }
```

8.4 Types and Declarations

The compiler uses four classes to provide support for CPRL types. Class `Type` is the base class for all CPRL types, and predefined types such as `Boolean`, `Integer`, and `String` are declared in class Type. Classes `ArrayType`, `EnumType`, and `RecordType` extend `Type` to provide additional support for arrays, enumerated types, and records.

Class `Type` encapsulates the predefined language type names and sizes (number of bytes) for predefined CPRL types. Predefined types are declared as static constants within the class. Using class `Constants`, type sizes are initialized to values appropriate for the CPRL virtual machine; e.g., 4 for `Integer`, 2 for `Char`, 1 for `Boolean`, etc.

Class `Type` is defined as follows.

```
public class Type
  {
    private String typeName;
    private int    size;

    // predefined types
    public static final Type Boolean
               = new Type("Boolean", Constants.BYTES_PER_BOOLEAN);
    public static final Type Byte
               = new Type("Byte", 1);
    public static final Type Integer
               = new Type("Integer", Constants.BYTES_PER_INTEGER);
    public static final Type Char
               = new Type("Char", Constants.BYTES_PER_CHAR);
    public static final Type String
               = new Type("String", Constants.BYTES_PER_ADDRESS);
```

```
    // an address of the target machine
    public static final Type Address
                = new Type("Address", Constants.BYTES_PER_ADDRESS);

    // compiler-internal types
    public static final Type UNKNOWN = new Type("UNKNOWN");
    public static final Type none    = new Type("none");
    ...
  }
```

Class `Type` also contains several helper methods including boolean methods `isScalarType()`, `isCompositeType()`, and `isNumericType()`, and static method `typeOf()` that returns the type of a literal symbol.

Class `ArrayType` extends class `Type`, and therefore array types are also types. In addition to the total size of the array, class `ArrayType` also needs the number of elements in the array and the element type. The constructor for `ArrayType` is declared as follows.

```
public ArrayType(String typeName, int numElements, Type elementType)
```

When the parser parses an array type declaration, the constructor for class `ArrayTypeDecl` creates an `ArrayType` object.

Similarly, classes `EnumType` and `RecordType` extend class `Type` for enumerated types and records. Details of creating arrays, enumerated types, and records are covered in subsequent chapters.

Parsing ConstDecl

As an example of using class `Type`, consider the following code for parsing a `ConstDecl`.

```
private InitialDecl parseConstDecl() throws IOException
  {
    try
      {
        match(Symbol.constRW);
        var constId = scanner.token();
        match(Symbol.identifier);
        match(Symbol.assign);

        ...   // handle negative literals as a special case

        var constDecl = new ConstDecl(constId,
                                      Type.typeOf(literal), literal);
        idTable.add(constDecl);

        match(Symbol.semicolon);
        return constDecl;
      }
```

```
      catch (ParserException e)
        {
          errorHandler.reportError(e);
          recover(initialDeclFollowers());
          return EmptyInitialDecl.instance();
        }
    }
```

The Scope Level of a Variable Declaration

During code generation, when a variable is referenced in the statement part of a program or subprogram, we need to be able to determine whether the variable was declared at global or local scope. Class `IdTable` contains a method named `scopeLevel()` that returns the current scope level; i.e., it returns `GLOBAL` for objects declared at the outermost (program) scope and it returns `LOCAL` for objects declared within a subprogram. As discussed in later chapters, it also returns `RECORD` for fields declared within a record, but for now we want to focus on the distinction between `GLOBAL` and `LOCAL`.

When parsing a variable declaration, the declaration is initialized with the current scope level.

```
var varDecl = new VarDecl(identifiers, varType,
                          initialValue, idTable.scopeLevel());
```

CPRL scope levels `GLOBAL` and `LOCAL` are illustrated in the following example program.

```
var x : Integer;   // scope level of declaration for x is GLOBAL
var y : Integer;   // scope level of declaration for y is GLOBAL

proc p()     // scope level of declaration for proc p is GLOBAL
  {
    var x : Integer;  // scope level of declaration for x is LOCAL
    var b : Integer;  // scope level of declaration for b is LOCAL

   ... x ...    // x was declared at LOCAL scope
   ... b ...    // b was declared at LOCAL scope
   ... y ...    // y was declared at GLOBAL scope
  }

proc main()
  {
    var y : Integer;   // scope level of declaration for y is LOCAL

    ... x ...      // x was declared at GLOBAL scope
    ... y ...      // y was declared at LOCAL scope
    ... p() ...    // p was declared at GLOBAL scope
  }
```

8.5 Structural References versus Nonstructural References

AST classes often contain properties or lists of properties that reference instances of other AST classes, and most such references correspond to the edges of the "tree". These structural (edge) references are created by the parser when parsing nonterminal symbols on the right side of rules in the context-free grammar.

Here are some specific examples of structural references.

- Class `Program` has a list of initial declarations and a list of subprogram declarations. This structure is derived from the grammar rule for `program`.

  ```
  program = initialDecls subprogramDecls .
  ```

- Class `AssignmentStmt` has references to the variable on the left side of the assignment symbol and the expression on the right side. This structure is derived from the grammar rule for `assignmentStmt`.

  ```
  assignmentStmt = variable ":=" expression ";" .
  ```

- Class `IfStmt` has references to a boolean expression, a "`then`" statement, and an "`else`" statement. The reference to the optional "`else`" statement can be null. This structure is derived from the grammar rule for `ifStmt`.

  ```
  ifStmt = "if" booleanExpr "then" statement [ "else" statement ] .
  ```

- Abstract class `BinaryExpr` and its concrete subclasses have an operator token plus references to left and right operands; both operands are expressions. This structure is not derived directly from the context-free grammar but from our knowledge of expressions. The grammar for expressions is somewhat contorted by the need to incorporate precedence, but instances of concrete subclasses are created in a straightforward manner when parsing the grammar rules for various types of binary expressions.

But some AST classes have references to instances of other AST classes that do not correspond to the edges of the "tree". These nonstructural references are introduced to assist with constraint analysis and/or code generation, but they are not suggested or motivated by the context-free grammar. All nonstructural references in AST classes are commented as such in the source code.

Nonstructural references fall into two general categories.

1. References from a class representing an applied occurrence of an identifier to its corresponding declaration.
2. References from a statement to its enclosing context (as described later in this chapter in Section 8.7).

Note that all nonstructural references are created by looking up an identifier in either the identifier table or one of the context classes.

Here is a list of all nonstructural references created during parsing. The first five fall into category one, and the last two fall into category two.

- Class `Variable` has a reference to the corresponding variable declaration.
- Class `FunctionCallExpr` has a reference to the corresponding function declaration.
- Class `ProcedureCallStmt` has a reference to the corresponding procedure declaration.
- Class `ConstValue` is used to encapsulate both literal values and constant declarations, and for the latter, it contains a reference to the corresponding constant declaration.
- Class `FieldExpr` has a reference to the corresponding field declaration.
- Class `ExitStmt` has a reference to its enclosing loop statement.
- Class `ReturnStmt` has a reference to its enclosing subprogram declaration.

The following example provides a visual illustration of structural and nonstructural references in an abstract syntax tree.

Example: Abstract Syntax Tree

Consider the following small CPRL program.

```
var x : Integer;

proc main()
  {
    x := 5;
    writeln x;
  }
```

We can visualize the associated abstract syntax tree as shown in the diagram below. This diagram uses solid lines to indicate the structural references for the tree and dotted lines to indicate the nonstructural references back to declarations.

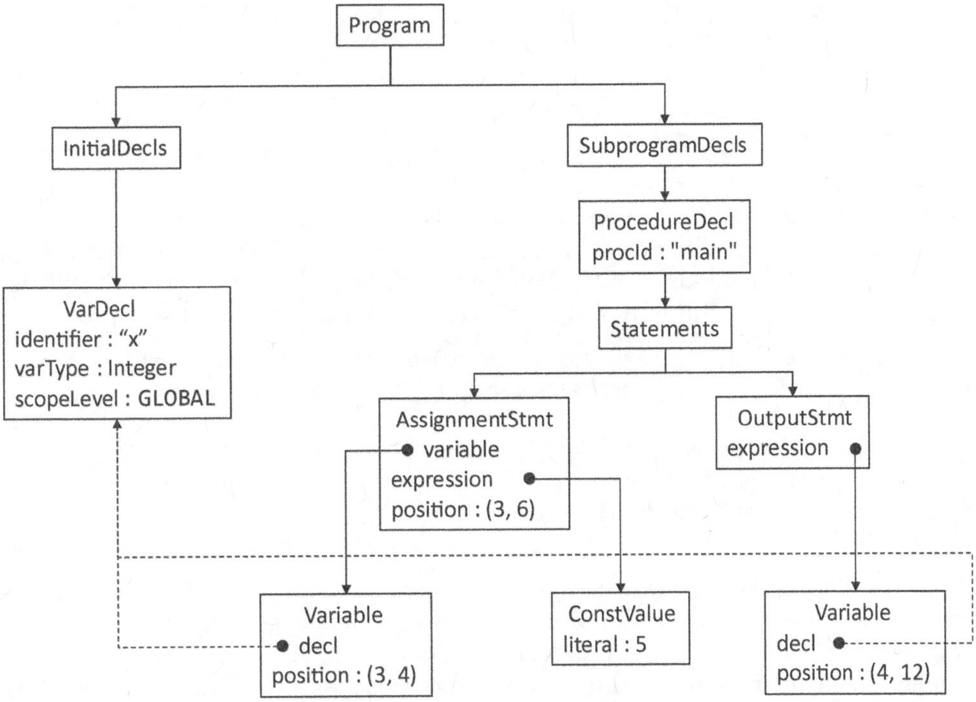

8.6 Determining Types of Variables and Expressions

Since CPRL is statically typed, it is possible to determine the type of every variable and expression at compile time, and AST class `Expression` has a property named "`type`" that is inherited by all expression subclasses. But where within the compiler should type determination take place? Possible answers include the parser, the constructors for the expression classes, or the `checkConstraints()` methods for the expression classes. In general, the approach taken in this book is to determine the type of an expression in the constructor for the expression's AST class when possible, but for programmer-defined types (e.g., arrays or records), we need to do additional work in method `checkConstraints()`. Let's look at some examples.

`ConstValue`: We use AST class `ConstValue`, a subclass of `Expression`, to encapsulate both literal values and constant declarations. Therefore, class `ConstValue` has two constructors, and both constructors determine the type of the constant value as shown below.

```
public ConstValue(Token literal)
  {
    super(Type.typeOf(literal), literal.position());
    this.literal = literal;
    this.decl    = null;
  }
```

```
public ConstValue(Token identifier, ConstDecl decl)
  {
    super(decl.type(), identifier.position());
    this.literal = decl.literal();
    this.decl    = decl;
  }
```

RelationalExpr: A relational expression is a binary expression where the operator is a relational operator such as "<=" or ">". A simple example would be "`x < 5`". Regardless of the types of the two operands, a relational expression always has type `Boolean`. Here is an excerpt from the constructor for `RelationalExpr` showing its type being set to `Boolean`.

```
public RelationalExpr(Expression leftOperand, Token operator,
                      Expression rightOperand)
  {
    super(leftOperand, operator, rightOperand);
    setType(Type.Boolean);
    assert operator.symbol().isRelationalOperator();
}
```

AddingExpr: For most "real" programming languages, determining the type of an adding expression can be somewhat complicated. For example, languages such as C and Java have multiple numeric types with lots of rules about automatic conversions (a.k.a. promotions or coercions) when an operator has different operand types. And for Java, Kotlin, and C#, an adding expression can also have string operands. Things are a little less complicated for CPRL. In CPRL, there are only two numeric types, `Integer` and `Byte`, and values of type `Byte` are promoted to type `Integer` when used as expressions. CPRL also allows the use of operator "+" for concatenation of strings. The constructor for `AddingExpr` initializes the type to `Integer` since that is the most common case, and the type is changed to `String` during constraint analysis if it is determined that both operands have type `String`.

Variable: The type for a variable is initialized to the type specified in the variable's declaration. Here is the primary constructor for `Variable` showing how the type is initialized.

```
public Variable(VariableDecl decl, Token idToken,
                List<Expression> selectorExprs)
  {
    super(decl.type(), idToken.position());
    this.decl = decl;
    this.idToken = idToken;
    this.selectorExprs = selectorExprs;
  }
```

The initialized type for a variable is correct for predefined scalar types such as `Integer` or `Char`, but additional work is required for composite types. Variables of composite types can be followed by selector expressions, which are either index expressions of the form "`[3]`" or field expressions of the form "`.name`". A selector expression effectively changes the type of the variable. Consider the following examples.

```
type Month = record
  {
    name    : String;
    maxDays : Integer;
  };
type Months = array[13] of Month;   // 1 for "January"
var  months : Months;
...
months                   // type is Months (an array type)
months[3]                // type is Month (a record type)
months[3].maxDays        // type is Integer
months[3].name           // type is String
months[3].name.length    // type is Integer
months[3].name[2]        // type is Char
```

This idea will be explored in more detail in subsequent chapters, but here is an outline of how selector expressions are handled in method `checkConstraints()` of class `Variable`.

```
// in method checkConstraints()
for (var expr : selectorExprs)
  {
    expr.checkConstraints();

    if (type() instanceof ArrayType arrayType)
        checkArraySelectorExpr(expr, arrayType);
    else if (type() instanceof RecordType recType)
        checkRecordSelectorExpr(expr, recType);
    else if (type() == Type.String)
        checkStringSelectorExpr(expr);
    else
      {
        var errorMsg = "Selector expression not allowed ...";
        throw error(expr.position(), errorMsg)
      }
  }
...

// in method checkArraySelectorExpr()
setType(arrayType.elementType());
...

// in method checkRecordSelectorExpr()
var fieldDecl = recType.get(fieldId.text());
setType(fieldDecl.type());
...
```

Using a Variable as an Expression

Recall from Chapter 6 the discussion of variables, variable expressions, and parsing methods `parseVariable()` and `parseVariableExpr()`. Method `parseVariable()` is called, for example, when parsing the variable on the left side of an assignment statement. Method `parseVariableExpr()` is called when we need the value of the variable as part of an expression; e.g., on the right side of an assignment statement. Both parsing methods call `parseVariableCommon()`, which implements the common parsing logic. Relative to abstract syntax trees, all three methods return an instance of AST class `Variable`. So how does class `Variable` distinguish between a variable and a variable expression?

Class `Variable` has a private boolean property `useAsExpression` and a public "set" method that let us distinguish how the variable is being used.

```
/**
 * Set to true if this variable is used as an expression.
 */
public void setUseAsExpression(boolean useAsExpression)
```

The default value of `useAsExpression` is false, which is the correct value for `parseVariable()`. Method `parseVariableExpr()` will need to set the value to true before returning the variable. Here is the relevant excerpt from method `parseVariableExpr()`.

```
var variable = parseVariableCommon();
variable.setUseAsExpression(true);
return variable;
```

8.7 Maintaining Context During Parsing

Certain CPRL statements need access to an enclosing context for constraint checking and proper code generation. Consider, for example, the following `exit` statement.

```
exit when n > 10;
```

An `exit` statement has meaning only when nested inside a loop. Correct code generation for an `exit` statement requires knowledge of which loop encloses it. Similarly, a `return` statement requires knowledge of its enclosing subprogram. Classes `LoopContext` and `SubprogramContext` will be used to maintain contextual information in these cases.

Following are three key methods from class `LoopContext`.

```
/**
 * Returns the loop statement currently being parsed.
 * Returns null if not currently parsing a loop.
 */
public LoopStmt loopStmt()
```

```
/**
 * Called when starting to parse a loop statement.
 */
public void beginLoop(LoopStmt stmt)

/**
 * Called when finished parsing a loop statement.
 */
public void endLoop()
```

Similarly, here are three key methods from class `SubprogramContext`.

```
/**
 * Returns the subprogram declaration currently being parsed.
 * Returns null if not currently parsing a subprogram.
 */
public SubprogramDecl subprogramDecl()

/**
 * Called when starting to parse a subprogram declaration.
 */
public void beginSubprogramDecl(SubprogramDecl subprogDecl)

/**
 * Called when finished parsing a subprogram declaration.
 */
public void endSubprogramDecl()
```

As an example using context, consider the following code for parsing a `loop` statement.

```
var stmt = new LoopStmt();
...
loopContext.beginLoop(stmt);
stmt.setStatement(parseStatement());
loopContext.endLoop();
```

Then when parsing an exit statement (e.g., as one of the statements inside a compound statement for the loop body), we gain access to the enclosing loop by doing the following.

```
// save position for error reporting
var exitPosition = scanner.position();
...
var loopStmt = loopContext.loopStmt();
if (loopStmt == null)
    throw error(exitPosition,
                "Exit statement is not nested within a loop.");
match(Symbol.semicolon);
return new ExitStmt(whenExpr, loopStmt);
```

> Class `LoopContext` exists solely to help associate an `exit` statement with its enclosing `loop` statement, and class `SubprogramContext` exists solely to help associate a `return` statement with its enclosing subprogram. But both classes can be eliminated if we were to add parent references to the AST classes. For example, if parent references existed, an `exit` statement could simply follow the chain of parent references to find its enclosing `loop` statement. See related exercise in Appendix B for additional discussion about adding parent references.

8.8 Declarations, Statements, and Expressions Revisited

Recall from Chapter 4 that the three major syntactic categories in CPRL are declarations, statements, and expressions. We conclude this discussion of abstract syntax trees by showing the inheritance hierarchy for each of these syntactic categories. "`Empty`" classes `EmptyInitialDecl`, `EmptySubprogramDecl`, `EmptyStatement`, etc. are omitted from the diagrams. The roles of most classes shown in these diagrams should be apparent from their names.

Inheritance Hierarchy for Declarations

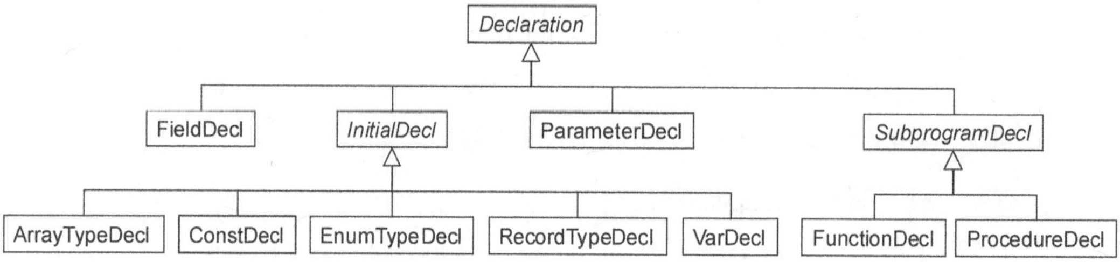

Inheritance Hierarchy for Statements

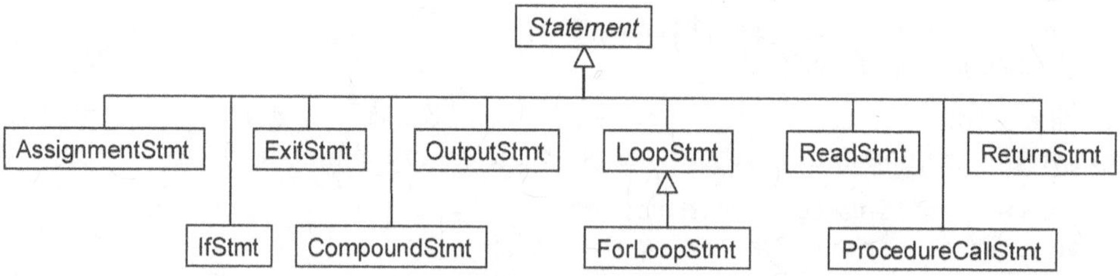

Inheritance Hierarchy for Expressions

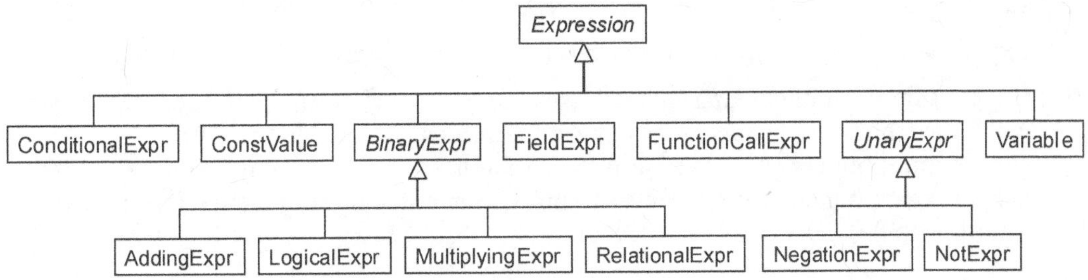

8.9 Essential Terms and Concepts

abstract syntax tree (AST)

`AST` (class)

`checkConstraints()` (method)

`GLOBAL` scope

initializers

`LoopContext` (class)

`RECORD` scope

return values for parsing methods

`SubprogramContext` (class)

`VarDecl` (class)

`ArrayType` (class)

binary expression

`emit()` (method)

`IdTable` (class)

`LOCAL` scope

nonstructural references (in the AST)

`RecordType` (class)

scope level

`Type` (class)

`VariableDecl` (interface)

8.10 Exercises

1. **Project Assignment.** Implement **Project 4: Abstract Syntax Trees** as described in Appendix A.
2. Describe the structure defined by the properties (instance variables) of the following AST classes.
   a. `AssignmentStmt`
   b. `LoopStmt`
   c. `BinaryExpr`
3. The AST class `BinaryExpr` is an abstract Java class. What are some of the concrete classes that extend `BinaryExpr`?
4. Explain the difference between structural references and nonstructural references in AST classes.
5. Describe the role of class `LoopContext` in parsing loops and `exit` statements.

6. Describe the role of class `SubprogramContext` in parsing subprograms and `return` statements.
7. Explain what is meant by the "scope level" of a var declaration.
8. If you study the implementation of classes `LoopContext` and `SubprogramContext`, you will notice that class `SubprogramContext` maintains a reference to only one subprogram; but `LoopContext` has a stack of loop statements. Why is it necessary for `LoopContext` to maintain references to more than one loop statement? (Hint: What can be nested?)

Chapter 9
Constraint Analysis

9.1 Overview of Constraint Analysis

Recall that the definition of a programming language involves the specification of its syntax, contextual constraints, and semantics. Syntax requires defining the basic language symbols and the allowed structure of symbols to form programs. Syntax is almost always specified by a context-free grammar, and that is the approach we have taken in defining CPRL.

Contextual constraints are program rules and restrictions that cannot be specified (or cannot be easily specified) in a context-free grammar. For CPRL these constraints consist primarily of type and scope rules. Note that what we are calling "constraint analysis" is sometimes referred to as "contextual analysis" or "analysis of static semantics". For CPRL, contextual constraints are specified informally using English descriptions.

The semantics of a programming language is its meaning; i.e., the behavior of a program when it is run on a machine. Semantics is often specified using informal descriptions in a natural language.

Syntax Analysis versus Constraint Analysis

Syntax analysis verifies that a program conforms to the formal syntax of the language as defined by a context-free grammar. Syntax analysis is performed by the parser. Constraint analysis verifies that a program conforms to the additional language rules and requirements that are not expressed in a context-free grammar. While there exist formal notations for expressing these additional rules, these formal notations are much more complex than context-free grammars, and therefore the additional rules that go beyond context-free grammars are often expressed informally in a natural language such as English.

As implemented in the compiler project for CPRL, constraint analysis is performed partly by the parser using helper classes `IdTable`, `LoopContext`, and `SubprogramContext`, and partly by the abstract syntax trees in constructors and in methods named `checkConstraints()`.

Our constraint rules fall into three general categories.

- Scope rules: Rules associated with declarations and applied occurrences of identifiers.
- Type rules: Rules associated with the types of expressions and their uses in certain contexts.
- Miscellaneous rules: Language constraints that do not fall into either of the above categories. Some of the rules we define for CPRL represent internal errors within the compiler.

Scope Rules in CPRL

CPRL has a relatively flat block structure in that subprograms can't be nested, which is allowed in some programming languages. There are three basic scope levels in CPRL. Declarations are either global in scope, local to a subprogram, or, in the case of field declarations, local to a record type declaration. In addition, names (identifiers) for enum constants must be unique within an enumerated type declaration. The scope rules for CPRL are fairly simple. There are essentially only two scope rules.

1. Every programmer-defined identifier (constant, variable, type name, subprogram name, etc.) must be declared. When we encounter an applied occurrence of an identifier, we must be able to discover its declaration and associate the declaration with the identifier. Further, CPRL requires that initial declarations (declarations of constants, variables, and types) appear before the name being introduced can be used (i.e., before any applied occurrence), but this restriction does not apply to subprogram declarations.
2. All identifiers appearing in declarations must be unique within their respective scopes. In other words, the same identifier must not be used twice in the same scope.

Scope analysis (a.k.a. identification) is the process of verifying the scope rules. Scope analysis is implemented primarily within the parser using class `IdTable`. Currently all scope errors are reported by the parser as syntax errors, but technically they are not really syntax errors since they are not defined in the context-free grammar. Reporting them as scope errors might make the error messages more meaningful. (See exercise 10 in Appendix B.)

We implemented a version of scope analysis in Chapter 6 and enhanced it in Chapter 8, where we associated an identifier with a reference to its actual declaration. Having a reference to the complete declaration will allow us to check additional constraints as outlined in this chapter. For example, having a reference to an identifier's declaration lets us know not only that the identifier was declared as a variable but also that it was declared to have type `Integer`.

Scope analysis using class `IdTable` is summarized below.

- When an identifier is declared, the parser will attempt to add a reference to its declaration to `IdTable` within the current scope. If a declaration with the same name (same token text) has been previously added in the current scope, then an exception will be thrown indicating that the program being compiled has a scope error.
- For an applied occurrence of an identifier (e.g., in a statement or in an expression), the compiler will check `IdTable` to see if the identifier has been declared. If the identifier has been declared, then the compiler will store a reference to its declaration as part of the AST where the identifier is used. If the identifier has not been declared, then a scope error has occurred. This check is performed by the parser for identifiers corresponding to initial declarations since initial declarations must appear before any applied occurrence. The check is performed in the appropriate `checkConstraints()`

methods for identifiers corresponding to subprograms; e.g., in class `ProcedureCallStmt` or `FunctionCallExpr`.

The CPRL/0 Subset of CPRL

Over the last few chapters we implemented a scanner and a parser for the full CPRL language. But in order to simplify the discussion and implementation of constraint analysis and code generation, we find it convenient to focus initially on a subset of CPRL. The "zero" subset of CPRL, denoted CPRL/0, is defined to be that part of the language **not** related to subprograms, enumerated types, and composite types. CPRL/0 includes the following.

- procedure `main()`, but no other subprograms
- global declarations for constants and variables, but no local variables within `main()`
- predefined scalar types `Boolean`, `Byte`, `Char`, and `Integer`
- string literals for output statements, but not programmer-defined string variables and operations
- most statements except those directly related to subprograms

Excluded are subprogram declarations other than `main()`, procedure call statements, function call expressions, return statements, and type declarations for arrays, enumerated types, and records.

The sample CPRL programs used to test various parts of your compiler are organized into separate directories to clearly indicate which examples are based only on the CPRL/0 subset.

Our current version of the compiler already implements scope analysis correctly for CPRL/0 since the parser can perform all necessary checks for initial declarations, but we will revisit scope analysis briefly in subsequent chapters, especially when covering subprograms in Chapter 13.

Static Typing versus Dynamic Typing

CPRL is a statically-typed language, which means that every variable and expression has a type and that type compatibility is a static property; i.e., it can be determined by the compiler. Other examples of statically-typed languages include Java, C#, C++, and Rust. But some programming languages (e.g., Python and JavaScript) are dynamically typed, which means that the type of a variable is determined by its current value, not by its declaration. The following examples use CPRL-like syntax to illustrate the distinction.

```
// static typing                 // dynamic typing
var x : Integer;                 var x;
...                              ...
x := 7;        // o.k.           x := 7;        // o.k.; x has type Integer
...                              ...
x := "Abby"    // *** error      x := "Abby"    // o.k.; x now has type String
```

In general, programs written using statically-typed languages tend to have fewer run-time errors since many such errors are caught at compile time, and compiler-generated code tends to execute more efficiently. In contrast, dynamically-typed languages tend to be more flexible and easier to use, but they execute less efficiently since, for example, type checking must be performed at run time.

Languages that use static typing are usually compiled, whereas languages that use dynamic typing are more likely to be interpreted. But recall from Chapter 1 that the distinction between compiled and interpreted languages is sometimes blurred. For example, Java initially uses a compiler, but the Java virtual machine (JVM) is a low-level interpreter for Java bytecode. In contrast, when you run a Python program, Python initially uses an interpreter, but the interpreter also converts the source code into an intermediate form that can speed up performance of subsequent executions.

Type Rules in CPRL

Type rules for CPRL define how and where certain types can be used. We define type rules in any context where a variable or expression can appear. Here are some examples.

For an assignment statement, the type of the expression on the right side of the assignment symbol must be assignment compatible with the type of the variable on the left side. Most of the time CPRL requires the two types to be exactly the same. For CPRL, we can assign an integer expression to an integer variable, and we can assign a boolean expression to a boolean variable, but we can't assign a boolean expression to an integer variable. Note that some languages have much weaker type rules for assignment. For example, in C (but not CPRL) it is perfectly acceptable to assign a character literal to a variable of type integer.

Since values of type `Byte` are coerced (automatically converted) to `Integer` values when used in expressions, strict type equality is relaxed slightly for numeric types. So for example, we can assign an `Integer` expression to a `Byte` variable and vice versa. We can also mix these types in expressions; e.g., we can add a `Byte` value to an `Integer` value – the result has type Integer.

As a third example of a type rule in CPRL, consider that for an `if` statement, the expression following the `if` symbol must have type `Boolean`.

Implementing Constraint Analysis

Constraint analysis is the process of verifying that all constraint rules have been satisfied. For CPRL, most type and miscellaneous rules are verified using `checkConstraints()` methods in the AST classes. Even AST classes that do not have associated constraints will implement the method `checkConstraints()` if they contain structural references to objects of other AST classes since they will need to call `checkConstraints()` on those AST objects.

We illustrate with a couple of examples. Here is the initial part of the implementation of method `checkConstraints()` in class `Program`, which has a list of global initial declarations and a list of subprograms.

```
@Override
public void checkConstraints()
  {
    try
      {
        for (var decl : initialDecls)
            decl.checkConstraints();

        for (var decl : subprogramDecls)
            decl.checkConstraints();
        ...
  }
```

Similarly, here is the implementation of `checkConstraints()` in class `CompoundStmt`, which is essentially a list of `Statement` objects.

```
@Override
public void checkConstraints()
  {
    for (var stmt : statements)
        stmt.checkConstraints();
  }
```

But beware. You should call `checkConstraints()` only for properties representing structural references (child nodes) of the tree, as described in Section 8.5. Calling `checkConstraints()` for nonstructural references (i.e., applied occurrences that reference declarations or statements that reference contexts) can cause problems. Recall that all properties represented as nonstructural references are commented as such.

As an example, consider that an `exit` statement has a nonstructural reference to its enclosing `loop` statement. What would happen if the `exit` statement called `checkConstraints()` for the `loop`? Since the `loop` statement calls `checkConstraints()` for the statement nested within the `loop` body, it would call `checkConstraints()` on the `exit` statement, setting up an infinite chain of recursive calls. Therefore an `exit` statement should not call `checkConstraints()` for the nonstructural reference to its enclosing `loop` statement. Similarly, a `return` statement should not call `checkConstraints()` for the nonstructural reference to its enclosing subprogram.

For another example, consider the diagram from Section 8.5, which we repeat below. The `checkConstraints()` method in `VarDecl` (for identifier `x`) should be called from `Program` as shown above and not by using the `decl` references in the two instances of `Variable` (shown with dotted lines). Calling `checkConstraints()` on the declaration referenced within the two instances of `Variable` would result in additional, redundant calls to `checkConstraints()` for the same instance of `VarDecl`. If there had been an error in the declaration, then the additional calls would generate redundant error messages.

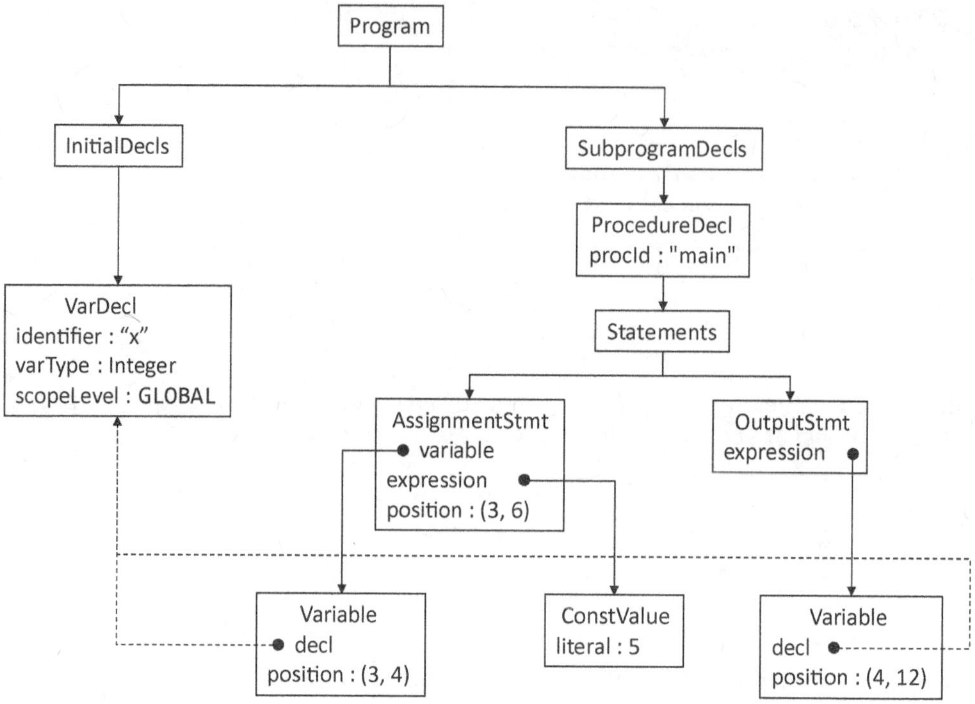

9.2 Constraint Rules for CPRL/0

This section lists the additional type and miscellaneous rules for CPRL/0 organized in terms of the AST classes whose constructors and `checkConstraints()` methods will be responsible for implementing the rules. Additional constraint rules for subprograms, arrays, enumerated types, strings, and records will be covered in subsequent chapters.

- **`AddingExpr` and `MultiplyingExpr`**
  - Type Rule: Both operands must have a numeric type (`Integer` or `Byte`) and the result has type `Integer`. (To support string concatenation, we will modify the constraint for `AddingExpr` in Chapter 16 to allow the plus ("+") operator for strings.)
- **`AssignmentStmt`**
  - Type Rule: The type of the expression on the right side of the assignment symbol must be assignment compatible with the type of the variable on the left side. Method `matchTypes()` in class `AST` can be used to check for assignment compatibility.

- **`ConstDecl` and `ConstValue`**
  - Miscellaneous Rule: If the literal value has type `Integer`, then it must be able to be converted to an integer value on the CPRL virtual machine. Class `IntUtil` in package `common.util` has a method named `toInt()` that can be used to check this. If the check fails for a constant declaration, after reporting the error we set the literal's value to `0`, a valid value for type `Integer`, in order to prevent additional error messages every time that the constant declaration is used.
- **`ConditionalExpr`**
  - Type Rule: The first expression (the one before "`?`") must have type `Boolean`. The other two expressions (on left and right of "`:`") must have exactly the same type, not merely assignment-compatible types. The requirement for exact types simplifies constraint checking and code generation for conditional expressions.
- **`ExitStmt`**
  - Type Rule: If a "`when`" expression is present, it must have type `Boolean`.
  - Miscellaneous Rule: The `exit` statement must be nested within a `loop` statement. (This constraint is handled by the parser using class `LoopContext`.)
- **`ForLoopStmt`**
  - Type Rule: Both expressions in the range of the `forLoop` must have a numeric type or an enumerated type. Class `Type` has a boolean method named `isRangeType()` that can be used to check this.
  - Type Rule: Both expressions in the range of the `forLoop` must have the same type.
  - Miscellaneous Rule: If both expressions in the range of the `forLoop` are constants, then the value of the first expression must be less than or equal to the value of the second expression.
- **`IfStmt`**
  - Type Rule: The expression following symbol `if` must have type `Boolean`.
- **`LogicalExpr`**
  - Type Rule: Both operands must have type `Boolean`, and the result has type `Boolean`.
- **`LoopStmt`**
  - Type Rule: If a "`while`" expression is present, it must have type `Boolean`.
- **`NegationExpr`**
  - Type Rule: The operand must have type `Integer`, and the result has type `Integer`.

- `NotExpr`
  - Type Rule: If the operator symbol is the reserved word `not`, then the operand must have type `Boolean`, and the result has type `Boolean`.
  - Type Rule: If the operator symbol is the bitwise negation operator ~, then the operand must have a numeric type, and the result has type `Integer`.
- `OutputStmt`
  - Type Rule: Each expression must have a scalar type or type `String`. Output is supported only for scalar types and strings. Note that class `Type` has a `boolean` method named `isOutputType()` that can be used when checking for valid output types.
- `Program`
  - Miscellaneous Rule: A program must contain a parameterless procedure named `main()`.
- `ReadStmt`
  - Type Rule: The variable must have type `Integer`, `Char`, `String`, or `Byte`. Input is supported only for numeric types, characters, and strings. Class `Type` has a boolean method named `isInputType()` that can be used to check this constraint.
- `RelationalExpr`
  - Type Rule: Both operands must have assignment compatible types, and the result has type `Boolean`.
  - Type Rule: Only scalar types (`Integer`, `Byte`, `Char`, or `Boolean`, or an enumerated type) are allowed for operands. For example, in CPRL, you can't have a relational expression where both operands are arrays, records, or strings. Method `isScalarType()` in class `Type` can be used to check this. Also, since the CVM comparison operators compare only integer values, values of type `Boolean` and `Char` will need to be promoted to `Integer` before comparing. Note that values of type `Byte` will have already been promoted to `Integer`.
- `VarDecl`
  - Type Rule: If the declaration has an initializer, the type of the value on the right side of the assignment symbol must be assignment compatible with the type of the variable being declared. For CPRL/`0`, method `matchTypes()` in class AST can be used to check for assignment compatibility. But method `checkConstraints()` becomes complicated when composite types are considered, especially since composite types can be nested. Example 3 in the next section illustrates some of the issues that need to be addressed. We will revisit type rules for class `VarDecl` in Chapters 14, 16, and 17.
  - Miscellaneous Rule: An initializer for a variable of type `Byte` must be in the range `0..255`.

Note that the type rules are much simpler for CPRL than for languages like C and C++ that support multiple numeric types with lots of special coercion rules for converting from one numeric type to another.

9.3 Examples of Constraint Analysis

This section provides complete implementations of method `checkConstraints()` for two AST classes plus a partial implementation for a third class.

Example 1. Constraint checking for class `AssignmentStmt`.

The implementation of method `checkConstraints()` shown below is valid for CPRL/`0`, but we will need to amend this method when we cover strings in Chapter 16. An additional check needs to be performed for strings. Since strings are immutable in CPRL, the variable on the left side of an assignment statement cannot have selector expressions if it has type `String`. The implementation shown below does not check for this constraint.

```
@Override
public void checkConstraints()
  {
    try
      {
        expr.checkConstraints();
        variable.checkConstraints();

        if (!matchTypes(variable.type(), expr))
          {
            var errorMsg = "Type mismatch for assignment statement";
            throw error(assignPosition, errorMsg);
          }
      }
    catch (ConstraintException e)
      {
        errorHandler().reportError(e);
      }
  }
```

Note the call to method `error()` in the `try` block above. Similar to what was done in class `Parser`, there are two overloaded methods named `error()` inherited from class `AST` that can be used to create constraint exceptions. One version of the method (the version called in Example 1 above) takes two parameters, both an error message and an explicit position to be used in creating the `ConstraintException`. The second version of method `error()` takes a single string parameter for the error message and returns a `ConstraintException` with that error message but without a position. The latter version is currently used only for reporting that procedure `main()` was never declared.

Example 2. Constraint checking for class `NegationExpr`.

```
@Override
public void checkConstraints()
  {
    try
      {
        operand().checkConstraints();

        // negation can only be applied to an integer expression
        if (operand().type() != Type.Integer)
          {
            var errorMsg = "Expression following \"-\" operator "
                         + "is not an Integer expression.";
            throw error(operand().position(), errorMsg);
          }
      }
    catch (ConstraintException e)
      {
        errorHandler().reportError(e);
      }
  }
```

Example 3. Constraint checking for class `Variable`.

For CPRL/`0`, there is not much to check in class `Variable`. But when we include arrays, strings, and records, `Variable` becomes one of the more difficult AST classes to implement. Both `checkConstraints()` and `emit()` are complicated by the fact that a variable can be followed by one or more selector expressions. Chapters 14, 16, and 17 will provide additional details, but for now, here is a preview of what we need to consider in order to implement `checkConstraints()` for class `Variable`.

Variables of programmer-defined types can be followed by one or more selector expressions, which are either index expressions of the form "`[i]`" or field expressions of the form "`.name`". A selector expression effectively changes the type of the variable. Consider the following declarations taken from one of the CPRL test examples.

```
type Month = record
  {
    name     : String;
    maxDays  : Integer;
  };
type Months = array[13] of Month;    // uses index 1 for "January"
var  months : Months;
```

While the declared type of variable months is Months, months can be followed by an index expression, which can be followed by a field expression, which can be followed by ..., as in the following.

```
months                    // type is Months (an array type)
months[3]                 // type is Month (a record type)
months[3].maxDays         // type is Integer
months[3].name            // type is String
months[3].name.length     // type is Integer
months[3].name[2]         // type is Char
```

When the parser encounters a reference of the form months[3].name in a program, it initializes the type to Months based on the declared type of the identifier. We determine the actual type of months[3].name in method checkConstraints() by looping through the selector expressions, getting the type associated with the expression, and then changing the type of the variable to the type determined by the selector expression. Here is an excerpt from method checkConstraints() for AST class Variable.

```
for (var expr : selectorExprs)
  {
    expr.checkConstraints();

    // Each selector expression must correspond to
    // an array type, a record type, or type String.
    if (type() instanceof ArrayType arrayType)
      {
        // Applying the selector effectively changes the
        // variable's type to the element type of the array.
        setType(arrayType.elementType());
        ...
      }
    else if (type() instanceof RecordType recType)
      {
        ...
        // Applying the selector effectively changes the
        // variable's type to the type of the field.
        ...
      }
    else if (type() == Type.String)
      {
        // Selector can be field expression .length (type Integer)
        // or an index expression for the characters (type Char).

        if (expr instanceof FieldExpr fieldExpr)
          {
            setType(Type.Integer);
            ...
          }
```

```
            else
              {
                // Must be an index expression.  Applying an index selector
                // effectively changes the variable's type to Char.
                setType(Type.Char);
                ...
              }
          }
        else
          {
            var errorMsg = "Selector expression not allowed ..."
            throw error(expr.position(), errorMsg);
          }
      }
```

9.4 Essential Terms and Concepts

`checkConstraints()` (method)	contextual constraint
flat block structure	`IdTable` (class)
miscellaneous rule	scope rule
statically typed	type rule

9.5 Exercises

1. **Project Assignment.** Implement **Project 5: Constraint Analysis** as described in Appendix A.
2. Describe the two scope rules for CPRL.
3. What does it mean when we say that a programming language is statically typed? Give an example of a programming language that uses static typing. What does it mean when we say that a programming language is dynamically typed? Give an example of a programming language that uses dynamic typing. Is CPRL statically-typed or dynamically-typed?
4. Give several examples of type rules for CPRL.
5. Give one example of a miscellaneous rule for CPRL.
6. Fill in the blanks.
   Constraint analysis is performed in two separate places within the CPRL compiler, ______________________________ and ______________________________.
   (Hints: Where are scope rules detected? Where are type rules detected?)

7. In Chapter 6 we implemented a form of scope analysis using classes `IdTable` and `IdType`. Describe the changes to scope analysis as implemented in this chapter. (Hint: Class `IdType` is no longer used.)
8. Select several type and miscellaneous rules for CPRL/0, and for each such rule, write two test programs in CPRL, one correct program that satisfies the rule and one incorrect program that does not satisfy the rule. The incorrect program should be valid CPRL except for the single rule violation. After completing Project 5 (Appendix A), use the test programs to check if your compiler correctly implements the rules.

Chapter 10
The CPRL Virtual Machine

This chapter presents an overview of the CVM (**C**PRL **V**irtual **M**achine), a hypothetical computer designed to simplify the code generation phase of a compiler for CPRL. Additional details of the CVM are provided in subsequent chapters as part of code generation, and Appendix E contains a detailed definition of the CVM, including complete descriptions of every machine instruction.

10.1 Overview of the CVM

CVM uses a stack architecture; i.e., most instructions either expect operands on the run-time stack, place results on the run-time stack, or both. Memory is organized into 8-bit bytes, and each byte is directly addressable. A word is a logical grouping of 4 consecutive bytes in memory. The address of a word is the address of its first (low) byte.

Boolean values are represented in a single byte, where a zero value means false and any nonzero value is interpreted as true. Character values use 2 bytes based on Unicode Basic Multilingual Plane (Plane 0). Character code points range from `U+0000` to `U+FFFF`. Integer values use a word and are represented using 32-bit 2's complement.

Each CVM instruction operation code (opcode) occupies one byte of memory. Some instructions take an immediate operand, which is always located immediately following the instruction in memory. Depending on the opcode, an immediate operand can be a single byte, two bytes (e.g., for a char), four bytes (e.g., for an integer or a memory address), or multiple bytes (e.g., for a string literal). Most instructions get their operands from the run-time stack. In general, the operands are removed from the stack whenever the instruction is executed, and any results are left on the top of the stack.

Here are some examples of CVM instructions.

- `ADD`: Remove two integers from the top of the stack and push their sum back onto the stack.
- `INC`: Add 1 to the integer at the top of the stack.
- `BGE` (Branch if Greater or Equal): Remove two integers from the top of the stack. If the first integer is greater than or equal to the second integer, then branch according to displacement operand immediately following the opcode; otherwise continue with the next instruction. Note that the immediate operand for the displacement can be positive or negative representing forward or backward branching.
- `LOADW` (Load Word): Load (push) a word onto the stack. A word is four consecutive bytes. The address of the first byte of the word is obtained by popping it off the top of the stack.
- `LDCINT` (Load Constant Integer): Fetch the integer immediately following the opcode (an immediate operand) and push it onto the top of the stack; e.g., `LDCINT 500`.

- `LDCINT0` (Load Constant Integer Zero): Optimized replacement for `LDCINT 0`. `LDCINT0` occupies only one byte in memory for the opcode, whereas `LDCINT 0` occupies five bytes – one for the opcode and four for the integer `0`. Also, `LDCINT0` executes slightly faster since there is no need to fetch the immediate operand. (This instruction is similar to the JVM instruction `iconst_0`.)

Note that CVM uses the term "load" whenever a value is pushed onto the run-time stack and "store" whenever a value is popped from the stack and saved in a memory location.

Appendix E describes ten functional groupings of the CVM opcodes.

- Arithmetic Opcodes. Examples include `ADD`, `SUB` (subtract), `MUL` (multiply), `INC` (increment), etc.
- Logical Opcodes. There is only one opcode in this grouping – `NOT` (logical not).
- Bitwise Opcodes. The four opcodes in this group operate at the bit level – `BITAND`, `BITOR`, `BITXOR`, and `BITNOT`.
- Shift Opcodes. There are only two opcodes in this grouping – `SHL` (shift left) and `SHR` (shift right).
- Type Conversion Opcodes. The four opcodes in this grouping convert between integers, characters, and bytes – `BYTE2INT`, `INT2BYTE`, `CHAR2INT`, and `INT2CHAR`.
- Branch Opcodes. Examples include `BR` (unconditional branch), `BE` (branch if equal), `BG` (branch if greater), `BGE` (branch if greater or equal), `BZ` (branch if zero), etc.
- Load/Store Opcodes. Examples include `LOADW` (load word), `LDCINT` (load constant integer), `LDGADDR` (load global address), `STOREB` (store byte), `STOREW` (store word), etc.
- Program/Procedure Opcodes. Examples include `PROGRAM`, `PROC` (procedure), `CALL`, `RET` (return), etc.
- I/O Opcodes. Examples include `GETINT` (get integer), `GETCH` (get character), `PUTINT` (put integer), `PUTSTR` (put string), etc.
- Special Opcode for String Concatenation. `STRCAT` is only one opcode in this grouping.

Note that for most real and virtual machines, string concatenation and I/O are implemented through calls to programming language or operating system (OS) library functions and not as machine instructions. The choice to implement them as machine instructions was made to simplify code generation for CPRL. To port CVM to a real machine one could use assembly language macros to mimic the opcodes for string concatenation and I/O.

CVM does not have any general-purpose registers, but it has five 32-bit internal (special purpose) registers as follows.

- `PC` (program counter, a.k.a. instruction pointer): holds the address of the next instruction to be executed.
- `SB` (stack base): holds the address of the bottom of the stack. When a program is loaded, `SB` is initialized to the address of the first free byte in memory, and its value never changes during program execution.
- `SP` (stack pointer): holds the address of the top of the stack. The stack grows from low-numbered memory addresses to high-numbered memory addresses. When the stack is empty, `SP` has a value of `SB - 1`, the address immediately before the first free byte in memory.
- `BP` (base pointer): holds the base address of the current activation record (a.k.a. frame); i.e., the base address for the subprogram currently being executed. `BP` and `SB` have the same value (i.e., both reference the same memory location) if there are no currently active subprograms.
- `HP` (heap pointer): holds the address of the top of the heap. The heap grows from high-numbered memory addresses to low-numbered memory addresses. When a program is loaded, `HP` is initialized to the number of bytes in memory; i.e., one more than the last valid memory address. `HP` is used in only two CPRL string-related opcodes, `GETSTR` (reads a string from standard input) and `STRCAT` (concatenates two strings).

  `BP` will be covered in more detail in Chapter 13. HP will be covered in more detail in Chapter 16.

10.2 Brief Comparison with the JVM

The Java Virtual Machine (JVM) is much more complicated than the CVM since the JVM must deal with object references, dynamic memory allocation, and other primitive types such as doubles and longs. The JVM has more than 200 opcodes, whereas the CVM has only 65. Plus, the CVM has several opcodes related to I/O and string concatenation while the JVM has no comparable opcodes. The JVM interacts with the operating system and Java library functions for these purposes. A major difference is how the run-time stack is implemented. The abstract specification for the JVM stack uses a 32-bit "slot"; i.e., all values of the stack logically occupy some multiple of 32-bits. (The physical implementation for the JVM on a 64-bit CPU often widens the stack slots to 64 bits for performance alignment.) The CVM uses an 8-bit "slot" for the runtime stack; i.e. all values on the stack.

Still, there are a number of similarities between the two virtual machines. The terms "big endian" and "little endian" are often used to describe how computers store multi-byte data items in memory. Like the CVM, the JVM also has a stack architecture, and both virtual machines use big-endian order for multibyte data items; i.e., the most significant byte of a multi-byte data item (character, integer, etc.) is stored at the lowest memory address. In addition, many of the CVM opcodes have corresponding opcodes in the JVM with similar or identical semantics. Below is a table showing CVM/JVM corresponding opcodes. In the table, the CVM opcodes use an all-uppercase naming convention, while those of the JVM are shown in all lowercase. Note that JVM opcodes that operate on integer values all start with the letter "`i`".

CVM Opcode	JVM Opcode
ADD	iadd
SUB	isub
MUL	imul
DIV	idiv
MOD	irem
NEG	ineg
INC	iinc
SHL	ishl
SHR	ishr
BR	goto/goto_w
BE	if_icmpeq
BNE	if_icmpne
BG	if_icmpgt
BGE	if_icmpge
BL	if_icmplt
BLE	if_icmple
BZ	ifeq
BNZ	ifne
LDCINT0	iconst_0
LDCINT1	iconst_1
INT2BYTE	i2b
BITAND	iand
BITOR	ior
BITXOR	ixor
CALL	invokestatic
RET	return/ireturn

10.3 CVM Uses Relative Addressing

At this point we need a basic understanding of how variables are addressed. All addressing in CVM is relative to an address contained in a register. Variables declared at global (program) scope are addressed relative to the `SB` register, while variables declared at local (subprogram) scope are addressed relative to the `BP` register. For example, suppose that we have a global variable named `x` with relative address `8`. If `SB` has the value `112`, then the absolute (physical) memory address of `x` is computed as `[SB] + relAddr(x)` or `120`, but rarely will we need to know the absolute memory address. Simply knowing the relative address is sufficient for understanding the CVM architecture and for code generation.

Let's work through an example that illustrates relative addressing. Suppose a program contains the following global declarations:

```
var m, n : Integer;
var c : Char;
var a, b : Boolean;
```

Based on the sizes (number of bytes) for types `Integer`, `Char`, and `Boolean`, the relative addresses of the variables are computed as follows.

- `m` has relative address `0`.
- `n` has relative address `4`.
- `c` has relative address `8`.
- `a` has relative address `10`.
- `b` has relative address `11`.

The total variable length for the program is `12`.

The layout of the variables in memory is illustrated by the diagram on the right.

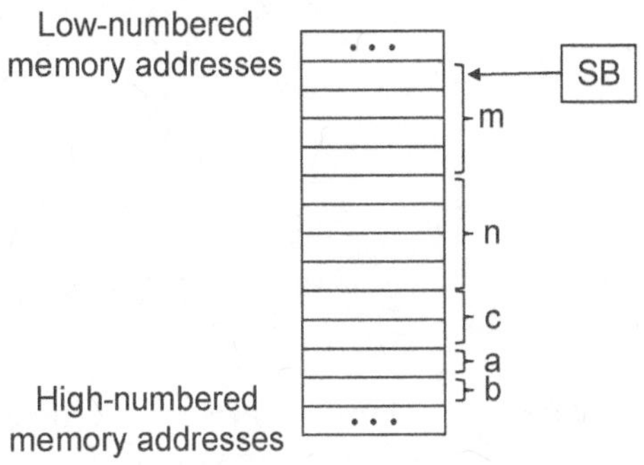

10.4 Loading a Program into Memory

When a program is run, the object code is loaded into the beginning of memory starting at address `0`. Register `PC` is initialized to `0`, the address of the first instruction. Registers `SB` and `BP` are initialized to the address following the last instruction, register `SP` is initialized to `BP - 1`, and register `HP` is initialized to the number of bytes in memory. The value in `SB` is fixed, but the other registers will change as the program executes.

If variables are declared at global scope, the first instruction has the form "`PROGRAM n`", where `n` is the total variable length of the program; e.g., `12` in the above example. When executed, this instruction allocates `n` bytes on the top of the stack for global variables. The following diagram depicts the layout for a program loaded in memory after a number of instructions have been executed.

As stated earlier, all variables are addressed using `SB` and `BP`. When preparing for code generation, the compiler needs to determine the relative address of every variable. The value of `SB` never changes after it is initialized to the address following the last instruction, but `BP` changes every time a subprogram is called.

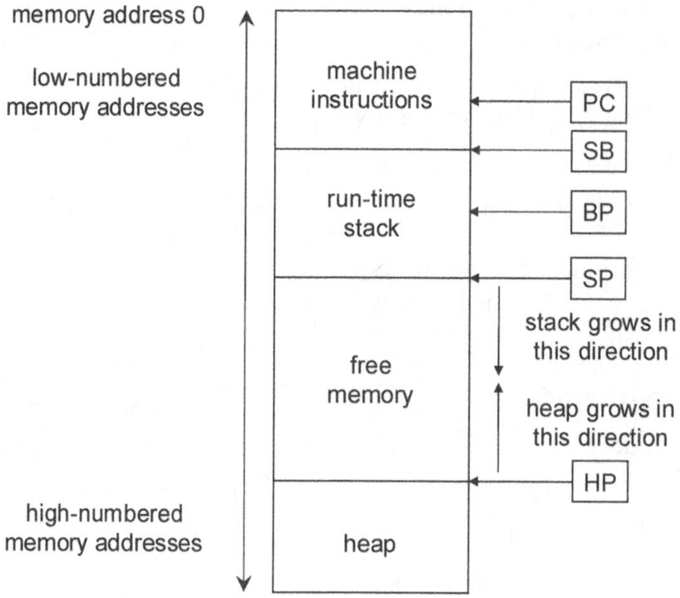

Code generation for CPRL/0 will involve only registers `PC`, `SB`, and `SP`. The role of register `BP` will become more apparent when we cover subprograms in Chapter 13. Similarly, discussion of the heap and register `HP` is postponed until we cover strings in Chapter 16.

Opcodes `LDGADDR` and `LDLADDR` are used to push the address of a variable onto the stack.

- `LDGADDR n`: Loads global address for variable at offset `n` by pushing `SB + n` onto the stack. This instruction is used for variables declared at global (program) scope.
- `LDLADDR n`: Loads local address for variable at offset `n` by pushing `BP + n` onto the stack. This instruction is used for variables declared at local (subprogram) scope.

Let's examine a CPRL example.

```
var   m, n : Integer;
var   c : Char;
const five := 5;

proc main()
  {
    m := 7;
    n := five*m;
    c := 'X';
    writeln "n = ", n;
    writeln "c = ", c;
  }
```

Compiling this program yields the following assembly code.

```
   PROGRAM 10
   CALL _main
   HALT
_main:
   LDGADDR 0
   LDCINT 7
   STOREW
   LDGADDR 4
   LDCINT 5
   LDGADDR 0
   LOADW
   MUL
   STOREW
   LDGADDR 8
   LDCCH 'X'
   STORE2B
   LDCSTR "n = "
   PUTSTR
   ...
   PUTEOL
   RET 0
```

After assembling this program, we can run the disassembler to see the actual layout of the object code with memory addresses as follows.

```
 0:  PROGRAM 10
 5:  CALL 1
10:  HALT
11:  LDGADDR 0
16:  LDCINT 7
21:  STOREW
22:  LDGADDR 4
27:  LDCINT 5
32:  LDGADDR 0
37:  LOADW
38:  MUL
39:  STOREW
40:  LDGADDR 8
45:  LDCCH 'X'
48:  STORE2B
49:  LDCSTR "n = "
62:  PUTSTR
...
92:  PUTEOL
93:  RET0
```

Note that instruction `RET 0` (5 bytes) has been optimized to `RET0` (1 byte).

When this program is loaded into memory, register `PC` will be initialized to `0`, register `SP` will be initialized to `93`, and registers `SB` and `BP` will be initialized to `94`. Execution of the first instruction will allocate space on the run-time stack for variables `m`, `n`, and `c`, and at that point, the three variables will have addresses as follows.

- `m`: relative address = `0` (absolute address = `94`).
- `n`: relative address = `4` (absolute address = `98`).
- `c`: relative address = `8` (absolute address = `102`).

CVM uses relative addressing; for global variables, the addresses are relative to `SB`. The absolute addresses are provided for informational purposes.

The diagram below shows the layout of this program in memory after the first instruction (`PROGRAM 10`) has been executed.

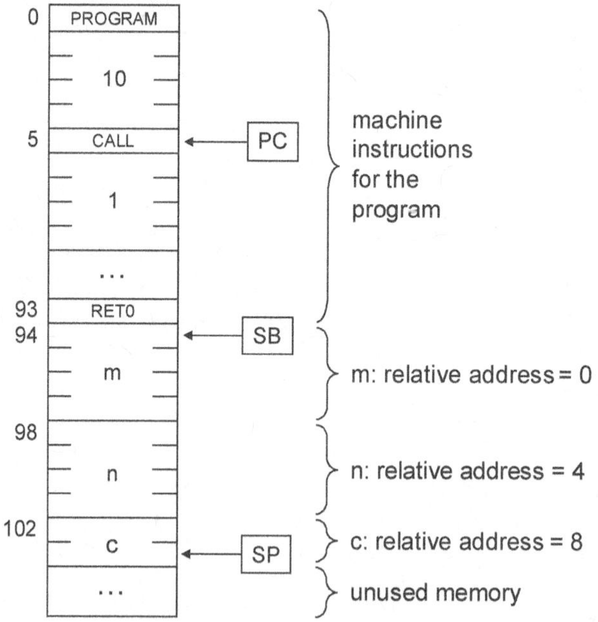

10.5 Using the Stack to Hold Temporary Values

The part of memory below the CVM instructions and global variables is used as a run-time stack that holds subprogram activation records (discussed in Chapter 13) and temporary, intermediate values. As machine instructions are executed, the stack grows and shrinks. The run-time stack is empty at both the start and end of each CPRL statement in the main program.

As an example showing the stack storing temporary values, let's assume the following.

- register `SB` has the value `100`
- integer variable `x` has relative address `0`
- integer variable `y` has value `5` and relative address `4`
- integer variable `z` has value `13` and relative address `8`

The CPRL assignment statement

```
x := 2*y + z;
```

will compile to the following CVM instructions.

```
LDGADDR 0
LDCINT 2
LDGADDR 4
LOADW
MUL
LDGADDR 8
LOADW
ADD
STOREW
```

We can visualize how the run-time stack is used to store temporary values by using a sequence of diagrams showing the state of the stack after execution of each machine instruction.

The stack is empty at the start of the CPRL assignment statement.

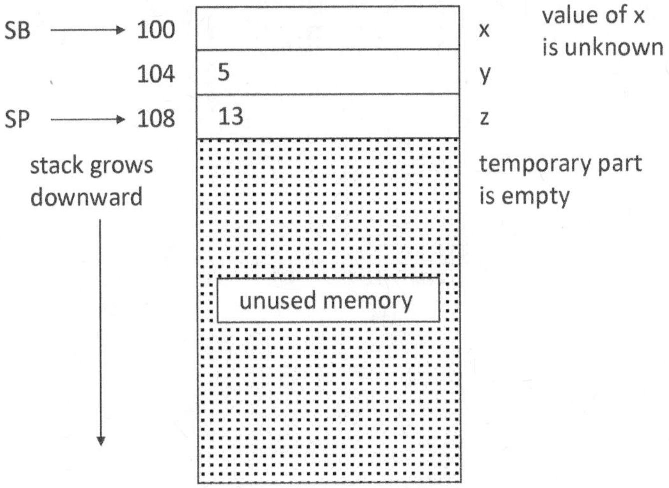

After execution of `LDGADDR 0`:

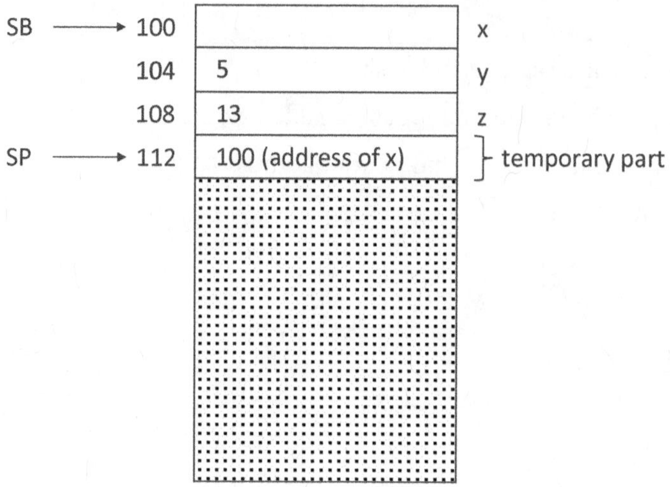

After execution of `LDCINT 2`:

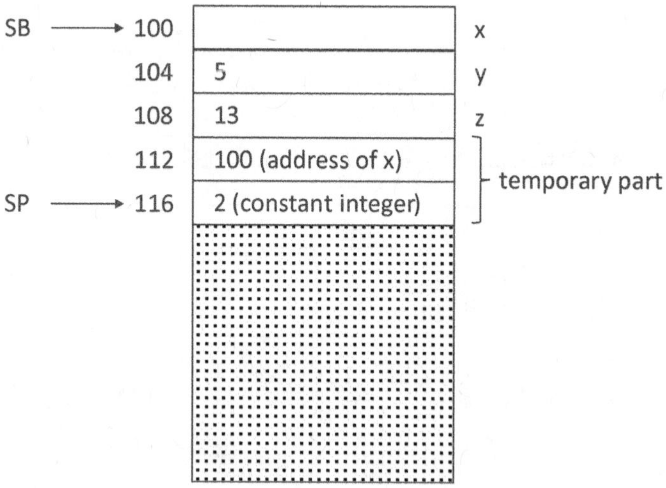

After execution of `LDGADDR 4`:

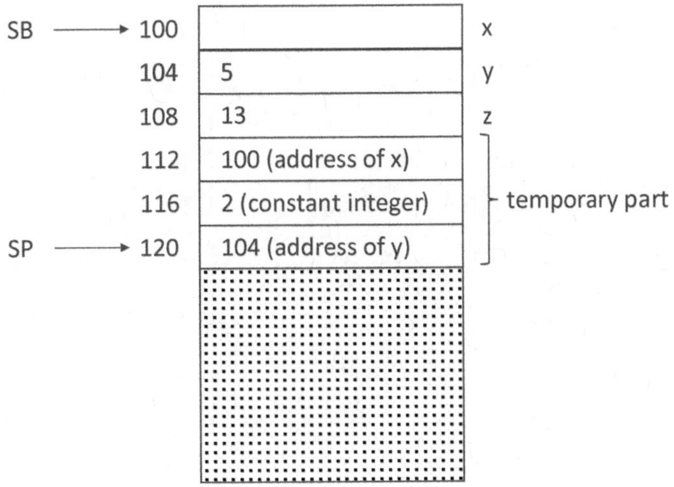

After execution of `LOADW`:

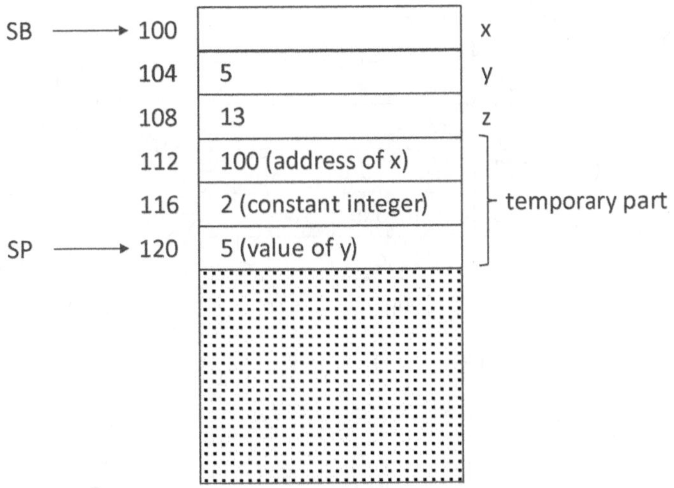

After execution of `MUL`:

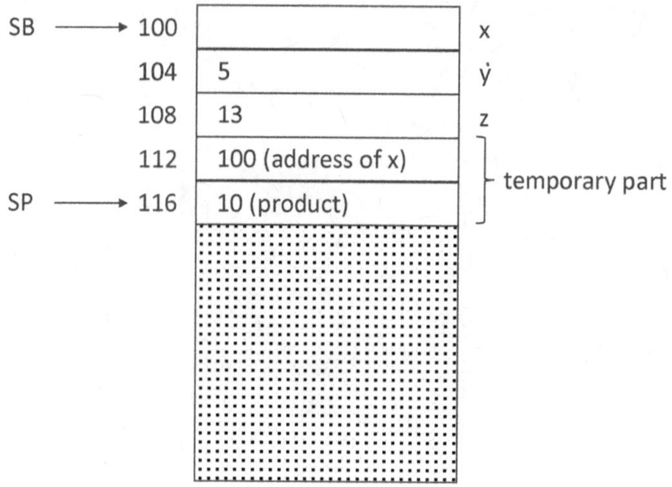

After execution of `LDGADDR 8`:

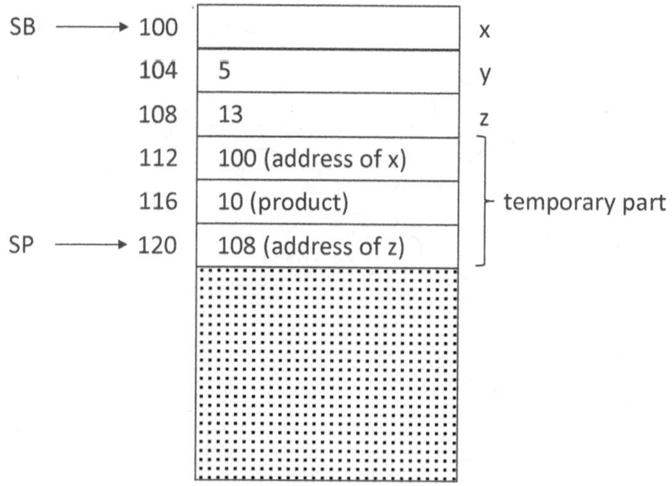

After execution of `LOADW`:

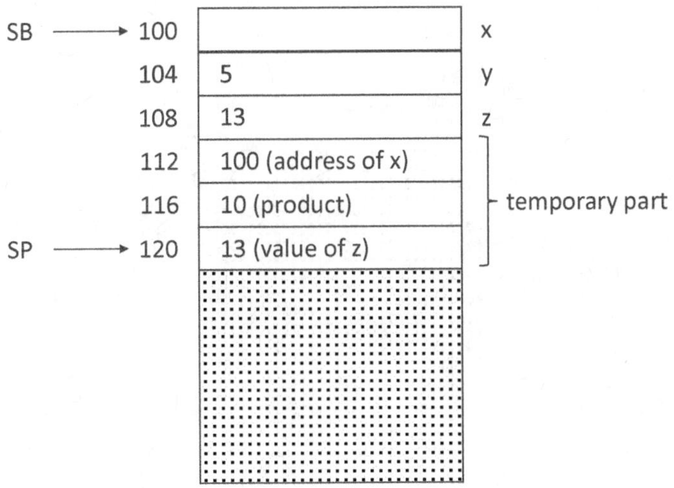

After execution of `ADD`:

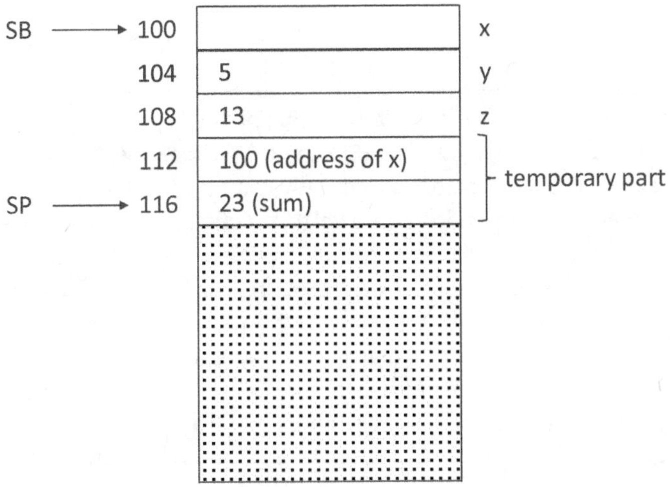

After execution of the final machine instruction `STOREW`:

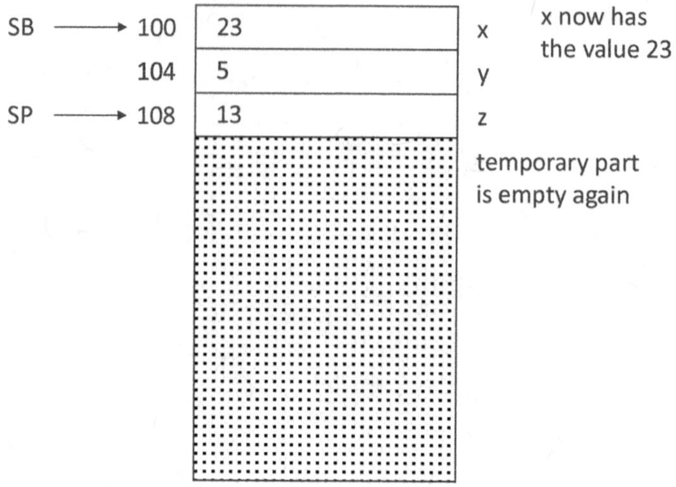

Note that at this point, variable `x` has now been assigned the value `23`, and the run-time stack is empty again.

> Many virtual machines use a stack architecture, including the Java Virtual Machine (JVM), the Microsoft .NET Common Language Runtime (CLR), and CPython, the Standard Python interpreter. But some virtual machines use explicitly named virtual registers as source and destination parameters for instructions. Noteworthy examples of register-based virtual machines include the Android Runtime (ART) and Google's V8 JavaScript Engine, which is used by Google Chrome and Node.js. For a stack architecture, the individual instructions are generally smaller, but a given task requires more instructions. Register-based virtual machines generally outperform stack-based virtual machines in raw execution speed, but the use of Just-In-Time (JIT) compilers minimizes the difference. One of the main advantages of a stack architecture is that it simplifies compiler development.

10.6 Essential Terms and Concepts

- arithmetic opcodes
- bitwise opcodes
- `BP`
- branch opcodes
- `HP`
- I/O opcodes
- logical opcodes
- load/store opcodes
- `PC`
- program/procedure opcodes
- relative address
- `SB`
- shift opcodes
- `SP`
- stack architecture
- string concatenation opcode
- type conversion opcodes
- word (in CVM)

10.7 Exercises

1. What does it mean when we say that CVM uses a stack architecture? Explain and give an example (e.g., explain how the `ADD` instruction works in CVM).
2. Name and describe the 5 internal/special purpose registers of CVM.
3. Fill in the blank relative to CVM.
   a. CVM has ______ internal (i.e., special purpose) registers. (How many?)
   b. A word consists of ______ byte(s). (How many?)
   c. Boolean values are represented using ________ byte(s). (How many?)
   d. Character values are represented using ________ byte(s). (How many?)
   e. Integer values are represented using ________ byte(s). (How many?)
   f. Each CVM opcode occupies ______ byte(s). (How many?)
   g. CVM is __________ -addressable. (Give a unit of memory.)
   h. All variable addressing is performed relative to ______ or ______. (Which registers?)
4. Suppose the first two global declarations in a program are as follows.

```
var x, y : Integer;
var b : Boolean;
```

   a. What is the relative address of `x`?
   b. What is the relative address of `y`?
   c. What is the relative address of `b`?

5. Assume that the first two global declarations in a program are as shown in exercise 4 above, and assume that `SB` has the value `102`.

   a. What is the absolute address of `x`?

   b. What is the absolute address of `y`?

   c. What is the absolute address of `b`?

Chapter 11
Code Generation

Code generation depends not only on the source language, but it also depends very heavily on the target machine, making it harder to develop general principles. However, we can describe some broad guidelines and templates for generating code.

During code generation, we must never lose sight of the most important rule.

> **First Rule of Code Generation: The resulting object code must be semantically equivalent to the source program.**

I remember vividly the first time I encountered a bug in a commercially available compiler. From that point on I had difficulty trusting that compiler. Fortunately, this turned out to be a very rare occurrence. While bugs might exist in commercially available compilers, most of them don't manifest in normal, day-to-day software development.

11.1 Overview of Code Generation

Other than I/O errors, any errors encountered during code generation represent internal errors and should never occur. We will report any errors, but there will be no attempt at error recovery. Also, we occasionally use assertions to make sure that everything is consistent, but recall that assertions are used only to help us debug the compiler. They should never occur, and any related error messages are intended for the compiler writer, not for the programmer using the compiler.

In this chapter we will concentrate on code generation for the CPRL/`0` subset; i.e., no subprograms other than `main()`; no arrays, enumerated types, strings, or records; only global declarations. Chapters 13-17 will discuss details of constraint analysis and code generation for subprograms, arrays, enums, strings, and records.

Using the CVM as the target machine simplifies some aspects of code generation that must be addressed on most "real" machines, such as I/O and the efficient use of general-purpose registers. Generating assembly language rather than actual machine language also simplifies code generation. For example, the assembler keeps track of the address of each machine instruction, maps labels to machine addresses, and handles the details of branch instructions. If we were targeting actual CVM machine code, these actions would need to be performed by the compiler.

Method `emit()`

Code generation is performed by the `emit()` methods in the AST classes. Similar to the implementation of the `checkConstraints()` methods, most of the AST classes delegate some or all code generation to component classes within the tree. Calls to `emit()` for component classes should use only structural references, as described in Section 8.5.

As an example, class `Program` contains a list of initial declarations and a list of subprogram declarations. Code generation for class `Program` contains two `for` loops, one that calls `emit()` for each of the initial declarations and another one that calls `emit()` for each of the subprogram declarations.

```
@Override
public void emit() throws CodeGenException
  {
    setRelativeAddresses();

    // no need to emit PROGRAM instruction if varLength == 0
    if (varLength > 0)
        emit("PROGRAM " + varLength);

    for (var decl : initialDecls)
        decl.emit();

    emit("CALL _main");
    emit("HALT");

    for (var decl : subprogramDecls)
        decl.emit();
  }
```

Class `AST` defines five methods that write assembly language to the target file.

```
protected void emitLoadInst(Type t)
protected void emitStoreInst(Type t)
protected void emitStoreInst(int numBytes)
protected void emitLabel(String label)   // appends ":" to label
protected void emit(String instruction)
```

These are the only methods that actually write to the assembly source code file. Since all abstract syntax tree classes are subclasses (either directly or indirectly) of class `AST`, all abstract syntax tree classes inherit these code-generation methods. All `emit()` methods involved in code generation must call one or more of these methods, or they must call another method that calls one or more of these methods, to write out the assembly language during code generation.

11.2 Labels and Branching

In the context of CVM assembly language, a label is simply a name for a location in memory. The compiler uses labels for branching, both forward and backward.

Here are a couple of examples.

- A `loop` statement needs to branch backward to the beginning of the loop.
- An `if` statement with an `else` part needs to branch to the `else` part if the condition is false. If the condition is true, it needs to execute the `then` statements and then branch over the `else` part.

Branches (a.k.a. jumps) are relative. The assembler computes the offset. For example, `BR L5` could translate to "branch `22`" (forward `22` bytes) or "branch `-12`" (backward `12` bytes).

Labels are implemented within the class `AST`. The key method is `newLabel()`, which returns a string to be used for a label.

```
/**
 * Returns a new value for a label.  This method should
 * be called once for each label before code generation.
 */
protected final String newLabel()
```

Labels returned from `newLabel()` are strings of the form "`L1`", "`L2`", "`L3`", ... During code generation, the compiler keeps track of label numbers so that a new label is returned each time the method is called.

As an example, let's consider the implementation of `emit()` for a loop statement. The AST class `LoopStmt` uses two labels.

```
private String L1 = newLabel();    // label for start of loop
private String L2 = newLabel();    // label for end of loop
```

The actual values assigned to the label variables by calls to `newLabel()` do not matter. What matters is that the values are unique and can be used as targets for branches. Note that `L1` and `L2` above are the local names for the label variables within class `LoopStmt`. The actual string values of `L1` and `L2` would be different; e.g., "`L12`" and "`L13`".

CVM Branch Instructions

CVM has nine branch instructions.

`BR`	unconditional branch
`BE`	branch if equal
`BNE`	branch if not equal
`BG`	branch if greater
`BGE`	branch if greater or equal
`BL`	branch if less
`BLE`	branch if less or equal
`BZ`	branch zero (branch if false)
`BNZ`	branch nonzero (branch if true)

These branch instructions are used to implement control flow logic within a subprogram.

Emitting Code for an Unconditional Branch

An unconditional branch in CVM has the form

```
BR Ln
```

where `Ln` is the label of the instruction that is the target of the branch; e.g., `L16`. The assembler converts

```
BR Ln
```

to a branch based on the relative offset of the target instruction. For example, depending on the relationship of the label to the branch instruction, "`BR L16`" would be converted to something like "`BR 22`" (branch forward 22 bytes) or "`BR -12`" (branch backward 12 bytes). At the machine level for CVM, each branch instruction occupies 5 bytes: 1 byte for the opcode and 4 bytes for the offset.

The actual code to emit an unconditional branch looks like the following.

```
emit("BR " + L2);
```

In this example `L2` is just the name of a string variable that holds the actual label value.

> Consider a disassembled instruction of the form
>
> ```
> 128:   BR 85
> 133:   ...
> ```
>
> where the address of the branch instruction is 128. When executing this branch instruction, the program counter (register PC) has already been updated to the next instruction prior to execution of the branch, and so the branch instruction would add 85 to the address of the instruction following the branch instruction; i.e., 85 + 133 or 218. Thus, after executing the branch instruction, the program counter would have the value 218.

Emitting Code for Branch Instructions

First consider code generation based on relational operators such as > or <=. The corresponding conditional branch instructions involve the comparison of two integer values which are already at the top of the run-time stack. These instructions remove the two integers from the top of the stack, compare them, and branch accordingly.

For example, suppose that we have loaded (pushed) two integer values `x` and `y` onto the stack in that order; i.e., `x` was pushed before `y`. The instruction

```
BGE Ln
```

will remove (pop) the two values from the stack and branch to the specified label if `x` is greater than or equal to `y`. Since branch instructions based on relational operators compare only integers, values with smaller types (e.g., `Boolean` or `Char`) will need to be "promoted" to integers before calling one of these instructions.

As a specific example, suppose we have a relational expression used as part of a while condition in a loop.

```
while x <= y loop ...
```

In this case, if the condition evaluates to **false**, we want to generate code to jump over the statements in the body of the loop; i.e., we want to generate code similar to the following.

```
... // emit code to leave the values of x and y on the top of the stack
BG L2
...
```

As a second example, consider the same relational expression used as part of an exit-when statement.

```
exit when x <= y;
```

In this case, if the condition evaluates to **true**, we want to generate code to branch to the end of the enclosing loop; i.e., we want to generate code similar to the following.

```
... // emit code to leave the values of x and y on the top of the stack
BLE L2
```

Note that in the first example we wanted to branch if the relational expression was false, and in the second example we wanted to branch if the relational expression was true.

Now consider branch instructions based on boolean expressions that don't involve relational operators. An example would be something like

```
if b then ...
```

where `b` is a boolean variable. In this case, code generation for the expression would leave the boolean value (one byte) on the top of the run-time stack, and we would want to branch based on this boolean value, where a value of zero is interpreted as false and a nonzero value is interpreted as true. For these situations we would use branch instructions `BZ` and `BNZ`, which pop a byte off the stack and branch accordingly.

In addition to the standard `emit()` method for an expression, which leaves the value of an expression on the top of the run-time stack, we introduce a couple of helper methods for branching. Class `Expression` defines a method named `emitBranch()` that emits code to push a boolean value on the run-time stack plus code that branches based on that value. It is implemented as follows.

```
public void emitBranch(boolean condition, String label)
    throws CodeGenException
  {
    ...
    emit();  // leaves boolean expression value on top of stack
    emit(condition ? "BNZ " + label : "BZ " + label);
  }
```

As pointed out in the previous examples, sometimes we want to emit code to branch if the expression evaluates to true, and sometimes we want to emit code to branch if the expression evaluates to false. The boolean parameter `condition` in method `emitBranch()` specifies which option we want to use.

The default implementation of `emitBranch()` defined in class `Expression` works correctly for boolean expressions that don't involve relational operators, but we need to override it for relational expressions.

Here is an outline of the implementation of `emitBranch()` for class `RelationalExpr`.

```
@Override
public void emitBranch(boolean condition, String label) throws
CodeGenException
  {
    emitOperands();
    switch (operator().symbol())
      {
        case equals         -> emit(condition ? "BE "  + label
                                              : "BNE " + label);
        case notEqual       -> emit(condition ? "BNE " + label
                                              : "BE "  + label);
        case lessThan       -> emit(condition ? "BL "  + label
                                              : "BGE " + label);
        ...
        case greaterOrEqual -> emit(condition ? "BGE " + label
                                              : "BL "  + label);
        default ->
          {
            var position = operator().position();
            var errorMsg = "Invalid relational operator.";
            throw new CodeGenException(...)
          }
      }
  }
```

11.3 Load and Store Instructions

Class `AST` provides three helper methods for emitting load and store instructions for various types. The code generated by all three methods assumes that the target address for the load or store instruction is already on the top of the stack.

```
/**
 * Emits the appropriate LOAD instruction based on the type.
 */
protected void emitLoadInst(Type t)

/**
 * Emits the appropriate STORE instruction based on the type.
 */
protected void emitStoreInst(Type t)

/**
 * Emits a STORE instruction based on the number of bytes.
 */
protected void emitStoreInst(int numBytes)
```

Method `emitLoadInst(`Type `t)` emits the appropriate load instruction based on the size (number of bytes) of a type; i.e., it will emit one of the following load instructions.

- `LOADB` (load byte)
- `LOAD2B` (load 2 bytes)
- `LOADW` (load word, 4 bytes)
- `LOAD n` (load n bytes)

Each of these instructions pops an address from the top of the stack and then pushes (loads) the appropriate number of bytes starting at that address onto the stack. While the general-purpose `LOAD` instruction (the fourth one above) could be used in all situations, the `LOADB`, `LOAD2B`, and `LOADW` instructions are shorter (no extra argument to specify the number of bytes), faster, and representative of the most common use cases. As such, using the first three instructions represents a small performance improvement for the generated code. (See Chapter 12 for additional details on code optimization.)

Method `emitLoadInst()` is implemented as follows.

```
protected void emitLoadInst(Type t)
  {
    switch (t.size())
      {
        case 4  -> emit("LOADW");
        case 2  -> emit("LOAD2B");
        case 1  -> emit("LOADB");
        default -> emit("LOAD " + t.size());
      }
  }
```

Similarly, the first method `emitStoreInst(`Type `t)` emits the appropriate store instruction based on the size of a type; i.e., it will emit one of the following store instructions.

- `STOREB` (store byte)
- `STORE2B` (store 2 bytes)
- `STOREW` (store word, 4 bytes)
- `STORE n` (store n bytes)

Each of these instructions pops an address from the top of the stack and then pops (removes) the appropriate number of bytes from the stack and stores them at memory locations starting at that address. Method `emitStoreInst()` is implemented similar to `emitLoadInst()` shown above.

11.4 Computing Relative Addresses for Variables

Since all addressing is performed relative to a register, we will need to compute the relative address (offset) for each variable plus the total number of bytes of all variables for the program and for each subprogram. In addition, for subprograms, we will need to compute the relative address for each parameter. Discussion of these computations for subprograms will be postponed to Chapter 13. Here we focus solely on computing the relative address for each variable declared at global scope. You should review the discussion of relative addressing in Section 10.3 before continuing.

Class `VarDecl` stores the relative address of each variable in a map that associates the variable name with its relative address.

```
private Map<String, Integer> relAddrMap = new HashMap<>();
```

Class `VarDecl` also has a method named `setRelAddr()` that can be called to update the map, as shown in the code below. Method `setRelativeAddresses()` in class `Program` computes the relative addresses by looping over all identifiers declared in a `VarDecl`.

```
private void setRelativeAddresses()
  {
    // initial relative address is 0 for a program
    int currentAddr = 0;

    for (var decl : initialDecls)
      {
        if (decl instanceof VarDecl varDecl)
          {
            // set relative address for each identifier
            for (var idName : varDecl.idNames())
              {
                varDecl.setRelAddr(idName, currentAddr);
                currentAddr = currentAddr + varDecl.size();
              }
          }
      }
```

```
    // compute length of all variables
    varLength = currentAddr;
  }
```

The instance variable `varLength` records the total number of bytes for all variables declared at the program level.

Code Generation for Variable Addresses

For variables not used as expressions (e.g., on the left side of an assignment statement or in a `read` statement), code generation must leave the address of the variable on the top of the run-time stack. The CVM instruction `LDGADDR` (load global address) will push the (global) address for a variable onto the top of the run-time stack. For CPRL/`0`, all variables can use this instruction since they all have global scope.

For CPRL/`0`, method `emit()` in class `Variable` can be implemented simply as follows.

```
@Override
public void emit() throws CodeGenException
  {
    emit("LDGADDR " + decl.relAddr());

    ...     // additional code if the variable is used as an expression
            // (see Code Generation for Variable Values in section 11.5)
  }
```

For full CPRL, we will need to modify `emit()` extensively to correctly handle parameters, variables declared at `local` scope level, index expressions for array and string variables, and field expressions for record and string variables. These details are covered in subsequent chapters.

11.5 Expressions

For expressions, code generation must leave the **value** of the expression on the top of the run-time stack. The size (number of bytes) of the value will depend on the type of the variable; e.g.,

- 1 byte for a boolean
- 2 bytes for a character
- 4 bytes for an integer
- 4 bytes for a string

A string is actually composed of several bytes (4 bytes for the length plus 2 bytes for each character) but we only need to generate code for the string address.

Code Generation Involving Type Byte

When a value of type `Byte` are used in expressions, it is promoted (a.k.a., coerced or automatically converted) to type `Integer` using the CVM instruction `BYTE2INT`, as illustrated by the following excerpt from AST class `Variable`.

```
if (type() == Type.Byte)
  {
    emit("BYTE2INT");
    setType(Type.Integer);
  }
```

Code Generation for `ConstValue`

An object of class `ConstValue` is either a literal or a declared `const` identifier. Class `ConstValue` has a method `intValue()` that returns the value of the constant as an integer. We can use this method together with the appropriate "load constant" instruction to generate code for the value of the constant.

Method `emit()` for class `ConstValue` is relatively straightforward. Note the calls to private helper method `intValue()`, which uses class `IntUtil` (in package `common.util`) to convert a string of digits representing an integer into an integer value.

```
@Override
public void emit() throws CodeGenException
  {
    if (type() == Type.Integer || type() instanceof EnumType)
        emit("LDCINT " + intValue());
    else if (type() == Type.Boolean || type() == Type.Byte)
        emit("LDCB " + intValue());
    else if (type() == Type.Char)
        emit("LDCCH " + literal.text());
    else if (type() == Type.String)
        emit("LDCSTR " + literal.text());
    else
      {
        var errorMsg = "Invalid type for constant value.";
        throw new CodeGenException(literal.position(), errorMsg);
      }
  }
```

Code Generation for Variable Values

When a variable is used as an expression, we need to generate code that pushes the value of the variable onto the stack. For example, consider the following assignment statement.

```
x := y;
```

As discussed in Section 11.4, code generation for variable x should leave the **address** of the variable on the top of the stack. However, we are using variable y as an expression, and code generation for y should push the **value** of y onto the stack. Class `Variable` has a boolean-valued property named `useAsExpression` which is initialized to `false`. When parsing a variable that is used as an expression (e.g., on the right side of an assignment statement), method `parseVariableExpr()` will set the value to `true`.

```
private Expression parseVariableExpr() throws IOException
  {
    try
      {
        var variable = parseVariableCommon();
        variable.setUseAsExpression(true);
        return variable;
      }
    catch (ParserException e)
      {
        ...
      }
  }
```

Initial code for method `emit()` in class `Variable` leaves the address of the variable on the top of the run-time stack. Then, if the value of property `useAsExpression` is `true`, method `emit()` calls `emitLoadInst()`, which pops the address off the stack and pushes the appropriate number of bytes (the variable value) onto the stack, starting at that memory address. In addition, a variable of type `Byte` is promoted to type `Integer`.

```
@Override
public void emit() throws CodeGenException
  {
    ...   // code that leaves the variable address on top of stack
          // (see Code Generation for Variable Addresses in section 11.4)

    if (useAsExpression)
      {
        // Previous code leaves address of this variable on top
        // of stack.  We need to emit the value at that address.
        // Promote Byte values to Integer if necessary.
        emitLoadInst(type());


        if (type() == Type.Byte)
          {
            emit("BYTE2INT");
            setType(Type.Integer);
          }
      }
  }
```

Code Generation for Unary Expressions

A unary expression contains an operator and one operand, where the operand is an expression. There are three types of unary expressions in CPRL.

- Unary negation for integer expressions: `-x`
- Bitwise not (complement) for numeric expressions: `~x`
- Logical not for boolean expressions: `not valid`

Note that the operand can be an arbitrary expression of the appropriate type, not simply a single variable; e.g., `-(2*x + y)`. For all three types of unary expressions, code generation uses the following pattern.

```
emit code for the operand
promote Byte operand to Integer for ~
emit code to perform the operation
```

Code Generation for Binary Expressions

A binary expression contains an operator and two operands, each of which is an expression. Examples of binary expressions include addition for integer expressions and relational expressions for integers, characters, etc. (e.g., `x <= y`). Code generation for a binary expression usually conforms to the following pattern.

```
emit code for the left operand
emit code for the right operand
emit code to perform the operation
```

Note that we are generating code that will evaluate the expression using a "postfix" (a.k.a. "reverse polish") notation approach.

The implementation of method `emit()` for class `AddingExpr` follows this pattern.

```
@Override
public void emit() throws CodeGenException
  {
    leftOperand().emit();
    rightOperand().emit();

    switch (operator().symbol())
      {
        case plus       -> emit("ADD");
        case minus      -> emit("SUB");
        case bitwiseOr  -> emit("BITOR");
        case bitwiseXor -> emit("BITXOR");
```

```
      default ->
        {
          var errorPos = operator().position();
          var errorMsg = "Invalid adding operator.";
          throw new InternalCompilerException(errorPos, errorMsg);
        }
    }
}
```

While the above code is correct for CPRL/0, we will need to revisit this method in Chapter 16 when we discuss concatenation of strings.

Code Generation for Logical Expressions

In general, code generation needs to consider whether or not the language requires logical expressions to use short-circuit evaluation (a.k.a. early exit). Similar to most high-level languages, CPRL has such a requirement.

Here are some examples of short-circuit evaluation. In these examples, `expr1` and `expr2` can be arbitrary Boolean expressions consisting of multiple operators and operands.

Example 1. Given an expression of the form $expr_1$ `and` $expr_2$, the left operand ($expr_1$) is evaluated. If the left operand is false, the right operand ($expr_2$) is not evaluated and the truth value for the compound expression is considered to be false. Otherwise, the right operand ($expr_2$) is evaluated, and its truth value becomes the value for the compound expression.

Example 2. Given an expression of the form $expr_1$ `or` $expr_2$, the left operand ($expr_1$) is evaluated. If the left operand is true, the right operand ($expr_2$) is not evaluated and the truth value for the compound expression is considered to be true. Otherwise, the right operand ($expr_2$) is evaluated, and its truth value becomes the value for the compound expression.

These examples are summarized in the following truth tables.

$expr_1$	$expr_2$	$expr_1$ and $expr_2$
true	true	true
true	false	false
false	not evaluated	false

$expr_1$	$expr_2$	$expr_1$ or $expr_2$
false	true	true
false	false	false
true	not evaluated	true

Using a code generation approach similar to that for `AddingExpr` will not result in short-circuit evaluation. For example, in generating code for an "`and`" expression, we can't simply emit code for left operand, emit code for the right operand, and then "`and`" them together.

From a programmer's perspective, it is almost always preferable for a programming language to use short-circuit evaluation for logical expressions, and not simply for performance reasons. Consider the following Java excerpt.

```
if (person != null && person.name().equals("John"))
  {
    statement₁;
    statement₂;
  }
else
  {
    statement₃;
    statement₄;
  }
```

If the first condition in the if statement (`person != null`) is false, then we don't want to evaluate the second condition, since doing so would throw the dreaded null pointer exception. Try to rewrite the above logic without assuming short-circuit evaluation of logical expressions. First, you will need to use nested if statements. But beyond that, you will need to determine how to handle the else statement. The most straightforward approach for the else statement is simply to repeat it for both if statements.

Even if we disregard the possibility of null references or pointers, the problem still exists. Consider, for example the following logic.

```
if (y != 0 && x/y > 0)
  {
    statement₁;
    statement₂;
  }
else
  {
    statement₃;
    statement₄;
  }
```

If the first condition is false, then an attempt to evaluate the second condition would result in division by zero.

Shown below is the CPRL code template for logical "`and`" with short-circuit evaluation. The actual code in the `emit()` method of class `LogicalExpr` is slightly more complicated since it interleaves the cases for both logical operators `and`/`or`.

```
    ...
    // if left operand evaluates to true, branch
    // to code that will evaluate right operand
    leftOperand.emitBranch(true, L1);
    LDCB 0
    BR  L2
L1:
    ...  // emit code for the right operand
         // (leaves boolean result on top of stack)

L2:
```

The branch instruction emitted by `leftOperand.emitBranch(...)` above is either `BNZ` or `BZ`, and when it is executed, the boolean value on the top of the stack is popped off. The instruction "`LDCB 0`" is needed to restore the expression value `0` (false) to the top of the stack. By default, the assembler will optimize "`LDCB 0`" to the single opcode instruction `LDCB0`.

Code Generation for a Conditional Expression

Recall that a conditional expression involves three expressions, where the first expression must have type `Boolean`, and the last two expressions must have exactly the same type. An example would be the right-hand side of the following assignment statement for integers.

```
x := n > m ? n : m;    // x := max of m and n
```

Within class `ConditionalExpr`, we call the first (boolean) expression `condition` and the last two expressions `exprTrue` and `exprFalse`. Since we already know how to generate code for branches, the code for method `emit()` in class `ConditionalExpr` is relatively straightforward. Here is the code template.

```
    ...  // branch to L1 if condition is false
    ...  // emit code for exprTrue
    ...  // branch to L2
L1:
     ...  // emit code for exprFalse
L2:
```

11.6 Statements

Code generation for statements can be described by showing several representative examples of code templates or patterns, where a code generation template specifies some explicit instructions and delegates portions of the code generation to nested components (child nodes in the abstract syntax tree). Code generation templates for control structures will often use labels to designate destination addresses for branches.

11.6.1 Code Generation for `AssignmentStmt`

Grammar Rule

```
variable ":=" expression ";" .
```

Here is a general description of the steps involved in code generation for an assignment statement.

- Emit code for the variable on left side of the assignment symbol. This code should leave the variable's address on top of the run-time stack.
- Emit code for the expression on right side of the assignment symbol. This code should leave the expression's value on top of the run-time stack.
- If both the variable and expression have the same type, emit the appropriate store instruction based on the expression's type. This code removes the value and the address from the top of the run-time stack and copies the value to the address using method `emitStoreInst(expr.type())`. If the variable has type `Byte` but the expression has type `Integer`, then we need to convert the expression type to `Byte` (using opcode `INT2BYTE`) before copying its value.

Code generation template when both the variable and the expression have type `Integer`

```
...  // emit code for variable
...  // emit code for expression
STOREW
```

Code generation template when both the variable and the expression have type `Boolean`

```
...  // emit code for variable
...  // emit code for expression
STOREB
```

Code generation for the assignment becomes a little more complicated when either the variable or the expression has type `Byte`, since we want to allow the assignment of byte values to a variable of type `Integer`, and vice-versa. These cases are handled by an `if` statement based on the two types. Here is the final code for method `emit()` in class `AssignmentStmt`.

Method emit() for class `AssignmentStmt`

```
@Override
public void emit() throws CodeGenException
  {
    variable.emit();
    expr.emit();

    // Emit the appropriate STORE instruction based on the types
    // of the variable and the expression being assigned.
```

```
    if (variable.type() == expr.type())
        emitStoreInst(expr.type());    // handle most common case quickly
    else if (variable.type() == Type.Byte && expr.type() == Type.Integer)
      {
        emit("INT2BYTE");
        emit("STOREB");
      }

    else
        emitStoreInst(expr.type());
  }
```

11.6.2 Code Generation for `CompoundStmt`

Grammar Rule

```
compoundStmt = "{" statements "}" .
```

Code generation template for a list of statements

```
for each statement in statements
    ...  // emit code for statement
```

Method `emit()` in class `CompoundStmt`

```
@Override
public void emit() throws CodeGenException
  {
    for (var stmt : statements)
        stmt.emit();
  }
```

11.6.3 Code Generation for `LoopStmt`

Grammar Rule

```
loopStmt = [ "while" booleanExpr ] "loop" statement .
```

Code generation template for loop without a `while` prefix

```
L1:
   ...  // emit code for statement
        // (usually a compound statement containing an exit statement)
   BR L1
L2:
```

Code generation template for loop with a `while` prefix

```
L1:
    ... // emit code to evaluate while expression
    ... // branch to L2 if value of expression is false
    ... // emit code for statement
    BR L1
L2:
```

Method `emit()` for `LoopStmt`

```
@Override
public void emit() throws CodeGenException
  {
    emitLabel(L1);

    if (whileExpr != null)
        whileExpr.emitBranch(false, L2);
    statement.emit();
    emit("BR " + L1);

    emitLabel(L2);
  }
```

11.6.4 Code Generation for `forLoopStmt`

Grammar Rule

```
forLoopStmt = "for" varId "in" expr ".." expr "loop" statement .
```

Code generation template for `forLoopStmt`

Code generation for a `forLoopStmt` is straightforward since it is equivalent to an assignment statement that initializes the loop variable followed by a while loop that updates the loop variable at the end of the loop.

For example,

```
for i in expr1..expr2 loop
    <statement>
```

is equivalent to

```
i := expr1;
while i <= expr2 loop
  {
    <statement>
    i := i + 1;
  }
```

11.6.5 Code Generation for `ExitStmt`

Grammar Rule

```
exitStmt = "exit" [ "when" booleanExpr ] ";" .
```

The `exit` statement must obtain the end label, say `L2`, from its enclosing loop statement.

Code generation template when the exit statement does not have a `when` boolean expression suffix

```
BR L2
```

Code generation template when the exit statement has a `when` boolean expression suffix

```
... // emit code that will branch to L2 if the
    // "when" boolean expression evaluates to true
```

Method `emit()` for `ExitStmt`

```
@Override
public void emit() throws CodeGenException
  {
    if (whenExpr != null)
        whenExpr.emitBranch(true, loopStmt.exitLabel());
    else
        emit("BR " + loopStmt.exitLabel());
  }
```

11.6.6 Code Generation for `IfStmt`

Grammar Rule

```
ifStmt = "if" booleanExpr "then" statement [ "else" statement ] .
```

Code generation template for an if statement

```
    ... // emit code that will branch to L1 if
        //     the boolean expression is false
    ... // emit code for then statement
    ... // if else statement is not null, emit "BR L2"
L1:
    ... // if else statement is not null
    ... //     emit code for else statement
L2:
```

11.6.7 Code Generation for ReadStmt

Grammar Rule

```
readStmt = "read" variable ";" .
```

Code generation template for a variable of type Integer

```
... // emit code for variable
    // (leaves variable's address on top of stack)
GETINT
```

Code generation template for a variable of type Char

```
... // emit code for variable
    // (leaves variable's address on top of stack)
GETCH
```

11.6.8 Code Generation for OutputStmt

Recall that an `OutputStmt` is returned by parsing methods `parseWriteStmt()` and `parseWritelnStmt()`.

Grammar Rules

```
writeStmt   = "write" expressions ";" .
writelnStmt = "writeln" [ expressions ] ";" .
expressions = expression { "," expression } .
```

An `OutputStmt` contains a list of expressions.

Code generation template for OutputStmt

```
for each expression
    ... // emit output instruction based on the expression type
```

Since there is no `PUTBYTE` opcode in the CVM, an expression value of type `Byte` or `Boolean` must first be converted to an integer value using opcode `BYTE2INT`. Opcode `PUTINT` is used for writing `Byte` and `Boolean` values.

11.7 Initial Declarations

Most initial declarations don't need to emit any code, but a variable declaration with a nonempty initializer must emit code to perform the initialization. In subsequent chapters we will need to address local variables and composite types, but for CPRL/0 we can ignore these features. Scalar types are initialized using constant values, and initialization in CPRL/0 looks very similar to that of an assignment statement.

Method `emit()` in class `VarDecl` (for CPRL/0)

```
@Override
public void emit() throws CodeGenException
  {
    // emit code only if the initializer is not empty
    if (!initializer.isEmpty())
      {
        for (var identifier : identifiers)
          {
            // load the address of the variable
            emit("LDGADDR " + relAddr(identifier.text()));

            if (initializer instanceof ConstValue constValue)
              {
                constValue.emit();
                emitStoreInst(constValue.type());
              }
            else
              {
               var errorMsg = "Unexpected initializer type.";
               throw new InternalCompilerException(position(), errorMsg);
              }
          }
      }
  }
```

11.8 Disassembler

An **assembler** translates from assembly language to machine code. A **disassembler** is a program that translates from machine code (binary file) back to assembly language (text file). A disassembler for CVM machine code is available for download from the book's GitHub repository – see Java source file `cvm.Disassembler.java`. While technically not required for the implementation of a compiler, the disassembler can be useful when debugging the generated code.

Here is an example showing the source code, disassembled object code, and an annotated version of the disassembled object code that illustrates more clearly how the source code statements are implemented in CVM. Note that the disassembler output has the machine address for each CVM instruction.

Code Generation Example

Source Code

```
var x : Integer;
const n := 5;

proc main()
  {
    x := 1;

    while x <= n loop
        x := x + 1;

    writeln "x = ", x;
  }
```

Disassembled Machine Code (includes optimizations)

```
 0:  PROGRAM 4
 5:  CALL 1
10:  HALT
11:  LDGADDR 0
16:  LDCINT1
17:  STOREW
18:  LDGADDR 0
23:  LOADW
24:  LDCINT 5
29:  BG 18
34:  LDGADDR 0
39:  LDGADDR 0
44:  LOADW
45:  INC
46:  STOREW
47:  BR -34
52:  LDCSTR  "x = "
65:  PUTSTR 4
70:  LDGADDR 0
75:  LOADW
76:  PUTINT
77:  PUTEOL
78:  RET0
```

Note that, without optimization,

- the single opcode instruction `LDCINT1` (1 byte) at memory address 16 would be `LDCINT 1` (5 bytes),
- the single opcode instruction `RET0` (1 byte) at memory address 78 would be `RET 0` (5 bytes),
- and the `INC` instruction (1 byte) at memory address 45 would look like the following two instructions (6 bytes).

```
LDCINT 1
ADD
```

Annotated Disassembled Object Code

```
// reserve 4 bytes for x
 0:  PROGRAM 4

// call main()
 5:  CALL 1
10:  HALT

// x := 1;
11:  LDGADDR 0
16:  LDCINT1
17:  STOREW

// while x <= n loop
18:  LDGADDR 0
23:  LOADW
24:  LDCINT 5
29:  BG 18

// x := x + 1
34:  LDGADDR 0
39:  LDGADDR 0
44:  LOADW
45:  INC
46:  STOREW

// end of loop
47:  BR -34

// writeln "x = ", x;
52:  LDCSTR  "x = "
65:  PUTSTR 4
70:  LDGADDR 0
75:  LOADW
76:  PUTINT
77:  PUTEOL

// return from main
78:  RET0
```

11.9 Essential Terms and Concepts

assembler	binary expression
branching/branch instructions	disassembler
`emit()` (method)	`emitBranch()` (method)
`emitLoadInst(Type t)` (method)	`emitStoreInst(Type t)` (method)
`newLabel()` (method)	label
relative addressing	short-circuit evaluation
unary expression	variable
variable expression	

11.10 Exercises

1. **Project Assignment.** Implement **Project 6: Code Generation for CPRL/`0`** as described in Appendix A.
2. Give the opcodes and descriptions for the nine branch instructions in CVM.
3. Fill in the blanks.
   a. Code generation is performed by method ____________________ in the AST classes.
   b. A/An ____________________ translates from assembly language to machine code.
   c. A/An ____________________ translates from machine code to assembly language.
4. True or False (T or F)
   a. Code generation depends on both the source language and the target machine.
   b. Most AST classes delegate some of the code generation to component classes.
   c. Code generation for a variable (e.g., on the left side of an assignment statement) leaves the variable's address on the top of the stack.
   d. Code generation for an expression leaves the value of the expression on the top of the stack.
   e. CPRL requires logical expressions to use short-circuit evaluation.
   f. A label is a name for a location in memory.
   g. Method `newLabel()` returns a different label (string) every time it is called.

5. Explain the difference between the instruction `LDCINT 1` and the instruction `LDCINT1`. Also, examine the set of CVM instructions defined in Appendix E for other similar instructions that can be optimized from an opcode plus an integer to a single opcode. (Hint: There are five additional instructions similar to `LDCINT1`.)

6. Suppose that programming language 1 supports short-circuit evaluation of logical operators "`and`" ("`&&`") and "`or`" ("`||`"), and that programming language 2 does not. That is, programming language 2 evaluates both operands before performing the logical operation. Consider the following skeletal code in programming language 1 (with short-circuit evaluation).

```
if condition_1 and condition_2 then
   statement;
```

This skeletal code can be written equivalently in programming language 2 (without short-circuit evaluation) as follows.

```
if condition_1 then
    if condition_2 then
        statement;
```

Now suppose that you have the following skeletal code in programming language 1.

```
if condition_1 and condition_2 then
    statement_1;
else
    statement_2;
```

Rewrite this skeletal code in programming language 2 (without short-circuit evaluation).

Chapter 12
Code Optimization

Code optimization refers to code generation techniques and transformations that result in a semantically equivalent program that runs more efficiently; i.e., the program runs faster, uses less memory, or both. The term "optimization" is actually used improperly since the generated code is rarely optimal. A better name might be "code improvements," but the phrase "code optimization" is in widespread use, and we will continue to follow that practice.

No study of compilers would be complete without covering this topic, but the compiler project outlined in this book does not include an assignment on optimization. All target code is generated in the most straightforward manner. So, for example, when adding constant `1` to a variable, the instructions

```
LDCINT 1
ADD
```

are generated rather than the more optimized "`INC`" instruction. However, by default, some optimizations are performed by the assembler. After reading this chapter, students are encouraged to study the assembler's source code to see how these optimizations are implemented. Students can also use the provided disassembler to examine the optimized code and compare it to the code generated by their compilers. It is not common for an assembler to perform optimizations, but it is common for a compiler to perform optimizations on a low-level representation of the source code, and we can consider CVM assembly language to be a low-level representation for CPRL source code. Assembler optimizations can be turned off with the command line switch "`-opt:off`" if desired.

Code optimization often involves a time-space tradeoff in that techniques that make the code faster often require additional memory, and conversely. However, there are usually some optimizations that improve both run-time performance and memory utilization. Most compilers perform at least some optimization, but some compilers devote significant resources to optimization. Such compilers are sometimes called "optimizing compilers." An optimizing compiler can often generate object code that will perform at a level equivalent to the best hand-coded assembly language.

12.1 Overview of Code Optimization

While a one-pass compiler might perform minor optimizations as part of code generation, most compilers perform optimization on intermediate representations of the program; e.g., on a high-level representation such as abstract syntax trees or on a low-level representation, possibly even on machine code.

Optimizations are often classified as local or global. A local optimization is one that examines only a few statements at a time, while a global optimization looks at an entire compilation unit. Local optimizations are common. Global optimizations are much more difficult to implement. Optimizing compilers do both.

Optimizations are sometimes classified as being either machine dependent or machine independent. Machine-independent optimizations are performed on an intermediate representation of the program without any specific knowledge of the target machine, while machine-dependent optimizations are customized for a specific machine.

> William A. ("Bill") Wulf, a computer scientist who spent most of his adult life working on optimizing compilers, was often quoted as saying that "There is no such thing as a machine-independent optimization. Not one! People who use the phrase don't understand the problem! There are lots of semantics-preserving transformations that improve code size or speed for some machines under some circumstances. But those same transformations may be pessimizations for another machine!"

Code Optimization Issues

As with most software systems, compiler development must support a variety of conflicting objectives including minimizing the cost of implementation, minimizing the schedule for implementation, minimizing compilation time, maximizing the run-time performance of the generated object code, and minimizing the size of the generated object code. Adding optimizations to a compiler can impact cost and schedule, and performing optimizations during compilation can impact compilation times. There is overhead involved in implementing compiler optimizations, and whole-program or global optimization is time consuming and often difficult or impractical. Remember that occasionally, especially during development, faster compile times can be more important than more efficient object code.

> **Personal Anecdote**: The Ada programming language was accompanied by an extensive validation test suite, and one of the earliest validated compilers was developed by Digital Equipment Corporation (DEC). In a conversation with one of the compiler developers, he revealed that one of the Ada test programs gave them a lot of problems. When they finally tracked it down, they discovered that the error was not in the Ada-specific part of the compiler but in a common global optimizer that was used for all of their compilers. They wrote an equivalent PL/I program, and sure enough, it had the same error. They corrected the error in the global optimizer, and both the Ada program and the PL/I program ran correctly.

One cost-effective approach to implementing compiler optimizations is to let someone else do it. For example, by using a common, low-level intermediate language such as the one provided by the LLVM project, compiler developers get compiler optimizations and code generation for most common computer architectures with little cost beyond the time required to understand the LLVM Intermediate Representation (IR). This concept is illustrated in the following figure.

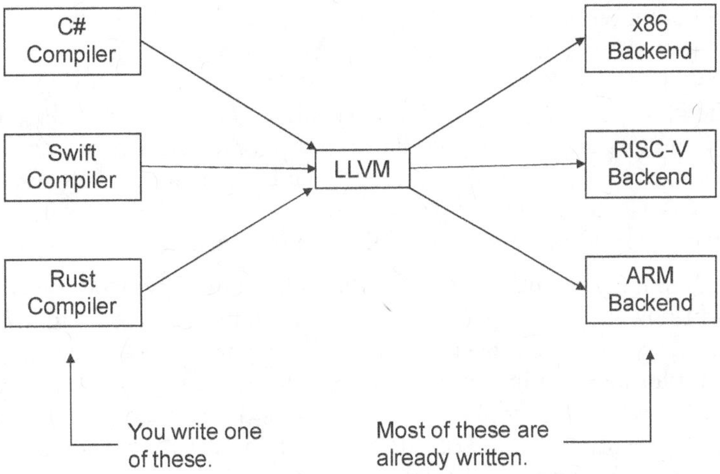

It is extremely difficult for a compiler to improve algorithmic complexity, and therefore the best source of optimization is often the programmer. No amount of compiler optimization is going to make a bubble sort run faster than a quick sort. Additionally, a programmer can use profiling to determine areas where optimization might have a significant impact and then rewrite time-critical code in assembly language.

There is an old programming adage that says you should "make the program correct before making it faster." With respect to compiler design, this means all optimizations should still produce semantically-equivalent object code. Compiler results should be tested both with and without optimizations to ensure that no optimization introduces an error.

Several common optimization themes have emerged over time and should be exploited by compiler developers. Here are just a few to think about.

- Optimize the common case even at the expense of a slow path. For example, suppose that there are two general approaches to implementing exception handling. One approach results in better overall performance of the generated code if no exceptions are thrown, but it results in slower performance whenever an exception is thrown and must be handled. The alternative approach implements the throwing and catching of exceptions more quickly, but it has a negative overall impact on the performance of the generated code if no exceptions are thrown. This guideline suggests that one should go with the first approach. (Note: This example involving exception handling was taken from a discussion the author had with a developer working on an actual commercial compiler.)
- Less code usually results in faster execution and lower product cost for embedded systems, where the code must be replicated in thousands of devices. If a compiler needs to make tradeoffs between faster execution and smaller code size, then there should be a compiler switch or pragma that the developer can use to give guidance to the compiler as to which one is preferred over the other.

- Exploit the computer architecture of the target machine. For example, generate code to exploit the memory hierarchy – registers first, then cache, then main memory, then disk (virtual memory). Register allocation is discussed in the following section, but in general, the idea is to improve locality by keeping related code and data as close together in memory as possible. Similarly, compiler developers can exploit parallelization in two ways, first by taking advantage of multiple processors to allow computations to be performed in parallel, and second by exploiting instruction pipelining; e.g., rearranging code to minimize pipeline hazards.

One interesting point about optimizations is that after some optimizations have been performed, additional potential optimizations can become more apparent. It is not uncommon for an optimization phase to make multiple passes over the code, with each pass looking for additional optimizations that might not have been detected during the previous pass. Compilers that implement extensive optimizations often provide a compiler switch or pragma that provides guidance to the compiler about how much time to spend in optimization, ranging from none to aggressive.

12.2 Common Optimizations

In this section we present several common optimizations that can be performed by a compiler.

Machine-Specific Instructions

The basic idea here is to make use of specific instructions available on the target computer. Here are some examples.

- Increment and decrement instructions are available on many (but not all) computer architectures and can be used in place of add and subtract instructions. This is usually an optimization that has a small improvement in both run-time performance and memory utilization. Although a single replacement of "`add 1`" by "`inc`" might not seem like much, the overall improvement can be more significant if done inside loops that are executed thousands of times.
- Some architectures provide block move instructions and block search instructions that can usually outperform the best hand-coded loops. For example, on the Intel x86, a "`rep`" prefix can be added to a "move byte" or a "move word" instruction to implement a block move from one part of memory to another.
- Many architectures provide special addressing modes or instructions to improve the processing of arrays. Sometimes array index computation can be improved by using addition to a constant pointer, a fact often exploited directly in C source code.
- Some architectures provide specific pre/post increment instructions that can be useful in certain situations. The early C compilers were developed on such architectures, and the use of ++ as both prefix and postfix operators allowed the programmer to provide an optimization "hint" to the compiler, similar to the use of the `register` directive in C.

Register Allocation

Most computer architectures have general-purpose registers, and register allocation is the process of assigning program variables to these registers. Since accessing a variable stored in a register is much faster than accessing a variable stored in memory, the efficient use of registers can have a significant effect on run-time performance. The overall process involves both register allocation – selection of variables that will reside in registers (e.g., a loop index) – and register assignment – selection of specific registers for the variables.

Register allocation is a very hard problem. One common approach uses a "graph coloring" algorithm, which is suitable for static compilation but often too time consuming for Just-In-Time (JIT) compilers, where the translation is performed at runtime.

Constant Folding

Constant folding is simply the compile-time evaluation of arithmetic expressions involving constants. For example, consider the following assignment statement.

```
c = 2*Pi*r;
```

Assuming `Pi` has been declared as a named constant, evaluation of `2*Pi` can be performed by the compiler rather than computed at runtime, and the resulting product can be used in the expression. Unless there is something very unusual going on in the instruction pipeline, this is one type of optimization that almost always results in better performance.

Algebraic Identities

Algebraic identities can often be used to simplify certain expressions. Here are some examples.

```
x + 0 = 0 + x = x
x - 0 = x
0 - x = -x
x*1 = 1*x = x
0/x = 0 (provided x ≠ 0)
```

But beware that not all algebraic identities from mathematics are applicable since arithmetic performed by computers is not always equivalent to the corresponding mathematical concepts. This is especially true for floating point computations, but it is also true for some integer computations. Problems result from the fact that computers use a fixed number of bits to represent mathematical numbers, but there are infinitely many mathematical numbers.

Strength Reduction

Strength reduction involves replacing operations with simpler, more efficient operations. Use of machine-specific instructions as discussed previously can be considered a form of strength reduction.

Here are some additional examples of this type of optimization.

`i = i + 1` → `inc i` (use increment instruction)
`i*2 or 2*i` → `i + i` (replace multiplication by 2 with addition)
`x/8` → `x >> 3` (replace division by 2^n with right-shift `n`)
`MOV EAX, 0` → `XOR EAX, EAX` (usually smaller and faster on x86 processors)

Common Subexpression Elimination

The basic idea is to detect a common subexpression, evaluate it only once, and then reference the common value as needed.

For example, consider the two following sets of statements.

```
a = x + y;                         a = x + y;
...                                ...
b = (x + y)/2;                     b = a/2;
```

These two sets of statements are equivalent provided that x and y do not change values in the intermediate statements. The set of statements on the right would be more efficient under normal circumstances.

Loop-Invariant Code Motion (a.k.a. Code Hoisting)

For this optimization we try to move calculations outside of a loop (usually before the loop) when doing so does not affect the semantics of the program. This optimization also facilitates storing constant values in registers. Consider the following example taken from Wikipedia.

```
while j < maximum - 1 loop
    j = j + (4+a[k])*Pi+5;    // a is an array
```

The calculation of "`maximum - 1`" and "`(4+a[k])*Pi+5`" can be moved outside the loop and precalculated. The optimized version of the code would look as follows.

```
int maxval  = maximum - 1;
int calcval = (4+a[k])*Pi+5;
while j < maxval loop
    j = j + calcval;
```

Dead Code Elimination

Dead (a.k.a. unreachable) code is code that can never be executed. For example, consider the following Java code, which adds debugging feedback to a program based on the value of a boolean variable.

```
private static final boolean DEBUG = false;
...

if (DEBUG)
  {
    ...
  }
```

Since DEBUG is final, both the declaration of DEBUG and the entire `if` statement can be removed without affecting the program results. Like many other compilers, the Java compiler will perform this optimization. If debugging feedback is desired at some point in the future, then simply changing `false` to `true` will cause the compiler to insert the debug code. Note that dead code elimination usually affects only the size of the generated code, not the speed at which it executes.

Subprogram Inlining (a.k.a. Function Inlining)

This optimization eliminates the call/return/parameter-passing overhead of subprograms by expanding the body of the called subprogram inline. It is similar to macro expansion available in C and many assemblers except that the optimization is performed by the compiler – the actual source code doesn't change as it would for macro expansions. Subprogram inlining can improve time performance, but there is a risk of increased object code size in certain cases. However, an added advantage of subprogram inlining is that it often reveals opportunities for additional optimizations. Subprogram inlining works best for small subprograms or for larger subprograms that are called infrequently.

Consider, for example, the following procedure.

```
proc inc(var x : Integer)
  {
    x := x + 1;
  }
```

For an integer variable n, replacing a call "`inc(n)`" by "`n := n + 1`" is not only faster at runtime, but in this case, it also results in smaller object code.

Recursive subprograms are not usually inlined unless the recursive call can be eliminated, which is sometimes possible with tail recursion.

Branch Elimination

One obvious optimization is to eliminate branches to other branches. For example,

```
    BR L10
    ...
L10:
    BR L14
```

Assuming that `L14` is within the reachable range of the first branch instruction, we can rewrite the above as

```
        BR L14
        ...
    L10:                // other code might still need this label
        BR L14
```

A slightly more complicated form of branch elimination is illustrated in the following subsection on peephole optimization.

Peephole Optimization

This is not so much a specific optimization as it is an approach to implementing certain types of local optimizations. This approach is usually applied to the generated target machine code or a low-level intermediate representation. In fact, this is the approach used by the CVM assembler for implementing optimizations. The basic idea is to analyze a small sequence of instructions at a time (the peephole) for possible performance improvements. The peephole is a small window into the generated code.

Examples of peephole optimizations include

- Elimination of redundant loads and stores
- Elimination of branch instructions to other branch instructions
- Use of algebraic identities and strength reduction. These are often easier to detect in the target machine code.

Example. Peephole Optimization

Consider the following source code excerpt.

```
loop
  {
    ...
    exit when x > 0;
  }
...
```

Straightforward code generation might result in something like the following, with the peephole shown as examining a sequence of two instructions.

```
L4:
   ...
   LDLADDR 0
   LOADW
   LDCINT 0
  +--------------------------+
  | BG L5         | peephole |
  | BR L4                    |
  +--------------------------+
L5:
   ...
```

As an optimization, we could replace the two instructions

```
BG L5
BR L4
```

with the following single instruction.

```
BLE L4
```

This example illustrates an actual example of an optimization performed by the CVM assembler. The assembler would also replace the instruction `LDCINT 0` (5 bytes) with the optimized instruction `LDCINT0` (1 byte).

12.3 Optimization in CPRL

As mentioned earlier in this chapter, none of the optimizations listed in the previous section are actually performed within the CPRL compiler projects as outlined in this book, but several are performed by the CVM assembler using a "peephole" optimizer. Here is a description of some of the optimizations performed by the assembler.

- Branch reduction (as illustrated in the above example).
- Constant folding for arithmetic operations. For example, the following three instructions

  ```
  LDCINT 5
  LDCINT 7
  ADD
  ```

  can be replaced with the single instruction

  ```
  LDCINT 12
  ```

- Constant folding for negation. For example, the following two instructions

  ```
  LDCINT 5
  NEG
  ```

  can be replaced with the single instruction

  ```
  LDCINT -5
  ```

  The assembler can handle negative integer values.
- Strength reduction using `INC` and `DEC` instead of adding or subtracting 1. For example, the following two instructions

  ```
  LDCINT 1
  ADD
  ```

  can be replaced with the single instruction

  ```
  INC
  ```

- Strength reduction using special constant instructions `LDCINT0`, `LDCINT1`, `LDCB0`, and `LDCB1`. For example, the instruction

  ```
  LDCINT 1
  ```

  can be replaced with the shorter, faster instruction

  ```
  LDCINT1
  ```

- Consider the following function.

  ```
  fun i2b(n : Integer) : Byte
    {
      var b : Byte;
      b := n;
      return b;
    }
  ```

  In the assignment statement variable b gets promoted to type Integer. Since the return type of the function is Byte, straightforward code generation will emit consecutive type conversions instructions `BYTE2INT` followed by `INT2BYTE`. This optimization will delete both instructions.

- Dead code is removed when an instruction without labels follows a return (`RET`) instruction. For example, since the first instruction below returns from a subprogram (covered in more detail in Chapter 13) and the second instruction is not preceded by a label, then the second instruction is unreachable and can be removed.

  ```
  RET 4
  BR L7
  ```

  This situation can occur for code that looks like the following.

  ```
  fun abs(n : Integer) : Integer
    {
      if n >= 0 then
          return n;
      else
          return -n;
    }
  ```

  Omitting details, code generation for the `if` statement looks like the following.

  ```
     ...   // code to compare n to 0
     BL L6
     ...   // code to load the value of n onto the stack
     RET 4
     BR L7
  L6:
     ...   // code to negate n and load its value onto the stack
     RET 4
  L7:
  ```

> Note that the instruction `BR L7` will never be executed since the function will return prior to getting to that instruction. Also, the label `L7:` can be removed since it can never be reached. The CVM assembler will eliminate both the branch instruction and the label `L7:` before final code generation.

Although not assigned as part of the compiler project, it is possible to perform some optimizations within the abstract syntax tree. One general approach to implementing optimizations in the abstract syntax tree would be to add an abstract method `optimize()` in class `AST` and to implement `optimize()` in each `AST` subclass. These `optimize()` methods would "walk" the tree in a manner similar to the `checkConstraints()` and `emit()` methods. Earlier versions of the project compiler assignments actually did this, but optimizations were moved from the compiler to the assembler in order to simplify the basic compiler project. In addition, another change that can simplify some optimizations within the abstract syntax tree is to add a parent reference to each node in the tree. In the current implementation, each AST object has references to its child objects, but the child objects don't maintain references to their parent.

12.4 Essential Terms and Concepts

- algebraic identities
- branch elimination
- code optimization
- common subexpression elimination
- constant folding
- dead code elimination
- global optimization
- local optimization
- loop-invariant code motion
- machine-dependent optimization
- machine-independent optimization
- machine-specific instructions
- peephole optimization
- register allocation
- subprogram inlining
- strength reduction

12.5 Exercises

1. True or false (T or F)
    a. Optimizations that reduce the size of the object code will always result in faster run-time performance.
    b. According to William A. Wulf, there are usually lots of machine-independent optimizations.
2. Study the peephole optimizations performed by the CVM assembler, and then implement an optimization for algebraic identities as discussed in Section 12.2 above. For example, replace occurrences of `x + 0` with `x`. Similarly, occurrences of `0 + x`, `1*x`, and `x*1` can all be replaced by `x`.
3. Give some examples of machine-specific instructions that can be used for optimization.

4. The CVM contains several optimized instructions including

   - `LDCINT0`, an optimized version of `LDCINT 0`
   - `LDCINT1`, an optimized version of `LDCINT 1`
   - `INC`, an optimized version of `ADD 1`
   - `DEC`, an optimized version of `SUB 1`
   - `RET0`, an optimized version of `RET 0`
   - `RET4`, an optimized version of `RET 4`

   Study the implementation of these optimized instructions within the CVM, and study the related peephole optimizations performed by the CVM assembler. Then add the following optimized instructions to the CVM and the assembler, and modify the optimization phase of the assembler to take advantage of these new instructions.

   - `LDLADDR8`, an optimized version of `LDLADDR 8`
   - `LDGADDR0`, an optimized version of `LDGADDR 0`

   Discussion: An analysis of the CPRL examples shows that `8` is the most common argument for the `LDLADDR`, which is not surprising since `LDLADDR 8` loads the address of the first variable declared in a subprogram. Similarly for `LDGADDR 0`, which loads the address of the first global variable.

   Hint: Unfortunately, adding an instruction to the CVM is quite complicated. It involves the following steps.

   a. In enum class `Opcode`, add an entry for the new opcode and modify helper methods as appropriate.
   b. In package `asssembler`:
      - Add an entry for the new opcode to enum class `Symbol`.
      - Add an AST class for the CVM instruction.
      - Add a case to the `switch` expression in `Parser` method `makeInstruction()`.
   c. In class `CVM`:
      - Add a method to "execute" the machine instruction corresponding to the new opcode.
      - Add a case to the `switch` statement in method `run()`.
      - Review debugging method `printMemory()` to determine if it needs to handle the instruction as a special case.
   d. In class `Disassembler`, review method `main()` to determine if it needs to handle the instruction as a special case.

Chapter 13
Subprograms

The term subprogram is used to mean either a procedure or a function. We have already addressed subprograms and issues of scope within the scanner, parser, and identifier table, so most of the remaining effort required to implement subprograms involves modifications of the AST classes. We begin with a review of relevant concepts.

13.1 Review of Subprograms, Scope, and Parameters

The grammar rules for subprograms give rise to the following methods in class `Parser`, where the return values of the methods are either AST classes or lists of AST classes.

```
private List<SubprogramDecl> parseSubprogramDecls()
private SubprogramDecl       parseSubprogramDecl()
private SubprogramDecl       parseProcedureDecl()
private SubprogramDecl       parseFunctionDecl()
private List<ParameterDecl>  parseParameterDecls()
private ParameterDecl        parseParameterDecl()
private Statement            parseProcedureCallStmt()
private List<Expression>     parseExpressions()    // for actual params
private Statement            parseReturnStmt()
private Expression           parseFunctionCallExpr()
```

The following diagram depicts the inheritance hierarchy for relevant AST classes.

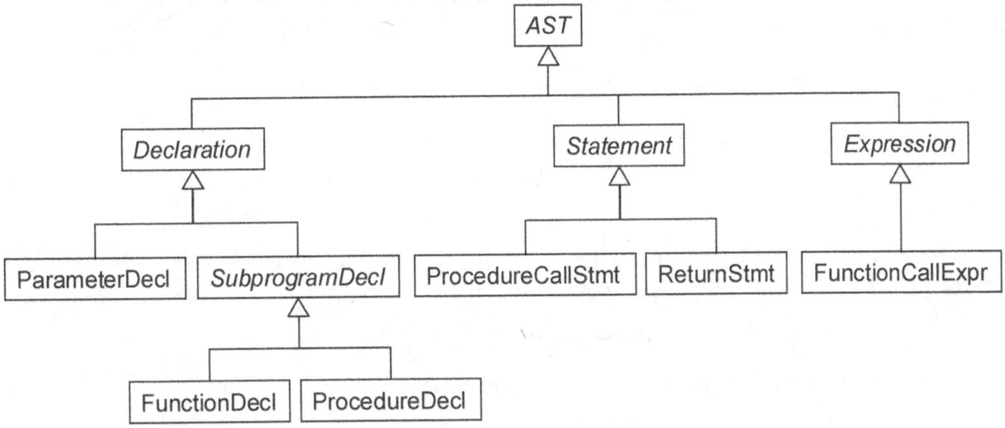

Variable Parameters and Value Parameters

The following example illustrates the use of parameters in CPRL.

```
var x : Integer;

proc main()
  {
    x := 5;
    inc(x);
    writeln x;
  }

proc inc(var n : Integer)
  {
    n := n + 1;
  }
```

What value is printed by this program? (Answer: 6) The integer parameter for procedure `inc()` above is a variable parameter, which means that the actual parameter is passed by reference. Any operation performed on the formal parameter `n` is effectively performed on the actual parameter `x`, so incrementing `n` inside procedure `inc()` will have the effect of incrementing `x`.

If "`var`" is removed from the parameter declaration in procedure `inc()`, what value is printed? (Answer: 5) Removing "`var`" from the parameter declaration means that the actual parameter is passed by value; i.e., the value of the actual parameter `x` is copied into the formal parameter `n`, but thereafter `x` and `n` are completely independent of each other. Changing the value of `n` inside procedure `inc()` would have no effect on `x`.

The Scope Level of a Var Declaration

Let's review the ideas of scope from Chapters 6 and 8. Recall that declarations introduce a name (identifier) into a scope. During code generation, when a variable is referenced in the statement part of a subprogram, we need to be able to determine its scope.

Class `IdTable` contains a method named `scopeLevel()` that returns the block nesting level for the current scope. It returns one of the three values in `enum` class `ScopeLevel`.

- `GLOBAL` for objects declared at the outermost (program) scope.
- `LOCAL` for objects declared within a subprogram.
- `RECORD` for objects (fields) declared within a record.

In this chapter we focus primarily on global and local scope.

When a variable is **declared**, the parser initializes the declaration with the current scope level.

```
var varDecl = new
    VarDecl(identifiers, varType, initialValue, idTable.scopeLevel());
```

The constructor for `VarDecl` adds this scope level to the declaration.

The following example illustrates scope levels.

```
var x : Integer;        // scope level of x is GLOBAL
var y : Integer;        // scope level of y is GLOBAL

proc p(n : Integer)     // scope level of p is GLOBAL
  {                     // scope level of n is LOCAL
    var x : Integer;    // scope level of x is LOCAL
    var b : Integer;    // scope level of b is LOCAL

    ... x ...           // x was declared at LOCAL scope
    ... b ...           // b was declared at LOCAL scope
    ... y ...           // y was declared at GLOBAL scope
  }

proc main()             // scope level of main is GLOBAL
  {
    var y : Integer;    // scope level of y is LOCAL

    ... x ...           // x was declared at GLOBAL scope
    ... y ...           // y was declared at LOCAL scope
    ... p(5) ...        // p was declared at GLOBAL scope
  }
```

Note that procedure `p()` is considered to be declared at `GLOBAL` scope, but its parameter `n` is declared at `LOCAL` scope.

Class `IdTable` supports the ability to open new scopes and to search for declarations, both within the current scope and in enclosing scopes. Class `IdTable` is implemented as a stack of scopes, where each scope is a map from identifier strings (names of things) to their declarations; i.e., the map key is the identifier string and the map value is the declaration corresponding to the identifier. Note that, since we don't allow subprograms to be nested and since there are no predefined subprograms, our stack usually has only three or four levels. In addition to the two scope levels shown above, a `record` declaration creates a new scope for its fields, an enumerated type declaration creates a new scope for the enum constants, and a `forLoop` creates a new, nested local scope for the `loop` variable. Some of the additional (optional) project exercises described in Appendix B would make use of additional stack levels.

When a new scope is opened, a new map is pushed onto the stack. When a scope is closed, the top map is popped off the stack. Within a subprogram, searching for a declaration involves searching within the current scope (top map in the stack containing identifiers declared at `LOCAL` scope) and then within the enclosing scope, which is usually the map under the top containing all identifiers declared at `GLOBAL` scope. (But the enclosing scope could be another local scope if the current scope was opened for a `forLoop`.)

Here are several key methods in class `IdTable`.

```
/**
 * Returns the current scope level.
 */
public ScopeLevel scopeLevel()

/**
 * Opens a new scope for identifiers.
 */
public void openScope(ScopeLevel scopeLevel)

/**
 * Closes the outermost scope.
 */
public void closeScope()

/**
 * Add an identifier token and its declaration to the current scope.
 *
 * @throws ParserException if the identifier already exists
 *         in the current scope.
 */
public void add(Token idToken, Declaration decl) throws ParserException

/**
 * Returns the declaration associated with the identifier name
 * (type String).  Returns null if the identifier is not found.
 * Searches enclosing scopes if necessary.
 */
public Declaration get(String idStr)
```

Constraint Rules for Subprograms

We close this section with a list of constraints for subprograms. The constraints are organized in terms of the AST classes whose `checkConstraints()` methods will be responsible for implementing the rules.

Note that implementing `checkConstraints()` in classes `ProcedureCallStmt` and `FunctionCallExpr` will require retrieving the corresponding subprogram declaration from the identifier table. Although subprograms can be called before they have been declared, these constraints aren't checked until after parsing has completed, and therefore the subprogram declarations will be in the identifier table when `checkConstraints()` executes.

- `FunctionDecl`
  - Miscellaneous Rule: Function parameters cannot be declared as `var` parameters. (However, array parameters are always passed by reference regardless of how they are declared, even for functions. We will revisit this idea in the next chapter.)
  - Miscellaneous Rule: There should be at least one return statement. (Note that this rule should be much stronger – the declared function should guarantee that it will always execute a return statement before reaching the end of the function. CPRL requires only the weaker rule since it is easier to implement.)
- `ProcedureCallStmt` **and** `FunctionCallExpr`
  - Miscellaneous Rule: The number of actual parameters should equal the number of formal parameters.
  - Type Rule: Each actual parameter expression should be assignment compatible with the corresponding formal parameter. Method `matchTypes()` inherited from class `AST` can be used to check for assignment compatibility.
- `ProcedureCallStmt`
  - Miscellaneous Rule: If the formal parameter is a `var` parameter, then the actual parameter must be a variable used as an expression (not an arbitrary expression).
  - Type Rule: If the formal parameter is a `var` parameter, then the type of the actual parameter must be equal to the declared type of the formal parameter. Note that this is a stronger form of type compatibility for `var` parameters.
- `ReturnStmt`
  - Miscellaneous Rule: If the return statement returns a value, then the return statement must be nested within a function declaration.
  - Miscellaneous Rule: If the return statement is nested within a function, then it must return a value.
  - Type Rule: If the statement returns a value for a function, then the type of expression being returned must equal the function return type.

13.2 Run-time Organization for Subprograms

Understanding the run-time organization for subprograms involves four major concepts.

1. CVM instructions for subprograms
2. Calling conventions; i.e., passing parameters and returning function values
3. Activation records
4. Variable addressing

We start with a brief overview of the CVM instructions mentioned in the first bullet above. These instructions are used specifically in the implementation of subprograms.

- PROC (procedure)
- CALL (call a subprogram)
- RET (return from a subprogram)

In addition, instructions LDLADDR (load local address) and LDGADDR (load global address) are used in subprograms to load relative addresses for variables and parameters.

We will discuss these instructions as we work through this chapter. Additional details are provided in Appendix E. Note that the CVM does not have separate instructions for procedures and functions. So, for example, instructions PROC, CALL, and RET are used in a similar manner for both.

Calling Conventions

A calling convention is a protocol describing how subprograms communicate at the machine architecture level. It specifies the responsibilities of the calling subprogram (a.k.a. the caller) and the called subprogram (a.k.a. the callee) with respect to passing parameters, returning values, and management of the run-time stack. In general, calling conventions are influenced by programming languages, operating systems, and machine architectures. For example, there could be a calling convention for interacting with C functions on Windows 11 or for making system calls in Linux on the x86-64 architecture.

Most real architectures use registers, and so a calling convention would specify the role of registers in subprogram communication. Most virtual machines are stack-based, and so the run-time stack is used almost exclusively for passing parameters and returning values. From the perspective of a compiler writer, a calling convention describes how to generate code in the context of the calling subprogram and the called subprogram.

Example. On x86-64 (a.k.a. AMD64 or x64) the calling convention followed by Linux, macOS, and other Unix-like operating systems is known as the System V AMD64 ABI (Application Binary Interface). Here is a brief summary of some of the key aspects of this calling convention (using the calling convention terminology, "argument" instead of "parameter" and "function" instead of "subprogram").

- Integer or pointer (address) arguments are passed in registers RDI, RSI, RDX, RCX, R8, and R9.
- Floating point arguments are passed in registers XMM0, XMM1, XMM2, XMM3, XMM4, XMM5, XMM6, and XMM7.
- Additional arguments are passed on the stack in reverse order.
- Integer values up to 64 bits are returned in RAX. Values up to 128 bits are returned in RDX:RAX (higher 64-bits go in RDX).
- Floating-point return values are returned in XMM0 or XMM1:XMM0.

- Registers RBP, RBX and R12-R15 "belong" to the calling function; the called function is required to preserve their values. Remaining registers "belong" to the called function.
- The calling function (caller) is responsible for cleaning up the run-time stack.

The next few sections provide the foundation for the CPRL calling conventions on the CVM.

Active Subprograms

When a program is running, a subprogram is said to be **active** if it has been called but has not yet returned. When a subprogram is called, we need to allocate space on the run-time stack for its parameters and local variables. When the subprogram returns, the allocated stack space is released. An active subprogram is one for which this space (activation record) is currently on the run-time stack.

Note that for functions, we also need to allocate space on the run-time stack for the return value, but this stack space is not released when the function returns – the return value remains on the stack so that it is accessible by the calling subprogram.

13.3 Activation Record

An activation record (a.k.a. frame or stack frame) is a run-time structure for each currently active subprogram.

Here is an important point. A new activation record is created every time a subprogram is called. If a subprogram is called recursively, there will be multiple activation records for that subprogram, one for each call.

The activation record consists of up to five parts as follows.

- The return value part. This part is only present for functions, not procedures.
- The parameter part, which may be empty if there are no parameters.
- The context part, which consists of the saved values for `PC` and `BP`. This part always uses two words (8 bytes) of memory on the run-time stack.
- The local variable part, which may be empty if there are no local variables.
- The temporary part, which holds operands and results as statements are executed. This part grows and shrinks as statements are executed, but it is always empty at the beginning and end of every statement of the subprogram.

Let's examine the parts of an activation record in more detail.

Return Value Part of an Activation Record

A function call must first allocate space on the run-time stack for the return value. The number of bytes allocated is the number of bytes for the return type of the function. Specifically, the `emit()` method in class `FunctionCallExpr` contains the following code.

```
// allocate space on the stack for the return value
emit("ALLOC " + funDecl.type().size());
```

Parameter Part of an Activation Record

For each value parameter, a subprogram call must emit code to leave the value of the actual parameter on the top of the run-time stack. For each variable (`var`) parameter, a procedure call must emit code to leave the address of the actual parameter on the top of the run-time stack. For variable parameters, the actual parameter must be a variable, not an arbitrary expression. Details of parameter passing are covered later in this chapter.

Context Part of an Activation Record

The context part of an activation record is never empty – it always contains exactly two word values (8 bytes).

- The dynamic link – the base address (`BP`) of the activation record for the calling subprogram.
- The return address – the address of the next instruction following the call to the subprogram. This is simply the value of the program counter (`PC`) after the call instruction has been "fetched" but before it has been executed.

The context part of an activation record is managed by the CVM `CALL` and `RET` instructions. The `CALL` instruction saves (pushes) the calling subprogram values for `BP` and `PC` onto the stack, and the RET instruction restores (pops) them back into the appropriate registers.

Local Variable Part of an Activation Record

If local variables are declared in a subprogram, then space must be allocated on the run-time stack for those variables. The CVM instruction `PROC` (procedure) has an integer argument for the variable length of the subprogram.

As an example, suppose that two integer variables and one boolean variable are declared in a procedure `p()` as follows.

```
proc p()
  {
    var m, n : Integer;
    var b : Boolean;
    ...
  }
```

Then this procedure will need to allocate nine bytes for local variables. The instruction `PROC 9` will be emitted to allocate the necessary space on the run-time stack. No `PROC` instruction is required for a subprogram without any local variables; the instruction `PROC 0` serves no purpose since it would simply allocate `0` bytes.

Temporary Part of an Activation Record

The temporary part of an activation record is analogous to the use of the run-time stack to hold temporary values as described in Section 10.5. As machine instructions for the subprogram are executed, the temporary part grows and shrinks, and it is empty at the start and end of each CPRL statement in the subprogram.

We illustrate with an example similar to the one in Section 10.5. Let's assume the following.

- Register `BP` has the value `200`.
- Local integer variable `x` has relative address `8`.
- Local integer variable `y` has value `6` and relative address `12`.

The CPRL assignment statement

```
x := y + 1;
```

will compile to the following CVM instructions.

```
LDLADDR 8
LDLADDR 12
LOADW
LDCINT 1      // will be optimized to LDCINT1 by the assembler
ADD
STOREW
```

We visualize the growing and shrinking of the temporary part by using a sequence of diagrams showing the state of the temporary part after execution of each machine instruction. The temporary part is empty at the start of the CPRL statement.

Initial diagram (immediately before execution of `LDLADDR 8`):

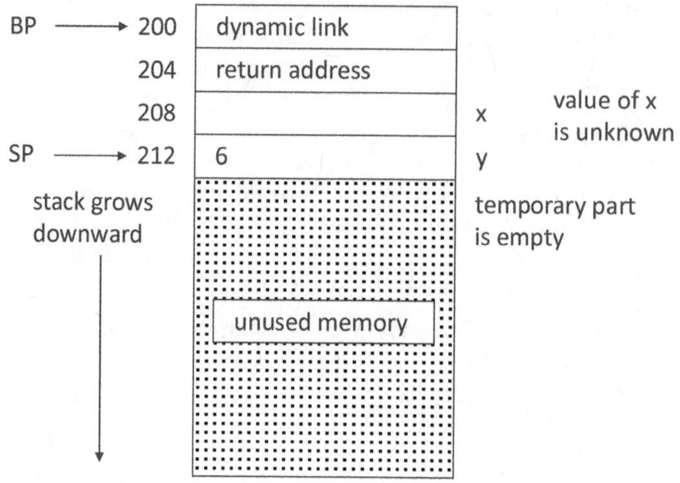

After execution of `LDLADDR 8`:

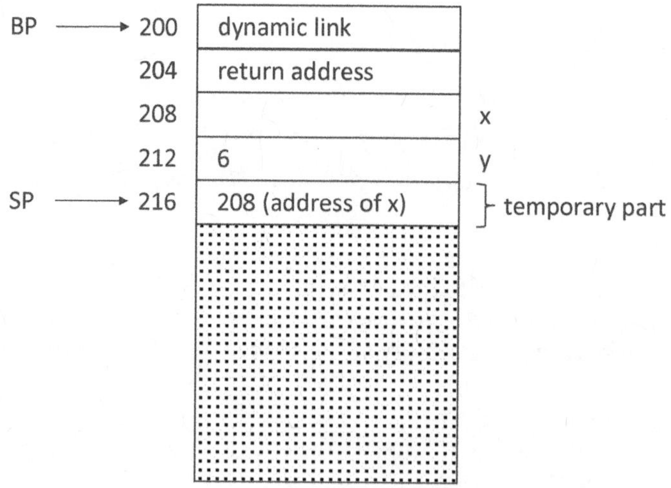

After execution of `LDLADDR 12`:

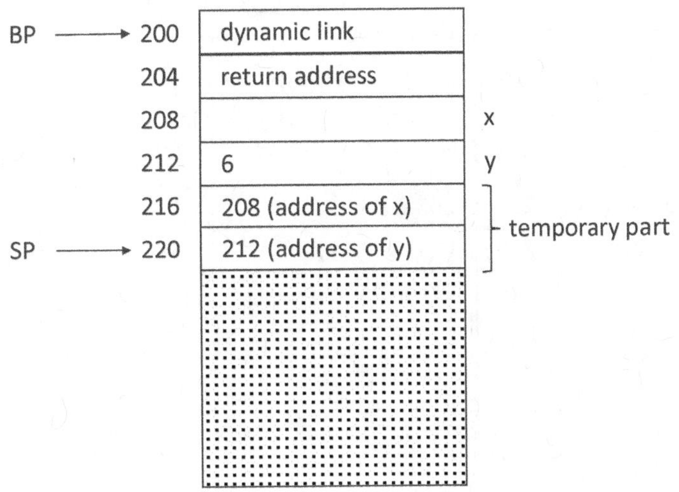

After execution of `LOADW`:

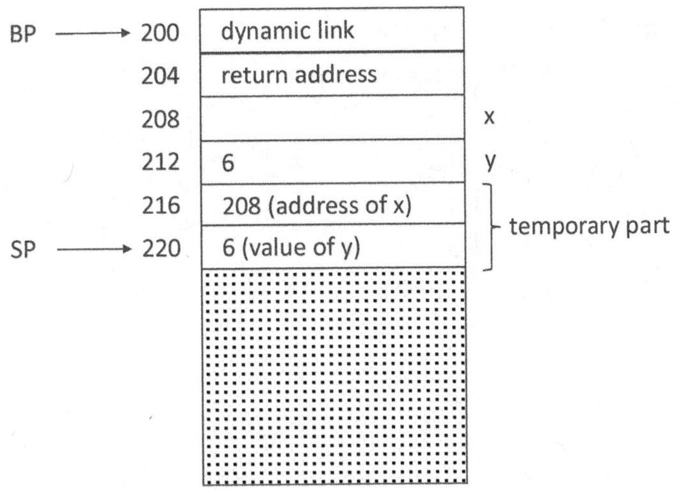

After execution of `LDCINT1`:

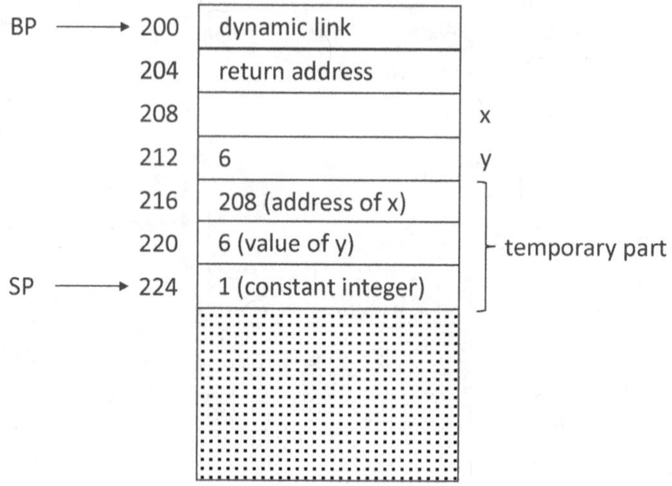

After execution of `ADD`:

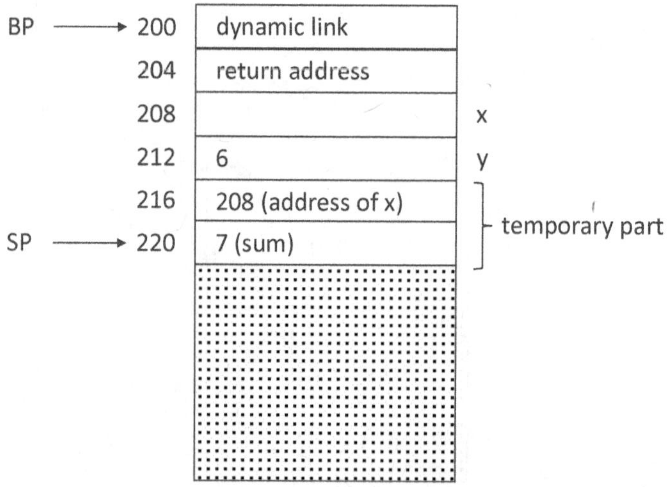

After execution of `STOREW`:

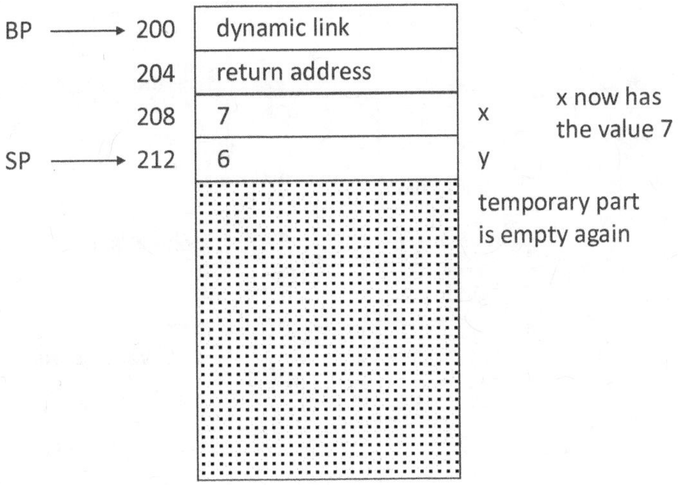

At this point the local variable `x` has been assigned the value `7`, and the temporary part is empty again.

Example: Subprogram with Parameters

Now let's examine the complete layout of an activation record for a procedure with parameters. Consider the following simple procedure.

```
proc p(a : Integer, b : Integer)
  {
     var n : Integer;
     ...
  }

proc main()
  {
    ...
    p(2, 5);
    ...
  }
```

The activation record for procedure `p()` is illustrated in the following diagram. Note that in this diagram, the memory addresses are shown as relative to the `BP` register and not in absolute values.

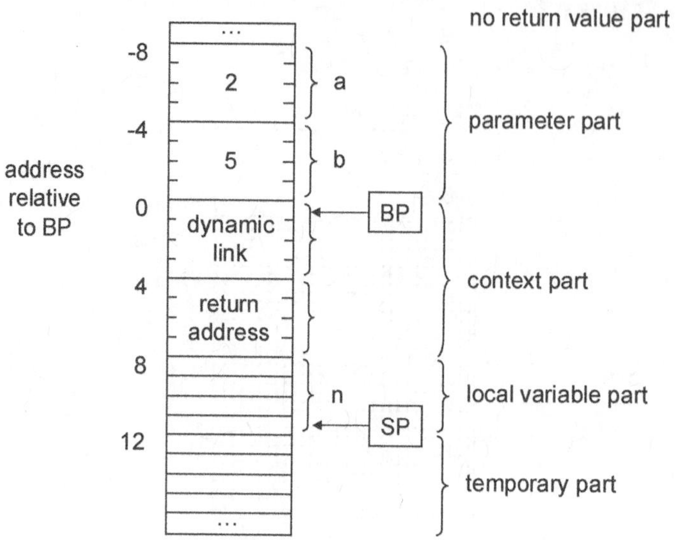

Recursion

Since a new activation record is created every time a subprogram is called, CPRL supports recursive calls. To illustrate, suppose that `main()` calls procedure `p()`, and then `p()` makes a recursive call to itself. **Each call to `p()` has its own activation record**, which means each call has its own copy of parameters, locally declared variables, etc. The following diagram illustrates this situation.

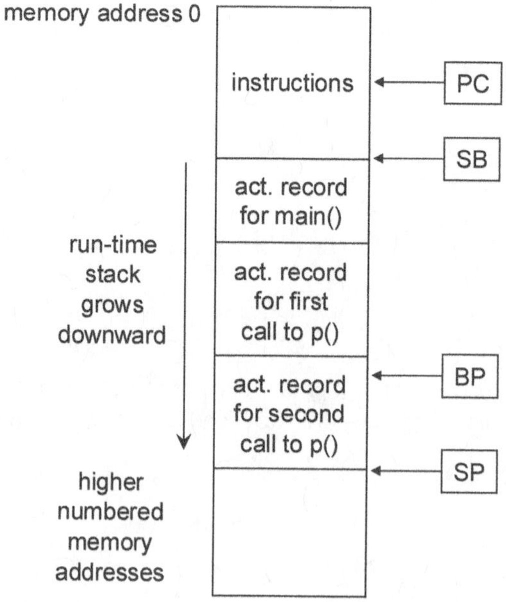

Note that recursion does not have to be direct; that is, procedure `p()` does not have to call itself. The approach that we use for calling subprograms works correctly for indirect recursion (a.k.a. mutual recursion), where a subprogram is called not by itself but by another subprogram that it called, either directly or indirectly.

Loading a Program

When a program is loaded into the CVM, the object code for the program is loaded into the beginning of memory starting at address `0`. Register `PC` is initialized to `0`, the address of the first instruction, and register `SB` is initialized to the address following the last instruction (i.e., the first free byte in memory). Register `BP` is also initialized to the address of the byte following the last instruction (i.e., the same as `SB`). Register `SP` is initialized to `BP - 1` since the run-time stack is empty.

13.4 Parameters

Functions can declare only value parameters, but procedures can have both variable (`var`) and value parameters. The code to implement the passing of these two kinds of parameters as part of a procedure call is somewhat analogous to the implementation of an assignment statement of the form "`x := y`", where we generate different code for the left and right sides. For the left side of an assignment statement, we generate code to leave the address on the run-time stack. For the right side of an assignment statement, we generate code to leave the value on the run-time stack.

As an analogy, for variable (`var`) parameters we generate code similar to the way we handle the left side of an assignment statement; that is, we want to leave the **address** of the actual parameter onto the run-time stack. For value parameters, we generate code similar to the way we handle the right side of the assignment statement; that is, we want to leave the **value** of the actual parameter onto the run-time stack.

When parsing the code for actual parameters, by default we always call `parseExpression()`. This method will generate code to leave the value of the expression on the run-time stack, which is correct for a value parameter but not for a variable parameter. Note that the code for AST class `Variable` contains a boolean property named `useAsExpression`. Calling `parseExpression()` will eventually result in a call to `parseVariableExpr()` for a variable, which will set the value for `useAsExpression` to `true`. When working with variable parameters, we will need to change this value to `false`.

Handling Variable Parameters

When you have a `Variable` corresponding to a `var` parameter, we want to generate code to leave the address of the variable on the top of the stack; i.e., we want to ensure that the value of `useAsExpression` for that variable is set to `false`. One possible approach, the approach that we adopt, is to explicitly set the value to `false` in the `checkConstraints()` method of class `ProcedureCallStmt`. When iterating through and comparing the list of formal parameters and actual parameters, if the formal parameter (as specified in the parameter declaration) is a `var` parameter and the actual parameter is not a `Variable`, then generate an error message since you can't pass an arbitrary expression as a `var` parameter. However, if the formal parameter is a `var` parameter, call `setUseAsExpression(false)` for the variable to ensure that code will be generated to leave the variable's address on the top of the run-time stack.

Following is an excerpt from method `checkConstraints()` in class `ProcedureCallStmt` that shows how we modify a parameter so that it can be used as a `var` parameter.

```
for (int i = 0; i < actualParams.size(); ++i)
  {
    var actualParam = actualParams.get(i);
    var paramDecl   = paramDecls.get(i);
    ...  // check that types match

    // check that only variables are passed for var parameters
    if (paramDecl.isVarParam())
      {
        if (actualParam instanceof Variable variable)
            variable.setUseAsExpression(false);
        else
          {
            var errorMsg = "Expression for a var parameter must be ...";
            throw error(expr.position(), errorMsg);
          }
      }
  }
```

In the next chapter we will need to modify the above to correctly handle arrays, but what we have now will work for CPRL programs that don't contain arrays.

13.5 Subprogram Calls and Returns

Calling a Subprogram

When a subprogram is called, we manage the non-temporary parts of its activation record as follows.

- For a function, space is allocated on the run-time stack for the return value.
- The actual parameters are pushed (loaded) onto the run-time stack.
  - Push expression values for value parameters.
  - Push addresses for variable parameters.
- The `CALL` instruction pushes the context part onto the run-time stack.
- The `PROC` instruction of the called subprogram allocates space on the run-time stack for the subprogram's local variables.

`PROC` Instruction versus `ALLOC` Instruction

For the CVM, the `PROC` instruction and the `ALLOC` instruction are equivalent and can be used interchangeably. Both instructions simply modify the stack pointer `SP` to allocate space on the run-time stack; e.g., for a function return value or a subprogram's local variable. In general, we prefer to use `PROC` at the beginning of a subprogram to allocate space for its local variables and `ALLOC` elsewhere, but this preference is entirely arbitrary.

Returning from a Subprogram

The CVM return instruction indicates the number of bytes used by the subprogram parameters so that they can be removed from the stack. Here is an example.

```
RET 8   // removes 8 bytes from the stack
```

When a return instruction is executed,

- `BP` is set to the dynamic link. This restores `BP` to point to the caller's activation record.
- `PC` is set to the return address. This restores `PC` to the instruction after the call.
- `SP` is set so as to restore the stack to its state before the call instruction was executed.
  - For procedures, `SP` is set to the memory address before the activation record.
  - For functions, `SP` is set to the memory address of the last byte of the return value. The return value remains on the stack.

Note that for functions, the space allocated on the run-time stack for the function's return value remains so that the return value can be used in an expression.

Code Generation for Class `ReturnStmt`

Most procedures don't have explicit return statements, but there is an implied return statement as its last statement. A function requires one or more return statements to return the function value. Recall the grammar rule for a return statement.

```
returnStmt = "return" [ expression ] ";" .
```

The optional return expression is `null` for procedures but not `null` for functions. Whether or not the expression is `null`, a return statement needs to emit a `RET` instruction to remove the number of bytes used by the subprogram parameters. Code generation for class `ReturnStmt` follows the following template.

```
if the return expression is not null
    emit the local address of the function
    emit the value of the expression
    emit the store instruction (stores the value at the address)
emit the RET instruction
```

There is one more issue to consider based on the constraint requiring that the type of expression being returned must equal the function return type. Similar to the implementation of an assignment statement, we need to consider the case where the return expression has type `Integer` but function return type is `Byte`. In this case, we need to convert the return expression type to `Byte` (using opcode `INT2BYTE`) before emitting the store instruction.

Method emit() for class `AssignmentStmt`

```
if (returnExpr != null)
  {
    var funDecl = (FunctionDecl) subprogramDecl;
    emit("LDLADDR " + funDecl.relAddr());
    returnExpr.emit();

    if (funDecl.type() == Type.Byte && returnExpr.type() == Type.Integer)
       emit("INT2BYTE");

    emitStoreInst(funDecl.type());
  }

emit("RET " + subprogramDecl.paramLength());
```

13.6 Calling Conventions for CPRL on the CVM

We are now in a position to summarize the calling conventions for CPRL on the CVM, which we illustrate with the following example. For this example, the calling subprogram (caller) is procedure `main()`, and the called subprogram (callee) is function `max()`.

```
proc main()
  {
    var n : Integer := 5;
    writeln "max = ", max(n, 10);
  }

fun max(x : Integer, y : Integer) : Integer
  {
    var result : Integer;
    result := x > y ? x : y;    // note use of conditional expression
    return result;
  }
```

- Before the call to function `max()`, the calling subprogram reserves space on the run-time stack for a function return value. Function `max()` in the above example returns an integer, so the calling program, `main()`, would emit an `ALLOC 4` instruction. This step is not necessary when calling a procedure since no value is returned.
- Next, the calling subprogram loads (pushes) the actual parameters onto the stack in the specified order. This step is not necessary when calling a subprogram that does not have parameters. For the above example, `main()` would emit the following instructions.

```
LDLADDR 8    // relative address of local variable n
LOADW        // replace relative address of n by its value
LDCINT 10    // push constant 10 onto the stack
```

- The calling subprogram then executes a `CALL` instruction, which pushes the context part onto the run-time stack. On most architectures, a call instruction pushes only the `PC` register, and separate instructions are required to handle the `BP` register. For the above example, `main()` emits a `CALL _max` instruction.
- Upon entry into the called subprogram, it reserves space on the stack for local variables. For the above example, function `max()` would emit a `PROC 4` instruction (equivalent to an `ALLOC 4` instruction) to reserve 4 bytes for the local variable `result`. This step can be omitted when the called subprogram does not have any local variables.
- The called subprogram puts the return value in the space previously allocated by the calling subprogram. This step can be omitted for procedures since they do not return a value. For the above example, the called program emits the following four instructions.

```
LDLADDR -12   // relative address of space allocated for return value
LDLADDR 8     // relative address of local variable result
LOADW         // replace relative address of result by its value
STOREW        // store result in space allocated for the return value
```

- The called subprogram returns by executing a `RET n` instruction, where `n` is the number of bytes allocated for the subprogram's actual parameters. For the above example, function `max()` emits a `RET 4` instruction. Executing `RET n` restores the stack pointer (`SP`) so that the actual parameters are effectively removed from the run-time stack. Note that the actual parameters were pushed onto the stack by the calling subprogram, but the called subprogram freed up the stack space occupied by the parameters. Some calling conventions require that the calling subprogram free up the stack space for actual parameters, which is necessary if a programming language allows different calls to have different numbers or different sizes of parameters.

13.7 Computing Relative Addresses

Similar to what we did for global variables, we need to compute the relative address (offset) for each variable plus the total number of bytes of all variables for each subprogram. In addition, for subprograms, we will need to compute the relative address for each parameter. There is one minor difference in computing the relative address of variables of a subprogram. Since addressing is relative to the `BP` register, and since `BP` points to the first byte of the activation record's context part, the starting relative address for the first variable is the number of bytes in the context part of an activation record (8 for CPRL activation records), not zero as it was for program-level variables.

Also, relative addresses for parameters are negative numbers since parameters are *above* `BP` in the stack. It is easier to compute relative addresses for parameters in reverse order, so we iterate backwards through the list of parameter declarations to compute their relative addresses.

Method `setRelativeAddresses()` in the AST class `SubprogramDecl` is defined as follows.

```
protected void setRelativeAddresses()
  {
    // initial relative address for a subprogram
    int currentAddr = Constants.BYTES_PER_CONTEXT;

    for (var decl : initialDecls)
      {
        if (decl instanceof VarDecl varDecl)
          {
            // set relative address for each identifier
            for (var idName : varDecl.idNames())
              {
                varDecl.setRelAddr(idName, currentAddr);
                currentAddr = currentAddr + varDecl.size();
              }
          }
      }

    // compute length of all variables by subtracting the
    // initial relative address
    varLength = currentAddr - Constants.BYTES_PER_CONTEXT;

    // set relative address for parameters
    if (paramDecls.size() > 0)
      {
        // initial relative address for a subprogram parameter
        currentAddr = 0;

        // we need to process the parameter declarations in reverse order
        var iter = paramDecls.listIterator(paramDecls.size());

        while (iter.hasPrevious())
          {
            var decl = iter.previous();
            currentAddr = currentAddr - decl.size();
            decl.setRelAddr(currentAddr);
          }
      }
  }
```

In addition to local variables, a function is considered to have a relative address, which is simply the relative address of the return value within the activation record. Since the space for the return value is allocated before any parameters are pushed onto the stack, the return value is *above* all parameters. Function `paramLength()` computes the sum of all parameter sizes. The relative address for a function is computed in class `FunctionDecl` as follows.

```
public int relAddr()
  {
    return -type().size() - paramLength();
  }
```

Referencing Variables and Parameters

Referencing Local Variables

The `LDLADDR` (load local address) instruction is used to load the address of variables local to the subprogram and the subprogram parameters. This instruction computes the absolute address of a local variable from its relative address with respect to `BP` and pushes the absolute address onto the run-time stack. Internally within the CVM machine emulator, instruction `LDLADDR` is implemented as follows.

```
pushInt(bp + displ);
```

The use of `LDLADDR` with subprograms is similar to the use of `LDGADDR` for global variables except that the relative address of the first local variable is `8` instead of `0` since there are `8` bytes in an activation record. Relative addresses can be negative to load the address of a parameter.

Referencing Global Variables

The `LDGADDR` (load global address) instruction is used within a subprogram to load the address of global variables. This instruction computes the absolute address of a global variable from its relative address with respect to `SB` and pushes the absolute address onto the run-time stack. Internally within the CVM machine emulator, instruction `LDGADDR` is implemented as follows.

```
pushInt(sb + displ);
```

The diagram on the next page illustrates the layout of the activation record for function `max()` as defined at the beginning of the previous section.

The following examples illustrate referencing variables and parameters for function `max()`.

```
LDLADDR -12  // loads (pushes) address of the return value onto the stack
LDLADDR -8   // loads (pushes) address of parameter x onto the stack
LDLADDR -4   // loads (pushes) address of parameter y onto the stack
LDLADDR 8    // loads (pushes) address of local variable result onto
             // the stack
```

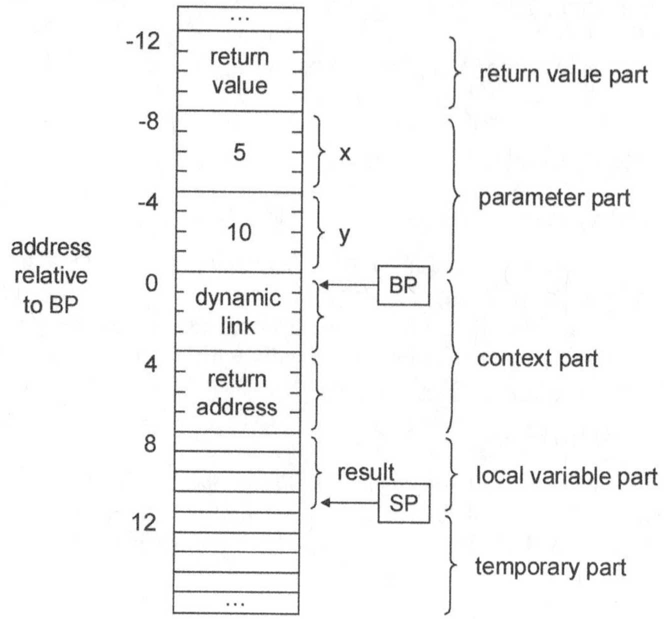

Variable (var) Parameters

For variable (var) parameters, the address of the actual parameter is passed; i.e., the value contained in the formal parameter is the address of the actual parameter. As an example, consider the following program, where procedure `p()` has a variable parameter named `a`.

```
var x : Integer;

proc main()
  {
    x := 5;
    p(x, 6);
  }
proc p(var a : Integer, b : Integer)
  {
    var n : Integer;
    ...
  }
```

The call `p(x, 6)` passes the address of `x` into parameter `a`; i.e., the value contained in parameter `a` is the address of `x`. Loading the value contained in parameter `a` onto the run-time stack is equivalent to loading the address of `x` onto the stack.

Let's assume that the absolute address of `x` is `325`. Then the activation record for `p()` is illustrated in the following diagram.

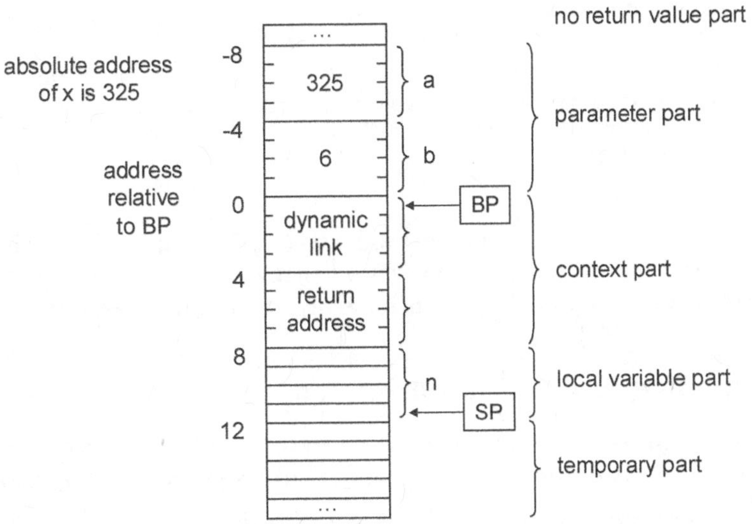

The two instructions

```
LDLADDR -8
LOADW
```

will push the address of the actual parameter `x` onto the run-time stack. Parameter `b`, local variable `n`, and global variable `x` are handled in the manner described earlier.

```
LDLADDR -4  // loads (pushes) address of parameter b onto the stack
LDLADDR 8   // loads (pushes) address of local variable n onto the stack
LDGADDR 0   // loads (pushes) address of global variable x onto the stack
```

Method `emit()` for class `Variable` loads the address of the variable onto the stack. Based on the above discussion, we can implement method `emit()` for class `Variable` as follows.

```
@Override
public void emit() throws CodeGenException
  {
    if (decl instanceof ParameterDecl pDecl && pDecl.isVarParam())
      {
        // address of actual parameter is value of var parameter
        emit("LDLADDR " + pDecl.relAddr());
        emit("LOADW");
      }

    else if (decl.scopeLevel() == ScopeLevel.GLOBAL)
        emit("LDGADDR " + decl.relAddr(idToken.text()));
    else
        emit("LDLADDR " + decl.relAddr(idToken.text()));

    // additional code will be needed for arrays, strings, and records
```

```
        if (useAsExpression)
          {
            // Previous code leaves address of this variable on top of stack.
            // We need to emit the value at that address.
            emitLoadInst(type());
          }
      }
```

Note that the above implementation of method `emit()` is incomplete in that it does not yet consider the case where the variable is an array, a string, or a record. Chapters 14, 16, and 17 will address the necessary modifications for array, string, and record variables.

13.8 Implementing Built-in Subprograms

Recommendation: Don't attempt to add a new built-in subprogram until after you have successfully completed Project 7: Subprograms in Appendix A.

None of the compiler projects in Appendix A require the implementation of an additional built-in subprogram, but one of the additional (optional) project exercises in Appendix B does, and the framework for implementing a new built-in subprogram is already in place.

Here is an outline of the steps for creating a new built-in subprogram.

1. Create a class in package `cprlc.builtins` for the declaration of the new subprogram. The class will need to be a subclass of either `ProcedureDecl` or `FunctionDecl` as appropriate, and it will need to implement interface `BuiltinSubprogram`. Method `checkConstraints()` can be empty, but method emit() will need to emit the assembly language code. Use the existing classes such as `FunChrDecl` and `ProcIncDecl` for guidance. To determine the assembly language that needs to be emitted, write a CPRL subprogram that is equivalent to (or nearly equivalent to) the one you want, and look at the generated assembly code. Better yet, look at the disassembled object code.
2. Modify the constructor for class `BuiltinSubprogramDecls` (in package `cprlc.builtins`) to add the new subprogram declaration.

To make the built-in subprograms available to the compiler, class `Cprlc` adds them to the identifier table immediately after creating it. Here is an outline of the code in `Cprlc`.

```
var idTable = new IdTable();

// Add built-in subprogram declarations to the identifier table at
// global scope and open a new global scope for the CPRL program.
var builtins = new BuiltinSubprograms();
for (var builtinDecl : builtins.subprogramDecls())
    idTable.add(builtinDecl.idToken(), builtinDecl);
idTable.openScope(ScopeLevel.GLOBAL);

var parser = new Parser(scanner, idTable, errorHandler);
```

Note that built-in subprograms are added at the initial global scope, and then a new global scope is opened before creating the parser. Using this approach, if there is a user-defined subprogram with the same name as one of the built-in subprograms, the user-defined subprogram will be found in the identifier table before the built-in subprogram.

Using this framework for built-in subprograms, assembly code for a built-in subprogram is not emitted unless the subprogram is actually called.

13.9 Example of Program Execution

To get a better understanding of the roles of the internal registers and run-time stack when executing subprograms, let's examine in detail the call to and return from a simple function. Consider the following CPRL program.

```
fun abs(n : Integer) : Integer
  {
    if n >= 0 then
       return n;
    else
       return -n;
  }

proc main()
  {
    var x : Integer;
    x := -12;
    writeln abs(x);
  }
```

Compiling this program yields the following assembly code.

```
   CALL _main
   HALT
_abs:
   LDLADDR -4
   LOADW
   LDCINT 0
   BL L2
   LDLADDR -8
   LDLADDR -4
   LOADW
   STOREW
   RET 4
   BR L3
L2:
   LDLADDR -8
   LDLADDR -4
   LOADW
   NEG
   STOREW
   RET 4
L3:
_main:
   PROC 4
   LDLADDR 8
   LDCINT 12
   NEG
   STOREW
   ALLOC 4
   LDLADDR 8
   LOADW
   CALL _abs
   PUTINT
   PUTEOL
   RET 0
```

After optimization and assembly, a disassembled version of the code would look as follows.

```
 0:  CALL 40
 5:  HALT
 6:  LDLADDR -4
11:  LOADW
12:  LDCINT0
13:  BL 13
18:  LDLADDR -8
23:  LDLADDR -4
28:  LOADW
29:  STOREW
30:  RET4
31:  LDLADDR -8
36:  LDLADDR -4
41:  LOADW
42:  NEG
43:  STOREW
44:  RET4
45:  PROC 4
50:  LDLADDR 8
55:  LDCINT -12
60:  STOREW
61:  ALLOC 4
66:  LDLADDR 8
71:  LOADW
72:  CALL -71
77:  PUTINT
78:  PUTEOL
79:  RET0
```

Below we present a subset of an execution trace of this code that shows memory contents, memory locations referenced by the registers, the run-time stack, etc.

Before execution of the first instruction, PC has the value 0, SB has the value 80, BP also has the value 80, and SP has the value 79. At this point no meaningful value is stored in memory location 80, as indicated by ?. We visualize this state as follows.

```
PC ->   0:  CALL 40
        5:  HALT
        6:  LDLADDR -4    <------------  first instruction for function abs()
       11:  LOADW
       12:  LDCINT0
       13:  BL 13
       18:  LDLADDR -8
       23:  LDLADDR -4
       28:  LOADW
       29:  STOREW
       30:  RET4
       31:  LDLADDR -8
       36:  LDLADDR -4
       41:  LOADW
       42:  NEG
       43:  STOREW
       44:  RET4
       45:  PROC 4        <------------  first instruction for procedure main()
       50:  LDLADDR 8
       55:  LDCINT -12
       60:  STOREW
       61:  ALLOC 4
       66:  LDLADDR 8
       71:  LOADW
       72:  CALL -71
       77:  PUTINT
       78:  PUTEOL
SP ->  79:  RET0
SB ->  80:  ?           <- BP
```

The first instruction, CALL 40, calls procedure main(), which starts at memory location 45. Note that function abs() starts at memory location 6. The partial execution trace shown on the next few pages will occasionally omit some instructions (indicated by ...) so that the most relevant instructions and the entire stack can be displayed on a single page.

After call to main():

```
         0:  CALL 40
         5:  HALT
         6:  LDLADDR -4     <------  first instruction for function abs()
        11:  LOADW
        12:  LDCINT0
        13:  BL 13
        18:  LDLADDR -8
        23:  LDLADDR -4
        28:  LOADW
        29:  STOREW
        30:  RET4
        31:  LDLADDR -8
        36:  LDLADDR -4
        41:  LOADW
        42:  NEG
        43:  STOREW
        44:  RET4
PC ->   45:  PROC 4         <------  first instruction for procedure main()
        50:  LDLADDR 8
        55:  LDCINT -12
        60:  STOREW
        61:  ALLOC 4
        66:  LDLADDR 8
        71:  LOADW
        72:  CALL -71
        77:  PUTINT
        78:  PUTEOL
        79:  RET0
SB ->   80:  0    ┐  <- BP
        81:  0    │
        82:  0    ├  80 = saved value for BP from call to main()
        83:  80   ┘
        84:  0    ┐
        85:  0    │
        86:  0    ├  5 = saved value for PC from call to main()
SP ->   87:  5    ┘
```

After executing `PROC 4`:

```
           0:  CALL 40
           5:  HALT
           6:  LDLADDR -4
          11:  LOADW
          12:  LDCINT0
          13:  BL 13
          18:  LDLADDR -8
          23:  LDLADDR -4
          28:  LOADW
          29:  STOREW
          30:  RET4
          31:  LDLADDR -8
          36:  LDLADDR -4
          41:  LOADW
          42:  NEG
          43:  STOREW
          44:  RET4
          45:  PROC 4
   PC ->  50:  LDLADDR 8
          55:  LDCINT -12
          60:  STOREW
          61:  ALLOC 4
          66:  LDLADDR 8
          71:  LOADW
          72:  CALL -71
          77:  PUTINT
          78:  PUTEOL
          79:  RET0
   SB ->  80:  0      ┐ <- BP
          81:  0      │
          82:  0      ├ 80 = saved value for BP from call to main()
          83:  80     ┘
          84:  0      ┐
          85:  0      │
          86:  0      ├ 5 = saved value for PC from call to main()
          87:  5      ┘
          88:  ?      ┐
          89:  ?      │
          90:  ?      ├ 4 bytes allocated on stack for x by instruction PROC 4
   SP ->  91:  ?      ┘
```

Fast-forward to the instruction that calls `abs(x)`:

```
             0:  CALL 40
             5:  HALT
             6:  LDLADDR -4
                 ...
            29:  STOREW
            30:  RET4
            31:  LDLADDR -8
            36:  LDLADDR -4
            41:  LOADW
            42:  NEG
            43:  STOREW
            44:  RET4
            45:  PROC 4
            50:  LDLADDR 8
            55:  LDCINT -12
            60:  STOREW
            61:  ALLOC 4
            66:  LDLADDR 8
            71:  LOADW
    PC ->   72:  CALL -71
            77:  PUTINT
            78:  PUTEOL
            79:  RET0
    SB ->   80:  0         <- BP
            81:  0
            82:  0          80 = saved value for BP from call to main()
            83:  80
            84:  0
            85:  0
            86:  0          5 = saved value for PC from call to main()
            87:  5
            88:  -1
            89:  -1
            90:  -1         -12 = value of x
            91:  -12
            92:  ?
            93:  ?
            94:  ?          4 bytes reserved for return value from abs
            95:  ?
            96:  -1
            97:  -1
            98:  -1         -12 = value of actual parameter pushed onto stack
    SP ->   99:  -12
```

After call to abs(x):

```
           0:  CALL 40
           5:  HALT
PC ->      6:  LDLADDR -4
          11:  LOADW
          12:  LDCINT0
          13:  BL 13
          18:  LDLADDR -8
          23:  LDLADDR -4
          28:  LOADW
          29:  STOREW
               ...
          72:  CALL -71
          77:  PUTINT
          78:  PUTEOL
          79:  RET0
SB ->     80:  0     ┐
          81:  0     │
          82:  0     ├ 80 = saved value for BP from call to main()
          83:  80    ┘
          84:  0     ┐
          85:  0     │
          86:  0     ├ 5 = saved value for PC from call to main()
          87:  5     ┘
          88:  -1    ┐
          89:  -1    │
          90:  -1    ├ -12 = value of x
          91:  -12   ┘
          92:  ?     ┐
          93:  ?     │
          94:  ?     ├ 4 bytes reserved for return value from abs
          95:  ?     ┘
          96:  -1    ┐
          97:  -1    │
          98:  -1    ├ -12 = value of actual parameter pushed onto stack
          99:  -12   ┘
BP ->    100:  0     ┐
         101:  0     │
         102:  0     ├ 80 = saved value for BP from call to abs()
         103:  80    ┘
         104:  0     ┐
         105:  0     │
         106:  0     ├ 77 = saved value for PC from call to abs()
SP ->    107:  77    ┘
```

Fast forward to the instruction that returns from `abs()` to `main()`:

```
             0:  CALL 40
             5:  HALT
             6:  LDLADDR -4
            11:  LOADW
            12:  LDCINT0
                 ...
            42:  NEG
            43:  STOREW
   PC ->    44:  RET4
            45:  PROC 4
                 ...
            72:  CALL -71
            77:  PUTINT
            78:  PUTEOL
            79:  RET0
   SB ->    80:  0
            81:  0
            82:  0         80 = saved value for BP from call to main()
            83:  80
            84:  0
            85:  0
            86:  0         5 = saved value for PC from call to main()
            87:  5
            88:  -1
            89:  -1
            90:  -1        -12 = value of x
            91:  -12
            92:  0
            93:  0
            94:  0         12 = return value from abs
            95:  12
            96:  -1
            97:  -1
            98:  -1        -12 = value of actual parameter pushed onto stack
            99:  -12
   BP ->   100:  0
           101:  0
           102:  0         80 = saved value for BP from call to abs()
           103:  80
           104:  0
           105:  0
           106:  0         77 = saved value for PC from call to abs()
   SP ->   107:  77
```

After return to `main()`:

```
           0:  CALL 40
           5:  HALT
           6:  LDLADDR -4
          11:  LOADW
          12:  LDCINT0
          13:  BL 13
               ...
          29:  STOREW
          30:  RET4
          31:  LDLADDR -8
          36:  LDLADDR -4
          41:  LOADW
          42:  NEG
          43:  STOREW
          44:  RET4
          45:  PROC 4
          50:  LDLADDR 8
          55:  LDCINT -12
          60:  STOREW
          61:  ALLOC 4
          66:  LDLADDR 8
          71:  LOADW
          72:  CALL -71
    PC -> 77:  PUTINT
          78:  PUTEOL
          79:  RET0
    SB -> 80:  0     ┐ <- BP
          81:  0     ├ 80 = saved value for BP from call to main()
          82:  0     │
          83:  80    ┘
          84:  0     ┐
          85:  0     ├ 5 = saved value for PC from call to main()
          86:  0     │
          87:  5     ┘
          88:  -1    ┐
          89:  -1    ├ -12 = value of x
          90:  -1    │
          91:  -12   ┘
          92:  0     ┐
          93:  0     ├ 12 = return value from abs
          94:  0     │
    SP -> 95:  12    ┘
```

Fast forward to instruction that returns from `main()`:

```
           0:  CALL 40
           5:  HALT
           6:  LDLADDR -4
          11:  LOADW
          12:  LDCINT0
          13:  BL 13
          18:  LDLADDR -8
          23:  LDLADDR -4
          28:  LOADW
          29:  STOREW
          30:  RET4
          31:  LDLADDR -8
          36:  LDLADDR -4
          41:  LOADW
          42:  NEG
          43:  STOREW
          44:  RET4
          45:  PROC 4
          50:  LDLADDR 8
          55:  LDCINT -12
          60:  STOREW
          61:  ALLOC 4
          66:  LDLADDR 8
          71:  LOADW
          72:  CALL -71
          77:  PUTINT
          78:  PUTEOL
   PC ->  79:  RET0
   SB ->  80:  0       ┐  <- BP
          81:  0       │
          82:  0       ├  80 = saved value for BP from call to main()
          83:  80      ┘
          84:  0       ┐
          85:  0       │
          86:  0       ├  5 = saved value for PC from call to main()
          87:  5       ┘
          88:  -1      ┐
          89:  -1      │
          90:  -1      ├  -12 = value of x
   SP ->  91:  -12     ┘
```

After return from `main()`:

```
           0:  CALL 40
  PC ->    5:  HALT
           6:  LDLADDR -4
          11:  LOADW
          12:  LDCINT0
          13:  BL 13
          18:  LDLADDR -8
          23:  LDLADDR -4
          28:  LOADW
          29:  STOREW
          30:  RET4
          31:  LDLADDR -8
          36:  LDLADDR -4
          41:  LOADW
          42:  NEG
          43:  STOREW
          44:  RET4
          45:  PROC 4
          50:  LDLADDR 8
          55:  LDCINT -12
          60:  STOREW
          61:  ALLOC 4
          66:  LDLADDR 8
          71:  LOADW
          72:  CALL -71
          77:  PUTINT
          78:  PUTEOL
  SP ->   79:  RET0
  SB ->   80:  ?          <- BP
```

13.10 Essential Terms and Concepts

activation record	active subprogram
calling convention	calling a subprogram
context part (of an activation record)	dynamic link
local variable part (of an activation record)	parameter part (of an activation record)
pass by reference	pass by value
referencing local variables	referencing global variables
return address	return value part (of an activation record)
returning from a subprogram	scope level
temporary part (of an activation record)	value parameter
variable parameter	

13.11 Exercises

1. **Project Assignment.** Implement **Project 7: Subprograms** as described in Appendix A.
2. True or False (T or F)
   a. A function can have variable parameter declarations.
   b. An expression value (e.g., a constant) can be passed as the actual parameter if the corresponding formal parameter is a variable parameter.
   c. If a return statement returns a value, then the return statement must be nested within a function declaration.
   d. CPRL supports recursion.
3. An activation record for a currently active subprogram consists of five parts. Name and briefly describe all 5 parts. (Note: Not every activation record contains all parts.)
4. Fill in the blanks.
   a. The scope level of a variable or parameter declaration can be one of two possible values, ________________________ or ________________________ .
   b. A subprogram is either a ________________________ or a ________________________ .
5. What is the difference between the two CVM instructions `PROC` and `ALLOC`?
6. Describe the calling conventions for CPRL on the CVM.

7. Select several type and miscellaneous rules for CPRL subprograms, and for each such rule, write two test programs in CPRL, one correct program that satisfies the rule and one incorrect program that does not satisfy the rule. After completing Project 7 (Appendix A), use the test programs to check if your compiler correctly implements the rules.

Chapter 14
Arrays

CPRL supports one-dimensional array types, but multidimensional arrays can be created as arrays of arrays. Array indices are integer values, and the index of the first element in the array is `0`. An array type declaration specifies the array type name (an identifier), the number of elements in the array (which must be a positive integer literal or constant), and the type of the elements in the array.

In the next chapter we will extend the idea of array indices to allow values of an enumerated type, but for now we will focus on integer-valued indices.

14.1 Using CPRL Arrays

To create array variables, you can declare an array type and then declare one or more variables of that type. Alternatively, you can declare an array variable using an array type constructor. Arrays can be initialized using composite initializers, which enclose constant values in braces. Here are some examples.

```
type T1 = array[100] of Integer;
type T2 = array[10] of T1;
var a1 : T1;  // contains 100 integers; indexed from 0 to 99
var a2 : T2;  // contains 10 arrays of integers; indexed from 0 to 9
const arraySize := 10;
var a : array[arraySize] of Integer := { 0, 1, 2, 3, 4, 5, 6, 7, 8, 9 };
...
a1[0]     // the integer at index 0 of a1 (the first integer)
a2[3]     // the array at index 3 of a2 (the fourth array)
a2[4][3]  // the integer at index 3 of the array at index 4 of a2
for i in 0..arraySize - 1 loop
    writeln a[i];   // print the elements in array a
```

Composite initializers can be nested for multidimensional arrays.

```
type Row    = array[3] of Integer;
type Matrix = array[3] of Row;     // a 3x3 matrix of integers
var m : Matrix := {
                    { 2, 0, 0 },
                    { 0, 1, 0 },
                    { 0, 0, 0 }
                  };
```

Type Equivalence for Arrays

Some programming languages use structural equivalence for array types; i.e., two array objects are considered to have the same type if they have the same number of elements and the element types are the same. So, for example, two array objects each containing 100 integers would be considered to have the same type.

In contrast, CPRL uses a variant of name equivalence for array types. Array objects in CPRL are considered to have the same type only if they are declared using the same type name or if they are declared with identical array type constructors. Thus, two distinct array type declarations define different types even if they are structurally identical.

Additionally, two array objects with the same type are assignment compatible. Two array objects with different types are not assignment compatible, even if they are structurally identical. This concept is illustrated through several examples.

Examples. Array Assignment

```
type T1 = array[5] of Integer;
var a1 : T1 := { 0, 1, 2, 3, 4 };
var a2 : T1;     // a1 and a2 have the same type

var a3 : array[5] of Integer := { 5, 4, 3, 2, 1 };
var a4 : array[5] of Integer;    // a3 and a4 have the same type

type T = array[5] of Integer;
var a : T;
...
a2 := a1;          // legal assignment (same type)
a4 := a3;          // legal assignment (same type)

a := a1;           // *** Illegal in CPRL (different types) ***
a := a3;           // *** Illegal in CPRL (different types) ***
```

Note that the last two assignment statements above are illegal in CPRL even though `a`, `a1`, and `a3` all have the same structure – arrays of `5` integers.

Reference Semantics versus Value Semantics

CPRL uses value semantics for assignment of arrays. In contrast, Java uses reference semantics by default; Java supports value semantics for array assignment via the static method `arraycopy()` in class `java.lang.System`. The following diagram illustrates the difference between the two for an assignment statement of the form `a1 := a2` involving arrays; i.e., both `a1` and `a2` are variables of the same array type.

Consider the effect of modifying `a2[0]` after the assignment. If array assignment used reference semantics, then modifying `a2[0]` will also modify `a1[0]` since both `a1` and `a2` reference the same array object. With value semantics, both `a1` and `a2` are independent copies of the same array values, and therefore modifying `a2[0]` will have no effect on the data in array `a1`.

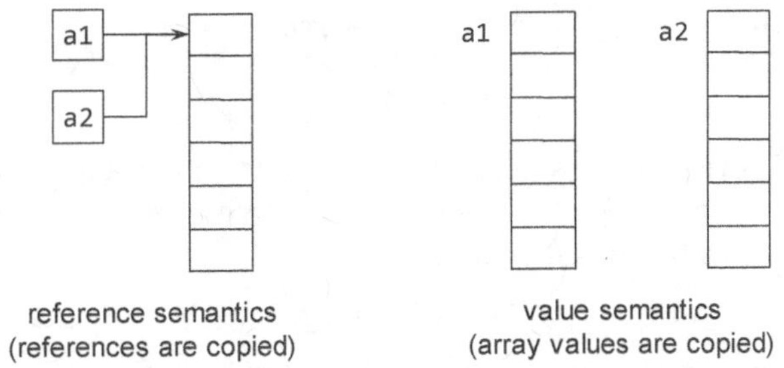

Here are some additional examples of array assignment with comments to explain the fact that CPRL uses value semantics for array assignment.

```
type T1 = array[100] of Integer;
type T2 = array[10] of T1;
var  x, y : T2;
...
x := y;                // array assignment (type T2); copies 1000 integers
x[2] := y[5];          // array assignment (type T1); copies 100 integers
x[2][7] := y[5][0];    // Integer assignment; copies 1 integer (4 bytes)
y[5][0] := 12;         // Integer assignment; has no effect on array x
```

Passing Arrays as Parameters and Returning Arrays from Functions

Similar to C, C++, and Java, but unlike parameters of scalar types in CPRL, array parameters are always passed as variable (`var`) parameters regardless of how the parameter is declared. This holds true even for function parameters, which cannot be declared as `var` parameters. This is simply a language design decision made for efficiency. Arrays can be large objects, and passing an array as a value parameter would require memory allocation and copying of the entire array. Passing an array as a variable parameter will allocate space only for the address of the array.

However, CPRL uses value semantics when returning arrays from functions; i.e., the entire array is returned on the run-time stack.

14.2 Implementing CPRL Arrays

We begin our discussion of implementing arrays by reviewing the relevant grammar rules, parser methods, classes, and constraints. Here are the grammar rules relevant to arrays.

```
varDecl = "var" identifiers ":" ( typeName | arrayTypeConstr )
          [ ":=" initializer ] ";" .
initializer = constValue | compositeInitializer .
constValue = ( [ "-" ] literal ) | constId .
compositeInitializer = "{" initializer { "," initializer } "}" .
arrayTypeDecl = "type" typeId "=" "array"  "[" intConstValue "]"
                "of" typeName ";" .
arrayTypeConstr = "array" "[" intConstValue "]" "of" typeName .
```

```
typeName = "Integer" | "Boolean" | "Byte"| "Char" | "String" | typeId .
variable = ( varId | paramId ) { indexExpr | fieldExpr } .
indexExpr = "[" expression "]" .
```

While it is possible to create arrays of arrays, the grammar rules require that the symbol following "`of`" (as in `array[10] of Integer`) be a type name. We can't nest array type constructors; i.e., the following is illegal in CPRL.

```
var x : array[10] of array[10] of Integer;  // *** Illegal in CPRL
```

The grammar rules for arrays are implemented in corresponding parser methods as follows.

```
private InitialDecl parseVarDecl()
private Initializer parseInitializer()
private Initializer parseCompositeInitializer()
private Expression parseIntConstValue()
private InitialDecl parseArrayTypeDecl()
private ArrayType parseArrayTypeConstr()
private Type parseTypeName()
private Variable parseVariable()
```

Note that method `parseIntConstValue()` is a specialized implementation of `parseConstValue()`. If an error is detected when parsing a constant value, or if the constant value does not have type `Integer`, then after the error has been reported, `parseIntConstValue()` will return a valid `ConstValue` of type `Integer`. This is done to prevent the reporting of extraneous errors.

Also note that an index expression is parsed within method `parseVariableCommon()`, which is called by `parseVariable()` as discussed in Section 6.9. There is no separate method named `parseIndexExpr()`.

Following is a diagram that shows the inheritance hierarchy of relevant classes for arrays.

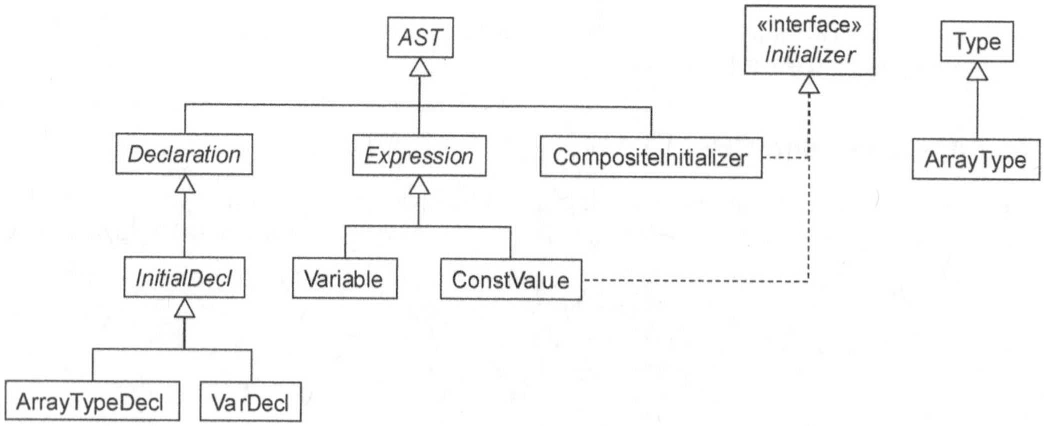

Class ArrayType

An array type declaration creates a new type – an array type. Class `ArrayType` encapsulates the following four properties of an array type.

- `typeName` – the name of the array type
- `numElements` – the number of elements in the array type
- `elementType` – the element type; i.e., the type of the elements in the array
- `size` – the size (number of bytes) of a variable with this type, which is computed as `numElements*elementType.size()`

Here is the constructor for class `ArrayType` showing the computation for `size`.

```
public ArrayType(String typeName, int numElements, Type elementType)
  {
    super(typeName, numElements*elementType.size());
    this.elementType = elementType;
  }
```

When creating an array object using an array type constructor, as in

```
var a : array[10] of Integer;
```

there is no simple identifier for the array type name, so the parser uses the entire array constructor string as the type name; i.e., the type name used for the above `var` declaration would be "`array[10] of Integer`".

The following excerpt from method `parseArrayTypeConstr()` illustrates the creation of this pseudo type name.

```
var numElements = parseIntConstValue();
match(Symbol.rightBracket);
match(Symbol.ofRW);
var elemType = parseTypeName();
var typeName = "array[" + numElements.intValue() + "] of " + elemType;
```

Array Object and Element Addresses

The relative address for a variable of an array type is the relative address of the first byte in the array. The relative address or offset for the element of the array at index `n` is the sum of the relative address of the array plus the offset of the nth element, computed as follows.

```
relAddr(a[n]) = relAddr(a) + n*elementType.size()
```

Since the `Boolean` type uses a single byte (size is `1`), for an array of `Boolean` the relative address for the element at index `n` can be simplified to the following.

```
relAddr(a[n]) = relAddr(a) + n
```

Let's consider an example. Suppose we have the following declarations.

```
type T = array[100] of Integer;
var  a : T;
```

We can visualize the layout of the array as shown in the following diagram.

If the actual physical memory address of a is 60, then the actual address of a[0] is 60, the actual address of a[1] is 64, the actual address of a[2] is 68, etc.

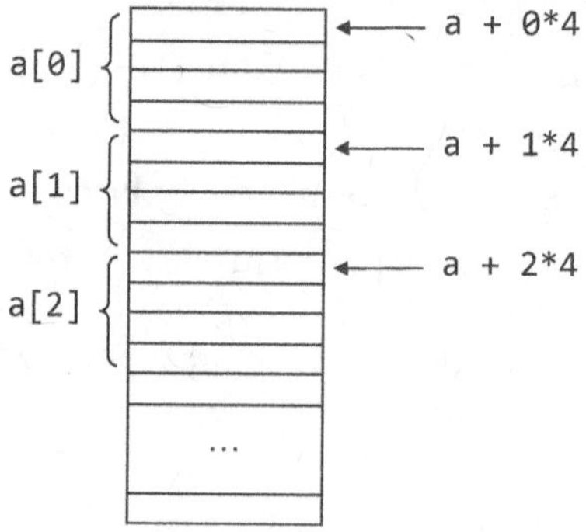

Constraint Rules for Arrays

Consider the following miscellaneous rule for arrays.

- Miscellaneous Rule: Array parameters are always passed as variable (var) parameters.

This rule is handled in the checkContraints() methods for AST classes FunctionDecl and ProcedureDecl. If the type of a formal parameter is declared as an array type, we simply force the parameter to be a variable parameter.

```
if (paramDecl.type() instanceof ArrayType)
    paramDecl.setVarParam(true);
```

The remaining constraint rules for arrays are organized according to the three AST classes where the rules are enforced.

- **ArrayTypeDecl**
  - Type Rule: The constant value specifying the number of items in the array must have type Integer, and the associated value must be a positive number.
- **VarDecl**
  - Miscellaneous Rule: An initializer for a variable of an array type must be a composite initializer, and the number of components in the composite initializer must equal the number of elements in the array type.
  - Type Rule: For arrays of arrays or arrays of records, the values in a composite initializer must also be composite initializers. For arrays of scalar types or arrays of type String, the values in a composite initializer must have the same type as the array element type.

- `Variable`
  - Miscellaneous Rule: Index expressions are permitted only for variables with an array type or type `String`. (Strings are covered in Chapter 16. The individual characters of a string are accessed using an index notation; as in `s[3]`.)
  - Type Rule: Each index expression must have a numeric type or an enum type. Class `Type` has a method named `isIndexType()` that can be used to check this. Note that index expressions of type `Byte` will have already been promoted to `Integer`.

Note that parser method `parseArrayTypeConstr()` returns an `ArrayType`, not an AST class. Therefore, this parser method must enforce a rule identical to the type rule stated above for `ArrayTypeDecl` – there is no AST class to check the constraint. For consistency, parser method `parseArrayTypeDecl()` is written using logic similar to that of parseArrayTypeConstr(), so enforcing the type rule in `ArrayTypeDecl` is technically redundant; it was already checked in the parser. So here we have a rare case of a type rule being checked in the parser.

Implementation of method `checkConstraints()` for class `VarDecl` is complicated by the fact that composite initializers can be nested. Nested initializers have a tree-like structure, and we need to "walk" down the tree to get to the constant values that are either scalar types or string types. We use a recursive method named `checkInitializer()` for this purpose. Below is an outline of this method.

```
private void checkInitializer(Type type, Initializer initializer)
    throws ConstraintException
  {
    if (type.isScalarType() || type == Type.String)
      {
        ...  // check that the initializer is a
             // ConstValue of the appropriate type
      }
    else if (type instanceof ArrayType arrayType)
      {
        ...  // check that the initializer is a composite
             // initializer with correct number of values

        // for each initializer i in the composite initializer
        //     call checkInitializer(arrayType.elementType(), i)
      }
    ...
```

In class `VarDecl`, method `checkConstraints()` simply calls `checkInitializer()` if the initializer is not empty.

```
if (!initializer.isEmpty())
    checkInitializer(type(), initializer);
```

We will need to revisit this method in the next three chapters, especially in Chapter 17 since we can declare arrays of records, and records can also have composite initializers.

Implementation of method `checkConstraints()` in class `Variable` needs additional explanation. Consider the following CPRL declarations.

```
type T = array[10] of Integer;
var  a : T;
```

Observe that `a` has type `T`, but `a[i]` has type `Integer`. Therefore, when checking constraints for an array type, for each selector expression `checkConstraints()` must perform the following actions.

- Set the type of the variable to the element type for the array. As an example, for an array of `Boolean`, an index expression could have type `Integer`, but the result of indexing into the array has type `Boolean`, and this variable type will need to be set in method `checkConstraints()`.
- Check that the selector expression is an index expression; i.e., that it is not a field expression.
- Check that the type of the selector expression is an allowed index type (`Integer`, `Byte`, or an enum type). Class `Type` has a `boolean` function named `isIndexType()` that can be used to check the type of an array selector expression.

Code Generation for Arrays

Many of the AST classes don't directly involve arrays, and some that do involve arrays don't need to be modified. For example, the implementation of `emit()` for class `AssignmentStmt` should work for arrays without any modifications. Most of the work involved in code generation for arrays takes place in the `emit()` method of class `Variable`. Here is a summary of the basic ideas.

First, as with non-array types, method `emit()` must emit code to leave the relative address of the variable being assigned on the run-time stack (i.e., the address of the first byte of the array). There is no change required to existing code for non-array variables.

Next, we get the type of the variable as found in its declaration.

```
var type = decl.type();
```

Then, for each selector (index) expression, if `type` is an instance of `ArrayType`, method `emit()` must perform the following actions.

- Generate code to compute the value of the selector (index) expression.

  ```
  expr.emit();
  ```

- Generate code to multiply this value by the element type's size to get the offset.

  ```
  emit("LDCINT " + arrayType.elementType().size());
  emit("MUL");
  ```

- Generate code to add the offset to the relative address of the variable.

  ```
  emit("ADD");
  ```

- Change the variable type to the element type of the array in case there are more selector expressions.

  ```
  type = arrayType.elementType();
  ```

As a simple optimization within method `emit()`, don't generate code for the second step above if the array's element type has size `1` (e.g., if the element type is `Boolean` or `Byte`). Generating code for the second step would simply multiply the value from the first step by one.

14.3 Essential Terms and Concepts

- array
- array type declaration
- index expression
- name equivalence for array types
- relative address of an array element
- value semantics (array assignment)
- `ArrayType` (class)
- array type constructor
- initializer/composite initializer
- reference semantics (array assignment)
- structural equivalence for array types

14.4 Exercises

1. **Project Assignment.** Implement **Project 8: Arrays** as described in Appendix A.
2. Explain the difference between reference semantics and value semantics for array assignment. Which one is used by CPRL? Which one is used by Java?
3. True or False (T or F)
   a. Array indices must be integer values.
   b. The index of the first element in an array is `1`.
   c. Array parameters are passed as value parameters (passed by value) for functions.
   d. Array assignment copies all values from the array on the right side of the assignment symbol to the array on the left side.
   e. An array type declaration creates a new type.

4. Use the following declarations in the questions below.

```
type T1 = array[100] of Integer;
type T2 = array[10] of T1;
var a1 : T1;
var a2 : T2;
```

   a. What is the type of `a1`?
   b. What is the type of `a1[5]`?
   c. What is the type of `a2[5]`?
   d. What is the relative address (offset) of `a1[5]`?
   e. If the actual memory address of `a1` is `100`, what is the actual memory address of `a1[5]`?
   f. If the actual memory address of `a2` is `500`, what is the actual memory address of `a2[5]`?

5. Select one of the constraint rules (either a type or a miscellaneous rule) for CPRL arrays and write two test programs in CPRL – one correct program that satisfies the rule and one incorrect program that does not satisfy the rule. After completing Project 8 (Appendix A), use the test programs to check if your compiler correctly implements the rules.

6. In CPRL, array parameters are always passed as variable (`var`) parameters. Suppose that arrays could be passed as value parameters. Explain an advantage of passing the array as a variable parameter even if the original array is not modified.

7. Use the following declarations in the question below.

```
type T1 = array[100] of Integer;
type T2 = array[100] of Integer;
var a1 : T1;
var a2 : T2;
var a3 : array[100] of Integer;
```

   a. Is the following assignment valid in CPRL (yes or no)? Justify your answer.

   ```
   a1 := a2;
   ```

   b. Is the following assignment valid in CPRL (yes or no)? Justify your answer.

   ```
   a1 := a3;
   ```

8. Explain why the following declaration is not valid in CPRL.

```
var a : array[10] of array[10] of Integer;
```

Chapter 15
Enumerated Types

Most modern programming languages provide a user-defined type that, at a minimum, allows assignment of meaningful names for integer-like constants. This language feature is commonly referred to as an enumerated type or an enum type. Enumerated types improve code readability and type safety, and they are more convenient than declaring a list of integer constants. CPRL supports a very simple form of enumerated type with minimal functionality. An enum type declaration specifies the type name (an identifier) plus the names (identifiers) for each enum constant. At the machine level, the first named constant has value `0`, the second named constant has value `1`, and so on.

Names of the enum constants are scoped to the enumerated type; i.e., they must be unique within the enum type declaration, but otherwise enum constant names can overlap other names in the program, including enum constant names for other enumerated types.

15.1 Motivation for Enumerated Types

Enumerated types improve readability by allowing the programmer to express ideas in the problem domain, and they enforce type safety. Instead of hard-coding integers, enumerated types use human-readable names. Consider the following three examples.

```
color := 32896;        color := 0x008080;        color := Color.Teal;
```

The first example uses a magic number that is not very meaningful to anyone. The second example is somewhat better for those who understand RGB color codes, but the third example is the most readable. It expresses the programmer's intent clearly.

Here are two more examples, one on the left and one on the right.

```
const Clubs    = 0;          type Suit = <Clubs, Diamonds, Hearts, Spades>;
const Diamonds = 1;          var suit : Suit := Suit.Hearts;
const Hearts   = 2;
const Spades   = 3;
var suit : Integer := Hearts;
```

The example on the right is not only more compact and more readable, but the use of enumerated types provides type safety in that we could never assign an invalid value to variable `suit`. The example on the left would not prevent such an assignment.

```
suit := 5;   // permitted, but doesn't match any declared suit
```

As a final example illustrating readability and type safety, let's assume that we are working on an application involving dates and that we have a `Date` type expressed as a record with three fields containing the year, month, and day. (Records are covered in more detail in Chapter 17.) We would likely want a function named something like createDate() to create a date from the three fields, possibly with some validation for the date fields. We could use integer values, and a call to `createDate()` might look like the following.

```
Date d = createDate(7, 10, 2026);
```

Looking at this function call we might assume that `2026` is the year, but what about the other two values? Is `7` the month or the day? Some countries prefer month first when expressing a date using three integers, and other countries prefer day first. We can't be sure without looking back at the details of the function definition, which hopefully provided meaningful names for parameters. Using enumerated types, the call might look like the following, which is much safer and more readable.

```
Date d = makeDate(Month.July, 10, 2026);
```

15.2 Using CPRL Enumerated Types

Enumerated types are declared using a type declaration that lists all possible values for the type. To use enumerated types, you must first declare an enumerated type and then declare one or more variables of that type. The values are ordered according to their order of appearance in the list, and relational operators can be used for comparison. Although enumerated types are distinct from type `Integer`, they are represented as integers at the machine level, and they can be used in `for` loops and as indices for array types. When used in `write` and `writeln` statements, the underlying integer value, not the enum value name, is written to standard output. Enum constants in CPRL are expressed in the form `TypeName.ValueName`. Here are some examples.

```
type Day = <Sun, Mon, Tue, Wed, Thu, Fri, Sat>;
type Suit = <Clubs, Diamonds, Hearts, Spades>;
type LogLevel = <Error, Warning, Info, Debug>;

var wed : Day := Day.Wed;

writeln "Day number for variable wed is ", wed;    // writes 3
writeln "Day number for Friday is ", Day.Fri;      // writes 5

for d in Day.Sun..Day.Sat loop
    writeln "day number = ", d;                    // writes 0, 1, ... 6
...

fun isWeekDay(d : Day) : Boolean
  {
    // note use of relational operators
    return d >= Day.Mon and d <= Day.Fri;
  }
```

Similar to type `Integer`, enumerated types use value semantics for assignment and value parameters for subprograms.

Even though enum constants are represented as integer values at the machine level, an enumerated type is distinct from type `Integer`. Assignment of an integer literal or variable to an enum variable is not allowed since they are considered to be different types, and vice versa. Enum variables are assignment-compatible only with enum constants and other enum variables of the same enumerated type.

Example.

```
type Day = <Sun, Mon, Tue, Wed, Thu, Fri, Sat>;

var n : Integer;
var d : Day;

n := Day.Mon;    // *** Illegal in CPRL ***
d := 4;          // *** Illegal in CPRL ***
```

Most programming languages provide built-in functionality to convert an enum constant to an integer value or to a more meaningful string value for output. This capability is not built into the CPRL programming language, but it can be implemented simply and efficiently using CPRL functions and parallel arrays as shown below.

Examples.

```
type Day = <Sun, Mon, Tue, Wed, Thu, Fri, Sat>;
var  dayNums  : array[7] of Integer := { 0, 1, 2, 3, 4, 5, 6 };
var  dayNames : array[7] of String
       := { "Sun", "Mon", "Tue", "Wed", "Thu", "Fri", "Sat" };
...

fun pos(day : Day) : Integer
  {
    return dayNums[day];
  }

fun toString(d : Day) : String
  {
    return dayNames[d];
  }
...

var n : Integer;
n := pos(Day.Fri);          // legal since pos() returns an integer

for d in Day.Sun..Day.Sat loop
    writeln toString(d);   // writes string values "Sun", "Mon", ...
```

In addition, most programming languages also provide built-in functionality to compute the predecessor or successor of an enum value. One design issue here is how to respond to an attempt to find the predecessor of the first enumerated value or the successor of the last enumerated value. It is common in these cases to generate a run-time error. Again, CPRL does not automatically provide this functionality, but it can be implemented (although somewhat inefficiently) as shown below in functions `pred()` and `succ()`.

```
fun pred(day : Day) : Day
  {
    var saveDay: Day := Day.Sun;

    if day > Day.Sun then
      {
        for d in Day.Mon..Day.Sat loop
          {
            if d < day then
                saveDay := d;
          }

        return saveDay;
      }
    else
      {
        writeln "Can't compute pred(Day.Sun)";
        return Day.Sun;
      }
  }

fun succ(day : Day) : Day
  {
    if day < Day.Sat then
      {
        for d in Day.Mon..Day.Sat loop
          {
            if d > day then
                return d;
          }
      }
    else
      {
        writeln "Can't compute succ(Day.Sat)";
        return Day.Sat;
      }
  }
```

15.3 Implementing CPRL Enumerated Types

As usual we begin by reviewing the relevant grammar rules, parser methods, classes, and constraints, but we don't need to revisit many related concepts such as variables, variable declarations, assignment, initializers, etc., since they all work the same way as for integers. We'll focus primarily on two grammar rules, their two corresponding parser methods, and classes `EnumType`, `EnumTypeDecl`, and `ConstValue`. The two grammar rules and their corresponding parser methods are as follows.

```
enumTypeDecl = "type" typeId "=" "<" identifiers ">" ";" .
enumConstValue = enumTypeId "." enumConstId .

private InitialDecl parseEnumTypeDecl()
private Expression parseEnumConstValue()
```

Constraint Rules for Enumerated Types

There is a single scope rule for enumerated types: names (identifiers) for enum constants must be unique within an enumerated type declaration.

Method `parseEnumTypeDecl()`

Method `parseEnumTypeDecl()` parses the enum type name and the list of enum constants (identifiers), and it uses that information to create and return an instance of `EnumTypeDecl`. The constructor for class `EnumTypeDecl` is as follows.

```
public EnumTypeDecl(Token typeId, List<Token> enumNames)
```

Method `parseEnumTypeDecl()` calls `parseIdentifiers()` to get the list of declared enum constant names. It uses the list of identifiers to create an enum type declaration and then adds the declaration to the identifier table in the current scope.

```
var enumTypeDecl = new EnumTypeDecl(typeId, identifiers);
idTable.add(typeId, enumTypeDecl);
```

The main issues with implementing method `parseEnumTypeDecl()` are ensuring that the enum constant names are unique and reporting any errors if they aren't unique. Using the identifier table would be cumbersome since all we have is a set of identifier tokens – no declaration to add to `IdTable`. Rather than using the identifier table to check for duplicates and report errors, we use a **set** of strings to help filter out duplicates and then report an error message identical to the one that would have been generated by the identifier table for duplicate names in the current scope.

```
var enumStrings = new HashSet<String>(identifiers.size());
for (var identifier : identifiers)
  {
    if (!enumStrings.contains(identifier.text()))
        enumStrings.add(identifier.text());
    else
      {
        // Report an error identical to that of the identifier table.
        var errorMsg = "Identifier \"" + identifier.text()
                     + "\" is already defined in the current scope.";
        var e = error(identifier.position(), errorMsg);
        errorHandler.reportError(e);
      }
  }
```

Class EnumType

An enumerated type declaration creates a new type – an enum type. Class `EnumType` encapsulates the type name and the list of enum constants. The constructor and a key method for class EnumType are outlined below.

```
/**
 * Construct an enum type with the specified type name
 * and list of enum constants.
 */
public EnumType(String typeName, List<Token> enumNames)

/**
 * Returns the numeric value associated with the enum identifier
 * string.  Returns -1 if the identifier string is not found.
 */
public int getValue(String idStr)
```

Method parseEnumConstValue()

This method returns an instance of AST class `ConstValue` with appropriate enum type but with an integer literal based on the underlying integer value for the enum constant. Relevant code is given below. Note the call to `enumType.getValue()` to obtain the underlying integer value for the enum constant.

```
// create a ConstValue representing this enum value
var enumTypeDecl = (EnumTypeDecl) decl;
var enumType = (EnumType) enumTypeDecl.type();
var enumValue = enumType.getValue(enumConstId.text());

if (enumValue < 0)
  {
    var errorMsg = "\"" + enumConstId.text() + "\" is not a valid ... "
    throw error(enumConstId.position(), errorMsg);
  }

var enumValStr = Integer.toString(enumValue);
var position   = enumConstId.position();
var literal    = new Token(Symbol.intLiteral, position, enumValStr);

return new ConstValue(literal, enumType);
```

Thereafter, constraint checking and code generation are performed in class `ConstValue`. The only modification for enumerated types is in the `emit()` method, which treats enumerated types in the same way as type `Integer`.

```
if (type() == Type.Integer || type() instanceof EnumType)
    emit("LDCINT " + intValue());
```

15.4 Essential Terms and Concepts

`EnumType` (class)

`EnumTypeDecl` (class)

enumerated constant

ordering of enumerated constants

15.5 Exercises

1. **Project Assignment.** Implement **Project 9: Enumerated Types** as described in Appendix A. Note that most of the work for implementing enumerated types is provided for you.
2. True or False (T or F)
   a. Enumerated types can be used as indices for arrays.
   b. Enumerated types can be used as range values in `for` loops.
   c. A variable with an enumerated type can be assigned an integer value.
   d. A variable with type `Integer` can be assigned a value of an enumerated type.
   e. Names (identifiers) for enum constants must be unique within an enumerated type declaration.
3. Discuss advantages of enumerated types over named integer constants. (Hint: see the examples at the start of this chapter.)
4. How are enumerated constants ordered?
5. How are enumerated constants represented at the machine level? What AST class is used for enumerated constants?
6. Assume that type Day is defined as follows.

   ```
   type Day = <Sun, Mon, Tue, Wed, Thu, Fri, Sat>;
   ```

   What value is written in the following `writeln` statement?

   ```
   writeln Day.Mon;
   ```

7. Select a programming language other than Java or CPRL and discuss how enumerated types are defined in that language.

Chapter 16
Strings

Like most programming languages, CPRL supports sequences of characters called character strings, or simply strings. String literals are enclosed in (double) quotation marks, as in `"Hello, world."` A string in CPRL has a run-time integer property named `length` as described below.

16.1 Using CPRL Strings

`String` is a predefined composite type in CPRL. String variables can be initialized using string literals or declared string constants. For a string variable, the length is determined when it is assigned a value, either via initialization, an assignment statement, or a read statement.

Consider the following examples.

```
var month : String := "January";
var name  : String;
var line  : String;
name := "Keira";
read line;
```

In the above examples, `month` is a string variable initialized to string literal `"January"`. After initialization, it has length `7`. Similarly, after assignment, variable `name` has length `5`. Since variable `line` was not initialized, its length is undefined at the point it is declared. After the `read` statement, the length of variable `line` would be determined based on the string of characters entered at the command line. Note that `length` is a run-time property of a string variable; i.e., the length of a string variable is based on its current value and can change at run-time if the variable is used on the left side of an assignment statement or in a read statement.

String variables use the array index notation to provide access to the individual characters and the dot notation to provide access to the string length.

```
name[0]        // the character at index 0 (the first character)
name.length    // the length of the string
```

Observe that variable `name` has type `String`, but `name.length` has type `Integer` and `name[i]` has type `Char`. An expression that follows a string variable (i.e., `.length` or `[i]`) is called a **selector** expression. Selector expression "`.length`" is called a field expression, and selector expression "`[i]`" is called an index expression. We have already encountered index expressions when working with arrays in Chapter 14. Field expressions will be discussed in more detail in the next chapter where we cover records.

String concatenation is supported using the plus ("+") operator.

```
var firstName : String := "Bennett";
var lastName  : String := "Smith";
var fullName  : String;
...
fullName := firstName + " " + lastName;    // "Bennett Smith"
```

Reference Semantics Versus Value Semantics

Similar to Java, CPRL uses reference semantics for assignment of strings. A string variable doesn't actually contain the sequence of characters. Rather, it contains a reference to the characters – in CPRL it contains the address of the characters. After an assignment statement of the form `s1 := s2`, both `s1` and `s2` refer to the same sequence of characters. In contrast, C++ uses value semantics. The difference between reference semantics and value semantics is illustrated in the following diagram.

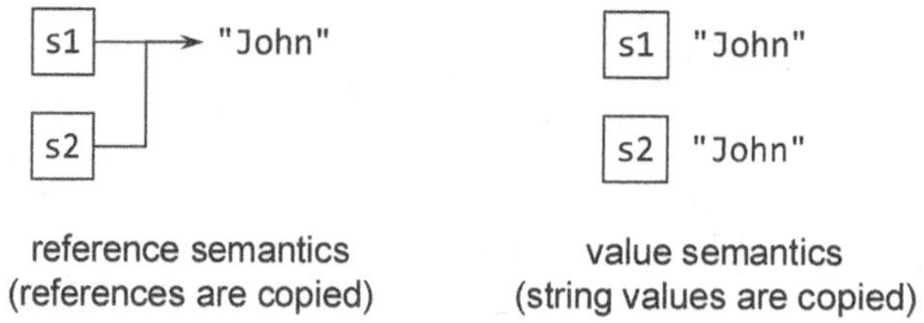

Using value semantics, variable `s1` and `s2` would contain independent copies of the sequence of characters. An assignment of the form

```
s2[2] := 'a'
```

would change `"John"` to `"Joan"` for variable `s2`, but it would have no effect on variable `s1`. Using reference semantics, the assignment would effectively change the string value referenced by both s1 and s2. But in CPRL, as in Java, strings are immutable. While a string variable can be reassigned, the length and the individual characters in the string can't be modified, so the above assignment statement would generate an error message in CPRL.

Examples.

```
var month : String := "Mar";   // month has length 3
var c : Char;
var n : Integer;
...
n := month.length;          // n has value 3
c := month[0];              // c has value 'M';
month[2] := 'y';            // *** Illegal in CPRL ***
month.length := 5;          // *** Illegal in CPRL ***
month := "May";             // assignment of string value is o.k.
```

Passing Strings as Parameters and Returning Strings from Functions

Since CPRL strings use reference semantics, the reference (address) of the string value is actually passed as a parameter. Passing a string as a value parameter will allocate space for and copy the reference (address) of the string. Passing a string as a variable parameter will allocate space for the address of the actual parameter, which means that you can reassign it, but you still can't modify the length or individual characters.

```
proc changeName(var n : String)   // pass by reference
  {
    n := "Johnny";    // reassigns value for the actual parameter
  }
```

Similarly, CPRL uses reference semantics when returning strings from functions; i.e., the string address is returned on the run-time stack.

```
fun boolToStr(b : Boolean) : String
  {
    if b then
        return "true";     // returns a reference to this string literal
    else
        return "false";    // ditto
  }
```

16.2 Implementing CPRL Strings

We begin with a discussion of how strings are represented in memory. At runtime, a string **value** is stored as an integer followed by an array of characters. The integer holds the current length of the string; i.e., the number of characters. Unlike arrays, the length of the string is actually stored as part of the string value. Records aren't covered in detail until the next chapter, but if you are familiar with records or structures (structs) in other languages, you will recognize that a string is essentially implemented similar to a record with two fields – one for the length and a second for an array of characters. The number of bytes of a string value in memory is 4 for the length plus 2 for each character.

A string **variable** contains the address for a string value, so the size of a string variable is always 4 in the CVM. For the following declaration,

```
var greet : String := "Hello";
```

the size of variable `greet` is 4 and the number of bytes in memory occupied by the string value `"Hello"` is 14 (`4 + 2*5`). We can visualize this representation as shown in the following diagram.

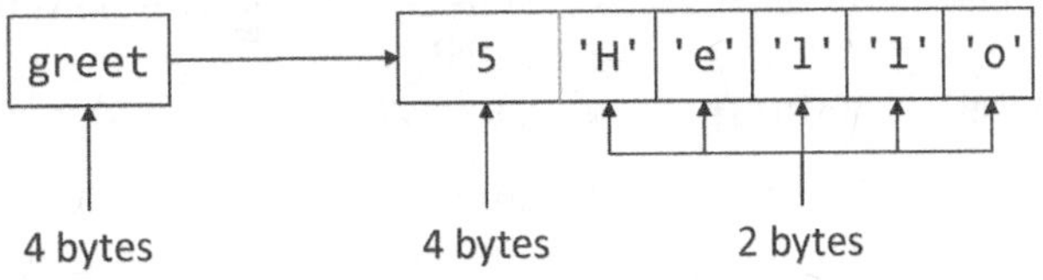

Constraint Rules for Strings

The constraint rules for strings are organized according to the AST classes where the rules are enforced.

- `AddingExpr`
  - Type Rule: Operands of type String are allowed, but only for the plus ("+") operator. (The plus operator is used for string concatenation.)
- `AssignmentStmt`
  - Type Rule: Strings are immutable in CPRL. We can assign new values to string variables, but we can't modify the string's length or its individual characters.
- `OutputStmt`
  - Each expression must have a scalar type or type `String`. Output is supported only for scalar types and strings. Note that class `Type` has a `boolean` method named `isOutputType()` that can be used when checking for valid output types.
- `ReadStmt`
  - Type Rule: The variable must have type `Integer`, `Byte`, `Char`, or `String`.
- `VarDecl`
  - Type Rule: An initializer for a variable of a string type must be a constant value (either a string literal or a declared constant) of type `String`.
- `Variable`
  - Miscellaneous Rule: Index expressions are permitted only for variables with an array type or type `String`.
  - Miscellaneous Rule: Field expressions (see records in Chapter 17) are permitted only for variables with a record type or type `String`. For strings, the only allowed field name is "`length`".
  - Type Rule: An index expression must have either a numeric type or an enumerated type.

Implementing String-Related Classes

The implementation of strings in the CPRL compiler is addressed in nine classes, but the string-related code in most of those classes is simple and straightforward. Below is the list of classes that contain code relevant to the implementation of strings. Classes `Parser` and `Type` are in package `cprlc`, and the other seven are AST classes in the subpackage `cprlc.ast`. The only class where the string-related code is moderately complicated is the last class listed below, class `Variable`.

- `Parser`
- `Type`
- `AddingExpr`
- `AssignmentStmt`
- `ConstValue`
- `OutputStmt`
- `ReadStmt`
- `VarDecl`
- `Variable`

We will address the relevant code in each of these classes in the order listed above.

- **`Parser`:** The only parser method that explicitly addresses strings `parseTypeName()`, which returns `Type.String` whenever the lookahead symbol from the scanner is the reserved word `StringRW`.

```
case StringRW ->
  {
    matchCurrentSymbol();
    return Type.String;
  }
```

- **`Type`:** Class `Type` declares `String` as a predefined type similar to types `Integer` and `Boolean`, and it has a static method `typeOf()` that returns the type of a literal token.

```
public static Type typeOf(Token literal)
  {
    return switch (literal.symbol())
      {
        ...
        case Symbol.stringLiteral -> Type.String;
        ...
      };
  }
```

- **`AddingExpr`:** Method `checkConstraints()` allows string operands for the plus operator, and method `emit()` writes the opcode `STRCAT` for adding (concatenating) string operands.

- **`AssignmentStmt`:** Method `checkConstraints()` needs to enforce the constraint that strings are immutable in CPRL. The logic here uses the variable on the left side of the assignment statement. If the declared type of the variable is `String`, then the list of selector expressions should be empty. Otherwise, we have detected an attempt to modify either the string length or a character within the string, neither of which is allowed.

- **`ConstValue`:** This class has code to emit the appropriate opcode and operand for a constant of type `String`.

```
else if (type() == Type.String)
    emit("LDCSTR " + literal.text());
```

  The entire value of the string is stored in memory with the opcode, but opcode `LDCSTR` pushes only the address of the string literal onto the stack.

- **`OutputStmt`:** We need to check the constraint that each expression being written has either a scalar type or type `String`. Class `Type` has a `Boolean` method named `isOutputType()` that can be used to check this constraint. Also, method `emit()` must emit the opcode `PUTSTR` for an expression of type `String`.

- **ReadStmt:** Method checkConstraints() needs to make sure that the variable being read has one of the four allowed types – Integer, Byte, Char, or String. Class Type has a Boolean method named isInputType() that can be used to check this constraint. Method emit() needs to emit the opcode GETSTR if the variable has type String.
- **VarDecl:** Method checkConstraints() uses helper method checkInitializer() to verify that, for strings, an initializer is a constant value of type String.
- **Variable:** For string variables, this is where things get interesting. We need to consider string variables with selector expressions in both the checkConstraints() and emit() methods. We start with a discussion of how the individual string components are addressed.

Addressing String Components

A string variable holds the address of the string value; i.e., the address of the first byte of the length. The relative address or offset of the length is zero. The relative address or offset for the character of the string at index n is the sum of the address of the string plus 4 (number of bytes for the integer length) plus 2 (number of bytes in a character) times the index, computed as follows.

```
relAddr(s[n]) = s + 4 + 2*n
```

Let's consider an example. Suppose we have the following declaration.

```
var s : String := "abc";
```

We can visualize the layout of the string as shown in the following diagram.

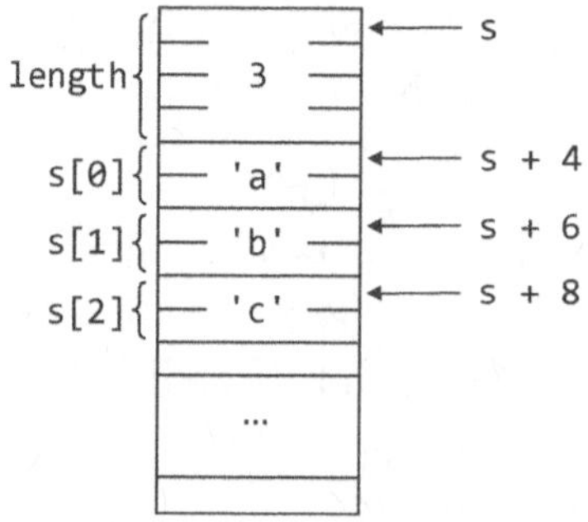

If s has memory address 100, then the actual address of length is 100, the actual address of s[0] is 104, the actual address of s[1] is 106, etc.

Consider the following declaration.

```
var name : String;
```

Observe that name has type String, but name.length has type Integer, and name[i] has type Char.

Method `checkConstraints()` in class `Variable` must perform the following actions for a selector expression following a string variable.

If the selector expression is a field expression, `checkConstraints()` will need to

- Set the type of the variable to `Integer`.
- Check that the field name is "`length`".

If the selector expression is not a field expression (and therefore must be an index expression), `checkConstraints()` will need to

- Set the type of the variable to `Char`.
- Check that the type of the index expression is a valid index type; i.e., that the type is either a numeric type (`Integer` or `Byte`) or an enumerated type. Class `Type` has a method named `isIndexType()` that can be used to check this constraint.

Similar to arrays, most of the work involved in code generation for strings takes place in the emit() method of `Variable`. Here is a summary of the basic ideas.

First, as with non-string types, method `emit()` must emit code to leave the relative address of the variable on the run-time stack (i.e., the address of the first byte of the string). There is no change required to that part of the existing code for non-string variables.

Next, consider a selector expression for a string variable. Recall that a selector expression can be an index expression of the form "`[3]`" providing access to an individual character in the string, or it can be a field expression of the form "`.length`" providing access to the current length of the string. Array variables have only index expressions, record variables have only field expressions, but a string variable can be followed by either type of selector expression. However, only one selector expression can follow a string variable.

If the selector expression is a field expression, no additional code needs to be emitted. The only allowed field expression for strings is "`.length`", which is at offset `0`. We don't need to emit any additional code for this offset.

If the selector expression is not a field expression (and therefore must be an index expression), method `emit()` must perform the following actions.

- Generate code to push the address of the string value on the stack.

  ```
  emit("LOADW");    // push address of string value on the stack
  ```

- Generate code to skip over the `length` field, which has type `Integer`, resulting in the relative address of the first character in the string.

  ```
  emit("LDCINT " + Type.Integer.size());
  emit("ADD");
  ```

- Generate code to compute the value of the index expression.

  ```
  expr.emit();
  ```

- Generate code to multiply this value by the size of type `Char` to get the offset.

```
emit("LDCINT " + Type.Char.size());
emit("MUL");
```

- Generate code to add the offset to the relative address of the first character.

```
emit("ADD");
```

Note that no code is generated to check that the index is within bounds; i.e., that the index is between `0` and the string length.

Heap Memory

In general, most programming languages need to allocate memory dynamically separate from the run-time stack. The part of memory used for dynamic allocation is commonly referred to as the "heap" or the "free store". Languages like Java, C++, and C# use the keyword `new` to request dynamic memory allocation on the heap. While memory allocated on the run-time stack is automatically reclaimed when a subprogram returns, memory allocated on the heap remains until either it is manually freed (e.g., using a `free()` function or a `delete` operator) or until a garbage collector identifies it as unused and reclaims it.

For CPRL, dynamic memory is needed only in two string-related CVM instructions.

- `GETSTR` allocates memory on the heap for the string entered at the command line.
- `STRCAT` allocates memory on the heap to store the concatenated string.

To simplify the implementation, the CVM uses a simple bump allocator that allocates heap memory when needed, and heap memory is never reclaimed; i.e., it is never deallocated. A special-purpose register named `HP` (heap pointer) points to the top of the heap. The heap pointer is initialized to the number of bytes in memory, so it contains a value one more than the address of the last byte. The heap grows from higher- numbered memory addresses toward lower-numbered memory addresses. We can visualize the heap as part of memory layout at run time as shown in the following diagram.

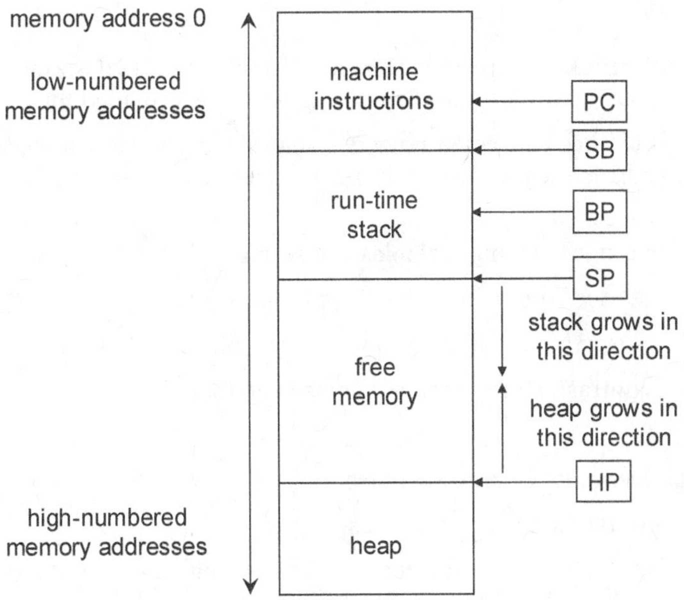

16.3 Essential Terms and Concepts

bump allocator

HP

length (of a string)

reference semantics (string assignment)

relative address of the string length

size (number of bytes) of a string variable

`String` (class)

string concatenation

`s.length` (access string length)

heap

immutable (string value)

plus ("+") operator for strings

relative address of a string character

selector expressions for strings

size (number of bytes) of a string value

string initialization

value semantics (string assignment)

`s[n]` (access character at index `n`)

16.4 Exercises

1. **Project Assignment.** Implement **Project 10: Strings** as described in Appendix A. Note that most of the work for implementing strings is provided for you.
2. Explain the difference between reference semantics and value semantics for string assignment. Which one is used by CPRL? Which one is used by Java? Which one is used by C++??
3. How many bytes does a string variable occupy in memory?
4. How many bytes does the string value `"abcde"` occupy in memory?
5. When passing a string as a value parameter, how many bytes are passed on the stack?
6. Compare and contrast: stack memory versus heap memory.
7. True or False (T or F)
   a. String indices must be integer values.
   b. The index of the first character in a string is 1.
   c. String assignment copies all values from the string on the right side of the assignment symbol to the string on the left side.
   d. The length of a string is a static property.
8. Explain the role of the heap pointer with respect to strings in the CVM. Which two CVM instructions make use of the heap.
9. Use the following declarations in the questions below.

   ```
   var  s : String := "compiler";
   ```

   a. What is the type of `s`?
   b. What is the type of `s.length`?
   c. What is the type of `s[5]`?
   d. What is the length of `s`?
   e. What is the relative address (offset) of `s.length`?
   f. What is the relative address (offset) of `s[5]`?
   g. If `s` contains the value `150`, what is the actual memory address of `s.length`?
   h. If `s` contains the value `150`, what is the actual memory address of `s[5]`?

10. Use the following declaration in the question below.

```
var s1, s2 : String;
var c : Char := 'r';
```

Which of the following assignment statements are valid in CPRL?

a. `s1 = "Haley";`

b. `s1 := s2;`

c. `s1[2] := c;`

d. `c := s1[2];`

e. `s1.length := 3;`

11. Select one of the constraint rules (either a type or a miscellaneous rule) for CPRL strings and write two test programs in CPRL – one correct program that satisfies the rule and one incorrect program that does not satisfy the rule. After completing Project 10 (Appendix A), use the test programs to check if your compiler correctly implements the rules.

Chapter 17
Records

A record is a composite type of named components with potentially different types. Records are called structures (or simply structs) in most C-based languages such as C++, C#, Go, and Rust. Intuitively we can think of a record as being somewhat similar to a class with public data and no constructors or methods. The components of a record are called fields. A record type declaration specifies the record type name (an identifier) plus the name and type of each field.

> Java version 14 introduced a new kind of type declaration called a record. Analogous to data classes in Kotlin, a Java record is a restricted form of a class designed primarily to reduce the boilerplate for classes that are primarily data carriers. CPRL records are much more limited. The term "record" in CPRL is borrowed from Pascal and Ada, where records were more like structures in C than classes in Java and Kotlin.

In contrast with arrays, the components (fields) of a record can have different types, whereas arrays are homogeneous in the sense that all components (elements) of an array have the same type. Also, fields of a record are accessed by their name using the dot notation `r.x`, whereas elements of an array are accessed by their position number using the index notation `a[5]`.

Field names are scoped to the record; i.e., they must be unique within the record type declaration, but otherwise field names can overlap other names in the program.

17.1 Using CPRL Records

To create record objects, you must first declare a record type and then declare one or more variables of that type. Here are some examples.

```
type Point = record
  {
    x : Integer;
    y : Integer;
  };

type Month = record
  {
    name    : String;
    maxDays : Integer;
  };

var p : Point;   // contains 2 fields, x and y
var m : Month;   // contains 2 fields, name and maxDays
...
```

```
p.x := 5;             // the field x of point p (type Integer)
m.name := "March";    // the field name of month m (type String)
```

Note that records and arrays can be nested. That is, records can contain fields that are records or arrays, and vice versa, arrays can contain elements that are arrays or records. We illustrate with several examples below.

```
type Point = record
  {
    x : Integer;
    y : Integer;
  };

type Rectangle = record                      // fields are records
  {
    point1 : Point;
    point2 : Point;
  };

type PointArray = array[10] of Point;   // array of records

type Data = array[10] of Char;
type MyString = record
  {
    length : Integer;
    data   : Data;                           // field is an array
  };
```

Note that records don't have type constructors like arrays; i.e., the following is not permitted in CPRL.

```
var p : record { x : Integer; y : Integer };   // *** Illegal in CPRL
```

Type Equivalence for Records

Some programming languages use structural equivalence for record types; i.e., two record objects are considered to have the same type if they have the same number of fields and the corresponding field types are the same. So, for example, two record objects each containing 2 integer fields would be considered to have the same type.

CPRL uses strict name equivalence for record types. Record objects in CPRL are considered to have the same type only if they are declared using the same type name. Thus, two distinct record type definitions are considered different even though they may be structurally identical.

Additionally, two record objects with the same type are assignment compatible. Two record objects with different types are not assignment compatible, even if they are structurally identical. This concept is illustrated through several examples.

Examples. Record Assignment

```
type Point = record
  {
    x : Integer;
    y : Integer;
  };

type Pair = record
  {
    x : Integer;
    y : Integer;
  };

type Rectangle = record
  {
    point1 : Point;
    point2 : Point;
  };

var point1, point2 : Point;    // point1 and point2 have the same type
var pair1,  pair2  : Pair;     // pair1 and pair2 have the same type
var rect : Rectangle;
...
point1 := point2;        // legal assignment (same types)
pair1  := pair2;         // legal assignment (same types)
point1 := pair1;         // *** Illegal in CPRL (different types) ***
rect.point1 := point1;   // legal assignment (same types)
rect.point2.x := 5;      // legal (integer assignment)
```

Note that the assignment `point1 := pair1` above is illegal in CPRL even though `point1` and `pair1` are both records with exactly two integer fields, and the fields even have identical names.

Also, record variables can be initialized using composite initializers, similar to array variables.

```
type Date = record
  {
    day   : Integer;
    month : Integer;
    year  : Integer;
  };

var d3 : Date := { 29,  2, 2024 };    // this was a leap year
```

We can even initialize nested composite types (e.g., arrays of records) using nested composite initializers.

```
type Point = record
  {
    x : Integer;
    y : Integer;
  };

var points : array[3] of Point := { { 0, 5 }, { 1, 3 }, { 99, -99 } };
```

Reference Semantics versus Value Semantics

CPRL uses value semantics for assignment of records – all field values are copied. In contrast, Java uses reference semantics for assignment of classes. The following diagram illustrates the difference between the two for an assignment statement of the form `p1 := p2` involving records of type `Point` as described above; i.e., both `p1` and `p2` are variables of the same record type.

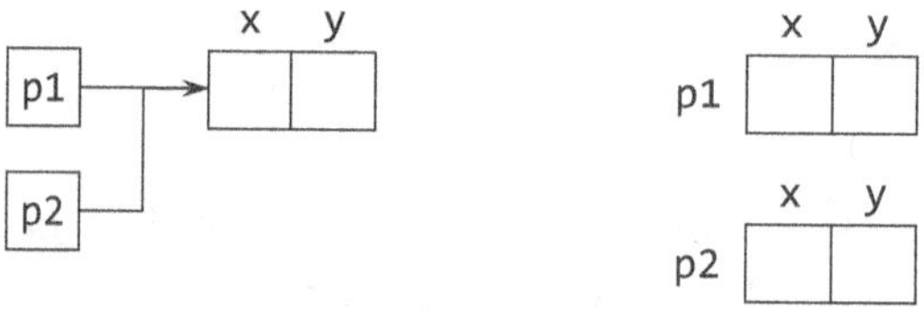

reference semantics (references are copied) value semantics (record values are copied)

Consider the effect of modifying `p2.x` after the assignment. If record assignment used reference semantics, then modifying `p2.x` would also modify `p1.x` since both `p1` and `p2` reference the same record object. With value semantics, both `p1` and `p2` are independent copies of the record's field values, and therefore modifying `p2.x` will have no effect on the data value in `p1.x`.

Here are some additional examples of record assignment with comments to explain the fact that CPRL uses value semantics for record assignment.

```
type Point = record
  {
    x : Integer;
    y : Integer;
  };

var point1, point2 : Point;
...
point1 := point2;         // record assignment (type Point);
                          // copies 2 integer fields (8 bytes)
point1.x := point2.x;     // Integer assignment; copies 1 integer (4 bytes)
point2.x := 5;            // Integer assignment; has no effect on point1.x
```

Passing Records as Parameters and Returning Records from Functions

As with parameters of scalar types, record parameters have semantics similar to assignment. Passing a record as a value parameter will allocate space for and copy the entire record, even if one of the fields is an array. Passing a record as a variable (`var`) parameter will simply allocate space for the address of the record.

Similarly, CPRL uses value semantics when returning records from functions; i.e., a copy of the entire record is returned.

17.2 Implementing CPRL Records

We begin our discussion of implementing records by reviewing the relevant grammar rules, parser methods, classes, and constraints. Here are the grammar rules relevant to records.

```
varDecl = "var" identifiers ":" ( typeName | arrayTypeConstr )
          [ ":=" initializer ] ";" .
initializer = constValue | compositeInitializer .
constValue = ( [ "-" ] literal ) | constId .
compositeInitializer = "{" initializer { "," initializer } "}" .
recordTypeDecl = "type" typeId "=" "record" "{" fieldDecls "}" ";" .
fieldDecls = { fieldDecl } .
fieldDecl = fieldId ":" typeName ";" .
typeName  = "Integer" | "Boolean" | "Byte" | "Char" | "String" | typeId .
variable  = ( varId | paramId ) { indexExpr | fieldExpr } .
fieldExpr = "." fieldId .
```

These grammar rules are implemented in corresponding parser methods as follows.

```
private InitialDecl parseVarDecl()
private Initializer parseInitializer()
private Expression parseConstValue()
private Initializer parseCompositeInitializer()
private InitialDecl parseRecordTypeDecl()
private List<FieldDecl> parseFieldDecls()
private FieldDecl parseFieldDecl()
private Type parseTypeName()
private Variable parseVariable()
```

As discussed in Section 6.9, method `parseVariable()` calls `parseVariableCommon()` to handle the parsing logic. Method `parseVariableCommon()` handles the work of parsing index and field expressions. There is no separate method named `parseFieldExpr()`.

Following is a diagram that shows the inheritance hierarchy of relevant classes for records.

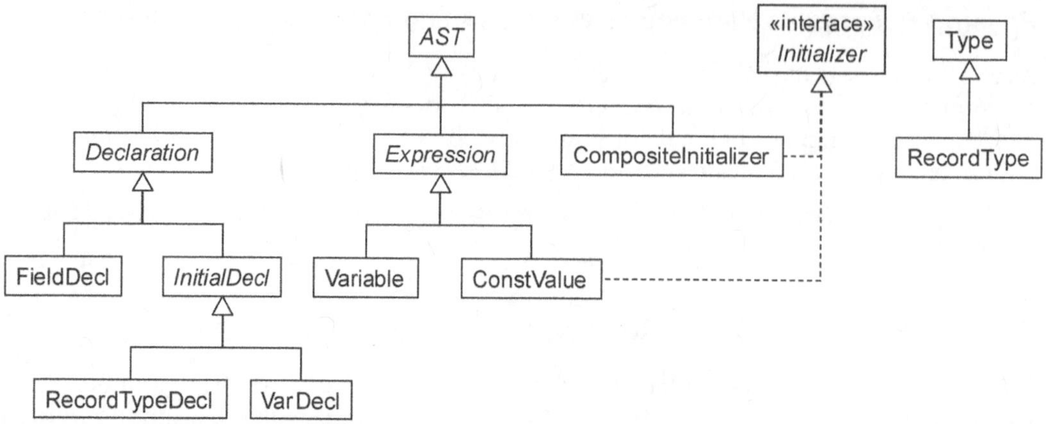

Class RecordType

A record type declaration creates a new type – a record type. Class `RecordType` encapsulates the following three properties of a record type.

- `typeName` – the name of the record type
- `fieldDecls` – a list of field declarations in the record type
- `size` – the size (number of bytes) of a variable with this type, which is computed as the sum of sizes for the fields

Here is the constructor for class `RecordType` showing the computation for `size` via a lambda expression.

```
public RecordType(String typeName, List<FieldDecl> fieldDecls)
  {
    super(typeName, fieldDecls.stream().mapToInt(decl ->
                                           decl.size()).sum());
    ...
  }
```

(Note the brief excursion into functional programming.)

Record Object and Field Addresses

A field declaration can appear only in the context of a record type declaration. One of the properties of a field declaration is `offset`, which is an integer representing the offset of the field within the record. Just as we use the index into an array to determine the address of an array element relative to the address of an array variable, we use the offset of a field to determine its address relative to the address of a record variable. The offset property is explained in more detail in the remainder of this subsection.

The relative address for a variable of a record type is the relative address of the first byte in the variable. Analogous to an array element at index `0`, the relative address or offset of the first field of the record is `0`, meaning that the first field has the same relative address as the variable. The relative address or offset for subsequent fields of the record is simply the sum of sizes of each previous field declarations. Consider, for example, the following declarations.

```
type Triple = record
  {
    x : Integer;
    y : Char;
    z : Boolean;
  };

var t : Triple;
```

We can visualize the layout of the record as shown in the following diagram.

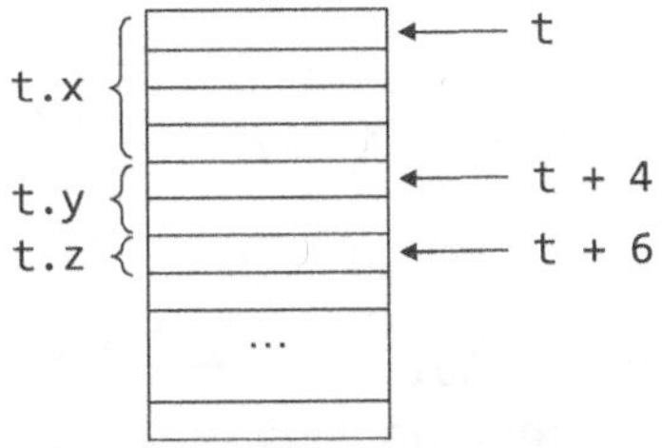

Relative to the address of `t`, field `x` has offset `0`, field `y` has offset `4` (size of `x`), and field `z` has offset `6` (size of `x` plus size of `y`).

Examples

```
relAddr(t.x) = relAddr(t)
relAddr(t.y) = relAddr(t.x) + 4     // = relAddr(t) + 4
relAddr(t.z) = relAddr(t.y) + 2     // = relAddr(t) + 6
```

If the actual physical memory address of `t` is `100`, then the actual address of `t.x` is `100`, the actual address of `t.y` is `104`, and the actual address of `t.z` is `106`.

Constraint Rules for Fields and Records

Field scopes are different from the scopes of other objects in that field names are scoped to the record; i.e., they must be unique within the record type declaration. Otherwise field names can overlap other names in the program. For example, two different record declarations can have fields with the same name, and variables can be created having the same name as a field. There is no ambiguity since fields are accessed using the dot notation `r.x`, where `r` is a variable of a record type that declares a field named `x`. Scope rules as previously implemented by the parser using class `IdTable` are still valid without any additional changes for records and fields.

In addition to constraints related to initializers, which are similar to those for arrays, there is one new major constraint rule to consider for records.

- **`Variable`**
  - Miscellaneous Rule: Field expressions are permitted only for variables with a record type or type `String`. (For strings, the only allowed field name is "`length`".)

Relative to the implementation of method `checkConstraints()` in class `Variable`, consider the following declarations.

```
type Point = record
  {
    x : Integer;
    y : Integer;
  };

type Rectangle = record                     // fields are records
  {
    point1 : Point;
    point2 : Point;
  };

var r : Rectangle;
```

Observe that `r` has type `Rectangle`, `r.point1` has type `Point`, and `r.point1.x` has type `Integer`. Therefore, for each selector expression applied to a record variable, method `checkConstraints()` in class `Variable` must perform the following actions:

- Verify that the selector expression is a field expression.
- Check that the field name in the expression is the name of a field declared within the record type.
- Set the declaration field in the field expression to the field declaration of the record.

  ```
  fieldExpr.setFieldDecl(fieldDecl);
  ```

- Set the type of the variable to the field type. Using the example above, `r` has type `Rectangle`, but `r.point1` has type `Point`, and this type will need to be set in method `checkConstraints()`.

Code Generation for Records

Similar to other composite types, many of the AST classes don't directly involve records, and some that do involve records don't need to be modified. For example, the implementation of `emit()` for class `AssignmentStmt` should work for records without any modifications. Only two classes require extra attention – `FieldExpr` and `Variable`.

Code generation in class `FieldExpr` is straightforward. We need to emit code to load the value for the field offset, which is just an integer whose value is known at compile time.

```
emit("LDCINT " + fieldDecl.offset());
```

Most of the work involved in code generation for records takes place in class `Variable`. Here is a summary of the basic ideas for implementing method `emit()` in class `Variable`.

First, as with non-record types, method `emit()` must emit code to leave the relative address of the variable on the run-time stack (i.e., the address of the first byte of the record). There is no change required to existing code for non-record variables.

Next, consider selector expressions for a record variable. Record variables can have only field expressions as selectors. For each selector expression, `emit()` must perform the following actions.

- Cast the selector expression to a field expression.

  ```
  var fieldExpr = (FieldExpr) expr;
  ```

- Generate code for the offset of the field.

  ```
  fieldExpr.emit();
  ```

- Generate code to add the offset to the relative address of the variable.

  ```
  emit("ADD");
  ```

- Change the type of the variable to the field type in case there are more selector expressions.

  ```
  type = fieldExpr.fieldDecl().type();
  ```

As an optimization, don't generate code for the second and third steps above if the field offset is `0` since doing so would simply add `0` to the relative address of the variable.

17.3 Essential Terms and Concepts

field	field declaration
field offset	name equivalence for record types
record	`RecordType` (class)
record type declaration	reference semantics (record assignment)
relative address of a field	structural equivalence for record types
value semantics (record assignment)	

17.4 Exercises

1. **Project Assignment.** Implement **Project 11: Records** as described in Appendix A. This will complete your compiler for CPRL.

2. The following declaration is not permissible in CPRL. Explain why.

   ```
   var r : record { x : Integer; y : Integer };
   ```

3. Explain the difference between reference semantics and value semantics for record assignment. Which one is used by CPRL? Which one is used by Java (for classes)?

4. Use the following declarations in the questions below.

   ```
   type Point = record
     {
       x : Integer;
       y : Integer;
       isVisible : Boolean;
       color : Integer;
     };
   type PointArray = array[10] of Point;
   var point  : Point;
   var points : PointArray;
   ```

   a. What is the type of `point`?

   b. What is the type of `point.x`?

   c. What is the type of `point.isVisible`?

   d. How many bytes does `point` occupy in memory?

   e. What is the type of `points`?

   f. What is the type of `points[5]`?

   g. What is the offset of `x` relative to `Point`?

   h. What is the offset of `y` relative to `Point`?

   i. What is the offset of `color` relative to `Point`?

   j. What is the relative address (offset) of `points[5]`?

   k. If the actual memory address of `point` is `200`, what is the actual memory address of `point.y`?

   l. If the actual memory address of `point` is `200`, what is the actual memory address of `point.isVisible`?

   m. If the actual memory address of `points` is `500`, what is the actual memory address of `points[5]`?

   n. If the actual memory address of `points` is `500`, what is the actual memory address of `points[5].y`?

5. True or False (T or F)

   a. Field names must be distinct from all other variable, type, and subprogram names in a CPRL program.

   b. Record assignment copies all field values from the record on the right side of the assignment symbol to the record variable on the left side.

   c. A record type declaration creates a new type.

6. When passing a record as a parameter to a procedure, the record can be passed as a value parameter or as a variable parameter. Explain an advantage of passing the record as a variable parameter even if the original record is not modified.

7. Use the following declarations in the question below.

```
type R1 = record { n : Integer; b : Boolean };
type R2 = record { n : Integer; b : Boolean };
var r1 : R1;
var r2 : R2;
```

   Is the following assignment valid in CPRL (yes or no)? Justify your answer.

```
r1 := r2;
```

8. Select one of the constraint rules (either a type or a miscellaneous rule) for CPRL records, and write two test programs in CPRL – one correct program that satisfies the rule and one incorrect program that does not satisfy the rule. After completing Project 11 (Appendix A), use the test programs to check if your compiler correctly implements the rules.

Appendix A
The Compiler Project

There are several general approaches for a compiler project in an academic course on compiler construction. One approach is to give detailed explanations and a **complete** implementation for a compiler for one source language but then concentrate the project around writing a compiler for a different source language. Another approach is to give explanations and a **partial** implementation for a compiler for a particular source language and then to concentrate the project around finishing the incomplete work and possibly extending the source language or targeting a different computer architecture. This book uses the latter approach.

The overall project of developing a compiler for CPRL is divided into 12 smaller projects (numbered 0-11) as described below. For most of the projects, the GitHub repository has lots of both complete and skeletal code to help you get started plus CPRL test programs that can be used to check your work. For each project you should test your compiler with both correct and incorrect CPRL programs as explained in the project descriptions.

Organizational Structure of the Compiler Project

It is useful to view the source code for the compiler project as being structured into four main organizational units (components) that we refer to as `common`, `cvm`, `assembler`, and `cprlc`. Each of these components has a primary top-level package with the name of the component, and some have one or two subpackages. There are explicit package dependencies among the organizational components as described below. Additionally, there are test classes that are not considered to be part of the main components. We view the test classes as being part of a fifth component named `test`. While it is possible to define these components in terms of Java modules, the use of modules is not required for the compiler project.

Following is a description of the five organizational components for the compiler project.

1. **The `common` Component**

   This component contains two packages, `common` and `common.util`. Classes in this component are not directly tied to the CPRL programming language and therefore are useful on other compiler-related projects. Examples include classes such as `Position`, `Source`, and `BoundedBuffer` defined in package `common`, plus utility classes such as `ByteUtil` and `CharUtil` defined in package `common.util`. This component has no dependencies on the other components.

2. **The `cvm` Component**

   This component has only one package, `cvm`. Two notable classes in this component are `CVM`, which implements the CPRL virtual machine, and `Disassembler`, which implements a disassembler for converting CVM object code into CVM assembly language. Classes in this component depend only on classes in the `common` component as described in item 1 above.

3. **The `assembler` Component**

   This component is comprised of four packages, `assembler`, `assembler.ast`, `assembler.builtins`, and `assembler.optimize`. Classes in this component implement an assembler for CVM assembly language. The assembler optionally performs several standard optimizations, such as converting an "`ADD 1`" instruction to an "`INC`" instruction. This component has a dependency on both the `common` and `cvm` components as described in items 1 and 2 above.

4. **The `cprlc` Component**

   This component contains the classes that implement the CPRL compiler. There are three packages, `cprlc`, `cprlc.ast`, and `cprlc.builtins`. Complete source code is provided for the other three components described above, but only portions of the source code are provided for this component. **Although students will need to refer occasionally to classes in the other three components to understand the roles those classes play in developing the CPRL compiler, all new development will take place only in this component.** Classes in the `cprlc` component depend only on classes in the `common` and `cvm` components, but they have no dependency on classes in the `assembler` component. However, knowledge of CVM assembly language is required for the code generation parts of this component.

5. **The `test` Component**

   There are three classes in this component, class `TestSource` in package `test.common` and classes `TestScanner` and `TestParser` in package `test.cprlc`. You will use these classes to test your work in the first few projects described below.

Overview of the Book's GitHub Repository

In addition to the standard license and readme files, the top level of the GitHub Repository at https://github.com/SoftMoore/CPRL-Java-5th contains four directories (a.k.a. folders). The `Book` directory contains PDF documents of several sections from this book including the Table of Contents, the Preface, and Appendix A. The `Handouts` directory contains several useful handouts. The `PowerPoint` directory contains PowerPoint slides that could be useful for college instructors who adopt this book as a course textbook. The slides correspond directly to the book chapters. The `Project` directory contains all files used for the compiler projects.

Warning: Several of the source files in the `Project` directory for later projects are replacements or enhancements for the same files in earlier projects. For example, there are three versions of class `Parser` and two versions of class `IdTable`. Don't try to download the source files and import all of them at the same time into the IDE for your compiler project. Follow the project instructions for each project in the order presented.

Project 0: Getting Started

- This is not a real project but more of an initialization of your working environment for the remaining compiler projects. Expand the green "Code" button on the GitHub Repository page, download the repository as a zip file, and unzip it into a directory on your computer. Under the `Project` directory you will see 9 immediate subdirectories and other nested subdirectories, partially illustrated as follows.

  ```
  Project
  ├── bin
  │   ├── bash
  │   └── windows
  ├── examples
  │   ├── Correct
  │   ├── Incorrect
  │   └── ScannerTests
  ├── src-assembler
  ├── src-common
  ├── src-cvm
  ├── src-parserV1
  ├── src-parserV2
  ├── src-parserV3
  └── src-scanner
  ```

  Directories with names beginning "src…" contain Java source files for the compiler project.

- Directory `bin` contains sample Bash shell scripts and Windows command scripts for running and testing various stages of the compiler. There are two subdirectories named "`bash`" and "`windows`" that contain the Bash and Windows script files, respectively. For each Windows "`.cmd`" script file there is a corresponding Bash script file without the "`.cmd`" suffix; e.g., `cprlc.cmd` and `cprlc`. Pick the collection of script files for your operating system and programming environment. For the Bash script files, you will need to run "`chmod +x script`" to make them executable.

  As an example of the contents of `bin` for Windows, there is a script `cprlc.cmd` that will run the CPRL compiler on a source file whose name is entered via standard input. Similarly, there is a script `assemble.cmd` for running the assembler on "`.asm`" files, a script `disassemble.cmd` for running the disassembler on "`.obj`" files, and a script `cprl.cmd` for executing a single compiled/assembled CPRL program on the CVM.

  ```
  cprlc Hello.cprl               // creates Hello.asm
  assemble Hello.asm             // creates Hello.obj
  cprl Hello.obj                 // executes Hello.obj on the CVM
  disassemble Hello.obj          // creates Hello.dis.txt
  ```

  The following will compile all CPRL source files in the current working directory.

  ```
  cprlc *.cprl
  ```

There are two scripts for testing correct programs. Script `testCorrect.cmd` can be used to test a single CPRL program, and script `testCorrect_all.cmd` can be used to test all CPRL programs in the current directory. Both test scripts execute ".obj" files on the CVM and compare the output with expected output. Starting with Project 6 you can also use script `testIncorrect_all.cmd` to compile all incorrect CPRL programs in the current directory and compare the results to the expected results.

Additionally, there are script files for testing the scanner and parser in the earlier projects, and there is a script file named `testEverything.cmd` (or simply `testEverything` for Bash) that can be used to test the completed compiler project.

You will need to edit the file `cprl_config.cmd` for Windows (or `cprl_config` for bash) so that the `COMPILER_PROJECT_PATH` variable "points to" the directories on your computer containing the Java class files for your project.

Most of the other script files use `cprl_config.cmd` to set the classpath appropriately. For example, my personal setup for Java uses an Eclipse workspace with source files structured in directories based on package names under a "`src`" subdirectory and class files structured similarly under a "`bin`" subdirectory. For example, the source code for `Parser.java` is in subdirectory `src\cprlc`, and the corresponding class file `Parser.class` in subdirectory `bin\cprlc`. When `cprl_config.cmd` is executed, it sets the `COMPILER_PROJECT_PATH` variable to include the `bin` directory.

Also, you will need to ensure that the directory containing the script files is included in your `PATH` environment variable so that the operating system can find them when you enter their names on the command line.

You can set the global `PATH` environment variable permanently for your computer, or you can either execute `setPath.cmd` (Windows) or source `setPath` (bash) as appropriate to set the `PATH` environment variable temporarily for the current terminal session. For Windows, simply change to the `windows` subdirectory of project folder `bin` and execute `setPath.cmd`. For Linux, change to the `bash` subdirectory of project folder `bin` and execute either "`source setPath`" or "`. setPath`".

- Directory `examples` contains examples of correct and incorrect CPRL programs that can be used to test various parts of your compiler. There are three subdirectories of `examples` as follows.
  - Subdirectory `Correct` contains numerous correct CPRL programs. The programs are organized into six subdirectories for testing different projects as you progress though the compiler implementation. For example, there is a subdirectory containing only test programs for CPRL/0, the zero subset of CPRL (no subprograms, enumerated types, or composite types) as outlined in Projects 5 and 6 below. **Testing should be performed cumulatively; i.e., you should always retest the CPRL/0 example programs when working on later projects to ensure that you haven't introduced an error that would cause one of the CPRL/0 programs to fail.**

  - Subdirectory `Incorrect` contains numerous incorrect CPRL programs that will be used for testing error detection and recovery. Similar to the correct programs, these programs are organized into six subdirectories for testing different projects as you progress through the compiler implementation.
  - Subdirectory `ScannerTests` contains both correct and incorrect files that can be used for testing your scanner as described in Project 1 below. These are not necessarily complete CPRL programs. For example, one of the files contains every valid symbol in CPRL including all reserved words, all operators, and numerous programmer-defined identifiers and literals.

  You are strongly encouraged to develop additional CPRL test programs as you work though the remaining projects described below.

- Directory `src-common` contains the source code for the `common` component as described above. These classes are used by the other three components, and they are potentially reusable on other compiler projects. All classes in this directory are complete and require no additional work for use on the compiler project. **Import the Java source code for this component into your preferred IDE for Java (e.g., Eclipse, IntelliJ IDEA, NetBeans, or Visual Studio Code).** All code should compile without any errors.
- Directory `src-cvm` contains classes that implement the `CVM`, the virtual machine that will be used on subsequent projects to run CPRL programs. These classes are described in the `cvm` component above. All classes in this directory are complete and require no additional work for use on the compiler project. **Import the Java source code for this component into your preferred IDE for Java.** All code should compile without any errors.
- Directory `src-assembler` contains classes that implement an assembler for `CVM` assembly language. You will run the assembler on assembly language files generated by your compiler to create machine code files that can be executed on the `CVM`. These classes are described in the `assembler` component above. All classes in this directory are complete and require no additional work for use on the compiler project. **Import the Java source code for this module into your preferred IDE for Java.** All code should compile without any errors.
- To check that source code has been imported successfully and that scrips have been edited correctly, let's test class `Source` as described in Section 5.2. Directory `src-common` contains a test driver named `TestSource` in package `test.common` that can be used together with the `testSource.cmd` (or `testSource` for bash) script file to "wrap" class `Source` and run it on any text file. **Run `testSource.cmd` (or `testSource` for bash) on the file `Source.java`.**

Project 1: Scanner

- Using the concepts from Chapter 5, implement a scanner for CPRL.
- Import the source files from directory `src-scanner` into your preferred IDE. Directory `src-scanner` contains several classes in package `cprlc`. It has complete implementations for classes `Symbol` and `Token` plus a partial implementation of class `Scanner`. Directory `src-scanner` also contains a test driver named `TestScanner` in package `test.cprlc` that can be used together with the `testScanner.cmd` (or `testScanner` for bash) script file to "wrap" your scanner and run it against the scanner example test files.
- **Complete the implementation for class `Scanner`.**
- Test your scanner with the scanner-specific test examples and multiple correct CPRL examples.

Project 2: Parser Version 1 – Language Recognition

- Using the concepts from Chapter 6, implement a parser that performs language recognition for the full CPRL language (not just the zero subset) based on the language definition and context-free grammar given in Chapter 4, Appendix C, and Appendix D.
- Import the source files from directory `src-parserV1` into your preferred IDE. Directory `src-parserV1` contains complete implementations of classes `IdType`, `IdTable`, `ScopeLevel`, and `Scope` in package `cprlc` as described in Chapter 6, and it contains a partial implementation of class `Parser` that performs only language recognition. Directory `src-parserV1` also contains a test driver named `TestParser` in package `test.cprlc` that can be used together with the script file `testParser.cmd` (or `testParser` for bash) to "wrap" both your scanner and parser together and run them against the example test files. The "incorrect" example subdirectories contain text files showing the results that you should expect when running this version of the parser against the incorrect test examples.
- **Complete the implementation for class `Parser`.**
- Do not implement error recovery for this project; i.e., when an error is encountered, simply report the error and exit compilation as described in Chapter 6. Some of the parser methods are fully implemented; study those as guides for the incomplete parser methods.
- Test with all correct and incorrect examples. At this point the parser should accept all correct programs and reject all incorrect programs **except** those with type errors and/or miscellaneous errors. Detection of type errors and miscellaneous errors will be implemented in subsequent projects. Use the text files showing expected results as guides.

Project 3: Parser Version 2 – Error Recovery

- Using the concepts from Chapter 7, add error recovery to your parser.
- Directory `src-parserV2` contains only one class in package `cprlc`, a partial implementation of class `Parser` that demonstrates how to add error recovery to the parser methods. Do **not** import this class into your IDE since you already have an implementation for class `Parser`. Instead, use the class provided in this directory as a guide to manually edit your existing parser in order to add error recovery. Use the test driver and script files from the previous project to run your parser against the example test programs. The "incorrect" example subdirectories contain text files showing the results that you should expect when running this version of the parser against the incorrect test examples.
- **Edit your parser from the previous project to implement error recovery as described in Chapter 7.**
- Test with all correct and incorrect examples. At this point the parser should accept and reject exactly the same example programs as for the previous project, but this time your parser should report more than one error for some of the incorrect programs. Use the text files showing expected results as guides.

Project 4: Parser Version 3 – Abstract Syntax Trees

- Using the concepts from Chapter 8, add generation of abstract syntax trees to your parser. Most parsing methods should return AST objects or lists of AST objects. From now on we will start referring to our implementation as a "compiler" even though it doesn't yet generate code.
- Directory `src-parserV3` contains full or partial implementations of more than 40 AST classes in package `cprlc.ast`. Approximately half of the AST classes are implemented completely, while the remaining AST classes have only partial implementations. You should import the AST classes into your IDE. For now there are empty bodies or partially incomplete bodies for methods `checkConstraints()` and `emit()` in the AST classes that are not fully implemented.

  Directory `src-parserV3` also contains full or partial implementations of several classes in package `cprlc` as follows.

  - A complete implementation for class `Cprlc`. For this project we will continue to use `TestParser`, but in the next project you will start using class `Cprlc` instead of `TestParser` to test your work.
  - Complete implementations for classes `LoopContext` and `SubprogramContext`. As described in Chapter 8, these classes are used to track entry to and exit from loops and subprograms. Use `LoopContext` when parsing loop statements and exit statements. Use `SubprogramContext` when parsing procedure declarations, function declarations, and return statements.

- Complete implementations for classes `Scope` and `IdTable`. As described in Chapter 8, `IdTable` now stores scopes with references to an identifier's declaration. These two classes replace the implementations of `Scope` and `IdTable` that we have been using in the previous two projects. Use the complete version of `IdTable` to check for declaration and scope errors. With this new implementation for `IdTable` your parser will now be able to detect additional scope errors when we implement subprograms in Project 7.
- A complete implementation for class `Type` and implementations for subclasses `ArrayType`, `EnumType`, and `RecordType`. The implementations for these three subclasses will compile, but at this point they are not correct. You will correct the implementations for these three classes as part of projects 8, 9, and 11. The correct implementations for `ArrayType`, `EnumType`, and `RecordType` are straightforward after studying the relevant chapters in the book; i.e., Chapters 14, 15, and 17.
- A partial implementation for class `Parser`. As described in Chapter 8, most parsing methods now return AST objects or lists of AST objects. Do **not** import this class into your IDE since you already have an implementation for class `Parser`. Instead, use the class provided in this directory as a guide to manually edit your existing parser in order to add generation of AST classes.

- **Edit your parser from the previous project to add generation of AST classes or lists of AST classes.**
- Test your parser with all correct and incorrect examples. The "incorrect" example subdirectories contain text files showing the results that you should expect when running this version of the parser against the incorrect test examples. The major differences in test results between versions 2 and 3 of your parser are that version 3 should also detect `exit` statements that are not nested within loops.

Project 5: Constraint Analysis for CPRL/0

- **Using the concepts from Chapter 9, implement `checkConstraints()` methods in the AST classes to perform full constraint analysis for the CPRL/0 subset (everything except subprograms, enumerated types, and composite types).** In addition to the syntax and scope errors previously detected by your compiler, your compiler should also detect all type and miscellaneous errors for the CPRL/0 subset. For this project, do **not** implement any constraint checks for class `Variable`. All constraint checks for class `Variable` involve arrays, strings, or records, which will be covered in subsequent chapters.
- Test with all correct and incorrect CPRL/0 examples. Henceforth you will use class `Cprlc` rather than `TestParser` to test your implementation with the CPRL examples. To invoke the compiler, use script `cprlc.cmd` or `cprlc` as appropriate, depending on whether you are developing in a Windows or bash environment. This script is designed to use class `Cprlc`. Recall that you can use "`cprlc *.cprl`" to compile all files in the current directory. At this point the compiler should accept all correct CPRL/0 examples and reject all incorrect CPRL/0 examples. The "incorrect" example

subdirectories contain text files showing the results that you should expect when running this version of the parser against the incorrect test examples.

> Here are some tips for working on the remaining projects.
>
> You will eventually want to run the scripts `testCorrect_all` and `testIncorrect_all` in the appropriate `examples` subdirectory, but start by running `cprlc *.cprl`.
>
> For correct programs, if you don't get a clean compile, then work on each problem example separately. Compile individual examples using something similar to
> `cprlc Correct_101.cprl`.
>
> Once you get a clean compile on every file, do the same thing with script `assemble`; i.e., start with `assemble *.asm` and use `assemble Correct_101.asm` (or similar) as needed. If there are problems, compare the `.asm` files you are generating to the `.asm` files downloaded from the book's GitHub repository. You can re-download the examples in the event that you overwrote yours when testing your compiler and didn't save copies in a different location.
>
> Once you get a clean compile and a clean assemble, you can run the example's `.obj` file using something like `cprl Correct_101.obj`, or you can simply run `testCorrect Correct_101`.

Project 6: Code Generation for CPRL/0

- **Using the concepts from Chapter 11, implement `emit()` methods in the AST classes to perform code generation for CPRL/0.** At this point you are actually generating assembly language for the CVM.
- Use the assembler provided in the `assembler` module (see Project 0 above) and script file `assemble.cmd` (`assemble` for bash) to generate machine code for all correct CPRL/0 examples.
- Use script files `cprl.cmd`, `testCorrect.cmd`, and `testCorrect_all.cmd` (or bash equivalents) to run and test all correct CPRL/0 examples. Use script file `testIncorrect_all.cmd` (or bash equivalent) to test all incorrect CPRL/0 examples.

Project 7: Subprograms

- **Using the concepts from Chapter 13, add constraint analysis and code generation for subprograms.**
- Correct any remaining errors.
- Test all correct and incorrect Subprogram examples. Retest all correct and incorrect examples from CPRL/0.

Project 8: Arrays

- **Using the concepts from Chapter 14, add constraint analysis and code generation for arrays.**
- Correct the implementation for class `ArrayType` plus any remaining errors.
- Test all correct and incorrect array examples. Retest all correct and incorrect examples from CPRL/0 and Subprograms.

Project 9: Enumerated Types

- **Using the concepts from Chapter 15, add constraint analysis and code generation for enumerated types.** Much of the work involved in implementing enumerated types is already provided in the GitHub repository, so this project is relatively simple.
- Correct the implementation for `EnumType` plus any remaining errors.
- Test all correct and incorrect enum examples. Retest all correct and incorrect examples from CPRL/0, Subprograms, and Arrays.

Project 10: Strings

- **Using the concepts from Chapter 16, add constraint analysis and code generation for strings.** Most of the work involved in implementing strings is already provided in the GitHub repository, so this project is relatively simple. Depending on student backgrounds and course prerequisites, instructors might elect to make this the last project and assign Project 11 as a reading assignment.
- Correct any remaining errors.
- Test all correct and incorrect string examples. Retest all correct and incorrect examples from CPRL/0, Subprograms, Arrays, and Enums.

Project 11: Records

- **Using the concepts from Chapter 17, add constraint analysis and code generation for records.** Completion of this project results in the final version of your compiler.
- Correct the implementation for `RecordType` plus any remaining errors.
- Test all correct and incorrect records examples. Retest all correct and incorrect examples from CPRL/0, Subprograms, Arrays, Enums, and Strings. Recall that there is a script file named `testEverything.cmd` (or simply `testEverything` for Bash) that can be used to test the completed compiler project.

Appendix B
Additional Project Exercises

For ambitious undergraduate or graduate students, below are suggestions for extensions to the basic compiler projects outlined in this book. Many of these ideas involve adding new features to the CPRL programming language. Warning: While a few of these additional projects are relatively easy, many are quite challenging. Some exercises are marked with one or two asterisks to indicate the level of difficulty, with two asterisks being the most difficult.

1. Create one or more CPRL correct or incorrect test programs that test features of the language not covered in the test examples supplied with the book resources.

2. Add a multiline comment to CPRL; e.g., along the lines of `/* ... */`. Most languages have a form for comments that can extend over multiple lines as shown below.

   ```
   /* comment line 1
      comment line 2
      comment line 3 */
   ```

   One design issue here is whether or not multiline comments can be nested. Equivalently, does each opening comment tag require its own closing comment marker, or does the first closing comment tag end all "open" comments?

3. Allow integer literals to use underscores, as in `1_000_000` for 1 million.

4. Create native executable images for your computer architecture/operating system. For example, create "cprlc`.exe`" file for a CPRL compiler on Windows. Investigate the Java Development Kit (JDK) packaging tool `jpackage` and the GraalVM tool `native-image`. See also the discussion of JIT versus AOT in Appendix G.

5. *Add bounds checking at runtime for array indices. As implemented in Chapter 14, the compiler does not perform bounds checking when indexing into an array, and therefore it is possible to reference a value beyond the end of the array. As an example, if `a` is an array of `100` integers, it is possible to access `a[150]`. Of course the result would not be valid, but the implementation doesn't prevent this from happening. With bounds checking at runtime, execution of the program would be halted, and an error message would be printed. One way to simplify bounds checking for arrays is to add special instructions to the CPRL virtual machine. For example, the virtual machine implemented by Brinch Hansen [Hansen 1985] has an `index` instruction that performs bounds checking. Also, consider storing the declared length of the array with the array itself (similar to the way that strings store their length), so that the offset of the first item in the array is 4 and not `0` as currently implemented. The JVM stores information about an array, including the declared length, in a class file, and JVM array load/store instructions such as `iaload`/`iastore` (for integer arrays) perform bounds checking.

6. Similar to the above, add bounds checking at runtime for string indices. Note that strings already store the length, so adding bounds checking for strings should be easier than adding bounds checking for arrays.

7. *Add a reference to the parent node for each node in the AST. In the current implementation of the compiler, each AST node has references to its children, but a child node doesn't have a reference to its parent.

   After adding references to parent nodes, remove classes `LoopContext` and `SubprogramContext` from your implementation of the compiler. These two classes exist solely so that an `exit` statement can find its enclosing `loop` statement and a `return` statement can find its enclosing subprogram. Both goals can be accomplished by following the chain of parent references.

   Here are some tips for one way to add parent references.

   - In class AST, add the following field plus methods `parent()` and `setParent()`.

     ```
     private AST parent;    // reference to parent node in the AST
     ```

   - For class `Program`, set the parent to `null` in its constructor, indicating that an instance of `Program` is the root of the tree and therefore has no parent.

     ```
     setParent(null);  // Program has no parent in the AST.
     ```

   - Other AST classes can use their constructors to set the parent reference for its children, passing "`this`" as the parameter. For example, the constructor for class `AssignmentStmt` could contain the following.

     ```
     variable.setParent(this);
     expr.setParent(this);
     ```

     Similarly, the constructor for class `BinaryExpr` could contain these statements.

     ```
     leftOperand.setParent(this);
     rightOperand.setParent(this);
     ```

8. *Add additional built-in subprograms; e.g., add procedure `dec` (decrement) and functions `abs` (absolute value), `max` (maximum), and `min` (minimum) for integers. Look through the examples for ideas about other possible subprograms to add. Look at the implementations of existing built-in CPRL subprograms for guidance. Note that some of the suggested functions are already defined in the CPRL test programs.

9. The constraint rules for AST class `FunctionDecl` require only that the declaration contain at least one `return` statement. Implement the much stronger constraint that the class should guarantee that it will always execute a `return` statement before reaching the end of the function.

10. Create a new class for scope exceptions and report all scope errors using this class. Recall from Chapter 9 that all scope errors are currently reported by the parser as syntax errors, but technically they are not really syntax errors since they are not defined in the context-free grammar. Reporting them as scope errors would likely make the error messages more meaningful.

11. *Allow nested subprograms. CPRL allows subprograms to be declared at the top level, but subprograms can't be declared within other subprograms. Many languages such as Pascal and Ada allow nested subprograms. Modify the definition of CPRL to allow subprograms to be declared within other subprograms. You will also need to address issues of scope, and the context part of an activation record will need to include a static link that references the activation record of the enclosing subprogram, similar to the way that the dynamic link references the activation record of the calling subprogram. See course references or other compiler texts for details.

12. Add a union type similar to that found in C. Unions are analogous to records except that all components have offset zero; i.e., they overlap. The size of a union is the size of its largest field. So, for example, if a union contained an integer field, a char field, and a boolean field, its size would be 4, the size of an integer in CPRL.

13. *Implement the CVM in C, Rust, or Go, which should make it much faster. The CVM is a good candidate for these languages since it is not very "object-oriented".

    - It doesn't use inheritance or polymorphism.
    - It consists mostly of constants and potentially static functions.
    - The primary control structure is a switch with function calls.

    The challenge, especially when working in C, is to write one version that will work on Linux/Mac and Windows. Implementing type `Char` (Unicode) and I/O can be difficult.

14. *Implement the compiler in a language other than Java. Languages that support recursion and object-oriented programming will work best with the approach used in this book. Examples include Kotlin, C++, C#, Python, Scala, Swift, and possibly Rust. Note that the existing Java implementations of the assembler and the CVM should still work without change.

15. **Add references/pointers and dynamic memory allocation for types other than strings.

16. **Implement constraint analysis and code generation using the visitor design pattern. This is the approach taken in the book by David A. Watt and Deryck F. Brown [Watt 2000].

17. **Modify the target language/machine.

    - Target a real machine or the assembly language for a real machine (e.g., x86, ARM, RISC-V, or x86-64).
    - Target the Java Virtual Machine (JVM) or assembly language for the JVM. (Yes, although not officially a part of the Java platform, there are assemblers for the JVM.) If you are using Java Version 24 or later, you should investigate the Java Class File API for this project. See https://openjdk.org/jeps/484.
    - Target the Common Language Runtime (part of Microsoft's .NET Framework).
    - Target another programming language such as WebAssembly or C. (Recall that the first C++ "compilers" targeted C rather than a low-level language.)

18. **Redesign code generation to allow for multiple targets.
    - Target a universal, machine-independent back end (e.g., LLVM).
    - Use design patterns to create a code-generation factory.
19. **Add classes similar to those in Java, Kotlin, C++, and C#.

Appendix C
Definition of the Programming Language CPRL

Introduction

CPRL (for **C**ompiler **PR**oject **L**anguage) is a small but complete programming language with constructs similar to those found in C, Java, and Ada. CPRL was designed to be suitable for use as a project language in an advanced undergraduate or beginning graduate course on compiler design and construction. Its features illustrate many of the basic techniques and challenges associated with language translation.

C.1 Lexical Considerations

General

CPRL is case sensitive. Upper-case letters and lower-case letters are considered to be distinct in all tokens, including reserved words.

Whitespace characters (space character, tab character, and end-of-line) serve to separate tokens; otherwise they are ignored. No token can extend past an end-of-line. Spaces may not appear in any token except character and string literals.

A comment begins with two forward slashes (`//`) and extends to the end of the line (or end of the file, whichever occurs first).

```
temp := x;    // swap values of x and y
x := y;
y := temp;
```

CPRL does not define a maximum line length for source code files.

Identifiers

Identifiers start with a letter and contain letters and digits. An identifier must fit on a single line, and all characters of an identifier are significant.

```
identifier = letter { letter | digit } .
letter = 'A'..'Z' + 'a'..'z' .
   // letter = [A-Za-z]   equivalent regular expression character class
digit  = '0'..'9' .
   // digit = [0-9]       equivalent regular expression character class
```

Reserved Words

The following 37 identifiers are keywords in CPRL, and they are all reserved.

```
Boolean   Byte      Char      Integer  String   and      array
class     const     else      exit     false    for      fun
if        in        loop      mod      not      of       or
private   proc      protected public   read     readln   record
return    then      true      type     var      when     while
write     writeln
```

Note that some keywords such as `class`, `private`, etc. are not currently used in CPRL but are reserved for possible future use. Such keywords are essentially terminal symbols in the context-free grammar that do not appear in any rule.

Literals

An integer literal can be defined using decimal, hexadecimal, or binary notation.

```
intLiteral = decimalLiteral | hexLiteral | binaryLiteral .
decimalLiteral = digit { digit } .
hexLiteral = ( "0x" | "0X" ) hexDigit { hexDigit } .
binaryLiteral = ( "0b" | "0B" ) binaryDigit { binaryDigit } .
```

In the above rules, `binaryDigit` and `hexDigit` have the usual definitions.

```
binaryDigit = '0'..'1' .
hexDigit = '0'..'9' + 'A'..'F' + 'a'..'f' .
```

A Boolean literal is either "`true`" or "`false`", and both of these words are reserved.

Similar to most C-based languages, CPRL uses the backslash (`\`) as a prefix character to denote escape sequences within character and string literals. The escape sequences used by CPRL are similar to those used in other languages.

`\t`	tab
`\n`	linefeed (a.k.a. newline)
`\r`	carriage return
`\"`	double quote
`\'`	single quote (a.k.a. apostrophe
`\\`	backslash

A character literal is a single printable character or an escaped character enclosed by a pair of apostrophes (sometimes called single quotes). Examples include `'A'`, `'x'`, and `'\''`. A character literal is distinct from a string literal with length one. A backslash is required for a character literal containing an apostrophe (single quote). Thus, `'\''` can be used to represent a character literal consisting of a single quote, but `'''` is not valid.

For convenience, we define a printable character as Unicode character encodable in 16 bits (using UTF-16) that is not an ISO control character, although there are some 16-bit Unicode characters that are not ISO control characters that are also not printable. The Java method `isISOControl()` in class `Character` can be used to test this condition.

A string literal is a sequence of zero or more printable or escaped characters enclosed by a pair of quotation marks (double quotes). Analogous to character literals, backslashes are required whenever a string literal contains quotation marks. Examples of string literals include `"Hello, world."`, `"It's Friday!\n"`, and `"He said, \"Good morning.\""`.

Other Symbols

The following symbols serve as delimiters, operators, and special symbols in CPRL.

```
// arithmetic, bitwise, and shift operators
+   -   *   /   &   |   ^   ~   <<   >>

// relational operators
=   !=   <   <=   >   >=

// assignment, grouping, and other symbols
:=   (   )   [   ]   {   }   ,   :   ;   .   ..   ?

// special scanning symbols
EOF, unknown
```

Note that CPRL uses the reserved word "`mod`" instead of the symbol `%` as the modulus or remainder operator. Similarly, CPRL uses the reserved word "`not`" instead of the symbol "`!`" for logical negation. (But the "not equal" relational operator is "`!=`".)

C.2 Types

CPRL is a statically-typed language.

- Every variable, constant, or expression in the language belongs to exactly one type.
- Type is a static property and can be determined by the compiler.

In general, static typing allows better error detection at compile time as well as generation of more efficient object code.

Scalar Types

There are four predefined scalar types in CPRL – `Boolean`, `Byte`, `Integer`, and `Char`. In addition, CPRL has a user-defined scalar type called an enumerated type (or simply an enum type).

Type `Boolean`

Type `Boolean` is treated as a predefined scalar type with two values, `false` and `true`. It is essentially equivalent to type `boolean` in Java, `Boolean` in Kotlin, and type `bool` in C++.

Type Byte

Type `Byte` is an **unsigned** 8-bit numeric type with values in the range `0..255`. Values of type `Byte` are promoted to type `Integer` when used as expressions.

Type `Integer`

Type `Integer` is a numeric type that is equivalent to type `int` in Java or `Int` in Kotlin.

Type `Char`

Type `Char` is a predefined character type that is roughly equivalent to type `char` in Java except that all characters in CPRL must be encodable in 2 bytes (16 bits) using UTF-16. This restriction greatly simplifies the treatment of `Char` values in CPRL since they all occupy exactly 2 bytes.

Enumerated Types

An enumerated type is defined by listing the identifiers that are the actual values of the type enclosed in angle brackets. Each enumerated identifier defines a constant value whose name is scoped to the enum type.

Example

```
type Day = <Sun, Mon, Tue, Wed, Thu, Fri, Sat>;
```

An enumerated type is distinct from all other types. In particular, while the enumerated constants have some properties similar to those of type `Integer`, an enumerated type is distinct from type `Integer`.

Composite Types

There are three composite types in CPRL – array types, record types, and the predefined type `String`. Array types and record types must be declared before the type name can be referenced, but array variables can be created without first declaring a type, as in

```
var a : array[10] of Integer;
```

Array Types

CPRL supports one dimensional array types, but arrays of arrays can be declared. An array type is defined by giving the number of elements in the array and the component (element) type.

Examples

```
type T1 = array[10] of Boolean;
type T2 = array[10] of Integer;
type T3 = array[10] of T2;
```

If `n` is the number of array elements, then array indices are integers ranging from `0` to `n-1` or enumerated constants with similar underlying range values. No bounds checking is performed when accessing an element of an array.

Type String

`String` is a predefined composite type in CPRL. String variables can be initialized using string literals or declared string constants. For a string variable, the length is determined when it is assigned a value, either via initialization, an assignment statement, or a read statement.

Examples

```
var name  : String := "Davis";
var month : String;
```

Similar to arrays, the individual characters of a string can be accessed using the array index notation. Valid indices range from `0` to `n-1`, where `n` is the length of the string. No bounds checking is performed when accessing a character in a string. Similar to records, the length of a string is accessed using the dot notation, as in `name.length`.

Record Types

CPRL supports record types that are similar to `structs` in C and C#. A record type is defined by specifying the fields in the record. Unlike arrays, whose elements all have the same type, the fields of a record can have different types.

Examples

```
type Point = record
  {
    x : Integer;
    y : Integer;
  };

type Month = record
  {
    name    : String;
    maxDays : Integer;
  };
```

The fields of a record are accessed using the dot notation, as in `p.x` or `m.name`.

C.3 Constants and Variables

Constants and variables must be declared before they can be referenced.

Constants

A constant (a.k.a. named constant or manifest constant) is essentially a name for a literal value. Constants are introduced by declarations that conform to the following rule.

```
"const" constId ":=" [ "-" ] literal ";" .
```

The type of the constant identifier is determined by the type of the literal, which must be an integer literal, a character literal, a boolean literal, or a string literal. The optional minus sign ("-") is allowed only for integer literals.

Example

```
const arraySize := 100;
const errorSig  := -1;
```

Variables

Variables are introduced by declarations of the following form.

```
var varId₁, varId₂, ..., varIdₙ : typeName := initializer;
```

The type name can be one of the predefined scalar types such as `Boolean` or `Integer`, or it can be an identifier representing an array type, an enumerated type, or a record type. A variable declaration can contain an optional initialization value, which must have the same type as the variables being declared.

For array variables, the type name does not have to be an identifier; an array type constructor can be used. So, for example, the following is also allowed.

```
var x : array[100] of Integer;
```

Initializers for scalar types and string types are simply constant values; i.e., literals or declared constants. But array types and record types can have composite initializers, which are enclosed in braces and separated by commas. The number of initializers within the braces must equal the number of components in the composite type. Composite initializers can be nested; e.g., to initialize an array of records or an array of arrays.

Here are the grammar rules for initializers.

```
initializer = constValue | compositeInitializer .

constValue = ( [ "-" ] literal ) | constId .

compositeInitializer = "{" initializer { "," initializer } "}".
```

Examples

```
var x1, x2 : Integer;         // x1 and x2 are not initialized
var x3, x4 : Integer := 1;    // both x3 and x4 are initialized to 1
var found  : Boolean := false;
var name   : String  := "Jack";
var a : array[6] of Integer := { 0x00, 0x01, 0x02, 0xFD, 0xFE, 0xFF };

type DaysPerMonth = array[13] of Integer;
var maxDays : DaysPerMonth :=  { 0, 31, 29, 31, 30, 31, 30,
                                     31, 31, 30, 31, 30, 31 };

const numRows := 3;
const numCols := 3;
type Row    = array[numCols] of Integer;
type Matrix = array[numRows] of Row;   // a 3x3 matrix of integers
var a : Matrix := {
                    { 2, 7, -3 },
                    { 1, 1,  5 },
                    { 7, 8,  9 }
                  };

var i : Matrix := {                    // the identity matrix
                    { 1, 0, 0 },
                    { 0, 1, 0 },
                    { 0, 0, 1 }
                  };

type Month = record
  {
    name    : String;
    maxDays : Integer;
  };
type Months = array[13] of Month;
var  months : Months := { { "invalid",    0 },
                          { "January",   31 }, { "February",  29 },
                          { "March",     31 }, { "April",     30 },
                          { "May",       31 }, { "June",      30 },
                          { "July",      31 }, { "August",    31 },
                          { "September", 30 }, { "October",   31 },
                          { "November",  30 }, { "December",  31 }
                        };
```

C.4 Operators and Expressions

Operators

The operators, in order of precedence, are as follows.

1. Boolean/bitwise negation	`not ~`	(highest precedence)
2. Multiplying/shift operators	`* / mod & << >>`	
3. Unary sign operators	`+ -`	
4. Adding/bitwise operators	`+ - | ^`	
5. Relational operators	`= != < <= > >=`	
6. Logical/conditional operators	`and or ?:`	(lowest precedence)

Expressions

For binary operators, in general both operands must have the same type except that we can mix types `Integer` and `Byte` since `Byte` values are promoted to type `Integer` when used in expressions. Objects are considered to have the same type if and only if they have the same type name or they are declared using identical array type constructors. Thus, two distinct type definitions are considered different even though they may be structurally identical. This is referred to as "name equivalence" of types.

Example 1

```
var x : array[10] of Integer;
var y : array[10] of Integer;
```

In this example, `x` and `y` have the same type, "`array[10] of Integer`".

Example 2

```
type T1 = array[10] of Integer;
type T2 = array[10] of Integer;

var x : T1;
var y : T1;
var z : T2;
```

In this example, `x` and `y` have the same type, but `x` and `z` do not even though they have the same structure.

Logical expressions (expressions involving logical operators "`and`" or "`or`") use short-circuit evaluation. For example, given an expression of the form "expr$_1$ `and` expr$_2$", the left operand (expr$_1$) is evaluated first. If the result is false, the right operand (expr$_2$) is not evaluated, and the truth value for the compound expression is false.

C.5 Statements

Assignment Statement

The assignment symbol is ":=". An assignment statement has the following form.

```
variable := expression;
```

Example 1

```
i := 2*i + 5;
```

The variable on the left and the expression on the right must have assignment compatible types. In general, CPRL uses named type equivalence, which means that two types are assignment compatible only if they share the same type name. Strict type equality is relaxed slightly for numeric types to allow the assignment of `Byte` expressions to `Integer` variables, and vice versa. Two composite types with identical structure but different type names are not assignment compatible.

Example 2

```
type T1 = array[10] of Integer;
type T2 = array[10] of Integer;

var x : T1;
var y : T1;
var z : T2;
...
x := y;   // allowed
x := z;   // *** Illegal in CPRL ***
```

String literals, and constants representing string literals, can be assigned to a variable of type `String`.

Example 3

```
var emailAddr1, emailAddr2 : String;
...
emailAddr1 := "natem@gmail.com";
emailAddr2 := "john_smith@hamptoncommunitycollege.edu";
```

Compound Statement

A compound statement is a sequence of zero or more statements enclosed in braces "{" and "}". A compound statement can be used anywhere a single statement can be used. Compound statements are commonly used in conjunction with `if` statements and `loop` statements. For example, the body of a `loop` is exactly one statement, but it may be a compound statement.

Example

```
while i < length loop
  {
    writeln a[i];
    i := i + 1;
  }
```

compound statement

If Statement

An `if` statement in CPRL is similar to an `if` statement in Java or Kotlin except that the boolean expression is followed by the keyword "`then`" and is not required to be enclosed in parentheses. An `if` statement can contain an optional `else` clause.

Examples

```
if a[i] = searchValue then
    found := true;

if x >= y then
    max := x;
else
    max := y;

if x < y then
  {
    // swap x and y
    temp := x;
    x := y;
    y := temp;
  }
```

Loop and Exit Statements

A general `loop` statement consists of the keyword "`loop`" followed by a statement, which is often a compound statement. A `loop` statement may be preceded by an optional "`while`" clause. An `exit` statement can be used to exit the innermost loop that contains it. Note that an `exit` statement must be nested within the body of a `loop` statement; it cannot appear as a standalone statement outside of a loop.

Example 1.

```
while i < n loop
  {
    sum := sum + a[i];
    i := i + 1;
  }
```

Example 2.

```
loop
  {
    read x;
    exit when x = SIGNAL;
    process(x);
  }
```

A `forLoop` statement can be used to iterate over a range of integer or enum values.

Example 3.

```
for i in 1..10 loop   // i has type Integer
    writeln a[i];
```

The loop variable, `i` in this example, is implicitly declared as a variable of type `Integer` and is scoped to the loop body. The starting and ending values of the loop can be arbitrary expressions; they are not required to be constants.

Range expressions in a `forLoop` can also have an enumerated type. In the example below, loop variable `d` has type `Day`.

Example 4.

```
for d in Day.Sun..Day.Sat loop   // d has type Day
    writeln dayNames[d];
```

Range expressions can also have type `Byte`, but the loop variable in this case will have type `Integer`.

Example 5.

```
var start : Byte := 0;
var end   : Byte := 9;
for b in start..end loop   // b has type Integer
    writeln b;
```

Input/Output Statements

CPRL defines only sequential text I/O for two basic character streams – standard input and standard output. I/O is provided by `read`, `write`, and `writeln` statements. Note that `readln` is a reserved word, but it is currently not used for input in CPRL.

The `write` and `writeln` statements can have multiple expressions separated by commas. The `writeln` statement appends an end-of-line after all expressions have been written, but the `write` statement does not. Both input and output are supported for integers, characters, and strings. Output for type `Boolean` is supported, but it writes out an integer representation instead of "`true`" or "`false`". Similarly, output for values of an enumerated type print the underlying integer value, not the name of the enum constant.

Examples

```
read x;      // assume that x has type Integer
writeln "The answer is ", 2*x + 1;
```

There is an important distinction between reading a value for an integer variable and reading a value for a byte variable. Reading a value for an integer variable will read a sequence of character digits and convert the sequence to an integer value. Reading a value for a byte variable will read a single binary byte value, not a sequence of characters representing the byte value. This difference is illustrated in the following example.

```
proc main()
  {
    var n : Integer;
    var b : Byte;

    writeln "Enter a value for n.";
    read n;         // enter 123<Return>
    writeln n;      // writes 123 as expected

    writeln "Enter a value for b.";
    read b;        // enter 123<Return>
    writeln b;     // writes 49, the ASCII/Unicode value for 1
  }
```

C.6 Programs

A program has an optional list of initial declarations (`const` declarations, `var` declarations, and `type` declarations) followed by a list of subprogram declarations. One of the subprograms must be a parameterless procedure named "`main()`", which serves as the starting point for program execution.

Example

```
var x : Integer;

proc main()
  {
    read x;
    writeln "x = ", x;
  }
```

C.7 Subprograms

CPRL provides two separate forms of subprograms – procedures and functions. A procedure does not return a value; it is invoked through a procedure call statement. A function must return a value and is invoked as an expression. Keywords "`proc`" and "`fun`" are used to start the declarations of procedures and functions, respectively. Recursive invocations of subprograms are allowed. Subprograms are not required to be declared before they are called. All subprogram names in a program must be distinct.

Procedures

Procedures are similar to void functions in C and programming languages derived from C. Explicit `return` statements are allowed within the subprogram body, but unlike functions, a `return` statement in a procedure must **not** be followed by an expression. Procedure calls are statements.

Example 1:

```
proc writeBoolean(b : Boolean)
  {
    if b then
        write "true";
    else
        write "false";
  }
```

Example 2 (Quick Sort)

```
proc quickSort(var a : A, fromIndex : Integer, toIndex : Integer)
  {
    var i, j, pivot, temp : Integer;

    i := fromIndex;
    j := toIndex;
    pivot := a[(fromIndex + toIndex)/2];

    // partition a[fromIndex]..a[toIndex] with pivot as the dividing item
    while i <= j loop
      {
        while a[i] < pivot loop
           i := i + 1;

        while a[j] > pivot loop
           j := j - 1;
```

```
            if i <= j then
              {
                // swap a[i] and a[j]
                temp := a[i];
                a[i] := a[j];
                a[j] := temp;

                // update i and j
                i := i + 1;
                j := j - 1;
              }
          }

        if fromIndex < j then
            quickSort(a, fromIndex, j);    // sort top part

        if i < toIndex then
            quickSort(a, i, toIndex);      // sort bottom part
      }
```

Assume that we have the following declarations.

```
const arraySize := 10;
type A = array[arraySize] of Integer;
var a : A;
```

Then we could call this procedure to sort the array as follows.

```
quickSort(a, 0, arraySize - 1);
```

Functions

Functions are similar to procedures except that functions return values. Function calls are expressions. A function returns a value by executing a "`return`" statement of the following form.

```
return <expression>;
```

Example 1

```
fun max(x : Integer, y : Integer) : Integer
  {
    return x > y ? x : y;
  }
```

Example 2

```
fun sgn(n : Integer) : Integer
  {
    if n > 0 then
        return 1;
    else if n < 0 then
        return -1;
    else
        return 0;
  }
```

Parameters

There are two parameter modes in CPRL – value parameters and variable parameters. Value parameters are passed by value (a.k.a. copy-in) and are the default. Variable parameters are passed by reference and must be explicitly declared using the "var" keyword. Unlike other types, arrays are always passed by reference to subprograms regardless of whether or not they are declared as variable parameters.

Example

```
proc inc(var x : Integer)
  {
    x := x + 1;
  }
```

Functions cannot declare variable parameters; only value parameters can be declared for functions. However, arrays are always passed by reference, even for functions, where they are not declared as var parameters.

Return Statements

A return statement terminates execution of a subprogram and returns control back to the point where the subprogram was called. A return statement within a function must be followed by an expression whose value is returned by the function. The type of the expression must be equal to the return type of the function. A return statement within a procedure must not be followed by an expression; it simply returns control to the statement following the procedure call statement.

A procedure has an implied return statement as its last statement, and therefore most procedures will not have an explicit return statement. A function requires one or more return statements to return the function value. There is no implicit return statement at the end of a function.

Built-in Subprograms

CPRL provides three built-in functions and one built-in procedure with the following signatures.

```
fun chr(n : Integer) : Char     // returns the character with the
                                // specified Unicode code point

fun eof() : Boolean             // returns true if standard input has
                                // reached the end of file

proc inc(var n : Integer)       // increments n

fun ord(c : Char) : Integer     // returns the ordinal value of a character
```

Functions `chr()` and `ord()`provide the capability to convert between CPRL types `Char` and `Integer`. For example, `ord('A')` returns the value `65`, and `chr(0x20AC)` returns the Euro sign `'€'`. When calling `chr()`, there is no checking that the integer parameter is a valid Unicode code point, but if it is, the two functions are inverses of each other; i.e., if `c` has type `Char` and `n` has type `Integer` (and if `n` is a valid Unicode code point) then `chr(ord(c)) = c` and `ord(chr(n)) = n`.

Procedure `inc()` simply increments its parameter. If n is an integer variable, writing `inc(n)` in CPRL is essentially equivalent to writing `++n` as a statement (i.e., on a line by itself followed by a semicolon) in C-based languages.

Function `eof()` signals end-of-file from standard input. Reading a file using the input redirection operator `<` works as expected, but the function does not detect end of file until a read is attempted. Following is an example function that reads and echoes the bytes in a binary file.

```
proc main()
  {
    var b : Byte;
    loop
      {
        read b;
        exit when eof();
        writeln b;
      }
  }
```

Assuming that the above program is in a CPRL source code file named `ReadBytes.cprl`, you could run the following to echo the bytes in the object code file.

```
cprl ReadBytes < ReadBytes.obj
```

Appendix D
The CPRL Grammar

```
// Structural Grammar
program = initialDecls subprogramDecls .
initialDecls = { initialDecl } .
initialDecl = constDecl | varDecl | typeDecl .
constDecl = "const" constId ":=" [ "-" ] literal ";" .
literal = intLiteral | charLiteral | stringLiteral | "true" | "false" .
varDecl = "var" identifiers ":" ( typeName | arrayTypeConstr )
          [ ":=" initializer ] ";" .
identifiers = identifier { "," identifier } .
initializer = constValue | compositeInitializer .
constValue = ( [ "-" ] literal ) | constId .
compositeInitializer = "{" initializer { "," initializer } "}" .
typeDecl = arrayTypeDecl | recordTypeDecl | enumTypeDecl .
arrayTypeDecl = "type" typeId "=" "array"  "[" intConstValue "]"
                "of" typeName ";" .
arrayTypeConstr = "array" "[" intConstValue "]" "of" typeName .
recordTypeDecl = "type" typeId "=" "record" "{" fieldDecls "}" ";" .
fieldDecls = { fieldDecl } .
fieldDecl = fieldId ":" typeName ";" .
enumTypeDecl = "type" typeId "=" "<" identifiers ">" ";" .
typeName = "Integer" | "Boolean" | "Byte" | "Char" | "String" | typeId .
subprogramDecls = { subprogramDecl } .
subprogramDecl = procedureDecl | functionDecl .
procedureDecl = "proc" procId "(" [ parameterDecls ] ")"
                "{" initialDecls statements "}" .
functionDecl = "fun" funId "(" [ parameterDecls ] ")" ":" typeName
               "{" initialDecls statements "}" .
parameterDecls = parameterDecl { "," parameterDecl } .
parameterDecl = [ "var" ] paramId ":" typeName .
statements = { statement } .
statement = assignmentStmt | procedureCallStmt | compoundStmt | ifStmt
          | loopStmt       | forLoopStmt       | exitStmt     | readStmt
          | writeStmt      | writelnStmt       | returnStmt .
```

```
compoundStmt = "{" statements "}" .
assignmentStmt = variable ":=" expression ";" .
variable = ( varId | paramId ) { indexExpr | fieldExpr } .
indexExpr = "[" expression "]" .
fieldExpr = "." fieldId .
ifStmt = "if" booleanExpr "then" statement [ "else" statement ] .
loopStmt = [ "while" booleanExpr ] "loop" statement .
forLoopStmt = "for" varId "in" expr ".." expr "loop" statement .
exitStmt = "exit" [ "when" booleanExpr ] ";" .
readStmt = "read" variable ";" .
writeStmt = "write" expressions ";" .
expressions = expression { "," expression } .
writelnStmt = "writeln" [ expressions ] ";" .
procedureCallStmt = procId "(" [ actualParams ] ")" ";" .
actualParams = expressions .
returnStmt = "return" [ expression ] ";" .
expression = relation { logicalOp relation } [ conditionalExpr ] .
logicalOp = "and" | "or" .
conditionalExpr = "?" expression ":" expression .
relation = simpleExpr [ relationalOp simpleExpr ] .
relationalOp = "=" | "!=" | "<" | "<=" | ">" | ">=" .
simpleExpr = [ signOp ] term { addingOp term } .
signOp = "+" | "-" .
addingOp  = "+" | "-" | "|" | "^" .
term = factor { multiplyingOp factor } .
multiplyingOp = "*" | "/" | "mod" | "&" | "<<" | ">>" .
factor = ("not" | "~") factor | literal | constId | variableExpr
       | enumConstValue | functionCallExpr | "(" expression ")" .
variableExpr = variable .
enumConstValue = enumTypeId "." enumConstId .
functionCallExpr = funId "(" [ actualParams ] ")" .
booleanExpr = expression .      // has type Boolean
intConstValue = constValue .    // has type Integer
```

```
// All symbols above with a suffix of "Id" are simply identifiers.
constId     = identifier .
enumConstId = identifier.
enumTypeId  = identifier .
fieldId = identifier .
funId   = identifier .
paramId = identifier .
procId  = identifier .
typeId  = identifier .
varId   = identifier .

// Common abbreviations used above:
//    constant    -> const
//    declaration -> decl
//    expression  -> expr
//    operator    -> op
//    parameter   -> param
//    statement   -> stmt
//    variable    -> var
//__________________________________________________________________

// Lexical Grammar

// All quoted terminals in the structural grammar given above are
// considered to be symbols of the lexical grammar.  In addition, all
// reserved words listed in Appendix C, Section C.1 are considered to be
// symbols of the lexical grammar even if they do not appear as terminal
// symbols in the structural grammar.

// The following four rules also define terminal symbols for the parser.
identifier = letter { letter | digit } .
intLiteral = decimalLiteral | hexLiteral | binaryLiteral .
charLiteral = "'" ( charLiteralElement | escapedChar ) "'" .
stringLiteral = "\"" { stringLiteralElement | escapedChar } "\"" .
```

```
// The remaining rules do not define terminal symbols for the parser.
// An integer literal can be expressed using decimal, hexadecimal, or binary
// notation

decimalLiteral = digit { digit } .
hexLiteral = ( "0x" | "0X" ) hexDigit { hexDigit } .
binaryLiteral = ( "0b" | "0B" ) binaryDigit { binaryDigit } .

// Character set notation: apostrophes (single quotes) for characters,
// two dots (periods) to denote ranges, a plus sign to denote set union,
// and a minus sign to denote set difference.  Equivalent definitions
// using regular expression character classes are shown in comments.

letter = 'A'..'Z' + 'a'..'z' .
   // regular expression character class: [A-Za-z]
digit = '0'..'9' .
   // regular expression character class: [0-9]
hexDigit = '0'..'9' + 'A'..'F' + 'a'..'f' .
   // regular expression character class: [0-9A-Fa-f]
binaryDigit = '0'..'1' .
   // regular expression character class: [0-1]
escapedChar = '\\' ('t' | 'n' | 'r' | '\"' | '\'' | '\\') .

// A graphic character is essentially any character that can be printed.
// For simplicity, this definition of graphic character excludes only ISO
// control characters, although some of the values in this range are not
// valid characters.  The ranges of allowable characters include space to
// tilde (~) plus NBSP to \uFFFF.
graphicChar = '\u0020'..'\u007E' + '\u00A0'..'\uFFFF' .
   // regular expression character class: [\u0020-\u007E\u00A0-\uFFFF]
   //                                 or: [^\u0000-\u001F\u007F-\u009F]

// A char literal element is any graphic character except single quote (')
// or backslash (\); i.e., includes space to ampersand, left paren to left
// bracket, right bracket to tilde, and NBSP to \uFFFF.
charLiteralElement = graphicChar - '\'' - '\\' .
   // regular expression character class: [ -&(-\[\]-~\u00A0-\uFFFF]
```

```
// A string literal element is any graphic character except double quote
// (") or backslash (\); i.e., includes space, exclamation point, hash
// tag to left bracket, right bracket to tilde, and NBSP to \uFFFF.
stringLiteralElement = graphicChar - '\"' - '\\' .
  // regular expression character class: [ !#-\[\]-~\u00A0-\uFFFF]
```

Appendix E
Definition of the CPRL Virtual Machine

E.1 Specification

CVM (CPRL Virtual Machine) is a hypothetical computer designed to simplify the code generation phase of a compiler for CPRL (the Compiler PRoject Language). CVM has a stack architecture; i.e., most instructions either expect operands on the stack, place results on the stack, or both. Memory is organized into 8-bit bytes, and each byte is directly addressable. A word is a logical grouping of 4 consecutive bytes in memory. The address of a word is the address of its first (low) byte. `Boolean` values are represented in a single byte, character values use 2 bytes (Unicode Basic Multilingual Plane or Plane 0, code points from `U+0000` to `U+FFFF`), and integer values use a word (four bytes).

CVM has five 32-bit internal registers that are usually manipulated indirectly as a result of program execution. There are no general-purpose registers for computation. The names and functions of the internal registers are as follows.

- `PC` (program counter, a.k.a. instruction pointer): holds the address of the next instruction to be executed.
- `SB` (stack base): holds the address of the bottom of the stack. When a program is loaded, `SB` is initialized to the address of the first free byte in memory, and its value never changes during program execution.
- `SP` (stack pointer): holds the address of the top of the stack. The stack grows from low-numbered memory addresses to high-numbered memory addresses. When the stack is empty, `SP` has a value of `SB - 1`, the address immediately before the first free byte in memory.
- `BP` (base pointer): holds the base address of the current activation record (a.k.a. frame); i.e., the base address for the subprogram currently being executed. `BP` and `SB` have the same value (i.e., both reference the same memory location) if there are no currently active subprograms.
- `HP` (heap pointer): holds the address of the top of the heap. The heap grows from high-numbered memory addresses to low-numbered memory addresses. When a program is loaded, `HP` is initialized to the number of bytes in memory; i.e., one more than the last valid memory address. `HP` is used in only two CPRL string-related opcodes, `GETSTR` (reads a string from standard input) and `STRCAT` (concatenates two strings).

Each CVM instruction operation code (opcode) occupies one byte of memory. Some instructions take an immediate operand, which is always located immediately following the instruction in memory. Depending on the opcode, an immediate operand can be a single byte, two bytes (e.g., for a char), four bytes (e.g., for an integer or a memory address), or multiple bytes (e.g., for a string literal). The complete instruction set for CVM is given in the next section. Most instructions get their operands from the run-time stack. In general, the operands are removed from the stack whenever the instruction is executed, and any results are left on the top of the stack. With respect to boolean values, zero means false and any nonzero value is interpreted as true.

The following diagram illustrates a program loaded into memory.

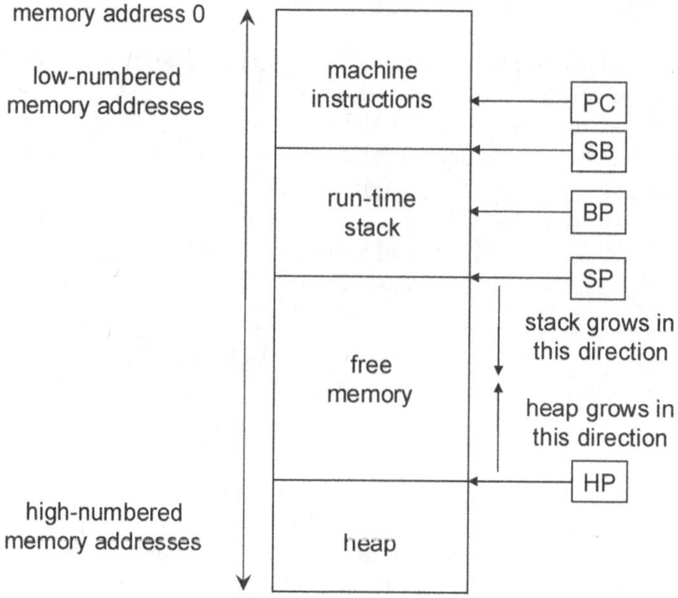

Variable Addressing

Each time that a subprogram is called, CVM saves the current value of `BP` and sets `BP` to point to the new activation record (a.k.a. frame). When the subprogram returns, CVM restores `BP` back to the saved value.

A variable has an absolute address in memory (the address of the first byte), but variables are more commonly addressed relative to a register. A local variable is addressed relative to register `BP`, and a global variable is addressed relative to register `SB`.

Various load and store operations move data between memory and the run-time stack.

E.2 Implementation

CVM is implemented by three classes in package `cvm`. Class `Constants` defines the number of bytes for primitive types plus the number of bytes for the context part of an activation record.

```
public static final int BYTES_PER_OPCODE  = 1;
public static final int BYTES_PER_INTEGER = 4;
...
public static final int BYTES_PER_CONTEXT = 2*BYTES_PER_ADDRESS;
```

Class `Opcode` is an enum class that defines the name and numeric values for each CVM opcode. In addition, this class defines several helper functions used by the CVM, the assembler, and disassembler, including static method `toOpcode(byte b)` that returns the opcode for the specified byte value.

```
public enum Opcode
  {
    // halt opcode
    HALT(0),

    // load opcodes (move data from memory to top of stack)
    LOAD(10),
    LOADB(11),
    LOAD2B(12),
    LOADW(13),
    LDCB(14),
    LDCCH(15),
    LDCINT(16),
    ...

    // arithmetic opcodes
    ADD(70),
    SUB(71),
    MUL(72),
    DIV(73),
    ...

    // program/procedure opcodes
    PROGRAM(90),
    PROC(91),
    CALL(92),
    RET(93),
    ...

    private final byte value;

    /**
     * Construct an opcode with its machine instruction value.
     */
    private Opcode(int value)
      {
        this.value = (byte) value;
      }

    ...
  }
```

Class CVM is the primary component of the implementation for the virtual machine. In addition to several helper methods, every opcode is implemented by a method. CVM method run() provides the basic control logic for the virtual machine using a large "switch" statement to dispatch opcodes to their corresponding method calls.

```
public void run()
  {
    running = true;
    pc = 0;

    try
      {
        while (running)
          {
            switch (Opcode.toOpcode(fetchByte()))
              {
                case ADD      -> add();
                case ALLOC    -> allocate();
                case BITAND   -> bitAnd();
                case BITOR    -> bitOr();
                case BITXOR   -> bitXor();
                case BITNOT   -> bitNot();
                case BR       -> branch();
                case BE       -> branchEqual();
                case BNE      -> branchNotEqual();
                case BG       -> branchGreater();
                case BGE      -> branchGreaterOrEqual();
                case BL       -> branchLess();
                ...
                case SHL      -> shl();
                case SHR      -> shr();
                case STORE    -> store();
                case STOREB   -> storeByte();
                case STORE2B  -> store2Bytes();
                case STOREW   -> storeWord();
                case STRCAT   -> strcat();
                case SUB      -> subtract();
                default       -> error("invalid machine instruction");
              }
          }
      }
    catch (Throwable t)
      {
        System.err.println("Virtual Machine Error: " + t.getMessage());
        t.printStackTrace();
      }
  }
```

E.3 CVM Instruction Set Architecture

Mnemonic	Short Description	Stack before / after	Definition
Arithmetic Opcodes			
ADD	Add: Pop two integers from the stack and push their sum back onto the stack.	n1 n2 ——— n1 + n2	n2 ← popInt() n1 ← popInt() pushInt(n1 + n2)
SUB	Subtract: Pop two integers from the stack and push their difference back onto the stack.	n1 n2 ——— n1 - n2	n2 ← popInt() n1 ← popInt() pushInt(n1 - n2)
MUL	Multiply: Pop two integers from the stack and push their product back onto the stack.	n1 n2 ——— n1*n2	n2 ← popInt() n1 ← popInt() pushInt(n1*n2)
DIV	Divide: Pop two integers from the stack and push their quotient back onto the stack.	n1 n2 ——— n1/n2	n2 ← popInt() n1 ← popInt() pushInt(n1/n2)
MOD	Modulo: Pop two integers from the stack, divide them, and push the remainder back onto the stack.	n1 n2 ——— n1 % n2	n2 ← popInt() n1 ← popInt() pushInt(n1 % n2)
NEG	Negate: Pop an integer from the stack, negate it, and push the result back onto the stack.	n ——— -n	n ← popInt() pushInt(-n)
INC	Increment: Pop an integer from the stack, add 1, and push the result back onto the stack.	n ——— n + 1	n ← popInt() pushInt(n + 1)
DEC	Decrement: Pop an integer from the stack, subtract 1, and push the result back onto the stack.	n ——— n - 1	n ← popInt() pushInt(n - 1)

Logical Opcodes			

NOT	Logical Not: Pop a byte from the stack and push its logical negation back onto the stack.	b
		———
		!b
			b ← popByte()
			if b = 0
			   pushByte(1)
			else
			   pushByte(0)

Shift Opcodes			
SHL	Shift Left: Pop 2 integers from the stack, shift the second integer left by the amount specified in the first integer using zero fill, and push the result back onto the stack. Note: Only the right most five bits of the first integer are used for the shift.	n1 n2 ——— n1 << n2	n2 ← popInt() n1 ← popInt() s ← n2 & 0b1111 pushInt(n1 << s)
SHR	Shift Right: Pop 2 integers from the stack, shift the second integer right by the amount specified in the first integer using sign extent, and push the result back onto the stack. Note: Only the right most five bits of the first integer are used for the shift.	n1 n2 ——— n1 >> n2	n2 ← popInt() n1 ← popInt() s ← n2 & 0b1111 pushInt(n1 >> s)
Branch Opcodes			
BR displ	Branch: Branch unconditionally according to displacement argument (may be positive or negative).		pc ← pc + displ

`BE displ`	Branch Equal: Pop two integers from the stack and compare them. If they are equal, then branch according to displacement argument (may be positive or negative); otherwise continue with the next instruction.	n1
		n2
		———
			`n2 ← popInt()`
			`n1 ← popInt()`
			`if n1 == n2`
			`   pc ← pc + displ`

`BNE displ`	Branch Not Equal: Pop two integers from the stack and compare them. If they are not equal, then branch according to displacement argument (may be positive or negative); otherwise continue with the next instruction.	n1
		n2
		———
			`n2 ← popInt()`
			`n1 ← popInt()`
			`if n1 != n2`
			`   pc ← pc + displ`

`BG displ`	Branch Greater: Pop two integers from the stack and compare them. If the second integer is greater than the first, then branch according to displacement argument (may be positive or negative); otherwise continue with the next instruction.	n1
		n2
		———
			`n2 ← popInt()`
			`n1 ← popInt()`
			`if n1 > n2`
			`   pc ← pc + displ`

`BGE displ`	Branch Greater or Equal: Pop two integers from the stack and compare them. If the second integer is greater than or equal to the first, then branch according to displacement argument (may be positive or negative); otherwise continue with the next instruction.	n1
		n2
		———
			`n2 ← popInt()`
			`n1 ← popInt()`
			`if n1 >= n2`
			`   pc ← pc + displ`

`BL displ`	Branch Less: Pop two integers from the stack and compare them. If the second integer is less than the first, then branch according to displacement argument (may be positive or negative); otherwise continue with the next instruction.	n1
		n2
		———
			`n2 ← popInt()`
			`n1 ← popInt()`
			`if n1 < n2`
			`   pc ← pc + displ`

`BLE displ`	Branch Less or Equal: Pop two integers from the stack and compare them. If the second integer is less than or equal to the first, then branch according to displacement argument (may be positive or negative); otherwise continue with the next instruction.	n1
		n2
		———
			`n2 ← popInt()`
			`n1 ← popInt()`
			`if n1 <= n2`
			`   pc ← pc + displ`

`BZ displ`	Branch if Zero: Pop one byte from the stack. If it is zero, then branch according to displacement argument (may be positive or negative); otherwise continue with the next instruction.	b
		———
			`b ← popByte()`
			`if b = 0`
			`   pc ← pc + displ`

`BNZ displ`	Branch if Nonzero: Pop one byte from the stack. If it is nonzero then branch according to displacement argument (may be positive or negative); otherwise continue with the next instruction.	b
		———
			`b ← popByte()`
			`if b ≠ 0`
			`   pc ← pc + displ`

Load/Store Opcodes			

`LOAD n`	Load multiple bytes onto the stack: The number of bytes to move is part of the instruction. Pop an address from the stack and push n bytes starting at that address onto the stack.	addr
		———
		b1
		b2
		...
		bn
			`addr ← popInt();`
			`for i ← 0..n-1 loop`
			`   pushByte(mem[addr + i])`

`LOADB`	Load Byte: Load (push) a single byte onto the stack. The address of the byte is obtained by popping it off the stack.	addr
		―――
		b
			`addr ← popInt()`
			`b ← mem[addr]`
			`pushByte(b)`

`LOAD2B`	Load Two Bytes: Load (push) two consecutive bytes onto the stack. The address of the first byte is obtained by popping it off the stack.	addr
		―――
		b0
		b1
			`addr ← popInt()`
			`b0 ← mem[addr + 0]`
			`b1 ← mem[addr + 1]`
			`pushByte(b0)`
			`pushByte(b1)`

`LOADW`	Load Word: Load (push) a word (four consecutive bytes) onto the stack. The address of the word is obtained by popping it off the stack.	addr
		―――
		w
			`addr ← popInt()`
			`w ← getWord(addr)`
			`pushInt(w)`

`LDCB b`	Load Constant Byte: Fetch the byte immediately following the opcode and push it onto the stack.	――― b	`pushByte(b)`
`LDCB0`	Load Constant Byte `0`: Optimized version of `LDCB 0`.	――― 0	`pushByte(0)`
`LDCB1`	Load Constant Byte `1`: Optimized version of `LDCB 1`.	――― 1	`pushByte(1)`
`LDCCH c`	Load Constant Character: Fetch the character immediately following the opcode and push it onto the stack.	――― c	`pushChar(c)`
`LDCINT n`	Load Constant Integer: Fetch the integer immediately following the opcode and push it onto the stack.	――― n	`pushInt(n)`
`LDCINT0`	Load Constant Integer `0`: Optimized version of `LDCINT 0`.	――― 0	`pushInt(0)`
`LDCINT1`	Load Constant Integer `1`: Optimized version of `LDCINT 1`.	――― 1	`pushInt(1)`

`LDCSTR s`	Load Constant String: The value of `pc` (which is the address of the constant string) is pushed onto the stack. Then `pc` is advanced so as to skip over the string.	`pc`	`// pc is address of string`
			`pushInt(pc)`
			`len ← getInt(pc)`
			`pc ← pc + 4 + len`

`LDLADDR n`	Load Local Address: Compute the absolute address of a local variable from its relative address `n` and push the absolute address onto the stack.	`bp + n`	`pushInt(bp + n)`
`LDGADDR n`	Load Global Address: Compute the absolute address of a global (program level) variable from its relative address `n` and push the absolute address onto the stack.	`sb + n`	`pushInt(sb + n)`

`STORE n`	Store n bytes: Remove `n` bytes from the stack followed by an absolute address and copy the `n` bytes to the location starting at the absolute address.	`addr`
		`b1`
		`b2`
		`...`
		`bn`
			`addr = mem[sp-n-3]`
			`for i ← n-1..0`
			`  mem[addr+i] ← popByte()`
			`popInt()    // remove addr`

`STOREB`	Store Byte: Store a single byte at a specified memory location. The byte to be stored and the address where it is to be stored are popped from the stack.	`addr`
		`b`
			`b ← popByte()`
			`addr ← popInt()`
			`memory[addr] ← b`

`STORE2B`	Store Two Bytes: Store two bytes at a specified memory location. The bytes to be stored and the address where they are to be stored are popped from the stack.	`addr`
		`b0`
		`b1`
			`b1 ← popByte()`
			`b0 ← popByte()`
			`addr ← popInt()`
			`mem[addr + 0] ← b0`
			`mem[addr + 1] ← b1`

`STOREW`	Store Word: Store a word (4 bytes) at a specified memory location. The word to be stored and the address where it is to be stored are popped from the stack.	`addr`
		`w`
			`w ← popWord()`
			`addr ← popInt()`
			`putWord(w, addr)`

Type Conversion Opcodes			

BYTE2INT	Byte to Integer: Pop a byte from the stack and push an int with the popped value as its low order (least significant) byte and zeros as the three high order bytes	b / n	`b ← popByte()`
			`n ← [0b0, 0b0, 0b0, b]`
			`pushInt(n)`

INT2BYTE	Integer to Byte: Pop an integer from the stack and push its low order (least significant) byte back onto the stack.	n / b	`n ← popInt()` `pushByte(n[3])`

CHAR2INT	Char to Integer: Pop a character from the stack and push an int with the popped value as the two low order (least significant) bytes and zeros as the two high order bytes	c / n	`c ← popChar()`
			`n ← charToInt(c)`
			`pushInt(n)`

INT2CHAR	Integer to Char: Pop an integer from the stack and push its two low order (least significant) bytes back onto the stack.	n / c	`n ← popInt()`
			`c ← intToChar(n)`
			`pushChar(c)`

Special Opcode for String Concatenation			

STRCAT	String concatenate: Concatenate two strings whose addresses are on the top of the stack. The concatenated string is stored on the heap. Register hp (address of the concatenated string) is pushed onto the stack.	s1addr s2addr / hp	`addr1 ← popInt()`
			`addr2 ← popInt()`
			`len1 ← getInt(addr1)`
			`len2 ← getInt(addr2)`
			`len ← len1 + len2`
			`copyStrToHeap(addr1)`
			`copyStrToHeap(addr2)`
			`hp ← hp - 4`
			`putInt(len, hp)`
			`pushInt(hp)`

Bitwise Opcodes			

`BITAND`	Bitwise `and`: Pop two integers from the stack, perform bitwise `and`, and push the result back onto the stack.	n1
		n2
		———
		n1 & n2
			`n2 ← popInt()`
			`n1 ← popInt()`
			`pushInt(n1 & n2)`

`BITOR`	Bitwise `or`: Pop two integers from the stack, perform bitwise `or`, and push the result back onto the stack.	n1
		n2
		———
		n1 | n2
			`n2 ← popInt()`
			`n1 ← popInt()`
			`pushInt(n1 | n2)`

`BITXOR`	Bitwise `xor`: Pop two integers from the stack, perform bitwise `xor`, and push the result back onto the stack.	n1
		n2
		———
		n1 ^ n2
			`n2 ← popInt()`
			`n1 ← popInt()`
			`pushInt(n1 ^ n2)`

`BITNOT`	Bitwise `not`: Pop an integer from the stack, perform bitwise `not`, and push the result back onto the stack.	n ——— ~n	`n ← popInt()` `pushInt(~n)`
Program/Procedure Opcodes			
`PROGRAM n`	Program: Initialize base pointer and allocate space on the stack for the program's local variables.		`bp ← sb` `sp ← bp + n - 1`
`PROC n`	Procedure: Allocate space on the stack for a subprogram's local variables.		`sp ← sp + n`

`CALL disp`	Call: Call a subprogram, pushing current values for `BP` and `PC` onto the stack.	———
		bp
		p
			`pushInt(bp)`
			`pushInt(pc)`
			`bp ← sp - 7`
			`pc ← pc + disp`

`RET n`	Return: Return from a subprogram, restoring the old value for BP plus space on stack previously allocated for the subprogram's local variables and parameters.		`bpSave ← bp`
			`sp ← bpSave - n - 1`
			`bp ← getInt(bpSave)`
			`pc ← getInt(bpSave + 4)`

`RET0`	Optimized version of `RET 0`.		`bpSave ← bp`
			`sp ← bpSave - 1`
			`bp ← getInt(bpSave)`
			`pc ← getInt(bpSave + 4)`

`RET4`	Optimized version of `RET 4`.		`bpSave ← bp`
			`sp ← bpSave - 5`
			`bp ← getInt(bpSave)`
			`pc ← getInt(bpSave + 4)`

`ALLOC n`	Allocate: Allocate space on the stack for future use.		`sp ← sp + n`
`HALT`	Halt: Stop the virtual machine.		`halt`
	I/O Opcodes		

`GETBYTE`	Get Byte: Read digits from standard input, convert them to a byte, and store the byte at the address on top of stack.	`addr`	`addr ← popInt()`
			`b ← readByte()`
			`putByte(b, addr)`

`GETEOF`	Get value of EOF flag: Push the value of the EOF flag onto the top of the stack.	`eofFlag`	`push(eofFlag)`

`GETINT`	Get Integer: Read digits from standard input, convert them to an integer, and store the integer at the address on top of stack.	`addr`	`addr ← popInt()`
			`n ← readInt()`
			`putInt(n, addr)`

`GETCH`	Get Character: Read character from standard input and store it at the address on top of stack.	`addr`	`addr ← popInt()`
			`c ← readChar()`
			`putChar(c, addr)`

`GETSTR`	Get String: Read string from standard input, store the string (length plus characters) on the heap, and write the heap pointer to the address on top of stack.	addr
		———
			`addr ← popInt()`
			`s ← readStr()`
			`heapAlloc(4 + 2*s.length)`
			`copyStringToHeap(s)`
			`addr ← hp`

`PUTINT`	Put Integer: Pop integer from top of the stack and write its value to standard output.	n ———	`n ← popInt()` `writeInt(n)`
`PUTCH`	Put Character: Pop character from top of stack and write its value to standard output.	c ———	`c ← popChar()` `writeChar(c)`

`PUTSTR n`	Put String: Write a string of n characters to standard output. The string (length plus characters) was previously pushed onto the stack.	s
		———
			`nBytes ← 4 + 2*n`
			`addr ← sp - nBytes + 1`
			`strLen ← getInt(addr)`
			`for i ← 0..strLen-1 loop`
			`   writeChar(mem[2*i])`
			`sp ← sp - n`

`PUTEOL`	Put End-of-Line: Write a line terminator to standard output.		`write(EOL)`

Appendix F
Searching for Reserved Words

An important task of the scanner is to distinguish between programmer-defined identifiers and reserved words. Since identifiers and reserved words account for a large percentage of the symbols in a typical program, this task needs to be implemented efficiently. Indeed, an analysis of the collection of correct CPRL test programs shows that almost half the symbols fall into one of these two categories.

The basic idea adopted by many hand-implemented scanners is to accumulate the characters for an identifier or reserved word into a string and then use a look-up mechanism to determine if the string is one of the reserved words. We encapsulate the details of the look-up mechanism in a scanner method with the following signature.

```
private Symbol getIdentifierSymbol(String idString)
```

The method will return either `Symbol.identifier` or one of the reserved word symbols such as `Symbol.IntegerRW`, `Symbol.ifRW`, `Symbol.loopRW`, `Symbol.varRW`, etc.

This appendix explores several algorithms for implementing this method, and it includes benchmark results for the performance of each algorithm. Other than the sequential algorithms, most of the algorithms discussed have either been used or suggested by compiler writers in the past. Details of the implementations and benchmark analyses are given in the remainder of this appendix, but the results displayed in the following table show that the performance differences can be substantial. Benchmark results were obtained using OpenJDK version 26.0.1.

Search Algorithm	Benchmark Time (in seconds)	Standard Deviation
Sequential 1	7.054	0.0525
Sequential 2	3.926	0.0132
Binary	4.055	0.0223
By Length	3.774	0.0183
By First Character	2.745	0.0078
Gperf Hash	2.100	0.0060
Switch Expression	2.021	0.0067
HashMap	1.722	0.0077

F.1 Benchmarking the Search Algorithms

The general approach to benchmarking was to use each algorithm to perform numerous searches for identifiers and reserved words. The run times for each algorithm were computed simply by reading the system monotonic (nano time) clock before and after the searches and then subtracting. While the timings are subject to some noise from other processes running in the background, every effort was made to minimize this effect, and multiple runs of the benchmarks produced comparable times. The results above are obtained by running the timed searches ten times and averaging the results.

Since not all reserved words are used with the same frequency, an analysis of the correct CPRL examples was performed to determine a rough order of magnitude. For example, the reserved word `proc` was used a lot more than the reserved word `loop`, and `loop` was used a lot more than the reserved word `false`. Among predefined type names, `Integer` was by far the most used. Also, recall that some reserved words are not yet used in CPRL but are reserved for possible future use. In addition, programmer-defined identifiers occurred almost as frequently as all reserved words combined.

Based on this analysis, a file was created to control the number of times each reserved word or identifier would be searched as part of the benchmarking process. Each line of the file contained either a reserved word or an identifier followed by the number of times it was to be searched. Below is an outline of the file.

```
Boolean        559000
Byte            23000
Char           380000
Integer       4090000
String        1073000
and            582000
array          760000
...
writeln       7531000
i            35000000
avg          15000000
main         15000000
maxIndex      1000000
thisIsAVeryLongIdentifier 1000000
```

The data in the list was used to initialize a large list of strings, with each identifier or reserved word appearing the specified number of times in the list. After initialization, values in the list were randomly rearranged using `Collections.shuffle()`, and the list was converted to an array named `testIds` for testing. Timed performance of each search algorithm was implemented as shown below.

```
timer.start();
for (var testId : testIds)
    search.getIdentifierSymbol(testId);
timer.stop();
```

Note that this code simply ignores the value returned by method `getIdentifierSymbol()`. Also, time required to initialize the search algorithm (e.g., a list or map) was not measured.

F.2 Sequential Search 1

This is the least efficient approach to searching for reserved words and is useful only for comparison purposes. This approach uses an array list of reserved word symbols and a sequential search through the array list. Its only advantage is that it is very easy to implement.

The code to declare and initialize the list is very simple.

```
private ArrayList<Symbol> reservedWords = new ArrayList<>(50);
...
for (var symbol : Symbol.values())
  {
    if (symbol.isReservedWord())
        reservedWords.add(symbol);
  }
```

We can visualize the contents of the list as follows.

```
{
  BooleanRW,
  ByteRW,
  CharRW,
  IntegerRW,
  StringRW,
  andRW,
  arrayRW,
  ...
  whileRW,
  writeRW,
  writelnRW
}
```

Using this list, the search method is implemented as shown below.

```
private Symbol getIdentifierSymbol(String idString)
  {
    for (var reservedWord : reservedWords)
      {
        if (idString.equals(reservedWord.toString()))
            return reservedWord;
      }

    return Symbol.identifier;
  }
```

The call to method `toString()` for retrieving the reserved word spelling makes this inefficient algorithm even more inefficient.

F.3 Sequential Search 2

This approach simply uses nested "else if" statements to determine the appropriate identifier symbol.

```
private Symbol getIdentifierSymbol(String idString)
  {
    if (idString.equals("Boolean"))
        return Symbol.BooleanRW;
    else if (idString.equals("Byte"))
        return Symbol.ByteRW;
    else if (idString.equals("Char"))
        return Symbol.CharRW;
    else if (idString.equals("Integer"))
        return Symbol.IntegerRW;
    else if (idString.equals("String"))
        return Symbol.StringRW;
    else if (idString.equals("and"))
        return Symbol.andRW;
    else if (idString.equals("array"))
        return Symbol.arrayRW;
    ...

    else if (idString.equals("while"))
        return Symbol.whileRW;
    else if (idString.equals("write"))
        return Symbol.writeRW;
    else if (idString.equals("writeln"))
        return Symbol.writelnRW;
    else
        // if you get this far, it must be a plain old identifier
        return Symbol.identifier;
  }
```

The performance of this algorithm was surprising. One might expect this algorithm to have roughly the same run-time performance as the **Sequential Search 1** algorithm, but, in fact, it was substantially better since it eliminates the overhead of looping through the array and retrieving the array values.

F.4 Binary Search

For this approach we use a binary search of the reserved words with the expectation that it will perform faster than the three sequential searches. Using big-Oh notation, we know that a sequential search has O(n) performance, while a binary search has O(log n) performance. It is not difficult to implement a binary search algorithm, but class `Arrays` (in package `java.util`) already does this for us.

First we create a sorted array of strings for the reserved words. We name this array `reservedWordStrs`, and we visualize its contents as follows.

```
{
  "Boolean",
  "Byte",
  "Char",
  "Integer",
  "String",
  "and",
  "array",
  ...
  "while",
  "write",
  "writeln"
}
```

Using `Arrays.binarySearch(reservedWordStrs, idString)` to search this list for string `idString` will return the array index if the string is found; otherwise, it will return a negative value. But when the value is found, we need to convert it to a `Symbol`. There are several ways to do this, but the most efficient way is to have a second (parallel) array of reserved word symbols and then use the index from the string search to retrieve the corresponding symbol. We name this second array `reservedWordSyms`, and we visualize its contents as shown below.

```
{
  BooleanRW,
  ByteRW,
  CharRW,
  IntegerRW,
  StringRW,
  andRW,
  arrayRW,
  ...
  whileRW,
  writeRW,
  writelnRW
}
```

The search algorithm can be implemented in Java as follows.

```
private Symbol getIdentifierSymbol(String idString)
  {
    int index = Arrays.binarySearch(reservedWordStrs, idString);
    return index >= 0 ? reservedWordSyms[index] : Symbol.identifier;
  }
```

The benchmark results show that **Binary Search** is much faster than **Sequential Search 1** but not faster than **Sequential Search 2**. Evidently the number of CPRL reserved words is too small to overcome the overhead of implementing a binary search. In other words, we would expect the **Binary Search** to be more efficient when searching through a larger list of strings. This conjecture was tested with Ada reserved words since Ada has approximately twice as many reserved words as CPRL. For Ada reserved words, **Binary Search** was faster than **Sequential Search 2**, but still not significantly faster. If the list was much larger, say over 10,000 words, we would expect the performance improvement to be substantial.

F.5 Search by Length

For this algorithm we create a Java record named `StrSymPair`, defined as follows.

```
private record StrSymPair(String rwString, Symbol rwSymbol) {}
```

We put the `(String, Symbol)` pairs in an array of subarrays according to the string length. We essentially use the length of the identifier string being searched as a hash to pick out the appropriate subarray, and we then use a sequential search of the subarray of reserved words having the desired length.

We declare and initialize the array of subarrays as follows.

```
private StrSymPair[][] reservedWordsByLength =
  {
    // first two subarrays (indices 0 and 1) are empty
    { },
    { },

    // reserved words with two characters
    {
      new StrSymPair("if", Symbol.ifRW),
      new StrSymPair("in", Symbol.inRW),
      new StrSymPair("of", Symbol.ofRW),
      new StrSymPair("or", Symbol.orRW)
    },

    // reserved words with three characters
    {
      new StrSymPair("and", Symbol.andRW),
      new StrSymPair("for", Symbol.forRW),
      new StrSymPair("fun", Symbol.funRW),
      new StrSymPair("mod", Symbol.modRW),
      new StrSymPair("not", Symbol.notRW),
      new StrSymPair("var", Symbol.varRW)
    },
```

```
    // reserved words with four characters
    {
      new StrSymPair("Byte", Symbol.ByteRW),
      new StrSymPair("Char", Symbol.CharRW),
      new StrSymPair("else", Symbol.elseRW),
      ...
      new StrSymPair("type", Symbol.typeRW),
      new StrSymPair("when", Symbol.whenRW)
    },

    ...

    // reserved words with eight characters
    { },

    // reserved words with nine characters
    {
      new StrSymPair("protected", Symbol.protectedRW)
    }
  };
```

Using this array of subarrays, the search algorithm can now be implemented as follows.

```
private Symbol getIdentifierSymbol(String idString)
  {
    // quick check based on length
    if (idString.length() > 9)
        return Symbol.identifier;

    // get array of reserved words based on length of idString
    var reservedWords = reservedWordsByLength[idString.length()];

    // perform a sequential search
    for (var pair : reservedWords)
      {
        if (idString.equals(pair.rwString()))
            return pair.rwSymbol();
      }

    return Symbol.identifier;
  }
```

Benchmark results indicate that this search algorithm performs faster than any of the sequential searches or **Binary Search**. It is possible that we could tweak out a few extra milliseconds by reordering the subarrays according to expected frequency of use (e.g., moving `Symbol.loopRW` to the beginning of the subarray for reserved words of length four and moving `Symbol.trueRW` to the end), but this was not tested since other algorithms give even better performance.

F.6 Search by First Character

This approach is somewhat similar to that of **Search by Length**, but, rather than organizing the array of subarrays according to string length, we organize according to the first character in the string. Then we use the first character of the identifier string being searched as a hash to pick out the appropriate subarray. The primary advantage here is that the subarrays are much shorter (average roughly 2 items per nonempty subarray versus 5 for **Search by Length**), so sequentially searching a subarray takes less time. The primary disadvantage is that it is a little more complicated to initialize the arrays.

We declare and initialize the array of subarrays as follows.

```
private StrSymPair[][] strSymPairs =
  {
    // first 65 subarrays (indices 0-64) are empty
    { }, { }, { }, { }, { }, { }, { }, { }, { }, { },
    ...
    { }, { }, { }, { }, { }, { }, { }, { }, { }, { },
    { }, { }, { }, { }, { },
    { },   // 'A'
    { new StrSymPair("Boolean", Symbol.BooleanRW),
      new StrSymPair("Byte",    Symbol.ByteRW) },
    { new StrSymPair("Char",    Symbol.CharRW) },
    { },   // 'D'
    ...
    { },   // '`'
    { new StrSymPair("and",     Symbol.andRW),
      new StrSymPair("array",   Symbol.arrayRW) },
    { },   // 'b'
    { new StrSymPair("class",     Symbol.classRW),
      new StrSymPair("const",     Symbol.constRW) },
    ...
    { new StrSymPair("then",      Symbol.thenRW),
      new StrSymPair("true",      Symbol.trueRW),
      new StrSymPair("type",      Symbol.typeRW) },    { },   // 'u'
    { new StrSymPair("var",     Symbol.varRW) },
    { new StrSymPair("when",    Symbol.whenRW),
      new StrSymPair("while",   Symbol.whileRW),
      new StrSymPair("write",   Symbol.writeRW),
      new StrSymPair("writeln", Symbol.writelnRW) },
    { },   // 'x'
    { },   // 'y'
    { }    // 'z'
  };
```

Using this array of subarrays, the search algorithm can now be implemented as follows.

```
private Symbol getIdentifierSymbol(String idString)
  {
    // get array of reserved word pairs based on first char of idString
    var reservedWordPairs = strSymPairs[(idString.charAt(0)];

    // perform a sequential search
    for (var rwPair : reservedWordPairs)
      {
        if (idString.equals(rwPair.rwString()))
            return rwPair.rwSymbol();
      }

    return Symbol.identifier;
  }
```

Benchmark results show that this algorithm is, indeed, faster than searching based on the length of the string, and it is slightly slower than **Gperf Hash Search**, which we cover next.

F.7 Gperf Hash Search

The need to perform a fast search for a list of words, reserved or otherwise, has been around since the early days of computing, so it should come as no surprise that there is a software utility that can provide assistance. Gperf is a perfect hash function generator for a list of strings. You give gperf a list of strings, and it produces a hash function and hash table in the form of C/C++ code for looking up an arbitrary string to see if it is one of those in the list. The hash function is perfect, which means that the hash table has no collisions, and the lookup needs only one single string comparison. Gperf uses extensive analysis of the list of strings (plus a little magic and trial and error) to generate the C/C++ code. Gperf is used for keyword recognition in several production and research compilers including GNU C and GNU C++.

Gperf is available primarily on Linux, but there are versions available for Windows or through Windows Subsystem for Linux 2 (WSL2). Gperf on Ubuntu (running on WSL2) was used to generate the C code for CPRL reserved words, and the C code was translated to Java and adapted for our use in distinguishing between programmer-defined identifiers and reserved words. The output of gperf is a little cryptic. It has three major components.

> Note that gperf was designed to work for the ASCII character set, but there are workarounds for strings that contain non-ASCII characters.

First, we have `hashCode`, an array that maps ASCII characters to integer values. Most of the positions in the array have a default of value 66, but characters that appeared in CPRL reserved words have different values. Here is the declaration for this array.

```
private int[] hashCode =
  {
    66, 66, 66, 66, 66, 66, 66, 66, 66, 66,
    66, 66, 66,  0, 66, 66, 66, 66, 66, 66,     // CR
    66, 66, 66, 66, 66, 66, 66, 66, 66, 66,
    66, 66, 66, 66, 66, 66, 66, 66, 66, 66,
    66, 66, 66, 66, 66, 66, 66, 66, 66, 66,
    66, 66, 66, 66, 66, 66, 66, 66, 66, 66,
    66, 66, 66, 66, 66, 66, 25, 40, 66, 66,     // B..C
    66, 66, 66, 15, 66, 66, 66, 66, 66, 66,     // I
    66, 66, 66,  5, 66, 66, 66, 66, 66, 66,     // S
    66, 66, 66, 66, 66, 66, 66,  0,  0, 30,     // a..c
    20, 10,  0, 66, 10, 10, 66, 66,  0, 10,     // d..f, h..i, l..m
     5,  0,  0, 66,  5, 35, 10,  5, 15,  5,     // n..p, r..w
    20, 25, 66, 66, 66, 66, 66, 66, 66, 66,     // x..y
    66, 66, 66, 66, 66, 66, 66, 66, 66, 66,
    66, 66, 66, 66, 66, 66, 66, 66, 66, 66,
    66, 66, 66, 66, 66, 66, 66, 66, 66, 66,
    66, 66, 66, 66, 66, 66, 66, 66, 66, 66,
    66, 66, 66, 66, 66, 66, 66, 66, 66, 66,
    66, 66, 66, 66, 66, 66, 66, 66, 66, 66,
    66, 66, 66, 66, 66, 66, 66, 66, 66, 66,
    66, 66, 66, 66, 66, 66, 66, 66, 66, 66,
    66, 66, 66, 66, 66, 66, 66, 66, 66, 66,
    66, 66, 66, 66, 66, 66, 66, 66, 66, 66,
    66, 66, 66, 66, 66, 66, 66, 66, 66, 66,
    66, 66, 66, 66, 66, 66, 66, 66, 66, 66,
    66, 66, 66, 66, 66, 66
  };
```

The idea is that, using this array, the letter '`B`' (line 7) is associated with the integer `25`, the letter '`d`' (line 11) is associated with the integer `20`, and the letters '`o`' and '`p`' (line 12) are both associated with the integer `0`. The selection of integer values is certainly not obvious at first glance. (I told you it was magic.)

Second, we associate a hash value (an integer) with a candidate string by adding `1`, the string's length, the hash code for the character at index zero, the hash code for the character at index one, and the hash code for the character at index two (or `0` for strings of length less than `3`). Assuming that `str` is the name of a candidate string, we compute a hash value for str as follows. (More magic!)

```
private int hash(String str)
  {
    return 1 + str.length()
        + hashCode[str.charAt(0)]
        + hashCode[str.charAt(1)]
        + (str.length() >= 3 ? hashCode[str.charAt(2)] : 0);
  }
```

Let's look at a few examples.

The hash value for reserved word "`Boolean`" is given by `1 + 7 + 25 +  0 +  0 = 33.`

The hash value for reserved word "`if`" is given by `1 + 2 + 10 +  0 +  0 = 13.`

The hash value for reserved word "`loop`" is given by `1 + 4 +  0 +  0 +  0 =  5.`

The hash value for identifier "`max`" is given by `1 + 3 + 10 +  0 + 20 = 34.`

The hash value for identifier "`guess`" is given by `1 + 5 + 66 +  5 + 10 = 87.`
(Note that the letter '`g`' has the default hash value of `66`.)

The hash value for identifier "`unknown`" is given by `1 + 7 +  5 +  5 + 66 = 84.`
(Note that the letter '`k`' has the default hash value of `66`.)

Third, we create an array of symbols that are indexed by hash values for our reserved words. Since the hash function isn't minimal, there will be entries in the array that do not correspond to a reserved word. For those entries we use the value `Symbol.unknown`. Our array contains 66 symbols (indexed from 0 to 65) and is defined as follows. (Yet more magic!)

```
private Symbol[] symbols =
  {
    Symbol.unknown,     Symbol.unknown,     Symbol.unknown,     //  0-2
    Symbol.ofRW,        Symbol.unknown,     Symbol.loopRW,      //  3-5
    Symbol.falseRW,     Symbol.returnRW,    Symbol.orRW,        //  6-8
    Symbol.forRW,       Symbol.procRW,      Symbol.unknown,     //  9-11
    Symbol.publicRW,    Symbol.ifRW,        Symbol.funRW,       // 12-14
    Symbol.protectedRW, Symbol.arrayRW,     Symbol.unknown,     // 15-17
    Symbol.inRW,        Symbol.notRW,       Symbol.readRW,      // 18-20
    Symbol.unknown,     Symbol.readlnRW,    Symbol.privateRW,   // 21-23
    Symbol.varRW,       Symbol.trueRW,      Symbol.writeRW,     // 24-26
    Symbol.StringRW,    Symbol.writelnRW,   Symbol.andRW,       // 27-29
    Symbol.whenRW,      Symbol.whileRW,     Symbol.returnRW,    // 30-32
    Symbol.BooleanRW,   Symbol.modRW,       Symbol.thenRW,      // 33-35
    Symbol.classRW,     Symbol.unknown,     Symbol.IntegerRW,   // 36-38
    Symbol.unknown,     Symbol.typeRW,      Symbol.constRW,     // 39-41
    Symbol.unknown,     Symbol.unknown,     Symbol.unknown,     // 42-44
    Symbol.exitRW,      Symbol.unknown,     Symbol.unknown,     // 45-47
    Symbol.unknown,     Symbol.unknown,     Symbol.elseRW,      // 48-50
    Symbol.unknown,     Symbol.recordRW,    Symbol.unknown,     // 51-53
    Symbol.unknown,     Symbol.CharRW,      Symbol.falseRW,     // 54-56
    Symbol.unknown,     Symbol.unknown,     Symbol.unknown,     // 57-59
    Symbol.unknown,     Symbol.unknown,     Symbol.unknown,     // 60-62
    Symbol.unknown,     Symbol.unknown,     Symbol.ByteRW       // 63-65
  };
```

Note that, as expected (based on the above examples), `Symbol.BooleanRW` is at index `33`, and `Symbol.ifRW` is at index `13`, and `Symbol.loopRW` is at index `5`.

With these three components in place, our search algorithm is implemented as follows.

```
private Symbol getIdentifierSymbol(String idString)
  {
    if (idString.length() >= 2 && idString.length() <= 9)
      {
        int key = hash(idString);
        if (key < symbols.length)
          {
            var symbol = symbols[key];
            if (idString.equals(symbol.toString()))
                return symbol;
          }
      }

    return Symbol.identifier;
  }
```

Benchmark results indicate that this search algorithm has excellent performance. The major drawbacks are that it is certainly not intuitive, and initialization of the arrays `hashCode[]` and `symbols[]` is rather lengthy.

F.8 Search Using Switch Expression

This algorithm is very efficient and very easy to implement. It consists primarily of a single, large `switch` expression as follows.

```
private Symbol getIdentifierSymbol(String idString)
  {
    return switch (idString)
      {
        case "Boolean"  -> Symbol.BooleanRW;
        case "Byte"     -> Symbol.ByteRW;
        case "Char"     -> Symbol.CharRW;
        case "Integer"  -> Symbol.IntegerRW;
        case "String"   -> Symbol.StringRW;
        case "and"      -> Symbol.andRW;
        case "array"    -> Symbol.arrayRW;
        ...
        case "while"    -> Symbol.whileRW;
        case "write"    -> Symbol.writeRW;
        case "writeln"  -> Symbol.writelnRW;
        default         -> Symbol.identifier;
      }
  }
```

Using a `switch` expression allows the compiler to build an efficient jump table, resulting in excellent performance. Plus, the implementation is straightforward.

F.9 Search Using HashMap

Our last search uses class `HashMap` from package `java.util`. `HashMap` maps keys to values, and, if the key type has an efficient `hashCode()` method, `HashMap` can be very fast. In our case we want to map objects of type `String` to objects of type `Symbol`, so we declare our map as a field within the scanner as follows.

```
private Map<String, Symbol> rwMap = new HashMap<>(100);
```

Fortunately for us, `String` is predefined in Java, and it already has a very efficient `hashCode()` method.

The map is initialized in the constructor for `Scanner`.

```
for (var symbol : Symbol.values())
  {
    if (symbol.isReservedWord())
        rwMap.put(symbol.toString(), symbol);
  }
```

Using the map to search reserved words is simple.

```
private Symbol getIdentifierSymbol(String idString)
  {
    return rwMap.getOrDefault(idString, Symbol.identifier);
  }
```

Searching for reserved words using a hash map is very straightforward, and based on the benchmark analysis, it is one of the fastest search algorithms. Short, easy to implement and fast, it is an excellent choice for the CPRL scanner.

Appendix G
JIT Compilation versus AOT Compilation

Recall from Chapter 1 that the Java Virtual Machine provides a Just-In-Time (JIT) compiler, which translates Java bytecode into native machine code at runtime. Plus, the JIT compiler profiles the code as it is running to discover methods (hot spots) where additional optimizations can be performed. Performance improvements can be significant for methods that are executed repeatedly. Note that Java's JIT compiler is part of the Java Virtual Machine (JVM), not the actual Java compiler that translates Java source files into bytecode. The term JIT typically applies to a virtual machine.

But many compilers use a different compilation model called Ahead-Of-Time (AOT) compilation, whereby the source code is translated completely into a native executable format for a specific environment; e.g., the compiler (possibly together with a linker) creates a ".exe" file for a Windows/x86-64 computer. All translation and optimization are done at compile time, and the native code is run directly on the processor, not as part of a virtual machine. Practically all C and C++ compilers use AOT compilation.

So which compilation model is better, JIT or AOT? The answer is ... it depends. Native executables created by AOT compilers typically start faster and run faster initially, but JIT compilers can often provide better overall optimization based on runtime execution patterns. Many server-based applications (e.g., web applications) are designed to run for extended periods of time – months to possibly years. For these types of applications, JIT compilation is an excellent choice. But for many applications, startup time and initial performance are more important, and for these applications, AOT compilation is usually a better choice. Compilers tend to fall in the second category of applications.

The three major applications discussed in this book are the CPRL compiler, the CVM (virtual machine), and the assembler for CVM assembly language. Complete source code for the latter two applications is available on the book's GitHub repository. Through the development of the CPRL compiler, we assume that all three applications will run on the JVM. But none of these applications are designed to run for extended periods of time, and so it seems likely that they could benefit from AOT compilation. Let's find out.

Creating a Native Executable

There are several tools that can be used to convert JVM applications into native executables, including the Java Development Kit (JDK) packaging tool `jpackage` and the GraalVM tool `native-image`. Since the GraalVM `native-image` tool creates a pure, native binary without a JVM layer, we will use it to create native applications for the compiler, the assembler, and the CVM. The discussion that follows will create native applications for Windows/x86-64 computers, but it is relatively straightforward to create native applications for Apple or Linux computers using the GraalVM `native-image` tool.

We start by assuming a Windows/x86-64 environment and a project setup as described in Appendix A. We also assume that GraalVM is installed and that its `bin` subdirectory is on the execution search path (included in the `PATH` environment variable). Then we create a subdirectory of the compiler project's `bin` directory (the one containing the scripts for compiling, assembling, and testing your CPRL test examples) named "`native`".

Using a text editor, add a script file named "`make_cprlc.cmd`" to directory `native` with the following contents.

```
@echo off

rem set config environment variables locally
setlocal
call ..\cprl_config.cmd

native-image -cp "%COMPILER_PROJECT_PATH%" -march=compatibility -O3 ^
   cprlc.Cprlc cprlc

rem restore settings
endlocal
```

The two key lines in the above listing are highlighted in bold. The "`-march`" and "`-O3`" options allow all features of the x86-64 with all optimizations for best performance. Note that the caret (`^`) character is the line continuation character for Windows command files. Typically you would just put everything on one line, but a single line was too long for the font and margins of this book.

For a bash/x86-64 environment, the script file "`make_cprlc`" (no "`.cmd`" suffix) would be written as follows, with the backslash (\) character serving as the line continuation character for bash scripts.

```
#!/bin/bash

# set config environment variables
source ../cprl_config

native-image -cp "$COMPILER_PROJECT_PATH" -march=compatibility -O3 \
   cprlc.Cprlc cprlc
```

In Windows, running `make_cprlc.cmd` from a command prompt will create the native executable file `cprlc.exe`. Follow a similar procedure to create native executables `assemble.exe` and `cprl.exe`.

Copy `setPath.cmd` and all `test...` files from the project's `bin` directory to the newly created `native` subdirectory. At this point the directory structure should look like the one shown on the next page (some files not shown).

Note that script files `assemble.cmd`, `cprl.cmd`, and `cprlc.cmd` in the parent directory have been replaced by native executables `assemble.exe`, `cprl.exe`, and `cprlc.exe` in the subdirectory. But since the other script files just call the executables by their base name (i.e., without the "`.cmd`" suffix), they will still run correctly from either directory. For example, when script file `testCorrect_all.cmd` calls `cprlc`, it will call either `cprlc.cmd` or `cprlc.exe` as appropriate.

Structure of the project `bin` directory with a subdirectory for native executables is as follows:

```
bin
├── assemble.cmd
├── cprl.cmd
├── cprlc.cmd
├── cprl_config.cmd
├── disassemble.cmd
├── setPath.cmd
├── testCorrect.cmd
├── testCorrect_all.cmd
├── testEverything.cmd
├── testIncorrect_all.cmd
└── native
    ├── assemble.exe
    ├── cprl.exe
    ├── cprlc.exe
    ├── make_assemble.cmd
    ├── make_cprl.cmd
    ├── make_cprlc.cmd
    ├── setPath.cmd
    ├── testCorrect.cmd
    ├── testCorrect_all.cmd
    ├── testEverything.cmd
    └── testIncorrect_all.cmd
```

Now let's see if the native executable files offer improved performance. Open two command prompts. In the first command prompt, change directory to the project's `bin` directory and run `setPath.cmd` in that directory to ensure that it is included in the execution search path. Then run `testEverything.cmd`, observing how long it takes to run. If the compiler project is correct and complete, then all tests should run with the expected results.

In the second command prompt, change directory to the `native` subdirectory and run `setPath.cmd` in that directory to ensure that it is included in the execution search path. Then run `testEverything.cmd`, observing how long it takes to run. You should observe that `testEverything.cmd` ran much faster in the `native` subdirectory than it did in the project's `bin` directory, but let's measure.

Measuring the Performance on Windows

Bash (and therefore Linux and Apple computers) has a `time` command that can be used to measure how long a given script takes to run. Windows PowerShell has a "cmdlet" (PowerShell term) called `Measure-Command` that does something similar, but the standard Windows Command Prompt doesn't seem to have a standard equivalent. There is an open-source utility called `ptime` that can be used for this purpose, but the web page for ptime says that it was last tested under Windows XP in 2005 and may be obsolete. Let's write our own utility for this purpose in Java.

Omitting error checking for arguments, method main() for our timing program can be implemented similar to the following.

```
public static void main(String[] args)
    throws IOException, InterruptedException
  {
    System.out.println();
    System.out.println("===  " + args[0] + " ===");

    // for windows
    ProcessBuilder pb = new ProcessBuilder("cmd.exe", "/c", args[0]);

    // for bash
    //ProcessBuilder pb = new ProcessBuilder("bash", "-c", args[0]);
    pb.redirectErrorStream(true);

    ...   // call System.nanoTime() to get start time

    Process p = pb.start();
    var reader =
          new BufferedReader(new InputStreamReader(p.getInputStream()));
    String line;
    while ((line = reader.readLine()) != null)
        System.out.println(line);

    ...   // call System.nanoTime() to get stop time
    ...   // compute and write out elapsed time
  }
```

Using the approach outlined in this appendix, we can create a native executable named wtime that can be used to measure the time needed to run testEverything.cmd as follows.

```
wtime testEverything
```

The execution of the script file testEverything.cmd can be timed using all three timing tools described previously in this appendix.

1. Windows PowerShell cmdlet Measure-Command
2. ptime (Yes, it still works on Windows 11!)
3. wtime (as described above)

All three timing tools give very similar results, with the native versions of the applications running much faster than the non-native (Java) versions.

For Windows PowerShell users, run these two commands separately in a PowerShell prompt.

```
$env:Path = "$PWD;" + $env:Path  # set path to include current dir
Measure-Command { testEverything | Out-Default }
```

But what happens if we run `testEverything` several times in a row? With Java, we would expect improved performance on the second run due to the "warm up" of the Java virtual machine, but there are additional factors at play for both the native and non-native versions of the applications. When we study topics such as computer organization and/or operating systems, we learn about cache memory and virtual memory via paging. With frequently-used blocks of memory already loaded into cache and virtual pages already moved into main memory, we would expect to get the best performance. In other words, when an application is run a second time or third time, we could expect it to run more quickly. Exact performance improvements can vary greatly across different computers based on relative processor speeds, operating systems, amount of cache memory, etc.

The following numbers were measured on my computer running Windows 11, The Java version was tested using OpenJDK version 26.0.1. The native (`.exe`) versions of the applications were created using GraalVM version 25.0.5. Before testing each version, I rebooted (restarted) the computer and then waited several minutes for the operating system to finish all initialization. I then ran `testEverything` multiple times consecutively, measuring the number of seconds for each run.

Run Times for the CVM

	Java Version	GraalVm (.exe) Version
1st Run	31.181 seconds	24.653 seconds
2nd Run	14.245 seconds	11.892 seconds
3rd Run	13.896 seconds	6.161 seconds

As might be expected, the second and third runs showed improved performance, even with the native (`.exe`) versions. Fourth and subsequent runs showed no meaningful improvement. As an aside, I should note that I have created versions of the compiler using C++, C#, and Kotlin, and although the actual numbers were different, all three of those compiler versions exhibited similar improvements over the first three runs.

So for Windows, the native versions of the compiler, assembler, and virtual machine proved to be faster than the JVM versions when run against the test examples. But what about Linux and other Unix-based operating systems such as macOS?

Measuring the Performance on Linux

Using a process similar to the one described above, native applications were also created for Linux. When script `testEverything` was run with these versions of the applications, the results were disappointing at first. But the initial tests were performed on Windows Subsystem for Linux 2 (WSL2), a lightweight virtual machine that runs on Windows.

> For software developers that run Windows most of the time, WSL2 is a great tool that offers a nearly complete Linux environment in a lightweight virtual machine. Plus, it is possible to access the Linux files from Windows, and vice versa. For developers that use Windows but also want a native Linux experience without a virtual machine, it is possible to configure a single computer that dual boots either Windows or Linux; however, the two environments are totally separate.

So all testing was moved to a different computer that ran Linux directly (not as part of a virtual machine). Without going into details, here is a summary of the differences between the results measured on the first computer running Windows and the second computer running (Ubuntu) Linux. Note that only the Java versions of the applications were tested on Linux; i.e., no native executables were created.

- The first runs were only slightly faster on the second machine.
- The second and third runs on Linux showed no significant difference in run-time performance.

Measuring Application Size

What about application size? When GraalVM generates a native executable for an application, it needs to include a lot of the JVM environment as well as the application-specific code. But, surprisingly, the GraalVM-generated version of the CVM was approximately twice as large as the GraalVM-generated version of the compiler, even though the source code for the CVM was smaller. One would expect that a C version of the executable for the CVM would be much smaller. That was, indeed, the case for both the Windows and Linux versions as shown in the following table.

Sizes of Native Executables for the CVM

	GraalVM Version	C Version
Windows	16,992 KB	241 KB
Linux	17, 283 KB	33 KB

Plus, the C version ran slightly faster. Implementing the CVM in C is clearly a worthwhile exercise in performance improvement. However, it should be noted that other important factors such as development time and maintainability could be impacted negatively.

For reference, source code for the C implementation used in the above tests is provided in the `Handouts` directory of the GitHub repository for this book. (But don't peek until you have attempted exercise 13 in Appendix B yourself.)

Ahead-of-Time Caching

Every time a Java application starts, the Java Virtual Machine rebuilds the same classes from scratch, and the JIT compiler optimizes the same classes from scratch, which results in slow startup and warmup times. Introduced via JDK Enhancement Proposal (JEP) 483 in JDK 24, and enhanced in JDK 25 and 26, Ahead-of-Time (AOT) caching reduces application startup and warmup times by loading an AOT cache directly from a disk file. The AOT cache is based on method execution profiles from a previous run of the application.

Using AOT caching is a two-step process. First a training run is used to build the cache. A training run is one performed deliberately, ahead of time, to let the JDK observe the running application and build the cache from what it observes. For optimal results, the training run should use workloads as close to production workloads as possible. Real users never see the training run. A production run, by contrast, is the deployment of the application using the finished cache to improve startup performance.

Here is a summary of the two steps.

1. Generate the AOT Cache

Run the application using the `-XX:AOTCacheOutput` flag.

```
java -XX:AOTCacheOutput=app.aot -cp app.jar com.example.App
```

2. Run the application with the AOT Cache

Launch the application in production with the created cache file.

```
java -XX:AOTCache=app.aot -cp app.jar com.example.App
```

Caution: The generated `.aot` file is coupled exclusively to the exact application code, library versions, and JDK patch version. Any modification to the source code or platform requires a complete cache regeneration.

The impact of AOT caching was tested for the three main applications of the compiler project – the compiler, the assembler, and the CVM. The training runs used the CPRL test examples to create separate AOT caches for each application. Extensive testing using the `testEverything` script showed that, for these applications, using an AOT cache improved the overall performance of the applications by more than 19%. Testing of longer running server-based applications has shown more significant improvements, especially during startup.

> If you are interested in AOT for Java, you should follow the progress of the OpenJDK project Leyden (see https://openjdk.org/projects/leyden/). In particular, the latest version of the Java Enhancement Proposal (JEP) entitled "Ahead-of-Time Code Compilation", currently in draft form, gives you a good idea of future directions of Java with respect to AOT.

Annotated Compiler References and Websites

What follows is not a comprehensive bibliography for compiler research but more of a listing of useful books, articles, and websites that complement or extend many of the ideas presented in this book.

[Aho 2006] Alfred V. Aho, Monica S. Lam, Ravi Sethi, Jeffrey D. Ullman, *Compilers: Principles, Techniques, And Tools* (Second Edition – a.k.a. Purple Dragon), Addison Wesley, 2006, ISBN 978-0321486813.

> The Purple Dragon is a classic, and many people learned how to write compilers from the Purple Dragon or its predecessor, the Red Dragon. It goes into much more detail about almost every compiler topic and is therefore much better suited for a two-semester course for graduate students or very advanced undergraduates.

[ANTLR] ANTLR (ANother Tool for Language Recognition), https://www.antlr.org/.

> ANTLR is a parser generator for reading, processing, executing, or translating structured text or binary files. It provides support for generating scanners and parsers, for building parse trees, and for generating tree walkers that can be used to visit the nodes of those trees to execute application-specific code. See also https://github.com/antlr/, the GitHub repository for ANTLR, and [Parr 2013] below.

[Appel 2002] Andrew W. Appel and Jens Palsberg, *Modern Compiler Implementation in Java* (Second Edition), Cambridge University Press, 2002, ISBN 978-0521820608.

> Andrew Appel has written several highly acclaimed and widely adopted books on compilers. This one uses Java as the implementation language, but there are parallel versions of the book that use implementation languages C and ML.

[Bloch 2018] Joshua Bloch, *Effective Java* (Third Edition), Addison-Wesley, 2018, ISBN 978-0134685991.

> This book has essentially nothing to do with compilers but everything to do with developing software using Java. Every Java programmer should own a copy of this book. I have owned copies of all three editions, and I refer to them frequently.

[Campbell 2013] Bill Campbell, Swami Iyer, and Bahar Akbal-Delibas, *Introduction to Compiler Construction in a Java World*, CRC Press, 2013, ISBN 978-1439860885.

> This book uses Java exclusively. The source language being compiled is a subset of Java, the implementation language is Java, and the target machine is the JVM. The authors start by providing a working compiler, and most of the exercises are involved in updating the compiler to add new features to the language being compiled. There is also a chapter on translating JVM byte code to MIPS machine code.

[Cilloni 2023] Marco Cilloni, "Unicode is harder than you think", https://mcilloni.ovh/2023/07/23/unicode-is-hard/.

The details of Unicode can be difficult to master. This article explains the evolution of Unicode and describes many of the issues encountered by programmers when working with the latest versions.

[Coco/R] The Compiler Generator Coco/R, https://www.ssw.uni-linz.ac.at/Research/Projects/Coco/.

Coco/R is a tool for generating scanners and recursive-descent parsers based on a context-free grammar. It accepts LL(k) grammars for arbitrary k. I used Coco/R to double check first and follow sets for CPRL.

[CompOpt] Compiler Optimizations, https://en.wikipedia.org/wiki/Category:Compiler_optimizations.

This Wikipedia web page provides links to dozens of other Wikipedia web pages with details on specific compiler optimizations.

[Delporte 2023] Frank Delporte, "The Anatomy of a JVM", https://www.azul.com/blog/the-anatomy-of-a-jvm/ .

This article includes a great discussion of the JVM's approach to just-in-time compilation.

[Elder 1994] John Elder, *Compiler Construction: A Recursive Descent Model*, Prentice Hall, 1994, ISBN 978-0132911399.

The book by John Elder is another excellent, very readable book whose scope and level of presentation are similar to the one taken in this book. The compiler source language Model is similar to CPRL, and the implementation language is Modula-2.

[Hansen 1985] Per Brinch Hansen, *Brinch Hansen on Pascal Compilers*, Prentice Hall, 1985, ISBN 978-0130830982.

Although somewhat out of date now, the book by Brinch Hansen presents a very readable introduction to compilers. Its scope and level of presentation are similar to the one taken in this book except that it uses Pascal as the implementation language, and a subset of Pascal as the source language.

[ISO/IEC 14977] Information technology – Syntactic metalanguage – Extended BNF.

ISO/IEC 14977 is an international standard for the EBNF notation used in this book for the syntactic grammar. For example, the standard uses curly braces "{" and "}" to enclose syntax expressions that can be repeated zero or more times, and it uses square brackets "[" and "]" to enclose optional syntax expressions. You can purchase a copy at https://www.iso.org/standard/26153.html, but you can also find publicly available PDF copies online.

[Jenkov 2022] Jakob Jenkov, "Unicode", https://jenkov.com/tutorials/unicode/index.html.

This is another excellent and short tutorial on Unicode and the UTF-8 encoding.

[LLVM] The LLVM Compiler Infrastructure, https://llvm.org/.

> LLVM is a professional grade collection of modular and reusable compiler tools. LLVM was originally written to be a replacement for the existing code generator in the GCC suite, and many of the GCC front ends have been modified to work with it. Apple's Swift, Mozilla's Rust, and many other programming languages make use of LLVM as a back end. In 2012 the Association for Computing Machinery presented Vikran Adve, Chris Lattner, and Evan Cheng with the ACM Software System Award for their work on LLVM.

[Moore 2024] John I. Moore, Jr., *Compiler Design Using Kotlin: An Object-Oriented Approach* (Third Edition), SoftMoore Consulting, 2024, ISBN 978-1734139174.

> The book referenced above is an alternate version of a previous edition of this book that uses Kotlin instead of Java as the implementation language for the compiler. Plus, another alternate version of this edition using C# is currently in the early stages of development.

[Nystrom 2021] Robert Nystrom, *Crafting Interpreters*, Genever Benning, 2021, ISBN 978-0990582939.

> This is a great book if you want to learn more about interpreters and dynamically typed languages. Personally, I prefer the print book, but there is also an online version at https://craftinginterpreters.com/contents.html.

[Parr 2010] Terence Parr, *Language Implementation Patterns*, Pragmatic Bookshelf, 2010, ISBN 978-1934356456.

> Terence Parr has devoted most of his adult life to compiler research, teaching, and implementation. I learned a lot from this book, and I highly recommend it to anyone interested in learning about compilers. The two chapters covering symbol tables are worth the price of the book.

[Parr 2013] Terence Parr, *The Definitive ANTLR 4 Reference* (Second Edition), Pragmatic Bookshelf, 2013, ISBN 978-1934356999. (See also https://www.antlr.org/.)

> ANTLR is a tool for generating scanners and recursive descent parsers that is somewhat similar in scope to Coco/R described above. ANTLR was developed and is maintained by Terence Parr. If you want to learn more about ANTLR, you should read this book. See also [ANTLR] above.

[ParseGen] Comparison of parser generators (Wikipedia), https://en.wikipedia.org/wiki/Comparison_of_parser_generators.

> This Wikipedia article provides a fairly comprehensive list of scanner and parser generators for various languages.

[RegEx1] Regular-Expressions.info, https://www.regular-expressions.info/.

> There are lots of good books and articles about regular expressions, but this website probably has everything you need to know except possibly for details about how to use regular expressions in a specific programming language.

[RegEx2] Regular expression (Wikipedia), https://en.wikipedia.org/wiki/Regular_expression.

Not surprisingly, Wikipedia also has a good treatment of regular expressions, which complements the website listed above.

[Siek 2023] Jeremy G. Siek, *Essentials of Compilation: An Incremental Approach in Racket*, MIT Press, 2023, ISBN 978-0262047760

In contrast to the object-oriented approach used in the book you are currently reading, this book by Jeremy Siek uses a functional approach to compiler construction. Racket (a dialect of Lisp and a descendant of Scheme) is used as both the source language and the implementation language, and the target language is x86 assembly language.

[Spolsky 2003] Joel Spolsky, "The Absolute Minimum Every Software Developer Absolutely, Positively Must Know About Unicode and Character Sets (No Excuses!)," https://www.joelonsoftware.com/2003/10/08/the-absolute-minimum-every-software-developer-absolutely-positively-must-know-about-unicode-and-character-sets-no-excuses/.

Although it is a little out of date now, this article remains one of the most entertaining and best written treatments of Unicode and Unicode encodings.

[Watt 2000] David A. Watt and Deryck F. Brown, *Programming Language Processors in Java: Compilers and Interpreters*, Prentice Hall, 2000, ISBN 978-0130257864.

The book by Watt and Brown is similar in scope to this one, and it also uses Java as the implementation language. Its coverage of tombstone diagrams was the inspiration for much of Chapter 1. One key difference is that the book by Watt and Brown uses the visitor pattern to "walk" the abstract syntax trees. I highly recommend this book.

[Westrelin 2021] Roland Westrelin, "How the JIT compiler boosts Java performance in OpenJDK," https://developers.redhat.com/articles/2021/06/23/how-jit-compiler-boosts-java-performance-openjdk.

Great explanation of the inner workings of the JVM JIT compiler.

[Wirth 1996] Niklaus Wirth, *Compiler Construction*, Addison Wesley, 1996, ISBN 978-0201403534. (A slightly revised version of this book is available online at https://people.inf.ethz.ch/wirth/CompilerConstruction/CompilerConstruction1.pdf.)

Niklaus Wirth wrote compilers and designed programming languages for most of his adult life. Notable languages designed by Wirth are Pascal, Modula-2, and Oberon. He was also the first person to propose the use of extended grammars, and the main parts of his notation were adopted by [ISO/IEC 14977] above. Wirth's book *Compiler Construction* is similar to this book in many ways except that it uses a subset of Oberon as both the source language and the implementation language for a compiler.

Index

A

B

C

www.ingramcontent.com/pod-product-compliance
Lightning Source LLC
LaVergne TN
LVHW060437061126
851857LV00016B/1656
9781734139143